The Use of Risk
in Portfolio Op

Albina Unger

The Use of Risk Budgets in Portfolio Optimization

With a foreword by Prof. Dr. Thorsten Poddig

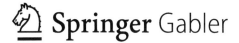 Springer Gabler

Albina Unger
Friedrichsdorf, Germany

Dissertation University of Bremen, Germany, 2014

ISBN 978-3-658-07258-2   ISBN 978-3-658-07259-9 (eBook)
DOI 10.1007/978-3-658-07259-9

The Deutsche Nationalbibliothek lists this publication in the Deutsche Nationalbibliografie; detailed bibliographic data are available in the Internet at http://dnb.d-nb.de.

Library of Congress Control Number: 2014949923

Springer Gabler
© Springer Fachmedien Wiesbaden 2015

Springer Gabler is a brand of Springer DE.
Springer DE is part of Springer Science+Business Media.
www.springer-gabler.de

Foreword

Today's active asset management is mainly based on the theory of portfolio selection, which was founded by H. Markowitz and J. Tobin in the 1950s. Since then, it was continuously developed. However, there arose quickly several points of criticism in practical applications. Practitioners complained about the results of the portfolio optimizations as unintuitive, since the resulting portfolio structures are usually characterized by high concentrations in a few assets. In addition, portfolio structures are very sensitive to minor changes in the input parameters, which are necessary for the portfolio optimization. While the use of this theory was accompanied by a degree of skepticism ever since, the course and outcome of the recent financial market crisis represented another significant drawback for the application of this theory. In the financial market crisis, both private and institutional investors suffered considerable losses in their portfolios, although they should be apparently well-diversified.

In the light of this practical experience, a 'new', highly propagandized investment approach emerged: Risk Parity or Equal Risk Contribution (ERC) portfolios. These are approaches to portfolio construction, which do not, or not primarily, take the return component into account, but are completely or mainly based on risk parameters. Albeit such approaches are not really new; the so-called minimum-variance portfolio, which is part of the classical theory of portfolio selection, accomplishes this since the beginning in a similar manner. In this respect, this leads consequently to the research question of this work: What aspects of the 'new' approaches are really 'new', what are they able to achieve? Or in other words: Are these approaches capable to accurately solve those problems, for which the classical models are discredited?

The present work deals with these issues. It analyzes the topic of risk-based asset allocations encompassing the theoretical, methodological and empirical point of view. In addition to common approaches in the investment industry, own extensions are presented and their quality is analyzed. The basic question is whether these approaches, including the developed extensions, denote a progress with respect to the classical theory and if so, what the difference exactly is. Whereas the achieved results are rich in detail and can hardly be summarized in a foreword, the basic result is anticipated. Despite some favorable results in individual cases, on the whole, a superiority of the risk-based budgeting portfolios cannot be ascertained. Overall, the risk budgeting models do not offer a real alternative to the well-known minimum-variance portfolio. Insofar, the currently in the investment practice propagandized approach seems more likely to be a 'fad' than a noticeable progress.

Prof. Dr. Thorsten Poddig

Preface

This PhD thesis contains the result of research undertaken at the Department of Finance of the University of Bremen under the supervision of Prof. Dr. Thorsten Poddig.

Many people have contributed to the success of the thesis, whom I would like to express my gratitude.

First of all, I thank my supervisor Prof. Dr. Thorsten Poddig for his excellent support during the years of research. His constructive suggestions as well as the critical comments were essential for this work. I have learned a lot during the time of my doctoral studies and have developed professionally and personally. Therefore, for enabling the PhD study and for his granted support in all aspects, I am extremely grateful. Also a heartfelt thank you to Prof. Dr. Diethelm Würtz for his continued support during my dissertation. His valuable suggestions, the research stays in Zurich and not least the introduction to the software R, which has now become a passion, have also contributed to the success of this work.

I also thank my former colleagues for the friendly cooperation and the numerous valuable discussions. A special thanks goes to Geraldine Tchegho for her willingness for spontaneous discussions and the many funny moments. I will always have fond memories of our time together in the office. I also thank Petra Sebbes for the versatile support and the nice talks, which made the doctorate more enjoyable.

Special thanks go to my husband and family for their essential support and the sometimes necessary free space. Especially in difficult situations, my husband has always given me confidence and courage. Without his encouragement, patience, trust and love and without the support of my family, this work would not have been possible.

Albina Unger

Contents

1 Introduction   **1**
  1.1 Motivation and Problem Statement   1
  1.2 Outline of Thesis   7

2 Theoretical Background   **11**
  2.1 Modern Portfolio Theory   11
      2.1.1 Mean Variance Framework   11
      2.1.2 Separation Theorem   21
      2.1.3 Utility Theoretic Foundation   24
      2.1.4 Weaknesses of the Classical Portfolio Theory .   34
  2.2 Asset Pricing Theory   36
      2.2.1 Capital Asset Pricing Model - CAPM   36
      2.2.2 Empirical Evidence - Critique and Anomalies .   41
      2.2.3 Factor Models   44
      2.2.4 Methodology for Empirical Testing   47
  2.3 Summary   51

3 Alternative Approaches in Portfolio Management   **53**
  3.1 Risk Measures and Risk Contributions   53
      3.1.1 What Is Risk?   53
      3.1.2 Risk Measures   55
      3.1.3 Risk Contributions   63
  3.2 Portfolio Models   74
      3.2.1 Equally Weighted Portfolio (1/n)   74
      3.2.2 Minimum Risk Portfolios   75
      3.2.3 Equally Risk Contribution Portfolios   77
  3.3 Utility Theoretic Foundations   80
      3.3.1 Expected Utility Theory   80

3.3.2   Other Approaches   85
3.3.3   Summary 105

4   Literature Review   **107**
4.1   Minimum Risk Portfolios 107
    4.1.1   MV/Low Risk Anomaly 107
    4.1.2   Minimum-CVaR Portfolio 119
    4.1.3   Maximum Drawdown and Drawdown Measures 123
    4.1.4   Minimum-CDaR Portfolio 126
4.2   Risk Budgeting Portfolios 128
    4.2.1   Volatility Risk Budgets 128
    4.2.2   CVaR Risk Budgets 137
    4.2.3   Summary of the Risk Budgeting Studies 140

5   Robustness   **147**
5.1   Definition of Robustness 147
5.2   Approaches to Robust Portfolios: A Short Review . . 149
5.3   Review of the Robustness of the Markowitz Approach   152
5.4   Robustness of the Volatility Risk Budgeting Portfolio . 155
5.5   Summary 158

6   Empirical Studies   **159**
6.1   Organization of Studies 159
6.2   Performance Study 161
    6.2.1   Methodology 162
    6.2.2   European Fund 173
    6.2.3   Global Portfolio 192
    6.2.4   German Market 215
    6.2.5   Summary of the Performance Studies 240
6.3   Exploring Risk-Based Pricing Anomalies 241
    6.3.1   Methodology 242
    6.3.2   Global Portfolio 246
    6.3.3   Germany 1973 250
    6.3.4   Rolling Regressions 257
    6.3.5   US Industry Indices 262

      6.3.6   US MSCI 264
      6.3.7   German Industry Indices 266
      6.3.8   German MSCI 270
      6.3.9   Four-Factor Model 274
      6.3.10 Summary of the Factor Regressions 275
  6.4 Robustness Study 276
      6.4.1   Methodology 277
      6.4.2   Simulation Study 280
      6.4.3   Empirical Study 304
      6.4.4   Results of the Robustness Study 318

7 Extensions of Empirical Studies   321
  7.1 Fat Tailed Distributions 321
  7.2 Binary Stability Portfolio 335
  7.3 Hierarchical Clustering 348
      7.3.1   Global Portfolio 352
      7.3.2   German Market 355
      7.3.3   Different Clustering Algorithm 359
      7.3.4   Summary 361

8 Conclusion   363

A Appendix   371
  A.1 Germany1973 Dataset 371
  A.2 Regressions 372
      A.2.1   Global Dataset 372
      A.2.2   Germany 1973 Dataset 377
      A.2.3   US Industry Dataset 383
      A.2.4   US MSCI Dataset 384
      A.2.5   German Industry Dataset 385
      A.2.6   German MSCI Dataset 387
  A.3 Robustness Study 388

Bibliography   391

List of Figures

1.1   Outline of Thesis 8

2.1   Efficient Frontier 21
2.2   Tangency Line 22
2.3   Utility Functions 29
2.4   Security Market Line 40

3.1   Value and Weighting Function under Prospect Theory   88
3.2   Weighting Function under Cumulative Prospect Theory   91

6.1   Outline of Empirical Studies 160
6.2   In-Sample and Out-of-Sample Periods 167
6.3   Bear Phases - European Fund 187
6.4   Relative Performance of Risk Budgeting Portfolios - Global Portfolio 199
6.5   Bull/Bear Phases - Global 211
6.6   Annualized Asset Means - Germany 1973 217
6.7   Annualized Standard Deviations - Germany 1973 . . . 218
6.8   Relative Performance of Risk Budgeting Portfolios - Germany 1973 222
6.9   Bull/Bear Phases - Germany 1973 237
6.10 Rolling Alpha - Global Portfolio 258
6.11 Rolling Regressions of the MV Portfolio - Global Portfolio259
6.12 Rolling Alpha - Germany 1973 260
6.13 Rolling Regressions of the MV Portfolio - Germany 1973261

7.1   Bayesian Change Point Method 337
7.2   SX5T Stability 338

7.3   Stability Portfolio Components 341
7.4   Binary Stability Portfolio Weights 345
7.5   Hierarchical Clustering Algorithm 350
7.6   Different Hierarchical Clustering Algorithm 359

A.1   Rolling Regressions (Global) 373
A.2   Rolling Regressions (Germany 1973) 378

List of Tables

4.1   MV Anomaly/Volatility-Return - Empirical Results   . 113
4.2   ERC Portfolio - Empirical Results 141

6.1   Notations of Portfolios 173
6.2   Notations of Indices - European Fund 174
6.3   Component Statistics - European Fund 174
6.4   Correlations of Indices - European Fund 175
6.5   Portfolio Statistics - European Fund 175
6.6   Performance per Calender Year - European Fund . . . 176
6.7   Statistical Significance of Mean Differences - European
      Fund 177
6.8   Jensen's Alpha - European Fund 178
6.9   Analysis of Jensen's Alpha Regression - European Fund 179
6.10 Significance of Difference in Variances - European Fund 180
6.11 Risk Figures - European Fund 181
6.12 Risk Ratios - European Fund 181
6.13 Turnover and Trades - European Fund 182
6.14 Weight Allocations - European Fund 183
6.15 Risk Budget Allocations of the MV Portfolio - European
      Fund 184
6.16 Risk Budget Allocations of the sampleCOV Portfolio -
      European Fund 184
6.17 Bull/Bear Characteristics of Minimum Risk Portfolios
      - European Fund 188
6.18 Bull/Bear Characteristics of Risk Budgeting Portfolios
      - European Fund 188

6.19 Significance in Means in the Bull Period - European
     Fund 189
6.20 Significance in Means in the Bear Period - European
     Fund 190
6.21 Significance in Variances in the Bull Period - European
     Fund 190
6.22 Significance in Variances in the Bear Period - European
     Fund 191
6.23 Notations of Indices 192
6.24 Component Statistics - Global Portfolio 193
6.25 Correlation of the Indices - Global Portfolio 195
6.26 Portfolio Statistics - Global Portfolio 196
6.27 Performance per Calender Year - Global Portfolio . . . 198
6.28 Statistical Significance of Mean Differences - Global
     Portfolio 200
6.29 Jensen's Alpha - Global Portfolio 201
6.30 Analysis of Jensen's Alpha Regression - Global Portfolio 202
6.31 Significance of Difference in Variances - Global Portfolio 202
6.32 Risk Figures - Global Portfolio 203
6.33 Risk Ratios - Global Portfolio 204
6.34 Turnover and Trades - Global Portfolio 205
6.35 Weights Allocations - Global Portfolio 206
6.36 Risk Budget Allocations of the MV Portfolio - Global
     Portfolio 207
6.37 Risk Budget Allocations of the sampleCOV Portfolio -
     Global Portfolio 208
6.38 Bull and Bear Periods - Global Portfolio 209
6.39 Bull/Bear Characteristics of Minimum Risk Portfolios
     - Global Portfolio 210
6.40 Bull/Bear Characteristics of Risk Budgeting Portfolios
     - Global Portfolio 210
6.41 Significance in Means in the Bull Period - Global Portfolio 212
6.42 Significance in Means in the Bear Period - Global Portfolio 213
6.43 Significance in Variances in the Bull Period - Global
     Portfolio 213

6.44 Significance in Variances in the Bear Period - Global
Portfolio 214
6.45 Correlations of Portfolio Returns - Global Portfolio . . 215
6.46 Main Performance Statistics - Germany 1973 219
6.47 Performance per 5 Calender Years - Germany1973 . . 220
6.48 Statistical Significance of Mean Differences - Germany
1973 223
6.49 Jensen's Alpha - Germany 1973 224
6.50 Analysis of Jensen's Alpha Regression - Germany 1973 225
6.51 Significance of Difference in Variances - Germany 1973 225
6.52 Risk Figures - Germany 1973 226
6.53 Risk Ratios - Germany 1973 227
6.54 Turnover and Trades - Germany 1973 227
6.55 Weights Allocations - Germany 1973 230
6.56 Risk Budget Allocations of the MV Portfolio - Germany
1973 231
6.57 Risk Budget Allocations of the sampleCOV Portfolio -
Germany 1973 232
6.58 Bull and Bear Periods - Germany 1973 233
6.59 Bull/Bear Germany1973 - Minimum Risk Portfolios . 234
6.60 Bull/Bear Germany1973 - Risk Budgeting Portfolios . 234
6.61 Significance in Means in the Bull Period - Germany 1973 236
6.62 Significance in Means in the Bear Period - Global Portfolio 237
6.63 Significance in Variances in the Bull Period - Germany
1973 238
6.64 Significance in Variances in the Bear Period - Germany
1973 238
6.65 Correlations of Portfolio Returns - Germany 1973 . . . 239
6.66 Overview of Regressions 245
6.67 Fama-French Global Factors - Statistics 247
6.68 Correlations of the Global Factor Returns 247
6.69 CAPM Regression Results for the Minimum Risk Portfolios - Global Portfolio 248
6.70 CAPM Regression Results for the Risk Budgeting Portfolios - Global Portfolio 248

6.71 Fama-French Regression Results for the Minimum Risk
      Portfolios - Global Portfolio 249
6.72 Fama-French Regression Results for the Risk Budgeting
      Portfolios - Global Portfolio 249
6.73 Fama-French German Factors (Artmann et al., 2012) -
      Statistics 251
6.74 Correlations of the German Factor Returns 251
6.75 CAPM Regression Results for the Minimum Risk Port-
      folios - Germany 1973 (Artmann et al., 2012) 252
6.76 CAPM Regression Results for the Risk Budgeting Port-
      folios - Germany 1973 (Artmann et al., 2012) 252
6.77 Fama-French Regression Results for the Minimum Risk
      Portfolios - Germany 1973 (Artmann et al., 2012) . . . 253
6.78 Fama-French Regression Results for the Risk Budgeting
      Portfolios - Germany 1973 (Artmann et al., 2012) . . . 254
6.79 Fama-French German Factors of Hanauer et al. (2013)
      - Statistics 255
6.80 Correlations of the German Factor Returns of Hanauer
      et al. (2013) 255
6.81 Fama-French Regression Results for the Minimum Risk
      Portfolios - Germany 1973 Hanauer et al. (2013) . . . 256
6.82 Fama-French Regression Results for the Risk Budgeting
      Portfolios - Germany 1973 Hanauer et al. (2013) . . . 256
6.83 CAPM Regression Results for the Minimum Risk Port-
      folios - US Industry 262
6.84 CAPM Regression Results for the Risk Budgeting Port-
      folios - US Industry 262
6.85 Fama-French Regression Results for the Minimum Risk
      Portfolios - US Industry 263
6.86 Fama-French Regression Results for the Risk Budgeting
      Portfolios - US Industry 264
6.87 CAPM Regression Results for the Minimum Risk Port-
      folios - US MSCI 265
6.88 CAPM Regression Results for the Risk Budgeting Port-
      folios - US MSCI 265

6.89 Fama-French Regression Results for the Minimum Risk
Portfolios - US MSCI 266

6.90 Fama-French Regression Results for the Risk Budgeting
Portfolios - US MSCI 266

6.91 CAPM Regression Results for the Minimum Risk Portfolios - German Industry (Artmann et al., 2012) 267

6.92 CAPM Regression Results for the Risk Budgeting Portfolios - German Industry (Artmann et al., 2012) 267

6.93 Fama-French Regression Results for the Minimum Risk
Portfolios - German Industry (Artmann et al., 2012) . 268

6.94 Fama-French Regression Results for the Risk Budgeting
Portfolios - German Industry (Artmann et al., 2012) . 268

6.95 Fama-French Regression Results for the Minimum Risk
Portfolios - German Industry (Hanauer et al., 2013) . 269

6.96 Fama-French Regression Results for the Risk Budgeting
Portfolios - German Industry (Hanauer et al., 2013) . 270

6.97 CAPM Regression Results for the Minimum Risk Portfolios - German MSCI (Artmann et al., 2012) 271

6.98 CAPM Regression Results for the Risk Budgeting Portfolios - German MSCI (Artmann et al., 2012) 271

6.99 Fama-French Regression Results for the Minimum Risk
Portfolios - German MSCI (Artmann et al., 2012) . . . 272

6.100 Fama-French Regression Results for the Risk Budgeting
Portfolios - German MSCI(Artmann et al., 2012) . . . 272

6.101 Fama-French Regression Results for the Minimum Risk
Portfolios - German MSCI (Hanauer et al., 2013) . . . 273

6.102 Fama-French Regression Results for the Risk Budgeting
Portfolios - German MSCI (Hanauer et al., 2013) . . . 273

6.103 Minimum and Maximum Portfolio Weights for the Minimum Risk Portfolios in the Simulation 283

6.104 Minimum and Maximum Portfolio Weights for the Risk
Budgeting Portfolios in the Simulation 284

6.105 Standard Deviations of Minimum Risk Portfolio Weights
in the Simulation 285

6.106 Standard Deviations of Risk Budgeting Portfolio Weights
in the Simulation 285
6.107 Performance Statistics for the Simulation - Minimum
Risk Portfolios 287
6.108 Performance Statistics for the Simulation - Risk Budgeting Portfolios 288
6.109 Performance Statistics for the Worst Case Simulation
- Minimum Risk Portfolios 291
6.110 Performance Statistics for the Worst Case Simulation
- Risk Budgeting Portfolios 292
6.111 True Means of the Assets in the Realistic Simulation . 293
6.112 True Correlations of the Assets in the Realistic Simulation 294
6.113 True Asset Weights of the Portfolios in the Realistic
Simulation 294
6.114 Minimum and Maximum Portfolio Weights for the Minimum Risk Portfolios in the Realistic Simulation . . . 296
6.115 Minimum and Maximum Portfolio Weights for the Risk
Budgeting Portfolios in the Realistic Simulation 297
6.116 Standard Deviations of the Minimum Risk Weights in
the Realistic Simulation 297
6.117 Standard Deviations of the Risk Budgeting Weights in
the Realistic Simulation 298
6.118 Performance Statistics for the Realistic Simulation -
Minimum Risk Portfolios 298
6.119 Performance Statistics for the Realistic Simulation -
Risk Budgeting Portfolios 299
6.120 Significance in Actual Means (μ actual) in the Realistic
Simulation across the 10.000 Simulations 300
6.121 Performance Statistics for the Worst Case Simulation
in the Realistic Simulation - Minimum Risk Portfolios 301
6.122 Performance Statistics for the Worst Case Simulation
in the Realistic Simulation - Risk Budgeting Portfolios 302
6.123 Significance in Actual Means (μ actual) in the Worst
Case of the Realistic Simulation 303

6.124 Minimum and Maximum Portfolio Weights for the Minimum Risk Portfolios in the Global Dataset 305

6.125 Minimum and Maximum Portfolio Weights for the Risk Budget Portfolios in the Global Dataset 305

6.126 Average Standard Deviations of Minimum Risk Portfolio Weights in the Empirical Dataset 306

6.127 Standard Deviations of Risk Budgeting Weights in the Empirical Dataset 306

6.128 Performance Statistics of the Minimum Risk Portfolios for the Global Dataset 307

6.129 Performance Statistics of the Risk Budgeting Portfolios for the Global Dataset 308

6.130 Significance in Actual Means (μ actual) in the Empirical Dataset 310

6.131 Annualized Returns, Annualized Volatilities and Correlations of the Assets in the Crisis Period 311

6.132 Performance Statistics of the Minimum Risk Portfolios in the Empirical Worst Case 312

6.133 Performance Statistics of the Risk Budgeting Portfolios in the Empirical Worst Case 313

6.134 Significance in Actual Means (μ actual) in the Empirical Worst Case 314

6.135 Performance Statistics of the Minimum Risk Portfolios in the Hypothetical Worst Case 315

6.136 Performance Statistics of the Risk Budgeting Portfolios in the Hypothetical Worst Case 316

6.137 Significance in Actual Means (μ actual) in the Hypothetical Worst Case 317

7.1 Notations of Portfolios with Simulated Returns 328

7.2 Main Statistics - sampleCVaR with Distributions . . . 328

7.3 Differences in Mean Returns - sampleCVaR with Distributions 328

7.4 Main Statistics - sampleCOV with Distributions . . . 329

7.5   Differences in Mean Returns - sampleCOV with Distributions 329

7.6   Main Statistics - sampleCDaR with Distributions . . 330

7.7   Differences in Mean Returns - sampleCDaR with Distributions 330

7.8   Risk Figures - sampleCVaR with Distributions 331

7.9   Risk Figures - sampleCOV with Distributions 331

7.10 Risk Figures - sampleCDaR with Distributions 332

7.11 Risk Ratios - sampleCVaR with Distributions 332

7.12 Risk Ratios - sampleCOV with Distributions 333

7.13 Risk Ratios - sampleCDaR with Distributions 333

7.14 Turnover - sampleCVaR with Distributions 333

7.15 Turnover - sampleCOV with Distributions 334

7.16 Turnover - sampleCDaR with Distributions 334

7.17 Main Statistics - Binary Stability Portfolio 340

7.18 Statistical Significance of Mean Differences - Binary Stability Portfolio 342

7.19 Significance of Difference in Variances - Binary Stability Portfolio 342

7.20 Returns per Calendar Year - Binary Stability Portfolio 343

7.21 Risk Figures - Binary Stability Portfolio 344

7.22 Risk Ratios - Binary Stability Portfolio 344

7.23 Statistics - Portfolios with Stabilized Assets 347

7.24 Abbreviations of Hierarchical portfolios 352

7.25 Statistics of the Hierarchical portfolios - Global portfolio 353

7.26 Statistical Significance of Mean Differences of the Hierarchical Portfolios - Global Portfolio 353

7.27 Risk Figures of the Hierarchical Portfolios - Global Portfolio 354

7.28 Risk Ratios of the Hierarchical Models - Global Portfolio 354

7.29 Turnover of the Hierarchical Portfolios - Global Portfolio 355

7.30 Statistics of the Hierarchical Portfolios - Germany 1973 356

7.31 Statistical Significance of Mean Differences of the Hierarchical Portfolios - Germany 1973 356

7.32 Risk Figures of the Hierarchical Portfolios - Germany
     1973 357
7.33 Risk Ratios of the Hierarchical Portfolios - Germany
     1973 358
7.34 Turnover of the Hierarchical Portfolios - Germany 1973 358
7.35 Statistics of the Hierarchical Portfolios with an Altern-
     ative Clustering Technique - Global Portfolio 360
7.36 Statistics of the Hierarchical Portfolios with an Altern-
     ative Clustering Technique - Germany 1973 361

A.1 Notifications and Asset Names of the Germany 1973
     Dataset 371
A.2 Four-Factor Model Regression Results for the Minimum
     Risk Portfolios - Global Portfolio 372
A.3 Four-Factor Model Regression Results for the Risk
     Budgeting Portfolios - Global Portfolio 372
A.4 Four-Factor Model Regression Results for the Minimum
     Risk Portfolios - Germany 1973 377
A.5 Four-Factor Model Regression Results for the Risk
     Budgeting Portfolios - Germany 1973 382
A.6 US Industry Indices of Datastream 383
A.7 Four-Factor Model Regression Results for the Minimum
     Risk Portfolios - US Industry 383
A.8 Four-Factor Model Regression Results for the Risk
     Budgeting Portfolios - US Industry 384
A.9 Four-Factor Model Regression Results for the Minimum
     Risk Portfolios - US MSCI 384
A.10 Four-Factor Model Regression Results for the Risk
     Budgeting Portfolios - US MSCI 385
A.11 German Industry Indices of Datastream 385
A.12 Four-Factor Model Regression Results for the Minimum
     Risk Portfolios - German Industry (Artmann et al., 2012)386
A.13 Four-Factor Model Regression Results for the Risk
     Budgeting Portfolios - German Industry (Artmann
     et al., 2012) 386

A.14 Four-Factor Model Regression Results for the Minimum
     Risk Portfolios - German MSCI (Hanauer et al., 2013) 387
A.15 Four-Factor Model Regression Results for the Risk
     Budgeting Portfolios - German MSCI (Hanauer et al.,
     2013) 387
A.16 Minimum and Maximum Portfolio Weights for the Min-
     imum Risk Portfolios in the Empirical Dataset 388
A.17 Minimum and Maximum Portfolio Weights for the Risk
     Budgeting Portfolios in the Empirical Dataset 389

1 Introduction

1.1 Motivation and Problem Statement

Risk budgeting models have recently gained great interest both from the academic as well as from the practical side. These are portfolio models which do not require expected returns as inputs and obtain the portfolio weights of the assets by equalizing risk contributions to a predefined risk measure.

Pearson (2002, p. 7) defines risk budgeting as a *'process of measuring and decomposing risk, using the measures in asset-allocation decisions, assigning portfolio managers risk budgets defined in terms of these measures, and using these risk budgets in monitoring the asset allocations and portfolio managers'*. More concretely, the process involves the determination of the sources of risk, measurement of the risk contributions, setting limits on the risk contributions, the asset allocation and afterwards the comparison of the realized risk contributions with the desired ones to remain within the limits. This process clarifies that the risk budgets are seen as an additional instrument to control the portfolio optimization (see also Sharpe (2002)). Only recently the risk contributions are used directly as a portfolio optimization criterion.

Risk contributions answer the question: 'Where does the risk come from?' (Rosen and Saunders, 2010, p. 336). As noted by Rosen and Saunders (2010, p. 336), the contributions to risk can be divided into two types: risk contributions to the individual assets in the portfolio or to specified risk factors (e.g. market risk factors such as interest rates, exchange rates, equity volatilities etc., macro-economic, geographic, or industry factors affecting market or credit risk). In both cases, the sum of the risk contributions yields the overall portfolio risk. However, the calculation of the contributions to risk factors is not straight forward and has yet received comparatively little attention in the literature. This can be explained through the fact that the risk factors have to be individually defined before the decomposition and there is no agreement in the asset pricing literature which risk factors exist and matter the most (see also Meucci (2007) for calculation of risk contributions to user-defined factors and chapter 2.2.2 for the review of asset pricing factors). Moreover, there are several factors which impact different assets in the portfolio, and thus the theory for deriving risk contributions cannot be directly applied (Rosen and Saunders, 2010, p. 337). Due to this reasons, this thesis focus on the risk contributions of the individual assets to different portfolio risk measures.

The risk contribution portfolios are a popular investment strategy. On the Asset Management side, Bridgewater Associates were the first to launch a risk parity fund to its clients in 1996 with the 'AllWeather' fund (Podolsky et al., 2010, Bridgewater Associates, 2010). Nowadays, many Asset Management Firms offer risk budgeting investments to their clients (to name a few: AQR Capital [1], Aquila Capital [2], Pan-Agora Asset Management [3], Putnam Investments [4] and Invesco [5]). The funds are based on the risk parity principle, but each of them is different, as the underlying assets and 'risks' (individual asset risks vs. macro-economic factors, etc.) are divergent. There are also equal risk contributions indices available (EURO iSTOXX 50 Equal Risk [6],

---

[1] http://www.aqr.com

[2] http://www.aquila-capital.de

[3] http://www.panagora.com

[4] https://www.putnam.com

[5] http://www.invesco.com

[6] http://www.stoxx.com/indices/index_information.html?symbol=SXERCE

Lyxor SmartIX ERC [7] and Salient Risk Parity Index [8]).

What are the reasons to use the equal risk contribution (ERC) portfolio as an investment strategy?

Usually an investment decision should be consistent with decision making under uncertainty. The utility or decision theory describes investors' preferences by utility functions. Thus, the theory explains the way investors think about risk. In case of the ERC portfolio, there is however a lack of explanation from the utility theory. Under this perspective, it is not clear what problem the risk budgeting portfolios should solve.

Moreover, the asset pricing theory states that investors should hold the 'market portfolio', that is the tangency portfolio with the maximum Sharpe ratio per definition (Sharpe, 1964). In the view of the theory, the minimization of risk on its own is meaningless (Scherer, 2010b, p. 653). However, despite the theoretical considerations, there is a large body of empirical literature which discovers a 'low risk anomaly', i.e., stocks with low risks have higher returns than stocks with higher risks (see 4.1.1). Related to this common finding is the observation that the MV portfolio earns higher returns than the market (capital-weighted index) while showing lower risk (Haugen and Baker, 1991). As the ERC portfolios consider also only risk estimations and mostly outperform the market, they can also be motivated through the low risk anomaly.

Despite the intuitive sounding statement that the equally distribution of risks across the assets provides 'true diversification' (Qian, 2005b, p. 1) and thus should better prevent the portfolio from losses than other portfolios, the use of risk budgeting models is also motivated by the fact that no expactations of future returns are needed. All

---

[7] http://www.ftse.com/Indices/LyxorSmartIXERCEquityIndices/index.jsp
[8] http://www.theriskparityindex.com/

risk budgeting models follow more or less mechanical or heuristical rules to construct a portfolio which does not rely on expected returns, but instead uses only risk information (covariance matrix, Conditional Value-at-Risk, Conditional Drawdown-at-Risk, see 3.1.2). This should lead to 'more robust' portfolios than in the Markowitz framework. According to DeMiguel et al. (2009b, p. 1947), the naive portfolio outperforms the mean-variance portfolio, as well its extensions (14 models in sum), with respect to Sharpe ratio and turnover due to estimation errors. Maillard et al. (2010, p. 66f) derive analytically that the ERC portfolio is located between the MV and the naive portfolio. Thus, the risk budgeting portfolios are supposed to display a superior trade-off than the naive portfolio among the effects of the estimation error on the one side and choosing an suboptimal portfolio on the other side (Schachter and Thiagarajan, 2011, p. 85). Or in the words of DeMiguel et al. (2009b, p. 1920), the trade-off consists of *'allocation mistakes caused by using the 1/N weights'* versus *'the error caused by using the weights from an optimizing model with inputs that have been estimated with error'*.

To sum up, although risk budgets are frequently used within the asset management industry and many studies state the outperformance of the equal risk contribution portfolio (based on the volatility) vs. the market-cap, naive or MV portfolio, less is done to investigate the reasons to use the risk budgeting models as an investment strategy. The comparison of the ERC portfolios is mostly done against the 60/40 benchmark (equity/bond) and only a few recent studies investigate the underlying exposures to known asset pricing factors like the Fama-French three factors. Additionally, as many studies substantiate the use of the ERC portfolio due to less estimation errors, no one has studied the impact of estimation errors on the risk budgeting portfolios. Moreover, only the ERC portfolio based on the volatility as a risk measure is considered.

The target of this thesis is to explore the ERC portfolios based on different risk measures in different ways. At first, the use of the portfolios from the theoretical side is analyzed. The question is, what decision or utility problem the ERC portfolio is trying to solve. Or in other words, under which circumstances could an investor choose the ERC portfolio as her investment decision? This is the microeconomic perspective. From the macroeconomic point of view, it is explored if the ERC portfolio implicitly picks up known asset pricing factors or captures an omitted risk factor.

From the 'practical' side of view, the analysis investigates the performance of the risk budgeting models in different datasets, the performance in bull and bear markets, the analysis of the allocations and their robustness behavior. Moreover, a first approach of hierarchical clustering to obtain a portfolio based on the risk contributions of the assets without optimization is examined. These aspects should give a clue about the characteristics and the use of the risk budgeting models in practical portfolio optimization. As the risk budgeting models are located in the area of risk management and serve to obtain portfolios without forecasting returns, they will mainly be compared to other existing risk focused portfolios, to examine if risk diversification is a good idea.

The research questions are:

1. Can the ERC portfolio be justified through the utility or decision theory?

2. Does the use of other risk measures improve the portfolio performance compared to the volatility (minimum risk and risk budgeting models)?

3. Does the use of risk budgets in the portfolio optimization process improve the risk-return balance compared to the downside risk optimization?

4. How sensitive is the performance of the approaches considering the estimation errors or how robust are the asset allocations based on risk budgets?

5. Can the performance of the risk budgeting models be explained through exposures to known asset pricing factors?

Thus, through answering these questions throughout the thesis, the main question will be answered, namely:

$\Rightarrow$ What are the benefits of the risk-budgeting models (compared to the minimization of risk)?

It has to be emphasized that in this thesis the term equal risk contribution, risk parity and risk-budgeting portfolio are used synonymously. In general, the literature does not distinguish between the two first terms, as the term 'risk parity' stems from the asset management industry. This is a better sounding label, whereas the equal-risk contribution portfolio names exactly how the portfolio is constructed and stems from the academic side. However, some studies define the weights of the risk parity portfolio proportional to the inverse of the volatility, thus disregarding the correlation ($w_i = 1/\sigma_i$, Chaves et al. (2012, p. 152)). In the famous example, where the 60/40 portfolio is used as the benchmark, which consists of an asset universe of two asset classes, equities and bonds, the solution of the two portfolios is the same. If the covariance between the assets is disregarded, the selection of assets is very important, as high correlation among the assets results in the same risk (Bhansali et al., 2012, p. 103). Especially the asset management industry emphasizes that the risk is spread across different risk sources, like equity, interest rate, credit and commodity risk. The term 'risk-budgeting portfolio' in specific simply means that the risk contributions are matched to specific risk budgets defined by the investor, but they do not have to be equal (Bruder and Roncalli, 2012, p. 3). In this thesis, it is always the case of the ERC portfolio, which equalizes the risk contributions by taking the correlations into account.

1.2 Outline of Thesis

Figure 1.1 shows the outline of the thesis. After this introduction and problem formulation, chapter 2 introduces the classical portfolio theory of Markowitz (1952) to obtain optimal portfolios. Although Markowitz developed the approach sixty years ago, this theory is still the foundation for all following portfolio models. The portfolio allocation process changes, if a riskless asset is included. This is outlined by the separation theorem of Tobin (1958). After the principles of the portfolio theory, the chapter focuses on the issue how an investor decides among certain alternatives and why she chooses a particular portfolio. This is the field of decision and utility theory, which is presented afterwards. At first, the expected utility is outlined and the description of risk averse investors. After this, it is analyzed if the portfolio theory is consistent with the expected utility theory framework. To conclude if the recent developed risk parity models have exposures to known risk factors and outperform the 'market', the asset pricing theory is also outlined in chapter 2. The asset pricing theory tries to explain the different returns of financial assets and constitutes the framework for empirical testing of return 'anomalies'.

The risk measures, risk contributions as well as the portfolio models used in this thesis are illustrated in chapter 3. This chapter represents at first a 'technical overview' of the risk measures and portfolios used in this thesis. But the conception of risk is also an essential part of the decision or utility theory. Thus, the classification of the portfolios into the decision theory takes also place in chapter 3 by presenting alternative utility theories and ideas of behavioral finance.

Before analyzing the equal risk contribution portfolios in different empirical studies, available studies of the portfolios are presented in chapter 4. The review comprises the minimum risk anomaly, the different risk measures as well as empirical studies of the risk budgeting models. Moreover, recent ideas to risk factor diversifications are presented.

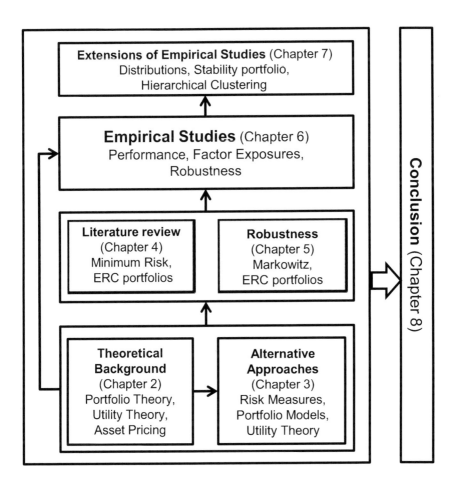

Figure 1.1: Outline of Thesis

A possible justification for the new portfolio models is the higher robustness compared to the Markowitz approaches. Chapter 5 presents
the field of robust portfolios, which deals with the sensitiveness as
well as estimation errors in the portfolios. Finally, the results of

empirical studies are presented in chapter 6. [9] The results in chapter 6 constitute the main part of the thesis and treat different aspects. At first, the empirical performances of the portfolios on three different data sets are investigated. The first dataset is an European fund, the second a global portfolio of different major indices and the third of individual assets. As the literature concentrates mostly on small datasets, it is important to analyze the different performances across the datasets. Thus, the first dataset can be seen as a strategic asset allocation, the second as a global diversified asset allocation and the third as an investment in individual securities. Moreover, the portfolio performances are analyzed in bull and bear phases. The next sub chapter investigates the exposures of the risk portfolios to known asset pricing factors in different data sets. It is examined, if the different risk based portfolios can generate an outperformance against the asset pricing factors. After this, the stimation errors of the different portfolios are examined in a simulation and an empirical study. [10]

Chapter 7 includes a few extensions to the empirical studies. An interesting aspect is to examine the influence of the simulation of returns by different distributions on the portfolio outcomes. This can be seen as a 'robustness check' of the performance results, as it is examined if the distribution assumption of the returns changes the portfolio outcomes. Moreover, an interesting alternative to the equal risk contribution portfolios, the Binary Stability portfolio, is outlined and compared to the ERC portfolios on the European fund dataset. Finally, another approach to use the risk contributions in asset allocation, but with hierarchical clustering is proposed and analyzed. The results are also compared to the risk contribution portfolios.

Chapter 8 summarizes and concludes the thesis.

---

[9]As this issue was already analyzed and published in an earlier study (Poddig and Unger, 2012), this chapter represents an expansion of the earlier work.

[10]This issue was already studied in Poddig and Unger (2012). The study in this thesis is a replication of the earlier work, but with more portfolio approaches and a slightly different setting.

2 Theoretical Background

This chapter presents the theoretical principles for this thesis. On the one hand, the Markowitz portfolio theory is outlined, which is the basis for the portfolio models. To obtain the investor's individual portfolio, the principles of the utility theory are needed, which are also presented. Moreover, the consistency of the Expected Utility Theory with the Markowitz portfolio theory is displayed. On the other hand, the asset pricing theory is presented, which is the theoretical explanation for different asset returns in the capital market and the fundament for testing return anomalies.

2.1 Modern Portfolio Theory

The foundation of the portfolio models consists of the modern portfolio theory of Markowitz and its extension through Tobin. Therefore the basis is outlined at first, before the new 'risk portfolio models' are presented in the next chapter.

2.1.1 Mean Variance Framework

Markowitz (1959) mean-variance optimization is the classical technique to allocate capital among a set of assets (Michaud, 1998, p. 1). Since the return is measured by the expected value of the random portfolio return, while the risk is quantified by the variance of the portfolio return, it is called mean-variance framework (Recchia, 2010, p.14). The portfolio allocation process implies the conflicting goals, return maximizing and risk minimizing. Markowitz was the first to show theoretically the observed diversification effect, that is, the reduction of the risk through splitting the capital to different assets. Given the returns, variances and correlations of the assets, the mean-variance approach allows to determine efficient portfolios through maximizing the return while constraining risk or minimizing the risk subject to a desired target return.

To outline the theory, at first, it is important to operationalize the relevant characteristics, that is returns and variances of the assets as well as of the portfolio. The returns can be calculated as discrete or logarithmic returns (Poddig et al., 2005, p. 31, p. 35):

$$r_t^D = \frac{p_t - p_{t-1}}{p_{t-1}} \tag{2.1}$$

with

r_t^D : discrete return for the period $t-1$ until t

p_t : asset price at time t

p_{t-1} : asset price at time $t-1$

$$r_t^S = ln\left(\frac{p_t}{p_{t-1}}\right) = ln(p_t) - ln(p_{t-1}) \tag{2.2}$$

with

r_t^S : logarithmic return for the period $t-1$ until t

p_t : asset price at time t

p_{t-1} : asset price at time $t-1$

Whereas in case of discrete returns, a discrete compounding of the capital is assumed (once at the end of the calculation period), in case of logarithmic returns a continuous compounding of the capital is assumed. The advantage of using the logarithmic returns lies in the transformation of the returns into different periods and the statistical properties. E.g., if there are daily returns, the monthly return can be simply calculated as the sum of the daily returns in this month. This is not so simple in case of discrete returns. Moreover, continuous returns display a symmetric density and are more in line with normal distribution, which is an assumption in many financial theories (Poddig et al., 2003, p. 105). However, discrete returns are easier to interpret. But both return calculations can simply be transformed into another and the differences are small if short periods are used.

The forecast of the mean return requires the knowledge of the returns in different scenarios and the probabilities of these scenarios (Poddig et al., 2005, p. 43):

$$\mu_i = \sum_{j=1}^{Z} p_j \cdot r_{ij} \tag{2.3}$$

with

μ_i : expected return of asset i

Z : amount of possible scenarios

p_j : probability of occurrence of scenario j

r_{ij} : return of asset i in scenario j

To measure the risk, Markowitz (1952) uses the variance. This is given by (Poddig et al., 2005, p. 44)

$$\sigma_i^2 = \sum_{j=1}^{Z} p_j (r_{ij} - \mu_i)^2 \tag{2.4}$$

$$\sigma_i = \sqrt{\sigma_i^2} \tag{2.5}$$

with

$$\sigma_i^2 : \text{variance of asset } i$$
$$\sigma_i : \text{standard deviation of asset } i$$

However, as the amount of possible scenarios and the probabilities of the scenarios are mostly unknown, the mean and the variance are estimated through historical returns (Poddig et al., 2005, p. 128f):

$$\mu_i = \frac{1}{T}\sum_{t=1}^{T} r_{it} \tag{2.6}$$

with

$$\mu_i : \text{empirical mean of asset } i$$
$$T : \text{amount of returns}$$

$$\sigma_i^2 = \frac{1}{T-1}\sum_{t=1}^{T}(r_{it} - \mu_i)^2 \tag{2.7}$$

with

$$\sigma_i^2 : \text{empirical variance of asset } i$$
$$\sigma_i : \text{empirical standard deviation of asset } i$$

The expected portfolio return is calculated through the sum of the products of the asset returns with their asset weight in the portfolio (Poddig et al., 2005, p. 47):

$$\mu_p = \sum_{i=1}^{n} w_i \mu_i \tag{2.8}$$

with

$$\mu_p : \text{expected return of portfolio } p$$
$$w_i : \text{weight of asset } i$$
$$\mu_i : \text{mean return of asset } i$$

Or in vector form:

$$\mu_p = \boldsymbol{w}'\boldsymbol{r} \tag{2.9}$$

with

$$\boldsymbol{w} : \text{nx1 vector of asset weights}$$
$$\boldsymbol{r} : \text{nx1 vector of mean asset returns}$$

The portfolio variance is calculated as follows (Poddig et al., 2005, p. 51f):

$$\sigma_p^2 = \sum_{i=1}^{n} w_i^2 \sigma_i^2 + \sum_{j=1}^{n} \sum_{\substack{i=1 \\ i \neq j}}^{n} w_i w_j \sigma_{ij}. \tag{2.10}$$

with

$$\sigma_p^2 : \text{portfolio variance}$$
$$\sigma_i^2 : \text{variance of asset } i$$
$$w_i : \text{weight of asset } i$$
$$\sigma_{ij} : \text{covariance of asset } i \text{ and } j$$

where the empirical covariance between asset i and j is given by

$$\sigma_{ij} = \frac{1}{T-1} \sum_{i=1}^{T} (r_{it} - \mu_i)(r_{jt} - \mu_j). \tag{2.11}$$

with

$$\sigma_{ij} : \text{covariance of asset } i \text{ and } j$$

The portfolio variance is calculated in vector form as

$$\sigma_p^2 = \boldsymbol{w}'\boldsymbol{V}\boldsymbol{w} \tag{2.12}$$

with

$$\boldsymbol{V} : \text{variance-covariance matrix}$$

The observed diversification effect, which can reduce the portfolio risk through building a portfolio and has induced Markowitz (1959) portfolio theory, can be summarized as follows (Poddig et al., 2005, p. 53f). Assume a naive portfolio, where all n assets have the same weight $1/n$.

Then the portfolio variance is given by (Poddig et al., 2005, p. 54)

$$\sigma_p^2 = \sum_{i=1}^{n} \left(\frac{1}{n}\right)^2 \sigma_i^2 + \sum_{j=1}^{n}\sum_{\substack{i=1 \\ i \neq j}}^{n} \frac{1}{n}\frac{1}{n}\sigma_{ij}. \tag{2.13}$$

with

$$\frac{1}{n} : \text{asset weight}$$

$$\sigma_p^2 : \text{portfolio variance}$$

$$\sigma_i^2 : \text{variance of asset } i$$

$$\sigma_{ij} : \text{covariance of asset } i \text{ and } j$$

Rearranging the equation leads to

$$\sigma_p^2 = \frac{1}{n}\sum_{i=1}^{n}\frac{1}{n}\sigma_i^2 + \frac{n-1}{n}\sum_{j=1}^{n}\sum_{\substack{i=1 \\ i \neq j}}^{n}\frac{1}{n(n-1)}\sigma_{ij} \tag{2.14}$$

$$= \frac{1}{n}\left(\frac{1}{n}\sum_{i=1}^{n}\sigma_i^2\right) + \frac{n-1}{n}\left(\frac{1}{n(n-1)}\sum_{j=1}^{n}\sum_{\substack{i=1 \\ i \neq j}}^{n}\sigma_{ij}\right).$$

Both bracket terms can be interpreted as the mean of the variances and the mean of the covariances in the portfolio:

$$\sigma_p^2 = \frac{1}{n}\bar{\sigma}_{Var}^2 + \frac{n-1}{n}\bar{\sigma}_{Cov} \tag{2.15}$$

with

$\bar{\sigma}_{Var}^2$: average variance of an asset in portfolio p

$\bar{\sigma}_{Cov}$: average covariance of the assets in portfolio p

If the amount of assets in the portfolio gets large, $n \to \infty$, then

$$\frac{1}{n}\bar{\sigma}_{Var}^2 \to 0, \tag{2.16}$$

$$\frac{n-1}{n}\bar{\sigma}_{Cov} \to \bar{\sigma}_{Cov} \quad \text{and thus} \tag{2.17}$$

$$\sigma_p^2 \to \bar{\sigma}_{Cov} \tag{2.18}$$

The risk of the portfolio can be divided in two parts: the unsystematic, asset specific risk and the systematic, covariance or market risk. Whereas the first component can be diversified through building a portfolio, the second component influences all assets and remains with the investor.

This effect explains why it is wiser to invest in an portfolio rather to hold individual assets. Based on this effect, Markowitz (1959) formulates the Modern Portfolio Theory or the Mean-Variance Framework.

The Mean-Variance Framework has the following assumptions:

- Investors care only about mean and standard deviation of asset returns

- Investors are risk averse (prefer same return for less risk or higher return with same risk, the aspect of risk aversion is also an important part of the utility theory in section 2.1.3)

More formally, let a and b be two different Portfolios.

- *Portfolio a dominates portfolio b, if it has a higher expected return with the same variance or a smaller variance with the same expected return or both (Poddig et al., 2005, p. 79):*

$$\mu(a) \geq \mu(b), \; if \; \sigma^2(a) = \sigma^2(b),$$

or

$$\sigma^2(a) \leq \sigma^2(b), \; if \; \mu(a) = \mu(b),$$

or

$$\mu(a) \geq \mu(b), \; and \; \sigma^2(a) \leq \sigma^2(b).$$

- *The portfolio is efficient, if there does not exist another portfolio, which dominates it.*

The efficient frontier represents all efficient portfolios. Markowitz assumes risk-averse investors, as the choice of the efficient portfolios depends on the two assumptions, that investors prefer a higher return vs. a lower return given the same level of risk, and a lower risk of a portfolio with the same return.

The objective of the portfolio theory is to obtain efficient portfolios. As it is obvious from the dominance- and efficiency-criteria, a trade-off between return and risk exists. To obtain a portfolio on the efficient frontier, the following optimization problem has to be solved (Poddig et al., 2005, p. 81):

$$min \quad \sigma_P^2 = \sum_{i=1}^{N} \sum_{j=1}^{N} w_i w_j \sigma_{ij}$$

or in matrix-form

$$min \quad \sigma_P^2 = \boldsymbol{w}' \boldsymbol{V} \boldsymbol{w}$$

subject to

$$\sum_{i=1}^{N} w_i \mu_i = r^* \quad or \quad \boldsymbol{w}'\boldsymbol{r} = \boldsymbol{r}^*$$

and

$$\sum_{i=1}^{N} w_i = 1; \quad w_i \geq 0, \quad for\, all\, i = 1, ..., N$$

with

σ_P^2 : portfolio volatility

r^* : target return

$\boldsymbol{w}$: weights vector

$\boldsymbol{V}$: covariance matrix

Through varying the target return r^*, the efficient frontier can be obtained point by point. On the left and right end of the efficient frontier lies the Minimum-Variance (MV) portfolio and the Maximum-Return portfolio. For the MV portfolio, the risk is minimized without considering the return and for the Maximum-Return portfolio, the return is maximized without considering the risk (Poddig et al., 2005, p. 109f):

Minimum-Variance Portfolio

$$min \quad \sigma_P^2 = \boldsymbol{w}'\boldsymbol{V}\boldsymbol{w} \qquad\qquad (2.19)$$

subject to

$$\sum_{i=1}^{N} w_i = 1; \quad w_i \geq 0, \quad for\, all\, i = 1, ..., N$$

Maximum-Return Portfolio

$$\mu_P = \boldsymbol{w}'\boldsymbol{r} \Rightarrow max!$$

subject to

$$\sum_{i=1}^{N} w_i = 1; \quad w_i \geq 0, \quad for\ all\ i = 1, ..., N$$

Alternative formulations of the optimization problem lead also to efficient portfolios and are common in practice. Instead of minimizing the risk, one can maximize the return subject to a risk constraint (Fabozzi, 2007, p. 34):

$$max \quad \boldsymbol{w}'\boldsymbol{\mu} \qquad\qquad\qquad (2.20)$$

subject to

$$\boldsymbol{w}'\boldsymbol{V}\boldsymbol{w} = \sigma^{2*}$$
$$\sum_{i=1}^{N} w_i = 1; \quad w_i \geq 0, \quad for\ all\ i = 1, ..., N$$

Figure 2.1 illustrates the efficient frontier with 100 points (different target returns) for a dataset of nine assets (Swiss pension fund benchmark, dataset LPP2005.RET of the R package fPortfolio (Würtz and Rmetrics Core Team, 2011)). The points represent random generated (inefficient) portfolios, whereas the square represents the Minimum Variance Portfolio (2.19). (The other points represent the portfolio models which are explained in chapter 3.2: the circle is the tangency portfolio, the triangle the naive portfolio and the rhombus the equally risk contribution portfolio based on the covariance risk budgets.)

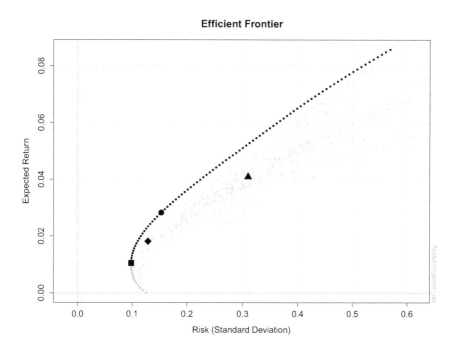

Figure 2.1: Efficient Frontier

2.1.2 Separation Theorem

If a risk-free asset exists, Tobin (1958) has shown that the efficient frontier can be reduced to a tangency line. If a risk-free asset exists, each investor invests a part in the risk free asset and the other part in a risky portfolio.

Figure 2.2 shows different combinations of the risk free rate with a risky portfolio. It is obvious that the efficient combination is the line H, since it offers greater returns for the same risk. This line is called the tangency line.

For the case of riskless lending and borrowing, an investor chooses the portfolio G in figure 2.2 as the risky asset. This is called the separation theorem.

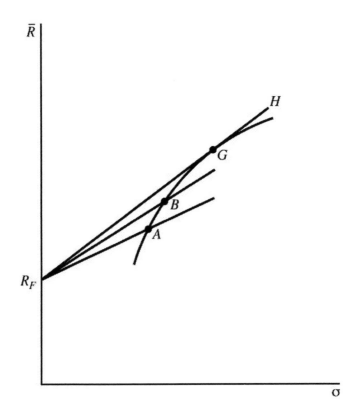

Figure 2.2: Tangency Line, Source: (Elton, 2003, p. 87)

The portfolio G is called the tangency portfolio and is obtained as follows (Elton, 2003, p. 104f):

$$max \quad \frac{R_P - R_f}{\sigma_P} \tag{2.21}$$

subject to

$$\sum_{i=1}^{N} w_i = 1; \quad w_i \geq 0, \quad for\,all\,i = 1,...,N$$

The expected return on the combination of riskless asset and the tangency portfolio is given by (Elton, 2003, p. 85)

$$E(R_C) = xE(R_{TP}) + (1-x)R_f \qquad (2.22)$$

which can be simplified to

$$E(R_C) = R_f + x[E(R_{TP}) - R_f] \qquad (2.23)$$

with

> R_C : Expected return of the combination portfolio
>
> R_{TP} : Expected return of the tangency portfolio
>
> x : fraction invested in the tangency portfolio

The risk of the combination portfolio is given by

$$\sigma_C = x\sigma_{TP} \qquad (2.24)$$

with

> σ_C : Standard deviation of the combination portfolio
>
> σ_{TP} : Standard deviation of the tangency portfolio

The risk of the combination portfolio depends only on the fraction of the tangency portfolio risk, as the standard deviation of the riskless asset and the covariance of the tangency portfolio with the riskless asset is zero (Elton, 2003, p. 85).

The weight x can also be expressed as

$$x = \frac{\sigma_C}{\sigma_{TP}} \tag{2.25}$$

Substituting x in the prior expression yields (Elton, 2003, p. 86)

$$E(R_C) = R_f + [\frac{E(R_{TP}) - R_f}{\sigma_{TP}}]\sigma_C \tag{2.26}$$

This is the equation of the tangency line, which will be useful in chapter 2.2.

2.1.3 Utility Theoretic Foundation

This section aims to analyze the investor's behavior towards risk and explains the principles why an investor chooses a specific portfolio. Decision theory provides concepts how investors make choices under risk or uncertainty. To make choices under several alternatives, the concept of utility is used. Utility theory deals with individuals' preferences in decision situations (Fishburn, 1970, p. 1). Thus, the decision and utility theory are closely related. Fishburn (1970, p. 1) points out: *'For a connection between decision and preference we shall assume that preferences, to a greater or lesser extent, govern decisions and that, generally speaking, a decision maker would rather implement a more preferred alternative than one that is less preferred.'*

The theories provide different explanations how investors make choices under risk or uncertainty. Thus, the utility theory can be seen as the theory behind risk measures and portfolio models. The expected utility theory provides theoretical foundations for the Markowitz portfolio model. Therefore, at first the expected utility framework is presented, before the link to the Markowitz portfolio models is made.

In decision theory, situations are usually distinguished in risky and uncertain situations. Knight (1921) was the first to make a distinction between decisions under risk and under uncertainty (Weber and

Johnson, 2003, p. 132). Risk is associated to situations where the probabilities of possible outcomes are known with certainty (Schmeidler (1989, p. 572) refers to these as 'objective probabilities'). Uncertainty refers to situations where the probabilities are not known with any mathematical precision (Weber and Johnson, 2003, p. 132). However, mostly it is assumed that uncertain situations can be reduced to risky situations through 'subjective probabilities' (Levy (2006, p. 8), Schmeidler (1989, p. 573)).

Expected Utility Theory
The most famous decision theory used (not only) in finance is the Expected Utility Theory. It is a normative theory for decisions under risk.

The beginning of the utility theory constitutes the work of Bernoulli in the 18th century. It was translated in English in (Bernoulli, 1954). He shows that two people facing the same lottery (this term is used in decision theory for uncertain outcomes) may value it differently because of a difference in their psychology. Before his work it was assumed that the value of a lottery is equal to its mathematical expectation and thus identical for all people, independently of their risk attitude. Bernoulli (1954) shows that the expectation of the utility of the wealth should be used instead of computing the expectation of the wealth ('[...] the determination of the value of an item must not be based on its price, but rather on the utility it yields' (Bernoulli, 1954, p. 24). The main insight of Bernoulli is to suggest that there is a nonlinear relationship between wealth and the utility of consuming the wealth (Eeckhoudt et al., 2005, p. 16).

The relationship between wealth and the utility of consuming the wealth is described by a utility function. As (Bernoulli, 1954, p. 24) points out: 'If the utility of each possible profit expectation is multiplied by the number of ways in which it can occur, and we then divide the sum of these products by the total number of possible cases, a mean utility [moral expectation] will be obtained, and the profit which corresponds to this utility will equal the value of the risk in question.'

The mean utility is called the Expected Utility and the profit which is equivalent to the utility is called certainty equivalent.

Moreover, he states that any increase in wealth results in an increase in utility. This increase is inversely proportional to the quantity of goods already possessed (*'[...] a poor man generally obtains more utility than does a rich man from an equal gain, [...]'* (Bernoulli, 1954, p. 24)).

The ideas of Bernoulli (1954) are formally developed in the book of Neumann and Morgenstern (1944) (vN/M). Therefore the utility function is also often called Bernoulli- or vN/M-function.

Four axioms have to be fulfilled to define a rational decision maker, who's preferences can be presented by an utility function (Elton (2003, p. 223), Danthine and Donaldson (2005, p. 39)):

- **Comparability**: Investors can make a comparison of different outcomes. This means that among alternatives A and B, a preference of A to B (A $\succeq$ B), B to A (B $\succeq$ A) or both (then she is indifferent between A and B, A $\sim$ B) can be expressed.

- **Transitivity**: Investors are consistent of their ranking of alternatives. For alternatives A, B and C, if A $\succeq$ B and B $\succeq$ C, then A $\succeq$ C.

- **Independence**: The preference of alternatives holds independent of the possibility of another alternative. For A, B and C with probability $p \in [0,1]$ that the alternative occurs, if A $\sim$ B, then pA + (1-p)C $\sim$ pB + (1-p)C.

- **Certainty Equivalent**: There exists a value (certainty equivalent), such that the investor is indifferent between the lottery (uncertain outcome) and the certainty equivalent (for sure).

The axioms are sufficient to guarantee an utility function U, which describes for every wealth level x the level of 'satisfaction' or 'utility' attained by the investor with this wealth (Eeckhoudt et al., 2005, p. 16). For any two alternatives of choice A and B,

$$A \succeq B$$

if and only if

$$U(A) \geq U(B) \tag{2.27}$$

with

$$U(x) : \text{Utility function of x}$$

The Expected Utility to choose among alternatives described above can then be represented by (Schmidt-von Rhein, 1996, p. 262)

$$EU(x) = \sum_{i=1}^{N} p_i U(x_i) \tag{2.28}$$

with

$$x_i : \text{Outcome/wealth in state i}$$
$$p_i : \text{Probability of state i}$$
$$U(x_i) : \text{Utility function of } x_i$$

Desirable Properties of Utility Functions

It is important to make assumptions about utility functions, which make sense in economics. This is based upon (Elton, 2003, p. 214ff).

The first property is known in the literature as 'nonsatiation': A higher level of x (more wealth) should induce a higher utility: the function should be increasing in x. Thus, more wealth is always preferred to less wealth. This implies a positive first derivative of the utility function respective to wealth: $U'(x) > 0$.

Another important property concerns the attitude of investors towards risk. Generally, risk aversion, risk neutrality and risk seeking is possible. However, in finance, and especially in portfolio theory, it is assumed that investors are risk averse. Risk aversion is defined by the reaction of the investor to a fair gamble. A fair gamble is a lottery where the expected utility of the gamble equals the cost or the bet of the lottery (e.g. invest 1\$ and win 2\$ with probability 0.5 or lose the bet with probability 0.5, expected value=1\$). Thus, the expected value of the option 'to invest' is equal to the option 'do not invest'. If an investor is risk-averse, he rejects the fair gamble. In the framework of utility, risk aversion means that the second derivative of the utility function must be negative: $U''(x) < 0$. This contains the decreasing marginal utility noticed by Bernoulli (1954, p. 24) and leads to a concave utility curve in the utility-wealth space and a convex indifference curve in the expected return - standard deviation space. Indifference curves show individual preferences of two alternatives with all combinations that yield the same level of satisfaction or utility and can be derived from utility curves. An indifference curve in the return risk space of the Mean Variance Framework shows the investor's preferences for return and risk and that hers utility is equal along the indifference curve and thus between different combinations of return and risk (Lee et al., 2010, p. 76). The level of risk aversion is determined by the shape of the indifference curve. Moreover, the utility level increases, if the indifference curves move higher northwest in the return - standard deviation space. Figure 2.3 shows that different utility curves lead to different investor's indifference curves between return and standard deviation. The risk averse investor requires a much higher increase in return for an increase in risk to stay on the same indifference curve.

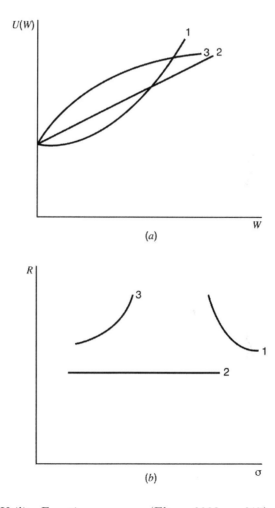

Figure 2.3: Utility Functions, source: (Elton, 2003, p. 217)
The upper chart shows the utility functions in the utility-wealth space and the lower chart the indifference curves in the expected return-standard deviation space for 1. a risk-seeking, 2. a risk-neutral and 3. a risk-averse investor.

Arrow (1971) and Pratt (1964) propose measures to describe the
risk aversion in detail (Elton, 2003, p. 217f):

$$A(x) = -\frac{U''(x)}{U'(x)} \qquad (2.29)$$

$$R(x) = -\frac{xU''(x)}{U'(x)} \qquad (2.30)$$

with

$$A(x) : \text{Absolute risk aversion}$$
$$R(x) : \text{Relative risk aversion}$$

The derivative of the absolute risk aversion with respect to wealth,
$A'(x)$, measures how the investor reacts to changes in wealth. If the
investor increases the amount in risky assets as wealth increases, she
has a decreasing absolute risk aversion $(A'(x) > 0)$. Otherwise it is
increasing $(A'(x) < 0)$. Is the amount unchanged, is the absolute risk
aversion constant $(A'(x) = 0)$.

The relative risk aversion considers the percentage of wealth invested in risky assets instead of the amount invested in risky assets.
The investor has a decreasing relative risk aversion, if she invests
more percentage in risky assets as wealth increases $(R'(x) < 0)$. If
she invests less percentage in risky assets with more wealth, then
she exhibits increasing relative risk aversion $(R'(x) > 0)$. If it is
unchanged, the relative risk aversion is constant $(R'(x) = 0)$.

Whereas it is generally assumed that most investors exhibit decreasing absolute risk aversion, the assumption concerning the relative risk
aversion is less clear (Elton, 2003, p. 218).

Implications for Markowitz Portfolio Theory

The expected utility theory is used within the Mean-Variance framework to obtain an investor-optimal portfolio. In the absence of a riskless asset, the investor's utility function is used to select a portfolio on the efficient frontier. Thus, the investor's preferences define how she chooses a portfolio among all efficient risky portfolios. In the case of a risk-free asset, all investors allocate their capital in the same risky portfolio, but the investor's utility function is needed to obtain the optimal combination of the tangency portfolio and the riskless asset (Elton, 2003, p. 210).

The portfolio selection process can be seen as a special case of decision theory with μ and σ as decision criteria (Schmidt-von Rhein, 1996, p. 227). The consistency of the expected utility and the portfolio framework can be obtained by assuming (Tobin, 1958, p. 74, 76)

- normal distributed returns or

- a quadratic utility function.

The first assumption guarantees that the investor's decision depends only on the mean and variance of returns and is also the assumption of Markowitz (1952). The focus on the mean and standard deviation can also be justified on the assumption that the utility function is quadratic (Hanoch and Levy, 1970, p. 182):

$$U(x) = a + bx + cx^2 \tag{2.31}$$

the expected value is

$$
\begin{aligned}
EU(x) &= a + bEx + cEx^2 \\
&= a + b\mu + c(\mu^2 + \sigma^2)
\end{aligned} \tag{2.32}
$$

with

$$\mu : Ex$$
$$\sigma^2 : E(x - \mu)^2 = Ex^2 - \mu^2$$

However, these necessary assumptions are subject of criticism in the literature. The first assumption of normally distributed returns is mostly rejected in empirical studies. The quadratic utility function implies thereby an increasing absolute and relative risk aversion, whereas empirical observations as well as rational considerations assume decreasing absolute risk aversion (Hanoch and Levy (1970, p. 182), Elton (2003, p. 220)). Levy (1994) tests two hypotheses: decreasing absolute vs. increasing relative risk aversion in an experiment among students with real money. The experiment consists of ten rounds of trades by changing the investor's amount of money depending on her performance. If the first hypothesis is true, the investor invests more money in risky assets, if wealth increases. If the other hypothesis is true, the investor invests more money in riskless assets, if she has more money at disposal. Levy (1994, p. 304) concludes:'*Investors tend to show decreasing relative risk aversion (DRRA) or, at best, constant relative risk aversion (CRRA) but by no means IRRA [(increasing relative risk aversion)].*' Thus, the Markowitz portfolio theory implies a behavior of investors, which is not empirically supported by experiments.

Due to the difficulty to determine a specific investor utility function, a simplified objective function is used for practical portfolio optimizations. The objective function to obtain an investor specific portfolio is given as follows (Poddig et al., 2005, p. 86):

$$U(P) = \mu_P - \lambda \sigma_P^2 \tag{2.33}$$

with

$$U(P) : \text{Utility of portfolio P}$$
$$\mu_P : \text{portfolio return}$$
$$\sigma^2 : \text{portfolio variance}$$
$$\lambda : \text{risk aversion parameter}$$

The objective function describes the trade-off of an investor between the mean and the variance of a portfolio. In fact, it is not a 'real' utility function in the sense of the expected utility theory, but an equivalent objective function that considers the investor's preferences through the risk-aversion parameter. Therefore, it can be named as the 'risk aversion formulation of the classical mean-variance optimization problem' (Fabozzi, 2007, p. 35). It can be motivated through the decision theory by the so called 'Förstner-rule', which measures the utility of an alternative through the mean and the standard deviation corrected by the parameter λ (Poddig et al., 2005, p. 85). However, the theoretical derivation is more complex. The consistency of this objective function with the expected utility theory can only be established for exponential utility functions with normal distributed returns ((Poddig et al., 2005, p. 105), see (Schneeweiß, 1967, p. 146ff), (Laux, 2003, p. 202ff)). For the derivation and discussion of this problem, see Schmidt-von Rhein (1996), Chopra and Ziemba (1993), Schneeweiß (1967) and Laux (2003). However, for practical purposes, even the explanation and determination of the risk aversion is not simple. Therefore, this method is usually preferred over determining a specific utility function (Poddig et al., 2005, p. 105ff).

The risk-aversion formulation reflects that the portfolio return (wealth) increases the utility and the variance (risk) decreases it. The risk aversion parameter specifies the risk preference of the investor. If $\lambda = 0$, the investor cares only about the portfolio return. If $\lambda > 0$, the investor is risk averse (which is the standard case according to the utility theory). In this case, portfolios with a higher variance become more highly penalized.

If the parameter is gradually increased from zero, the efficient frontier can be calculated. It is a common practice to calibrate the parameter such that a particular portfolio has the desired risk profile. The determination of λ can be performed in different ways and the approaches can be found in Poddig et al. (2005, p. 94ff). For most portfolio allocation decisions, the risk aversion is somewhere between 2 and 4 (Fabozzi, 2007, p. 35).

2.1.4 Weaknesses of the Classical Portfolio Theory

The criticism of the mean-variance approach results from two different research areas: risk measurement and robust asset allocation.

The mean-variance approach has limited generality since several authors have shown that mean-variance selection will only lead to optimal portfolios if the returns are jointly elliptically distributed, as the variance treats positive and negative deviations of the mean equally (Grootveld and Hallerbach, 1999, p. 305). The assumption of symmetrically distributed returns is however refuted in the literature (see Mandelbrot (1963), Fama (1965b), Rachev et al. (2005)). Moreover, empirical studies demonstrate that extreme events, which occur in the tail of the distribution, are more likely than predicted by the normal distribution, so called 'fat tails' (Rachev et al., 2005, p. 81).

Thus, other risk measures, which take the asymmetry or skewness and the 'fat tails' into account, have become very popular. As stated by (Grootveld and Hallerbach, 1999, p. 305): *'Indeed, the popularity of downside risk among investors is growing and mean return-downside risk portfolio selection models seem to oppress the familiar mean-variance approach.'*

The other criticism stems from the fact that the inputs are assumed to be 'true' and the optimizer does not account for uncertainty in the estimated values (Michaud, 2009, p.18; Drobetz, 2001, p. 59).). In reality the inputs are not known in advance, but can only be forecasted or estimated with large errors. These estimation errors are known to result in not well diversified 'optimal' portfolios, which tend to concentrate on a small subset of the available securities and are also often very sensitive to changes in input parameters (Tütüncü and Koenig, 2004, p. 2). Thus, the portfolios exhibit extreme weights, which vary in each optimization (DeMiguel et al., 2009b, p. 1916). For a review of more studies, see chapter 5.

Going back to figure 2.1, one can see that the amount of the possible portfolios, the 'feasible set', which lies under the efficient frontier has a much higher variability of portfolio with similar characteristics as the portfolios on the efficient frontier (there are much more points further down the efficient frontier than directly near the efficient frontier). Thus, small changes in the inputs change dramatically the composition of the portfolio on the efficient frontier, as no near neighbors are available, whereas changes in portfolios in the 'feasible set' affect far less the structure (weight allocation) of the portfolio (Würtz et al. (2011, p. 2), Würtz et al. (2012a, p. 1)). Moreover, the portfolios, which lie in the feasible set, are more diversified in terms of weights or in terms of risk. As one can see from figure 2.1, the naive and the equal risk contribution portfolio (which are introduced in chapter 3.2) lie under the efficient frontier, where the amount of possible portfolios (small black dots) is much higher. Therefore, the line under the efficient frontier can be called the 'ridge frontier' (Würtz et al., 2011, p. 2). Würtz et al. (2011) have shown that the investment in portfolios on the 'ridge frontier' can result in less drawdowns and quicker recovery times compared to the efficient tangency portfolio.

This thesis captures the criticisms of the classical portfolio optimization process: First, alternative portfolio models based on downside risk measures are studied and secondly, the estimation error/robustness of these approaches will be studied in a simulation and an empirical examination. Most often, the downside risk measures are 'statistically' motivated in the literature, i.e., to capture features of a return distribution. In chapter 3.3, it will also be analyzed if the downside risk measures can resemble an underlying utility theory. As the risk budgeting portfolios lie under the efficient frontier, in the 'feasible set', it can be suspected that the sensitivity to estimation errors are lower compared to the efficient portfolios (as the density of the available alternative portfolios is much higher, as explained in (Würtz et al., 2011, p. 2)). However, there is a lack of studies on robustness of the risk budgeting portfolios. The concept of robust portfolios is presented in chapter 5 and the examination of robustness is provided in 6.4.

2.2 Asset Pricing Theory

This thesis aims to examine if the different portfolios exhibit 'abnormal returns'. Therefore, the Asset Pricing Theory is going to be introduced in this section. This theory represents the basis for exploring pricing anomalies, which will be examined in chapter 6.

One of the central questions in finance is why different assets earn different returns. Asset pricing models try to give the answer to this profound question and explain expected returns. Whereas all models agree on the insight that returns are compensation for bearing systematic risk, what constitutes the systematic risk is less clear (Goyal, 2012, p. 3).

2.2.1 Capital Asset Pricing Model - CAPM

This section is based upon (Elton, 2003, p. 292ff).

The Capital Asset Pricing Model of Sharpe (1964), Lintner (1965b) and Mossin (1966) is the most famous model in asset pricing. It is valid in a 'mean-variance world'. That means that the investors make their portfolio decision following the Mean-Variance Framework (see section 2.1.1). Altogether, the following assumptions hold (Elton, 2003, p. 293):

- Investors follow the Mean-Variance framework.

- Unlimited short sales are allowed.

- Limitless lending and borrowing at the risk-free rate is possible.

- The market is in equilibrium.

- There are no transaction costs and no taxes.

- Assets are infinitely divisible and marketable.

- Investors have homogeneous expectations about the mean, variance and correlations of the assets. Thus, they build exactly the same risky portfolio.

The assumptions make sure that the market is perfect. If all investors hold the same risky portfolio, then in a state of equilibrium, it is the market portfolio. They hold a combination of the market portfolio and the riskless asset. In equilibrium, the tangency line (derived in chapter 2.1.2) is called the capital market line and is given by

$$E(R_e) = R_f + [\frac{E(R_M) - R_f}{\sigma_M}]\sigma_e \qquad (2.34)$$

with

$$
\begin{aligned}
E(R_e) &: \text{Expected return of an efficient portfolio} \\
E(R_M) &: \text{Expected return of the market portfolio} \\
R_f &: \text{risk free rate} \\
\sigma_M &: \text{Standard deviation of the market portfolio} \\
\sigma_e &: \text{Standard deviation of the efficient portfolio}
\end{aligned}
$$

This equation describes the expected return of an efficient portfolio, but not the expected return of a non-efficient portfolio or an individual security. For this, the individual security risk in equilibrium has to be derived.

The market risk is given by

$$\sigma_M = \sqrt{\sum_{i=1}^{N} x_i^2 \sigma_i^2 + \sum_{\substack{i=1 \\ }}^{N} \sum_{\substack{j=1 \\ i \neq j}}^{N} x_i x_j \sigma_{ij}} \qquad (2.35)$$

with

$$x_i : \text{market proportions}$$

As all investors hold the market portfolio, the individual security risk is the change in the risk of the market portfolio and results through the change of the individual security holdings in the market portfolio (Elton, 2003, p. 300). In other words, it is the marginal risk contribution of security i to the market portfolio and is calculated as the derivative of the market risk with respect to the the security holding (Elton, 2003, p. 300):

$$\frac{\partial \sigma_M}{\partial x_i} = \frac{\partial [\sum_{i=1}^{N} x_i^2 \sigma_i^2 + \sum_{i=1}^{N} \sum_{\substack{j=1 \\ i \neq j}}^{N} x_i x_j \sigma_{ij}]^{1/2}}{\partial x_i},$$

$$= \frac{\frac{1}{2}[2x_i \sigma_i^2 + 2\sum_{i=1}^{N} \sum_{\substack{j=1 \\ i \neq j}}^{N} x_j \sigma_{ij}]}{[\sum_{i=1}^{N} x_i^2 \sigma_i^2 + \sum_{i=1}^{N} \sum_{\substack{j=1 \\ i \neq j}}^{N} x_i x_j \sigma_{ij}]^{1/2}}$$

$$= \frac{x_i^2 \sigma_i^2 + \sum_{i=1}^{N} \sum_{\substack{j=1 \\ i \neq j}}^{N} x_j \sigma_{ij}}{\sigma_M}$$

$$= \frac{\sigma_{iM}}{\sigma_M} \tag{2.36}$$

Substituting the efficient portfolio risk through the security risk in equation 2.34 yields

$$E(R_i) = R_f + [\frac{E(R_M) - R_f}{\sigma_M}]\frac{\sigma_{iM}}{\sigma_M} \tag{2.37}$$

with

$E(R_i)$: Expected return of security i

$E(R_M)$: Expected return of the market portfolio

R_f : risk free rate

σ_M : Standard deviation of the market portfolio

σ_{iM} : Covariance between security i and the market portfolio.

This is called the security market line.
Define

$$\beta_i = \frac{\sigma_{iM}}{\sigma_M^2}, \tag{2.38}$$

then

$$E(R_i) = R_f + \beta_i(E(R_M) - R_f), \tag{2.39}$$

with

$E(R_i)$: Expected return of asset i

R_f : Risk-free return

β_i : systematic risk, market risk of asset i

$E(R_M)$: Expected return of the market portfolio

This is the well-known formula of the CAPM. It states that the expected return of any asset or portfolio i depends only on the β. Thus, the differences between asset returns results only through differences in their betas. The relationship between the expected return and the securities' β is linear. This is shown in figure 2.4.

In chapter 2.1.1 it was shown that the risk of a security can be divided into a systematic and an unsystematic part. The unsystematic part can be eliminated by holding a large enough portfolio. Thus, the CAPM establishes the relationship that only the systematic part matters in determining expected returns. The investor will only get a reward for holding systematic risk, which cannot be diversified away. There is no reward for holding unsystematic risk.

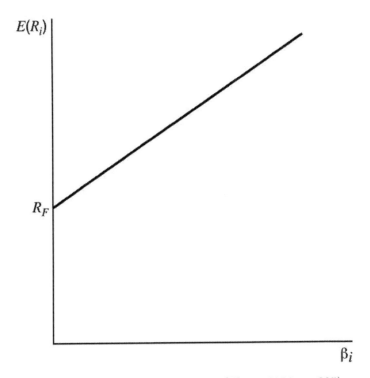

Figure 2.4: Security Market Line, Source: (Elton, 2003, p. 305)

Note that the CAPM is only valid in equilibrium. It does not mean that stocks with high beta earn higher returns in all times. But stocks with a higher beta are expected to earn a higher return. Thus, on average, over long periods of time the relationship should hold (Elton, 2003, p. 299).

2.2.2 Empirical Evidence - Critique and Anomalies

This review is based on Goyal (2012), Jagannathan et al. (2010) and Cochrane (2005, p. 436ff).

Since the development of the CAPM, the model was extensively tested in several empirical studies. Already in the beginning, not all results were validating the theory. Lintner (1965a) and Douglas (1969) do not find a significant relationship between expected returns and market betas. Miller and Scholes (1972) and Black (1972) state that the bias of the regression coefficients arises through the 'errors-in-variables' problem. Because of this problem, Black (1972) and Fama and MacBeth (1973) propose to group the stocks into portfolios. This method has since become standard in empirical testing. The assets are sorted into portfolios according to their estimated historical betas, which are rebalanced periodically. Then, the portfolio beta is calculated. Portfolio betas are a better measure, as the individual risks of the assets are smaller (lower residual variance) and the betas are more stable over time. Black (1972) and Fama and MacBeth (1973) find that the β is related to the excess return, which are conform with the CAPM. However, Black et al. (1972, p. 44) state that *'the intercept and slope of the cross-sectional relation varied in different subperiods and were not consistent with the traditional form of the capital asset pricing model'*. Moreover, all the early studies find that the relation between expected returns and market betas is too flat. The alpha is positive for assets with low betas and negative for assets with high betas. Thus, assets with low betas have a higher return than expected from the theory and assets with high betas lower than predicted from the CAPM (low-beta anomaly). Black (1972) provides a theoretical link for the low-beta anomaly through the theory of leverage aversion. He shows that if riskless borrowing is not allowed, the market equilibrium changes such that the slope of the security market line is lower than in the 'original' CAPM (Black, 1972, p. 455). Frazzini and Pedersen (2010) extend the idea of Black (1972) and point out that if leverage is not allowed, riskier assets (high beta assets) are over-weighted. This causes that the equilibrium price of high beta assets increases or that the expected return on high-beta assets is lower. The high beta assets have lower risk-adjusted returns than low-beta assets, which require leverage. Frazzini and Pedersen (2010) introduce a dynamic model of leverage constraints with two types of investors: the one group is allowed to use leverage and overweights high beta assets and the other group uses leverage, but the leverage is limited and thus sells short high beta assets and leverages low beta assets. In several empirical tests within U.S. equities and across 20 global equity markets, they show that this model leads to the flatter security market line and thus to the low-beta anomaly.

Roll (1977) argues that the CAPM is not testable due to the non-tradeability of the true market portfolio (since it has to contain all existing assets, e.g. human capital, real estate). He points out that the CAPM equation will hold, if any the 'market portfolio' is mean-variance efficient. Therefore, the test if the CAPM holds, can only be approached by testing the mean-variance efficiency of a proxy of the market portfolio. However, as stated by Elton (2003, p. 358), even if the empirical tests cannot provide a perfect test of the CAPM, the results give important implications for behavior in capital markets. Moreover, the empirical tests produce results which are in general consistent with the CAPM: investors are only rewarded for systematic risks.

The CAPM predicts that the return of an asset depends only on its β. However, many empirical studies document other factors, which are linear related to expected returns. The significance of the factors is proved through examining alphas from a time series regression on sorted portfolios and/or examining the factor risk premium through Fama and MacBeth (1973) regressions. Results detected by empirical investigations, which are not in line with the theory, are called 'puzzles' or 'anomalies', as they cannot be explained by the CAPM. Based on these anomalies, new asset pricing models were proposed.

As described by Cochrane (2005, p. 436), an anomaly is usually detected as follows:

1. Stocks are sorted into portfolios based on a characteristic, which is associated with average returns. Then it is examined if there is a difference in average returns between the portfolios. It has to be made sure that biases are eliminated, to get an acceptable result (like measurement errors, survival bias, etc.).

2. The betas for the portfolios are calculated and proved whether the average return spread is caused by the spread in betas (cross-sectional regressions).

3. If the betas cannot account for the spread, there is an anomaly. Multiple betas should be considered.

Thus, an anomaly is detected, if the assets or portfolios display 'abnormal returns' relative to the CAPM. Or in other words, abnormal returns are returns that cannot be explained by the market beta alone. In time series regressions, an anomaly or abnormal return is detected, if the intercept α is positive and significant. If the α is positive, it means that the asset return exceeds the equilibrium expected return of the CAPM:

$$\alpha = R_{i,t} - [R_f + \beta_i(E(R_M) - R_f)]$$

According to the CAPM, the α should be zero, as only the market beta defines the asset return. If the α is positive, the CAPM is rejected and there has to be a missing factor or missing factors which determine the return. Jensen (1968) uses the CAPM to measure the performance of mutual funds. He states that when a portfolio manager has an ability to forecast asset returns, the intercept will be positive. Therefore it is called the 'Jensen's alpha'.

Many anomalies were discovered in empirical studies. Subrahmanyam (2010) states in his literature review that he can *document at least fifty variables that the literature has used to predict stock returns*

*in the cross-section, where the cross-section essentially is the same
familiar universe of NYSE-Amex-Nasdaq stocks'* (Subrahmanyam,
2010, p. 27). He provides a classification of the different variables
into four groups:

- informal arguments or different firm characteristics (p/e ratio, size,
  momentum),

- risk-return model variants (decomposing beta, intertemporal CAPM,
  idiosyncratic risk),

- behavioral biases (over-/underreaction of investors) and

- market frictions (illiquidity, information risk, short selling)

A detailed review of the empirical studies is omitted here, as it
is beyond the scope of this thesis. For a review of the asset pricing
literature, see Campbell (2000), Jagganathan and Ma (2003), Fama
and French (2004), Subrahmanyam (2010) and Goyal (2012).

The most important variables for which anomalies were detected
are: price to earning ratio (Basu, 1977, Ball, 1978, Miller and Scholes,
1972), size (Banz, 1981, Fama and French, 1992), book-to market ratio
(Stattman, 1980, Rosenberg et al., 1985, Fama and French, 1992) and
past returns (Bondt and Thaler, 1985, Jegadeesh and Titman, 1993).
Other detected significant variables are idiosyncratic risk (Lehmann,
1990, Malkiel and Xu, 2002, Ang et al., 2006, Fu, 2009), liquidity
(Amihud and Mendelson, 1986, Brennan et al., 1998, Pástor and
Stambaugh, 2003), information risk (Easley and O'Hara, 1987, Easley
et al., 1996, 2002, Easley and O'Hara, 2004), short selling (Miller,
1977, Desai et al., 2002, Diether et al., 2002) and overreaction of
investors (Lakonishok et al., 1994).

2.2.3 Factor Models

Based on the detected anomalies, new asset pricing models were proposed. The most famous is the Fama-French three factor model.

Three-Factor Model

The book-to-market anomaly and the size anomaly inspired the development of the Fama-French three-factor model. Fama and French (1992) sort NYSE-AMEX-NASDAQ stocks in 25 value-weighted portfolios based on firm size and book-to-market value. They find that small stocks have abnormally high returns, which cannot be explained by the market beta. On the other side, 'growth' stocks (stocks with high market value relative to their book value) display a lower beta than their CAPM betas suggests. They also confirm the early evidence that the relation between average return and beta is too flat.

To explain these patterns in average returns, Fama and French (1993) and Fama and French (1996) propose a multifactor asset pricing model with the market return, the difference between the returns on diversified portfolios of small and big stocks and the difference between the returns on diversified portfolios of high and low book-to-market stocks as factors:

$$R_i - R_f = \alpha + \beta_{MKT}(R_M - R_f) + \beta_{SMB}SMB + \beta_{HML}HML + \varepsilon_i, \tag{2.40}$$

with

$$
\begin{aligned}
R_i &: \text{return of asset } i \\
R_f &: \text{Risk-free return} \\
\alpha &: \text{intercept / excess return} \\
SMB &: \text{return of small minus big stocks} \\
HML &: \text{return of high minus low stocks} \\
\beta &: \text{factor coefficients} \\
\varepsilon_i &: \text{residual return}
\end{aligned}
$$

The three-factor model is found to capture much of the variation in average returns for portfolios formed on size, book-to-market equity or other price ratios that cause problems for the CAPM (Fama and French, 2004, p. 39). It is widely used in empirical research to explain asset returns and to measure the performance of mutual funds or portfolios (Carhart, 1997). However, the problem of the model is the empirical motivation rather than a sound theoretical basis like in the case of the CAPM.

Fama (1995) suggests that the HML factor is a premium for relative distress. Thus, a premium for holding risks related to recession and economy-wide financial distress is provided (Cochrane, 2005, p. 450). Weak firms with low earnings seem to have high book-to market ratios and strong firms with high earnings seem to have low book-to-market ratios (Fama and French, 1996, p. 56). Cochrane (2005, p. 450) states also, that *'Value and small-cap stocks are typically distressed.'* Due to the fact that to take advantage of the value effect, the investor has *'to buy stocks or long-term bonds at the bottom, when stock prices are low after a long and depressing bear market; in the bottom of a recession or financial panic; a time when long-term bond prices and corporate bond prices are unusually low'* (Cochrane, 2005, p. 451). Then, the stocks or long-term bonds have to be selled in *'good times, when stock prices are high relative to dividends, earnings, and other multiples, when the yield curve is flat or inverted so that long-term bond prices are high'* (Cochrane, 2005, p. 451). However, other studies reject this distress hypothesis (Dichev, 1998, Griffin and Lemmon, 2002).

Four-Factor Model
Carhart (1997) find that funds with high returns in the last year exhibit higher expected returns in the next year. This is called the momentum effect and is already documented by Jegadeesh and Titman (1993). The momentum factor is constructed by subtracting the equal-weight average of firms with the lowest 30 percent eleven-month returns lagged one month from the equal-weight average of firms with the highest 30 percent eleven-month returns lagged one month. Thus, the factor is build through *'buying the winners and selling the losers'*, as the title of Jegadeesh and Titman (1993) reveals. This effect cannot be explained by the three-factor model of Fama and French (1993).

Thus, the momentum factor is added to the three-factor model and results in a four-factor model:

$$R_i - R_f = \alpha + \beta_{MKT}(R_M - R_f) + \beta_{SMB}SMB + \beta_{HML}HML \\ + \beta_{WML}WML + \varepsilon_i, \tag{2.41}$$

with

R_i : return of asset i

R_f : Risk-free return

α : intercept / excess return

SMB : return of small minus big stocks

HML : return of high minus low stocks

WML : return of winners minus losers

β : factor coefficients

ε_i : residual return

Performance measurement of fund managers are mostly accomplished using the four-factor model (Goyal, 2012, p. 28). However, whether the momentum factor is a reward for risk is doubtful (Goyal (2012, p. 28), Cochrane (2005, p. 447)). The factor lacks an economic interpretation and was not linked to business cycles or financial distress (Cochrane, 2005, p. 452). It is more a performance attribution factor and the performance measure literature interprets the factor simply as a diversified passive benchmark return that capture patterns in average returns (Goyal, 2012, p. 28).

2.2.4 Methodology for Empirical Testing

This section is mainly based upon Goyal (2012) and (Cochrane, 2005, p. 230ff).

Asset Pricing Models describe a cross-sectional relationship between expected returns and certain factors. However, they are adapted to derive time-series properties of the returns. Therefore, the two main approaches to test the models are the Time Series and the Cross Section regressions. The generalized method of moments (GMM) combines both methods, but will not be regarded in the following. For details of the GMM see e.g. Hansen (1982), Harvey (1989), Cochrane (2005).

For the CAPM or a model with one single factor, the Time Series Regression is accomplished as follows (Cochrane, 2005, p. 230):

$$R_i = \alpha_i + \beta_i F + \varepsilon_i, \quad i = 1, ..., N \tag{2.42}$$

with

R_i : Nx1 vector of excess returns of asset i

α_i : regression intercept of asset i

β_i : β of asset i

F : Nx1 vector of factor returns

ε_i : Nx1 matrix of residuals of asset i

If there are K factors, the Time Series Regression is accomplished as follows (Cochrane, 2005, p. 232):

$$R_i = \alpha_i + B_i F_K + \varepsilon_i, \quad i = 1, ..., N \tag{2.43}$$

with

R_i : Nx1 vector of excess returns of asset i

α_i : regression intercept of asset i

B_i : Kx1 vector of $\beta's$ of asset i

F_K : NxK vector of factor returns

ε_i : Nx1 matrix of residuals of asset i

The unknown parameters which are estimated are α_i, β_i or B_i and ε_i. The Time Series Regression is run for each asset, such that for each asset different α, $\beta's$ and $\varepsilon's$ are obtained. The factor risk premium λ is calculated as the mean of the factors: $\lambda = E(F_t)$.

The Cross-Section approach follows in two steps. At first, the β or $\beta's$ are estimated by the Time Series regression. Then, the estimated beta or betas are placed in a cross-sectional regression of average returns on the estimated betas (Goyal, 2012, p. 10). For the CAPM or an one-factor model, the second regression is as follows:

$$E(R_i, T) = \hat{\beta}_i \lambda + \alpha, \quad i = 1, ..., N \tag{2.44}$$

with

$$E(R_i, T) : \text{average return of the asset } i \text{ over}$$
$$\text{sample length } T, \text{ scalar}$$
$$\hat{\beta}_i : \text{estimated beta of the time series}$$
$$\text{regression, scalar}$$
$$\lambda : \text{factor risk premium, scalar}$$
$$\alpha : \text{residual, scalar}$$

For more factors, the regression of average returns on betas is as follows:

$$E(R_i, T) = \hat{B}_i{'}\Lambda + \alpha, \quad i = 1, ..., N \tag{2.45}$$

with

$$\hat{B}_i : \begin{array}{l}\text{Kx1 vector of estimated betas of}\\ \text{the time series regression}\end{array}$$
$$\Lambda : \text{Kx1 vector of regression coefficients}$$

In the Cross Section approach, the $\beta's$ are the explanatory variables and the $\lambda's$ are the regression coefficients. The $\lambda's$ are the factor risk premia and as it is obvious from equation 2.39, in case of the CAPM, the regression coefficient should be equal to $\lambda = E(R_M) - R_f$. The pricing error is given by the cross-sectional residual α instead of the intercept α in the time-series regression. The model predicts $\alpha = 0$. The cross-sectional regression can be run with or without an intercept. The theory states that the intercept should be zero (Cochrane, 2005, p. 236).

More generally, the Asset Pricing implication is that factors explain the expected returns. Thus, all the $\alpha's$ should be zero (Cochrane, 2005, p. 230).

Fama and MacBeth (1973) derived an alternative procedure for running cross-sectional regressions. Whereas the estimation of the $\beta's$ remains the same, the second-stage cross-sectional regression is given by

$$E(R_{i,T}) = \lambda_{0t} + \hat{B}_i{}' \Lambda_t + \alpha_t \tag{2.46}$$

with

$E(R_{i,T})$: average return of the asset i over sample length T

λ_{0t} : intercept at time t

Λ_t : Kx1 vector of factor risk premia at time t

The difference from the 'original' cross-section regression is that this regression is run in each period t (e.g. in each month instead of once over the whole period). The factor risk premium and pricing error estimates are then calculated as time-series averages of period by period estimates (Goyal, 2012, p. 13):

$$\hat{\lambda} = \frac{1}{T}\sum_{t=1}^{T}\hat{\lambda}_t, \quad \hat{\alpha} = \frac{1}{T}\sum_{t=1}^{T}\hat{\alpha}_t$$

The main advantage of the Fama and MacBeth (1973) procedure is that varying betas are possible. Fama and MacBeth (1973) use rolling

5-year regressions to estimate the betas in their tests. Moreover, it is possible to use only those stock returns which are available at time t, which could be different from those at another time period.

In both cross-section approaches, the so-called 'errors-in-variables' problem is present (first identified by Miller and Scholes (1972)). This results through the fact that the betas in the cross-sectional regression are themselves estimated via a time-series regression. The corrections for the estimators to circumvent this problem are provided in Shanken (1992).

2.3 Summary

Markowitz shows that the risk can be diversified through building a portfolio of several assets. If investors are risk averse and prefer the same return for less risk, they should hold efficient portfolios. If a risk-free asset exists, it is reasonable to invests a part in the risk free asset and the other part in a risky portfolio. The relevant parameters for the investors are thereby the mean and the variance of the assets. The utility theoretic foundation of the Modern Portfolio Theory outlined that the portfolio selection of Markowitz (1952) is only consistent with the Expected Utility Theory if the returns are normally distributed or the utility function is quadratic. However, both criteria are not quite desirable, as quadratic utility induces increasing absolute risk aversion, which is contrary to the observed decreasing absolute risk aversion and asset returns are seldom normally distributed. This is also the reason why the variance is mostly refuted empirically as a proper risk measure for asset returns, as the returns exhibit fat tails. Moreover, it is known that estimation errors in the inputs have a high impact on the portfolio structure and outcomes. This aspect is further treated in chapter 5 and 6.4.

As the asset returns are usually not normally distributed, the variance does not properly describe the 'risk'. Thus, other risk measures, which consider more the fat tails of returns are proposed in the literature. The alternative risk measures and the resultant portfolio models are outlined and presented in the next chapter. Moreover, the examination of investor's behavior towards risk leads in the literature to alternative utility theories, as experiments are in contradiction to the Expected Utility Theory. The alternatives to Expected Utility are also presented in the next chapter and it will be analyzed if the 'alternative' risk measures can be justified by the 'alternative' utility theories, as the Expected Utility Theory is not applicable. Thus, two literature strands, the 'statistical' as well the 'decision theoretical' side are combined.

Assuming the mean-variance framework for each investor leads to the Capital Asset Pricing Model. It states that the expected return of an asset depends only on its beta. This is calculated as the covariance of the security with the market divided by the market variance and is a measure for systematic risk. Thus, the difference of the asset returns result only through the differences in their systematic risks. But empirical results show that the CAPM is not always valid and anomalies are detected. These anomalies result in factor models, which are now popular to test the performance of different portfolio strategies. The analysis of abnormal returns and the exposures to the factors of the different portfolios will be analyzed by a time series regression. The three-factor as well as the four-factor model will be used to test if the portfolio returns can be explained through the underlying factors. Thus, it will be studied if the minimum risk as well as the risk budgeting portfolios implicitly pick up asset pricing anomalies and if they exhibit a positive alpha. The examination takes place in chapter 6.3.

3 Alternative Approaches in Portfolio Management

At first, this chapter introduces downside risk measures and the corresponding risk contributions from the analytical and statistical side. Moreover, the appropriate portfolio models are presented. After the technical introduction, the risk measures or the portfolio models are analyzed from the decision theoretical point of view.

3.1 Risk Measures and Risk Contributions

3.1.1 What Is Risk?

The term 'risk' is very difficult to define exactly. In every day life, risk is mostly associated with a hazard and has generally a negative meaning. However, it can also be associated with a chance, e.g. in a lottery or in an investment of an unsecured project (Cottin and Döhler, 2009, p. 1). In both cases, it is the possibility of a change or the uncertainty in future outcomes. Mathematically, it is usually not distinguished between positive and negative deviations and the risk is modeled as a random variable (Cottin and Döhler (2009, p. 2), Danthine and Donaldson (2005)). The random variable has a density, thus the risk is described by the density of the random variable.

In finance, risk is associated with a gain or a loss. Dowd (2002, p. 1) defines financial risk as follows: *'Financial risk is the prospect of financial loss - or gain - due to unforeseen changes in underlying risk factors.'* Moreover, there are different forms of financial risks. Usually it is distinguished between market risk, credit risk, operational risk and liquidity risk (McNeil and P., 2005, p. 2f):

- market risk: risk of a loss or a gain of a financial position due to changes in market prices or interest rates

- credit risk: risk of a loss due to a default of the borrower to repay the debt

- operational risk: risk of a loss due to inappropriate or failed internal processes, people and systems, or from external events

- liquidity risk: risk due to the lack of marketability of a financial position, so that it cannot be bought or sold quickly enough without losses

This thesis covers the aspect of market risk. As outlined by Dowd (2002, p. 1), market risk can itself be divided into different risks, depending on the underlying risk factor, e.g. interest rate risks, equity risks, exchange rate risks, commodity price risks, and so on.

As risk is modeled as a random variable, different risk measures have arisen, which characterize the density of the random variable. The variation of a random variable are measured by the variance, which is the first simple risk measure and was already presented in chapter 2.1.1. However, the variance is criticized as a risk measure, as investors usually associate risk with losses. Therefore, other risk measures that focuses on the losses are developed and can be summarized under downside risk measures (Poddig et al., 2003, p. 130).

Beside the mathematical or statistical side of modeling risk, it is important how investors think about risk measures (or they attitudes towards risk) and rely on them in financial decisions. Thus, risk is mostly subjective and depends on the situation (Dowd, 2005, p. 1). As outlined already in chapter 2.1.3, the attitude towards risk depends on subjective preferences, which can be conceptualized through the utility theory. It is distinguished, if a decision is made under risk or uncertainty. Hanisch (2006, p. 15) points out that a risk measure characterizes the investor's amount for the degree of uncertainty or the level of negative consequences in a decision situation under risk. Thus, on the one hand the risk measure captures the uncertainty about which of the possible outcomes will occur and on the other hand how bad outcomes influence the investor's decision. Through the choice of a specified risk measure, the investor chooses which aspects are taken into consideration. The question is then, which investor should choose which risk measure? This question can only be answered under the consideration of the investor's preferences and hence the utility theory (Hanisch, 2006, p. 120).

Thus, on the one side different risk measure quantify the density of a random variable and on the other side the risk measure reflects a subjective preference. Ideally, these two strands should be consistent. After presenting the risk measures, it will be analyzed if the downside risk measure can be consistent with an utility theory and which preferences of an investor are consistent with a particular risk measure or portfolio model.

3.1.2 Risk Measures

If returns were normally distributed there would be no need for downside risk measures as the volatility would perfectly describe the underlying risk. While the world is not normally distributed, other risk measures occurred which focus on the losses (Scherer, 2010a, p. 288).

The volatility is a symmetric measure which treats positive and negative returns symmetrically. This is not the way an investor usually thinks about risk. Instinctively risk is associated with unexpected losses (Scherer, 2010a, p. 289). So downside risk measures focuses on the left side of the return distribution. Under the assumption that returns are normally distributed, the mean-Value at Risk (see equation 3.3) and the mean-Conditional Value at Risk (see equation 3.4) optimization models deliver efficient frontiers which are subsets of the mean-variance efficient frontier (Fantazzini, 2004, p. 14).

The importance of downside risk measures for portfolio optimization has already been recognized by Roy (1952). He proposes a 'safety first' strategy to maximize portfolio expected return subject to a downside risk constraint (Fabozzi et al., 2010, p. 193). There are also other downside risk measures, like the lower partial moment (LPM, Bawa (1975)) or the mean absolute deviation (MAD, Konno and Yamazaki (1991)). Also Markowitz itself notice that the variance may be insufficient to measure the portfolio risk and proposes the semi-variance. However, these approaches did not prevail, perhaps due to computational difficulties (Fabozzi et al., 2010, p. 193). The VaR was disclosed by J.P. Morgan [1] in 1994 from the industry and was made publicly available by their system 'RiskMetrics' to calculate it. Since the concept is intuitively understood, it is not surprising that since then, the VaR has become the standard risk measure in the practice to measure investment losses and was also applied by the bank regulators (Basel I in 1996) to calculate a bank's required capital. However, in recent times, there is scepsis to use the VaR as a risk measure in the academic literature, due to its lack of subadditivity in some cases, according to the axioms of Artzner for coherent risk measures (Artzner et al., 1999).

Artzner et al. (1999, p. 209f) defined risk measure axioms for a coherent risk measure. After this, the concept has become the standard to evaluate a risk measure. A risk measure $\rho(\cdot)$ is said to be 'coherent' if it satisfies the following conditions.

Let X and Y be the random returns of two financial assets and α a real number, then the following rules apply for a coherent risk measure (Artzner et al., 1999, p. 209):

---

[1] http://www.jpmorgan.com/pages/jpmorgan

- Translation Invariance: $\rho(X + \alpha) = \rho(X) - \alpha$ for any constant α

- Subadditivity: $\rho(X + Y) \leq \rho(X) + \rho(Y)$

- Positive Homogeneity: For any number $a \geq 0$, $\quad \rho(aX) = a\rho(X)$

- Monotonicity: $\rho(Y) \leq \rho(X)$ if $X \leq Y$

In the following, popular downside risk measures will be outlined.

In what follows, $f(\boldsymbol{w}, \boldsymbol{r}) = -\boldsymbol{w}'\boldsymbol{r}$ is defined as the loss function depending on the weight vector $\boldsymbol{w}$ and the uncertain vector of asset returns $\boldsymbol{r}$ with density $p(r)$. Let $\Psi(\boldsymbol{w}, \varsigma)$ be the cumulative distribution function of the random variable $f(\boldsymbol{w}, \boldsymbol{r})$ and thus the probability of $f(\boldsymbol{w}, \boldsymbol{r})$ not exceeding a threshold ς (Rockafellar and Uryasev (2000, p. 24), Rockafellar and Uryasev (2002, p. 1447), Krokhmal et al. (2002a, p. 17), Krokhmal et al. (2003, p. 5)):

$$\Psi(\boldsymbol{w}, \varsigma) = \int_{f(\boldsymbol{w}, \boldsymbol{r}) \leq \varsigma} p(r)dr, \tag{3.1}$$

$$\Leftrightarrow \Psi(\boldsymbol{w}, \varsigma) = P[f(\boldsymbol{w}, \boldsymbol{r}) \leq \varsigma] \tag{3.2}$$

with

$$\varsigma : \text{threshold}$$
$$\Psi(\boldsymbol{w}, \varsigma) : \text{cumulative distribution function of}$$
$$\text{the}$$
$$\text{loss function } f(\boldsymbol{w}, \boldsymbol{r})$$

$\Psi(\boldsymbol{w}, \varsigma)$ is the cumulative distribution function for the loss associated with $\boldsymbol{w}$. For simplicity, it is assumed that $\Psi(\boldsymbol{w}, \varsigma)$ is everywhere continuous with respect to ς.

Value at Risk (VaR)

The Value at Risk is the maximum loss which will not be exceeded with a probability/confidence level and is the α - quantile of a distribution ((Dowd, 2005, p. 27). Formally it is defined as (Rockafellar and Uryasev (2000, p. 24), Rockafellar and Uryasev (2002, p. 1447)):

$$VaR_{\alpha} = \min_{\varsigma \in R}\{\Psi(\boldsymbol{w}, \varsigma) \geq \alpha\}, \qquad (3.3)$$

with

$$\alpha : \text{a chosen probability/confidence level}$$

VaR is not a coherent risk measure since it fails to hold the subadditivity axiom of coherence if the returns are not normally distributed and thus contrasts with portfolio diversification (Çobandağ and Weber, 2011, p. 1). Because of these features of VaR, academics and practioners have started to search for an alternative risk measure to VaR which is coherent (Acerbi and Tasche, 2002, p. 1). However, in practice the VaR remains the standard approach to measure financial risk (Jorion, 2007, p. x).

Conditional Value at Risk (CVaR)

The Conditional Value at Risk is the mean of the losses exceeding VaR (Dowd and Blake (2006, p. 200), Rockafellar and Uryasev (2000, p. 24), Krokhmal et al. (2002a, p. 17)):

$$CVaR_{\alpha} = \frac{1}{1-\alpha} \int_{f(\boldsymbol{w}, r) \geq VaR_{\alpha}} f(\boldsymbol{w}, r) p(r) dr, \qquad (3.4)$$

with

$$\alpha : \text{a chosen probability}$$

It can also be written as the conditional expectation (Scaillet (2004, p. 119), Sarykalin et al. (2008, p. 273)):

$$CVaR_\alpha = E[f(\boldsymbol{w}, \boldsymbol{r}) | f(\boldsymbol{w}, \boldsymbol{r}) \geq VaR_\alpha], \qquad (3.5)$$

with

$$\alpha : \text{a chosen probability}$$
$$E : \text{expectation}$$

Uryasev (2000, p. 24) shows that the CVaR can be characterized by the following function:

$$F_\alpha(\boldsymbol{w}, \varsigma) = \varsigma + \frac{1}{(1-\alpha)} \int_{r \in \mathbb{R}} [f(\boldsymbol{w}, \boldsymbol{r_t}) - \varsigma]^+ p(r) dr \qquad (3.6)$$

with

$$\boldsymbol{r_t} : \text{asset returns at time } t$$
$$\varsigma : \begin{array}{l} \text{threshold of the cumulative} \\ \text{distribution function } \Psi(\boldsymbol{w}, \varsigma) \end{array}$$
$$[f(\boldsymbol{w}, \boldsymbol{r_t}) - \varsigma]^+ : max\,(0, f(\boldsymbol{w}, \boldsymbol{r_t}) - \varsigma)$$

With this function, the $CVaR_\alpha$ and the VaR_α result by

$$CVaR_\alpha = \min F_\alpha(\boldsymbol{w}, \varsigma), \qquad (3.7)$$

$$VaR_\alpha = \text{left endpoint of} \quad \text{argmin}\, F_\alpha(\boldsymbol{w}, \varsigma) \qquad (3.8)$$

The integral in equation (3.6) can be approximated with a sample of the probability distribution (discrete distribution), then the function $F_\alpha(\boldsymbol{w}, \varsigma)$ is calculated as follows (Rockafellar and Uryasev (2000, p. 25), Rockafellar and Uryasev (2002, p. 1461)):

$$F_\alpha(\boldsymbol{w}, \varsigma) = \varsigma + \frac{1}{(1-\alpha)T} \sum_{t=1}^{T} [f(\boldsymbol{w}, \boldsymbol{r_t} - \varsigma]^+, \qquad (3.9)$$

By definition, the CVaR is always greater than the VaR for the same confidence level (for a theoretical proof see (Rockafellar and Uryasev, 2002, p. 1452)). It is also known as mean excess loss, expected shortfall (ES) or tail VaR (Rockafellar and Uryasev, 2000, p. 21). However, theoretically there are a few differences between these terms (Rockafellar and Uryasev, 2002, p. 1445). In this thesis, it will be throughout denoted as CVaR.

Drawdown and Maximum Drawdown (MaxDD)

A drawdown is the drop in the portfolio value comparing to the maximum achieved in the past (Cheklov et al., 2003, p. 2). It is a very intuitive risk measure since it measures the loss the portfolio might suffer. Moreover, some investors have the target that a drawdown larger than a prespecified amount is unacceptable (Grossman and Zhou, 1993, p. 242).

However, the use of drawdowns in portfolio optimization is not as much widespread as other common measures such as return volatility, VaR, or CVaR (Burghardt et al., 2003, p. 14). Grossman and Zhou (1993) were the first to study a portfolio optimization subject to drawdown constraints in an one-dimensional case by allocating current capital between one risky and one risk-free asset. Cvitanic and Karatzas (1994) generalized the model to a case with several risky assets. Alexander and Baptista (2006) study the impact of adding a maximum drawdown constraint to the mean-variance model. Cheklov et al. (2003) introduced the Conditional Drawdown at Risk as a new risk measure, but first Cheklov et al. (2005) extended the CDaR approach as an objective in portfolio optimization.

Assume $r_p(\boldsymbol{w}, t)$ is the cumulative portfolio return over the preceding portfolio holding time (e.g. one month) at time t with asset weights $\boldsymbol{w} = (\boldsymbol{w}_1, ..., \boldsymbol{w}_n)$. Then the drawdown function is obtained as follows (Cheklov et al. (2003, p. 3), Krokhmal et al. (2003, p. 8)):

$$D(\boldsymbol{w},t) = \max_{0\leq\tau\leq t}\{r_p(\boldsymbol{w},\tau)\} - r_p(\boldsymbol{w},t), \qquad (3.10)$$

with

$D(\boldsymbol{w},t)$: Drawdown function at time t

$\max_{0\leq\tau\leq t}\{r_p(\boldsymbol{w},t)\}$: maximum of the cumulative portfolio return

over the history preceding time t

For a sample-path of returns, the drawdown function $D(\boldsymbol{w},t)$ is defined for each time tick, e.g. $D(\boldsymbol{w},1), D(\boldsymbol{w},2), ..., D(\boldsymbol{w},t)$ corresponding to a time series vector of drawdowns at different times. Usually the drawdowns are calculated as negative numbers $-D(\boldsymbol{w},t)$ or $D(\boldsymbol{w},t) = \frac{r_p(w,t)}{\max_{0\leq\tau\leq t}\{r_p(w,\tau)\}}$, as the drawdowns are associated with losses. However, for reasons of consistency as the loss distributions is taken for the calculation of the CVaR, the Drawdown function will be seen as positive.

The maximum and the average drawdown are calculated as the maximum and the average of the drawdown function over the interval $[0,T]$ (Cheklov et al. (2003, p. 4), Krokhmal et al. (2003, p. 9), Jöhri (2004, p. 60)):

$$MaxDD(\boldsymbol{w}) = \max_{0\leq t\leq T}\{D(\boldsymbol{w},t)\}, \qquad (3.11)$$

$$AvDD(\boldsymbol{w}) = \frac{1}{T}\int_0^T D(\boldsymbol{w},t)dt, \qquad (3.12)$$

with

$MaxDD(\boldsymbol{w})$: Maximum Drawdown at time t

$AvDD(\boldsymbol{w})$: Average Drawdown at time t

Conditional Drawdown at Risk (CDaR)

The Conditional Drawdown at Risk was first suggested by Cheklov et al. (2003) and is defined as the mean of the worst $(1-\alpha)*100\%$ drawdowns experienced over some period of time on a sample-path with a confidence value α (Cheklov et al., 2003, p. 2) .The Drawdown at Risk (DaR_α) is the value, which corresponds to the VaR_α in case of the drawdown distribution. The DaR_α is thus a threshold, such that (1-α)*100% of the drawdowns exceed it. The Drawdown at Risk function is the α-quantile of the $D(\boldsymbol{w},t)$ distribution.

The CDaR is based on the CVaR concept to the case when the loss function is defined as the drawdown function $D(\boldsymbol{w},t)$ (Cheklov et al., 2003, p. 4):

$$CDaR(\alpha) = \frac{1}{(1-\alpha)T} \int_{D(\boldsymbol{w},t)\geq DaR_\alpha} D(\boldsymbol{w},t)dt, \qquad (3.13)$$

with

$$DaR_\alpha : \text{Drawdown at Risk (threshold)}$$

The CDaR measure includes the average drawdown and the maximum drawdown: when the confidence level $\alpha = 1$, the CDaR equals the MaxDD and when $\alpha = 0$, the CDaR equals the AvDD (Cheklov et al., 2003, p. 4).

Similar to the CVaR, the CDaR can be obtained by minimizing the following function ((Cheklov et al., 2005, p. 29), (Krokhmal et al., 2003, p. 11)):

$$CDaR(\alpha) = \min H_\alpha(\boldsymbol{w},y), \qquad (3.14)$$

$$H_\alpha(\boldsymbol{w},y) = y + \frac{1}{(1-\alpha)T} \int_0^T [(D(\boldsymbol{w},t)-y]^+ dt \qquad (3.15)$$

with

$$y : \text{threshold of the cumulative distri-}$$
$$\text{bution function of } D(\boldsymbol{w},t)$$

If the drawdown function is represented by a sample of returns, then the function $H_\alpha(\boldsymbol{w}, y)$ is obtained as follows (Krokhmal et al., 2003, p. 10):

$$H_\alpha(\boldsymbol{w}, y) = y + \frac{1}{(1-\alpha)T} \sum_{t=1}^{T} [(D(\boldsymbol{w},t) - y]^+$$

The CDaR can also be minimized by linear optimization (Cheklov et al., 2005, p. 28).

3.1.3 Risk Contributions

Risk decompositions help to identify the assets with the largest and lowest contribution to risk and can be very useful (Dowd, 2005, p. 265). As stated by Pearson (2002, p. 153), *'a risk measure is useful only to the extent that one understands the sources of risk'.*

Through applying Euler's theorem (that every linear homogeneous function can be represented by the partial differentials), Tasche (1999) shows that every homogeneous risk measure (the positive homogeneity axiom of Artzner et al. (1999)) can be decomposed into a weighted sum of its derivatives with respect to portfolio weights, the risk contributions. A risk measure is linear homogeneous, if it changes proportionally when one makes the same proportional change in all positions (Pearson, 2002, p. 154).

Sharpe (2002, p. 80) states that the additive decomposition of total portfolio risk is only correct for independent (non-correlated) returns, but Qian (2006) shows that the decomposition of the risk into absolute risk contributions is closely linked to contributions to the defined risk measure. Thus, *'risk contribution or risk budgeting can be regarded as loss contribution or loss budgeting' (Qian, 2006, p. 1)*.

Risk Contributions to Volatility

In recent years there is a growing amount and interest in portfolio construction approaches focused on risk contributions from volatility, called equal risk contribution portfolios or simply risk parity. The portfolio is obtained by equalizing risk contributions based on volatility from the assets of the portfolio (Allen, 2010, Foresti and Rush, 2010, Lee, 2011, Maillard et al., 2010, Demey et al., 2010, Levell, 2010, Barra, 2010).

Marginal risk contributions (MRC) are defined as the derivative of the portfolio risk after the weights and the absolute risk contributions (ARC) are obtained by multiplying the marginal contributions with the asset weights. MRC's represent the change in portfolio volatility induced by a small change in the asset weight and are already introduced in chapter 2.2.1 for the derivation of the CAPM equation. The focus of the equal risk contribution portfolios lie on the ARC, whereas the MV portfolio equalizes the MRC's (Maillard et al., 2010, p. 68). After what follows, the risk contributions will be named MRC and ARC, respectively.

The portfolio variance is given by (Poddig et al., 2005, p. 51):

$$\sigma_p^2 = \boldsymbol{w'Vw} = \sum_{i=1}^{N} w_i^2 \sigma_i^2 + \sum_{j=1}^{N}\sum_{i=1}^{N} w_i w_j \sigma ij.$$

The marginal risk contribution is defined as follows (Maillard et al., 2010, p. 64):

$$MRC_{\sigma,i} = \frac{\partial \sigma_p}{\partial w_i} = \frac{w_i \sigma_i^2 + \sum_{j \neq i}^{N} w_j \sigma ij}{\sigma_p}. \tag{3.16}$$

In vector form, the n marginal risk contributions are calculated as (Maillard et al. (2010, p. 64), Bruder and Roncalli (2012, p. 4))

$$MRC_\sigma = \Leftrightarrow \frac{Vw}{\sqrt{w'Vw}},$$

with

MRC_i : marginal risk contribution of asset i

MRC_σ : marginal risk contributions of all assets (vector)

V : covariance matrix

σ_{ij} : covariance of asset i and j

w : weight vector

σ_p : portfolio volatility

The absolute risk contribution is defined as $ARC_i = MRC_i * w_i$ and the portfolio risk equals the sum of the absolute risk contributions (Tasche (1999, p. 7), Maillard et al. (2010, p. 64)):

$$\sigma_p = \sum_{i=1}^{n} ARC_i \qquad (3.17)$$

Risk Contributions to CVaR

Since the CVaR is a tail risk measure, the decomposition of CVaR into risk contributions is also called tail risk budgeting (Stoyanov et al., 2010). The general derivative of the CVaR, with respect to the weights and without considering a special distribution of the returns, is as follows (Tasche (1999, p. 20), Yamai and Yoshiba (2002, p. 106), Stoyanov et al. (2010, p. 311), Scaillet (2004, p. 120), Sarykalin et al. (2008, p. 281) Meucci (2007, p. 4), Boudt et al. (2008, p. 85)):

$$MRC_{CVaR,i} = \frac{\partial CVaR_\alpha(-r_p)}{\partial w_i} = E[-r_i| -r_p \geq VaR_\alpha(-r_p)], \quad (3.18)$$

with

$MRC_{CVaR,i}$: marginal risk contribution of asset i
$\quad -r_i$: loss of asset i
$\quad -r_p$: portfolio loss
$VaR_\alpha(-r_p)$: portfolio VaR

Or in vector form:

$$MRC_{CVaR} = \frac{\partial CVaR_\alpha(-\boldsymbol{w}'\boldsymbol{r})}{\partial w_i} = E[-\boldsymbol{r}|-\boldsymbol{w}'\boldsymbol{r} \geq VaR_\alpha(-\boldsymbol{w}'\boldsymbol{r})],$$

$$(3.19)$$

with

MRC_{CVaR} : marginal risk contributions of all assets (vector)
$\quad -\boldsymbol{r}$: vector of asset losses $(-r_1, -r_2, ..., -r_n)'$
$-\boldsymbol{w}'\boldsymbol{r}$: portfolio loss

This is also called the 'conditional expectation', as the risk budgets can simply be calculated through the mean of the asset returns, if the portfolio return exceeds the portfolio VaR (Tasche (1999, p. 19), Yamai and Yoshiba (2002, p. 106)). As the historical returns are used for this, this calculation will be called 'sampleCVaR budgets'. To obtain equal risk budgets, this formula can be optimized, but to obtain more precise results, the method of the finite differences will be used (see below).

If a special distribution is considered, an analytical formula can be derived based on the distribution parameters. However, this is challenging for most distributions. In the literature, the explicit derivative can only be found for the normal and the t-distribution (Boudt et al. (2008, p.), Meucci (2007, p. 299), Meucci (2010, p. 90)).

As the normal distribution will be considered for the CVaR risk contributions, the 'normCVaR' is calculated as follows (Boudt et al., 2008, 2011):

$$normCVaR = -\boldsymbol{w}'\boldsymbol{\mu} + \sqrt{\boldsymbol{w}'\boldsymbol{V}\boldsymbol{w}}\frac{\phi[\Phi^{-1}(\alpha)]}{\alpha}, \qquad (3.20)$$

with

$\boldsymbol{\mu}$: vector of mean asset returns

ϕ : Gaussian density function

Φ^{-1} : Gaussian quantile function

Thus, the marginal risk contributions of the normCVaR result through the first derivation of the normCVaR (Boudt et al. (2008, p. 87), Boudt et al. (2011, p. 7)):

$$MRC_{normCVaR,i} = -\mu_i + \frac{w_i\sigma_i^2 + \sum_{j\neq i}^{N} w_j\sigma ij}{\sigma_p}\frac{\phi[\Phi^{-1}(\alpha)]}{\alpha}, \qquad (3.21)$$

with

ϕ : Gaussian density function

Φ^{-1} : Gaussian quantile function

Or in vector form:

$$\boldsymbol{MRC}_{normCVaR} = -\boldsymbol{\mu} + \frac{\boldsymbol{V}\boldsymbol{w}}{\sqrt{\boldsymbol{w}'\boldsymbol{V}\boldsymbol{w}}}\frac{\phi[\Phi^{-1}(\alpha)]}{\alpha}. \qquad (3.22)$$

Boudt et al. (2008) provide an analytical decomposition for the CVaR based on the Cornish-Fisher and Edgeworth approximations. They call it 'modified Expected Shortfall (mES)', because it can be considered as a parametrical normal CVaR adjusted for skewness and excess kurtosis (Boudt et al., 2008, p. 92). In this thesis, it will be called modified CVaR or 'modCVaR', respectively.For the derivation of the risk contributions, first, it is important that the portfolio return is expressed under its location-scale representation (Boudt et al., 2008, p. 88):

$$r_p = w'\mu + \sqrt{w'V w}\, u, \tag{3.23}$$

with

u : zero mean, unit variance random
variable with distribution function
$G(\cdot)$

The distribution function $G(\cdot)$ of the random variable is generally assumed to be normal. But it can be improved by adjusting for skewness and kurtosis in the data. This is done by using the rth order Edgeworth expansion of $G(\cdot)$ around the standard Gaussian distribution function $\Phi(\cdot)$ (Boudt et al., 2008, p. 88):

$$G_r(z) = \Phi(z) - \phi(z)\sum_{i=1}^{r} P_i(z), \tag{3.24}$$

with

$P_i(z)$: polynomial in z

The Cornish-Fisher expansion of the rth order of the quantile function $G^{-1}(\cdot)$ around the Gaussian quantile function $\Phi^{-1}(\cdot)$ equals then (Boudt et al., 2008, p. 88):

$$G_r^{-1}(\alpha) = z_\alpha + \sum_{i=1}^{r} P_i^*(z_\alpha), \tag{3.25}$$

with

$$z_\alpha : \Phi^{-1}(\alpha)$$

Draper and Tierney (1973) provide exact formulas for the first eight terms in the Edgeworth and Cornish-Fisher expansions. For the derivation of the modCVaR, only the terms related to the second order expansion are needed (Boudt et al., 2008, p. 89):

$$P_1(z) = P_1^*(z) = \frac{1}{6}(z^2 - 1)s_p, \qquad (3.26)$$

$$P_2(z) = \frac{1}{24}(z^3 - 3z)k_p + \frac{1}{72}(z^5 - 10z^3 + 15z)s_p^2, \qquad (3.27)$$

$$P_2^*(z) = \frac{1}{24}(z^3 - 3z)k_p - \frac{1}{36}(2z^3 - 5z)s_p^2 \qquad (3.28)$$

with

$$s_p : \text{skewness of the portfolio return}$$

$$k_p : \text{excess kurtosis of the portfolio return}$$

Under the location-scale representation 3.23, the modCVaR can be computed as follows (Boudt et al., 2008, p. 92):

$$modCVaR = -\boldsymbol{w}'\mu - \sqrt{\boldsymbol{w}'\boldsymbol{V}\boldsymbol{w}}\,E_{G_2}[z|z \leq G_2^{-1}(\alpha)], \qquad (3.29)$$

with

$$G_\alpha^{-1} : \alpha \text{ Cornish Fisher quantile around} \\ \text{the Gaussian quantile function } \Phi^{-1}$$

For a loss probability α, the modified CVaR is the expected value of all returns below the α Cornish-Fisher quantile. The calculation of $E_{G_2}[z|z \leq G_2^{-1}(\alpha)]$ yields (Boudt et al., 2008, p. 92):

$$E_{G_2}[z|z \leq G_2^{-1}(\alpha)] = -\frac{1}{\alpha}\Big\{\phi(g_\alpha) + \frac{1}{24}[I^4 - 6I^2 + 3\phi(g_\alpha)]k_p$$

$$+ \frac{1}{72}[I^6 - 15I^4 + 45I^2 - 15\phi(g_\alpha)]s^2_p \qquad (3.30)$$

$$+ \frac{1}{6}[I^3 - 3I^1]s_p\Big\},$$

where

$$
I^q =
\begin{cases}
\sum_{i=1}^{q/2} \left(\dfrac{\prod_{j=1}^{q/2} 2j}{\prod_{j=1}^{i} 2j} \right) g_\alpha^{2i} \phi(g_\alpha) + \left(\prod_{j=1}^{q/2} 2j \right) \phi(g_\alpha) & \text{for q even} \\[3ex]
\sum_{i=0}^{q*} \left(\dfrac{\prod_{j=0}^{q*} 2j+1}{\prod_{j=0}^{i} 2j+1} \right) g_\alpha^{2i+1} \phi(g_\alpha) - \left(\prod_{j=0}^{q*} (2j+1) \right) \phi(g_\alpha) & \text{for q odd}
\end{cases}
$$

with

$$q* : (q-1)/2$$

$$g_\alpha : G_2^{-1}$$

The derivative of the modified CVaR or the marginal risk contributions to the modified CVaR can be computed analytically by (Boudt et al., 2008, p. 119):

$$
\begin{aligned}
MRC_{modCVaR,i} = &-\mu_i - \frac{w_i \sigma_i^2 + \sum_{j\neq i}^{N} w_j \sigma ij}{\sigma_p} E_{G_2}[z | z \leq g(\alpha)] \\
&+ \sigma_p \frac{1}{\alpha} \Big\{ \frac{1}{24}[I^4 - 6I^2 + 3\phi(g_\alpha)] \partial k_p + \frac{1}{6}[I^3 - 3I^1] \partial s_p \\
&+ \frac{1}{36}[I^6 - 15I^4 + 45I^2 - 15\phi(g_\alpha)] s_p \partial s_p \\
&+ \partial g_\alpha [-g_\alpha \phi(g_\alpha) + \frac{1}{24}[\partial_i I^4 - 6\partial_i I^2 - 3g_\alpha \phi(g_\alpha)] k_p \\
&+ \frac{1}{6}[\partial_i I^3 - 3\partial_i I^1] s_p + \frac{1}{72}[\partial_i I^6 - 15\partial_i I^4 + 45\partial_i I^2 \\
&+ 15 g_\alpha \phi(g_\alpha)] s_p^2] \Big\}
\end{aligned}
$$

$$(3.31)$$

For $z_\alpha = \Phi^{-1}(\alpha)$,

$$
\begin{aligned}
\partial_i g_\alpha = &\frac{1}{6}(z_\alpha^2 - 1)\partial_i s_p + \frac{1}{24}(z_\alpha^3 - 3z_\alpha)\partial_i k_p \\
&- \frac{1}{18}(2z_\alpha^3 - 5z) s_p \partial_i s_p.
\end{aligned}
$$

For q even, the derivative of I^q yields

$$\partial_i I^q = \sum_{i=1}^{q/2} \left(\frac{\prod_{j=1}^{q/2} 2j}{\prod_{j=1}^{i} 2j} \right) g_\alpha^{2i-1} (2i - g_\alpha^2) \phi(g_\alpha)$$

$$- \left(\prod_{j=1}^{q/2} 2j \right) g_\alpha \phi(g_\alpha),$$

and for q odd

$$\partial_i I^q = \sum_{i=0}^{q*} \left(\frac{\prod_{j=0}^{q*} 2j+1}{\prod_{j=0}^{i} 2j+1} \right) g_\alpha^{2i} (2i+1 - g_\alpha^2) \phi(g_\alpha)$$

$$- \left(\prod_{j=0}^{q*} (2j+1) \right) \phi(g_\alpha),$$

with

$$q* : (q-1)/2$$

The formula appears complicated, but the calculation of the marginal risk contributions is obtained quickly. The calculation of the modCVaR risk contributions is included in the R package PerformanceAnalytics of Carl et al. (2012).

Risk Contributions to CDaR

Risk budgets based on the CDaR were not yet proposed or examined in the literature. As the CDaR risk measure concept is similar to the CVaR, the risk contributions can be obtained in the same way based on the drawdown function as the loss function through the conditional expectation:

$$MRC_{CDaR,i} = \frac{\partial CDaR_\alpha(D(\boldsymbol{w},t))}{\partial w_i} \tag{3.32}$$

$$= E[D(r_i,t)|D(\boldsymbol{w},t) \geq DaR_\alpha(D(w,t))],$$

with

$$D(\boldsymbol{w},t) : \text{drawdowns of the portfolio return}$$
$$D(r_i,t) : \text{drawdowns of the asset return i}$$

There does not exist an analytical derivative of the CDaR yet in the literature, as this risk measure depends on the drawdown distribution rather than on the return distribution. However, the CDaR budgets can like the sampleCVaR budgets directly be optimized through the conditional means of the asset drawdowns, if the individual asset drawdowns exceed the portfolio Drawdown-at-Risk. Another approach is given by the approximation of a derivative through finite differences (Gilli et al., 2011, p. 70). For a function $f(x)$, the approximation of the derivative $(f'(x))$ is as follows (Gilli et al., 2011):

$$f'(x) = \lim_{h \to 0} \frac{f(x+h) - f(x)}{h}, \tag{3.33}$$

with

$$h : \text{a small value}$$

This approximation is called the forward-difference, as the small value h is added to the function. It is also possible to subtract h (backward-difference: $(f(x) - f(x-h))/h$) or to do both (central difference: $(f(x+h) + f(x-h))/2h$).

For the calculation of the CDaR budgets it would also be possible to apply the extreme value theory (EVT), as the distribution of the drawdowns has no negative values (or no positive values depending on the interpretation, see Mendes and Brandi (2004), Mendes and Leal (2005)). Mendes and Brandi (2004) and Mendes and Leal (2005) propose the Generalized Pareto Distribution to model the distribution of the maximum drawdown. For the analytical formula of the CDaR budgets, one has to assume that the drawdowns are GPD distributed, obtain the analytical formula for the GPD-CDaR and then obtain the derivative with respect to the weights. As the derivation is not straightforward, this is left for further work.

After testing the expected mean approach and the finite difference approach for calculating the CVaR and the CDaR budgets, the 'sampleCVaR' as well as the 'sampleCDaR' budgets will be calculated through the finite differences approach. The finite differences approach provides more precise results, if there are only a few data points available. Otherwise, both approaches deliver the same results. As a rebalancing approach is going to be used for testing the portfolios, the finite differences approach is more reliable. For the CVaR or the CDaR, or in general a risk measure $\Gamma(\boldsymbol{w})$, the marginal risk contributions are obtained as follows:

$$\frac{\delta\Gamma}{\delta w_i} = \lim_{\Delta \to 0} \frac{\Gamma(\boldsymbol{w} + \Delta w_i) - \Gamma(\boldsymbol{w})}{\Delta w_i}, \tag{3.34}$$

with

$\Gamma(\boldsymbol{w})$: a specified risk measure, CVaR or CDaR

Δ : a small value

w_i : weight of asset i

The Δ value is set to 0.01, as this results in equal risk contributions (see also Zivot (2011) for the implementation of the derivative of the CVaR through finite differences in R). The optimization of the marginal risk contributions with the finite differences takes place with the nonlinear optimizer Rdonlp2 in R Tamura (2007). This is an implementation of Prof. Dr. Peter Spellucis DONLP2 [2]. To obtain precise results, the following options are set: $hessian = TRUE$, $difftype = 1$ and $nstep = 500$.

---

[2]http://www.mathematik.tu-darmstadt.de/fbereiche/numerik/staff/ spellucci/DONLP2/

3.2 Portfolio Models

This section gives an overview of the portfolio models, which are considered in this thesis for the simulation as well as for the empirical study. To obtain a fair comparison of the different approaches, the following constraints are applied for every optimization technique:

$$\sum_{i=1}^{n} w_i = 1, \tag{3.35}$$

$$w_i \geq 0, \qquad i = 1, ..., n \tag{3.36}$$

with

$$w_i : \text{weight of asset i}$$
$$n : \text{number of assets in the portfolio}$$

3.2.1 Equally Weighted Portfolio (1/n)

The equally weighted portfolio assigns to each asset the same weight. With respect to the asset weights, this strategy is well diversified. However, this may not be the case due to covariation between different asset returns (Lindberg, 2009, p. 465). There is no objective function associated with the EW portfolio, the strategy involves holding a portfolio weight $w = 1/n$ in each of the n risky assets (DeMiguel et al., 2009b, p. 1922). Obviously, this approach ignores both the return and risk prospects of the investments (Lee, 2011, p. 15).

$$\boldsymbol{w} = \begin{bmatrix} 1/n \\ \vdots \\ 1/n \end{bmatrix} \tag{3.37}$$

with

$$\boldsymbol{w} : \text{weight vector}$$

3.2.2 Minimum Risk Portfolios

Minimum-Variance-Portfolio (MV)

The minimum-variance portfolio, which was already presented above (2.19), has gained a lot of interest, since it relies solely on estimates of the covariance matrix (DeMiguel et al., 2009b, p. 1924). It is also the only portfolio that is on the efficient frontier without expected returns as inputs (Lee, 2011, p. 16). (Broadie, 1993, p. 32) states that along the efficient frontier, it is easier to estimate minimum variance portfolios than maximum return portfolios. This lies in the fact that *'the error in the estimate of mean returns is typically much larger than the error in the estimate of standard deviation of returns'* (Broadie, 1993, p. 35). The optimization is as follows:

$$min \quad \boldsymbol{w'Vw} \tag{3.38}$$

Minimum-CVaR-Portfolio (minCVaR)

The minimum CVaR portfolio minimizes the CVaR without considering a target return. It is the portfolio which lies on the Mean-CVaR efficient frontier with the minimum CVaR and thus the corresponding portfolio to the MV portfolio. The optimization of an integral is tricky, but Uryasev (2000) shows that the CVaR can be minimized through the linear optimization (Uryasev, 2000, p. 4):

$$CVaR_\alpha = \min_{\varsigma \in \mathbb{R}} F_\alpha(\boldsymbol{w}, \varsigma), \tag{3.39}$$

$$F_\alpha(\boldsymbol{w}, \varsigma) = \varsigma + \frac{1}{(1-\alpha)T} \sum_{t=1}^{T} [f(\boldsymbol{w}, \boldsymbol{r_t}) - \varsigma]^+ \tag{3.40}$$

with

$$T : \text{number of returns}$$

$$\boldsymbol{r_t} : \text{asset returns at time t}$$

$$[f(\boldsymbol{w}, \boldsymbol{r_t}) - \varsigma]^+ : max(0, f(\boldsymbol{w}, \boldsymbol{r_t}) - \varsigma)$$

By using auxiliary variables z_t for $t = 1, ..., T$ to replace the term $[f(\boldsymbol{w}, \boldsymbol{r}_t) - \varsigma]^+$, the minimization of $F_\alpha(\boldsymbol{w}, \varsigma)$ can be reduced to a linear program (Uryasev (2000, p. 4), Rockafellar and Uryasev (2000, p. 28), Krokhmal et al. (2002a, p. 21)):

$$min \quad \varsigma + \frac{1}{(1-\alpha)T} \sum_{t=1}^{T} z_t, \qquad (3.41)$$

subject to

$$z_t \geq f(\boldsymbol{w}, \boldsymbol{r}_t) - \varsigma$$
$$z_t \geq 0, \quad t = 1, ..., T$$

with

$$T : \text{number of returns}$$
$$z_t : \text{auxiliary variables}$$

Before the optimization, ς is a free variable, after the optimization it is the Value of Risk of the minCVaR portfolio.

Minimum-CDaR-Portfolio (minCDaR)
The CDaR is given as follows (Cheklov et al., 2003, p. 4):

$$CDaR_\alpha = \min_{\varsigma \in \mathbb{R}} H_\alpha(\boldsymbol{w}, y), \qquad (3.42)$$

$$H_\alpha(\boldsymbol{w}, y) = y + \frac{1}{(1-\alpha)T} \sum_{t=1}^{T} [(D(\boldsymbol{w}, t) - y]^+ \qquad (3.43)$$

The minimization of the CDaR or the minimum CDaR portfolio can similar to the CVaR be obtained by linear optimization through considering auxiliary variables (Cheklov et al. (2003, p. 7), Cheklov et al. (2005, p. 31), Kuutan (2007, p. 20)):

$$min \quad y + \frac{1}{(1-\alpha)T} \sum_{t=1}^{T} z_t, \qquad (3.44)$$

subject to

$$z_t \geq u_t - r_p(w,t) - y, \quad t = 1, ..., T$$
$$z_t \geq 0, \quad t = 1, ..., T$$
$$u_t \geq r_p(w,t), \quad t = 1, ..., T$$
$$u_t \geq u_{t-1}, \quad t = 1, ..., T$$

with

y : threshold value of the cumulative distribution function of the drawdown distribution $D(\boldsymbol{w},t)$

z_t, u_t : auxiliary variables

The constraints $u_t \geq r_p(w,t)$, and $u_t \geq u_{t-1}$ substitute linearly the highest value of the portfolio up to time t: $max\{r_p(w,t)\}$. The first constraint secures that u_t is always greater than or at least equal to the cumulated portfolio return at time t and the second constraint secures that u_t is always greater than or at least equal to the previous value (Kuutan, 2007, p. 20). Before the optimization, y is a free variable, after the optimization it is the DaR_α for the minCDaR portfolio. Thus, through minimizing the function $H_\alpha(\boldsymbol{w},y)$ both values are simultaneously obtained.

3.2.3 Equally Risk Contribution Portfolios

The equal risk contribution portfolios are obtained by equalizing risk contributions from the assets of the portfolio. The risk contribution of one asset is the share of total portfolio risk attributable to that asset. It is computed as the product of the asset weight with its marginal risk contribution, the latter one being given by the change in the total risk of the portfolio induced by an diminutively increase in holdings of the asset. The marginal risk contribution is the first derivative of the risk measure to the weights. The risk contributions to different risk measures are given in chapter 3.1.3. Starting from the definition of the risk contributions, the equally risk contribution strategy finds a risk-balanced portfolio such that the absolute risk contributions are the same for all assets of the portfolio. The absolute risk contributions are defined as $ARC_i = MRC_i * w_i$ and the portfolio risk equals the sum of the absolute risk contributions:

$$\Gamma_p = \sum_{i=1}^{n} ARC_i, \tag{3.45}$$

with

$$\Gamma_p : \text{a specified risk measure}$$
$$ARC_i : \text{absolute risk contribution of asset i}$$

Thus, the following optimization problem to obtain the equally risk contribution portfolio is considered (Maillard et al., 2010, p. 66) [3]:

$$\min \quad f(w) \tag{3.46}$$

$$where \quad f(w) = \sum_{i=1}^{n}\sum_{j=1}^{n}(ARC_i - ARC_j)^2$$

Obviously, the routine minimizes the variance of the (rescaled) risk contributions (Maillard et al., 2010, p. 66). Thus, the optimization problem can also be stated as follows:

$$\min \quad Var(\boldsymbol{ARC}) \tag{3.47}$$

---

[3]It is also possible to obtain the risk budgets without optimization through an iteration process, see Chaves et al. (2012).

with

$$Var(\boldsymbol{ARC}) : \text{variance of the ARC's}$$
$$\boldsymbol{ARC} : \text{vector of ARC's}$$

For better interpretation and comparison, it is better to use the 'risk budgets' (RB) or the percental risk contributions. They add up to one like the weights and show how the assets contribute to the risk measure on a percentage basis:

$$RB_i = \frac{ARC_i}{\Gamma_p}, \qquad \sum_{i=1}^{n} RB_i = 1 \tag{3.48}$$

with

RB_i : risk budget of asset i

Γ_p : a specified risk measure (volatility, CVaR or CDaR)

As the risk budgets do add up to one, the risk concentration can be directly observed and the risk budgets can easily be compared to the weights. The optimization problem is logically as follows:

$$\min \quad f(w) \tag{3.49}$$

$$where \quad f(w) = \sum_{i=1}^{n}\sum_{j=1}^{n}(RB_i - RB_j)^2$$

with

RB_i : risk budget of asset i

or

$$\min \quad Var(\boldsymbol{RB})$$

with

$$Var(\boldsymbol{RB}) : \text{variance of the risk budgets}$$
$$\boldsymbol{RB} : \text{vector of RB's}$$

3.3 Utility Theoretic Foundations

After establishing the link of the Markowitz portfolio to the expected utility theory in chapter 2.1.3, this section tries to provide also a link to utility theory of the different risk based portfolio models. For this, at first, it is outlined if the principles of the expected utility are consistent with the different risk measures and portfolio models. After this, different insights of several theories for decision under risk or uncertainty are explained and conclusions to risk measures and different portfolios are outlined.

3.3.1 Expected Utility Theory

The application of the expected utility theory to downside risk measures is difficult, as the explicit utility functions are hard to define. Among the downside risk measures, only for the Lower Partial Moment an adequate utility function is available. However, the consistence of a risk measure with the expected utility maximization can be accomplished through the concept of Stochastic Dominance.

As stated by Bawa (1975, p. 95), the expected utility theory is mostly not applicable due to a lack of a specified utility function. In such situations, selection rules are needed which are in line with the observed economic phenomena (Bawa, 1975, p. 96). A possible comparison of uncertain alternatives without the knowledge of the utility function can be made with the mean-variance criteria (Hadar and Russell, 1969, p. 25). However, as stated above, the same decisions can only be achieved in specific circumstances (normal returns or quadratic utility function). Stochastic dominance (SD) provides a useful criterion for portfolio choice and risk measurement (for the SD criterion see Hanoch and Levy (1969), Fishburn (1964), Hadar and Russell (1969), Rothschild and Stiglitz (1970, 1971) and Bawa (1975)). The stochastic dominance criteria provides the ranking of alternatives by making general assumptions of utility functions. Thus, the rules are non-parametric and independent of a distribution (Levy, 2009, p. 251).

The **First-Order Stochastic Dominance (FSD)** rule describes the preference of one alternative to another for all non-decreasing utility functions (Levy (2009, p. 251), Bawa (1975, p. 99)):

Let $F(x)$ and $G(x)$ be the cumulative distributions of two alternatives, where $x \in [a,b]$ denotes wealth. Then,

$$F \quad \text{dominates} \quad G \qquad\qquad (3.50)$$

if and only if

$$F(x) \quad \leq \quad G(x) \quad \forall \quad x \in R \quad \text{and} < \text{for at least one } x \qquad (3.51)$$

$$\Leftrightarrow E_F U(x) \quad \geq \quad E_G U(x) \quad \forall \quad U \in U_1$$

with

$$U(x) : \text{Utility function of x}$$
$$U_1 : \text{Set of all non-decreasing}$$
$$\text{utility functions, } U'(x) > 0$$

The **Second-Degree Stochastic Dominance (SSD)** describes the preference for all risk-averse utility functions (Levy (2009, p. 251), Bawa (1975, p. 101)):

$$F \quad \text{dominates} \quad G \qquad\qquad (3.52)$$

if and only if

$$\int_a^x [F(t)]dt \quad \le \quad \int_a^x [G(t)]dt \quad \forall x \in R \quad \text{and} < \text{for at least one } x$$

(3.53)

$$\Leftrightarrow E_F U(x) \quad \ge \quad E_G U(x) \quad \forall U \in U_2$$

with

$\qquad U(x)$: Utility function of x

$\qquad U_2$: Set of all non-decreasing and concave utility functions, $U'(x) > 0$, $U''(x) < 0$

The First-order Stochastic Dominance assumes that an investor prefers more to less. Thus, she prefers an alternative x to y, if the cumulative distribution function of x is never greater than the cumulative distribution function of y. Hence, the cumulative probability distribution F is a shift downward (or to the right) of the distribution G (Hanoch and Levy, 1969, p. 337). However, if the cumulative distribution functions cross, a choice under the FSD is no longer possible. Then, the Second-degree Stochastic Dominance is needed. This rule assumes additionally that an investor is risk averse. An investor prefers x to y, if the sum of the cumulative probabilities of x is never higher than the sum of the cumulative probabilities of y.

Under the normal distribution, the SSD and the mean-variance criterion lead to similar results, otherwise the choices differ (Bawa (1975, p. 98), Hanoch and Levy (1969, p. 343)).

Implications for Portfolio Models

minCVaR and minCDaR Portfolios

The CVaR risk measure is not explicitly consistent with the expected utility maximization, in the sense that the four prerequisite axioms for a utility function cannot be fulfilled. In detail, the Independence axiom is violated. This is shown in Hanisch (2006, p. 141ff). For the validation, Hanisch (2006) uses a so called 'hybrid-CVaR' decision model. The decision is based on the trade-off between the expected mean and the CVaR (Hanisch, 2006, p. 128):

$$\Phi_{\alpha,\lambda}(X) := (1-\lambda)E(X) - \lambda CVaR_\alpha(X), \ \lambda, \ \alpha \in (0,1)$$

with

$$\Phi_{\alpha,\lambda} : \text{Preference function}$$
$$\lambda : \text{Risk aversion parameter}$$

This function is similar to the objective function in equation 2.33. The risk aversion parameter λ defines the trade-off between the expected mean and the CVaR. For $\lambda = 0$, the decision is based only on the expected mean, for $\lambda = 1$, only on the CVaR.

Through constructing a situation with three different lotteries X, Y and Z and excluding the case $\lambda = 0$, it is shown, that X $\succ$ Y and simultaneously XβZ $\prec$ YβZ, where $\beta \in (0,1)$. This is against the Independence axiom outlined above, which is a precondition for the existence of an utility function (Hanisch, 2006, p. 143). Also under the assumption of the normal distribution there does not exist an utility function which is consistent with the 'hybrid-CVaR' decision model (Hanisch, 2006, p. 144).

However, even if an utility function for the CVaR is unavailable, the risk measure is consistent with the expected utility maximization in the sense of Second-degree Stochastic Dominance. This is shown in Yamai and Yoshiba (2002), Bertsimas et al. (2004) and Ma and Wong (2010). The CVaR risk measure is consistent with SSD, such that for two random variables X and Y, the following conditions are equivalent (Ma and Wong, 2010, p. 17):

$$X \succeq^{SSD} Y$$

$$\Leftrightarrow CVaR_\alpha(X) \leq CVaR_\alpha(Y)$$

$$\Leftrightarrow E[u(X)] \geq E[u(Y)]$$

The consistency of the CDaR risk measure with expected utility was not yet considered in the literature. As the CDaR risk measure is conceptually similar to the CVaR, but based on the drawdown distribution it can only be speculated that the CDaR is either consistent with the expected utility theory.

ERC Portfolio

The ERC portfolio is mean-variance efficient, if the Sharpe ratios of all assets are identical and the correlations among the assets are the same (Kaya and Lee, 2012, p. 3). The proof is outlined in Kaya and Lee (2012, p. 21) and also in Maillard et al. (2010, p. 9). If only the correlations are constant, Maillard et al. (2010) show that the ERC portfolio equals the MV portfolio. More precise, the ERC portfolio is similar to the MV portfolio when cross-diversification is the highest. That is the case, if the correlation matrix reaches its lowest possible value (for the proof see Maillard et al. (2010, p. 21)).

Thus, the choice of the ERC portfolio is equal to the μ-σ criterion under the assumptions of constant correlations of the assets. Otherwise, the ERC portfolio is not consistent with the expected utility theory. It will be analyzed in the next section, if the choice of the ERC portfolio can be explained through other utility considerations.

3.3.2 Other Approaches

Behavioral studies have shown that the expected utility framework does not always provide a good description of human behavior. Especially the Independence Axiom is violated in experimental results, known as 'Allais paradox' (Allais, 1953) or 'Ellsberg paradox' (Ellsberg, 1961). Several decision-making models have been suggested as alternatives to expected utility (Levy, 2009, p. 251). The most popular of them is the Prospect Theory developed by Kahneman and Tversky (1979), which is also a theory for decisions under risk.

Kahneman and Tversky (1979) draw several conclusions based on empirical studies through a questionnaire and experiments. They conclude that the decision process can be divided into two phases: editing and evaluation. An alternative or prospect $(x_1, p_1; ...; x_n, p_n)$ constitutes of an outcome x_i with probability p_i. The first phase comprises a preliminary analysis of the prospects and the second phase the evaluation and choice of the prospects with the highest value. The following key features constitute the Prospect Theory (Kahneman and Tversky (1979), Stracca (2002, p. 5)):

- People think in gains and losses, rather than in states of wealth. The gains and losses are determined through a reference point.

- People overweight certain alternatives relative to uncertain outcomes ('certainty effect'). This is the main observation of Allais (1953), known as the 'Allais paradox'. Ellsberg (1961) observed that people prefer risky to uncertain situations, as they assume that in uncertain situations the chances are worse. This is known as the 'Ellsberg paradox'. Both paradoxes violate the Independence axiom.

- The certainty effect leads to the 'reflection effect'. That is, preferences between negative prospects are the opposite of the preference between positive prospects. This includes risk aversion for gains and risk seeking for losses. A sure gain is preferred over a larger probable gain, but a probable loss is preferred to a smaller sure loss.

- The value function v is concave for gains ($v''(x) < 0$, for x >0) and convex for losses ($v''(x) > 0$, for x < 0). Thus, the marginal value of gains and losses decreases with their amount.

- Losses have a higher impact than gains with the same size ('loss aversion'). The asymmetry between gains and losses is too extreme to be explained by income effects or by decreasing risk aversion. This results in a steeper value function for losses than for gains. A hypothetical value function is shown in figure 3.1.

- Probabilities are substituted through subjective decision weights, so that the value of each outcome is multiplied by a decision weight. The decision weights are not probabilities, thus they do not comply with probability axioms and they should not be interpreted as measures of degree or belief. The subjective probability weighting function $\pi(p)$, where each $\pi(p)$ is a decision weight, describes the impact of a probability p on the value of the prospect. $\pi(p)$ is an increasing function of the probabilities p, with $\pi(0) = 0$ and $\pi(1) = 1$. In the general case, the probabilities are weighted nonlinearly. People overvalue the probabilities so that $\pi(p) < p$, except in the case of small probabilities, which are overvalued (so that $\pi(p) > p$ for small p). Another property is $\pi(p) + \pi(1-p) < 1, \forall\ 0 < p < 1$, which is called subcertainty. This means that the sum of two complementary events is less than the weight for a certain event. Moreover, people have a limiting ability to assess extreme probabilities, so that events of extremely low probability are either ignored or overweighted, and events with extremely high probability are either disregarded or overvalued. Thus, the weighting function π is not well-behaved near the end-points. The typical weighting function is shown in figure 3.1.

The Prospect Theory value is obtained as follows (Kahneman and Tversky, 1979, p. 276):

$$V(x_1, p_1; ...; x_n, p_n) = \pi(p_1)v(x_1) + ... + \pi(p_n)v(x_n) \qquad (3.54)$$

with

$\pi(p_i)$: decision weight function of probability p_i

$v(x_i)$: subjective value of outcome x_i

The value is obtained by the multiplication of subjective decision weights with subjective values of outcomes. Thus, additional to the expected utility theory, where the where the wealth or outcome is transformed by an utility function, the the probabilities are also transformed by a function into subjective decision weights.

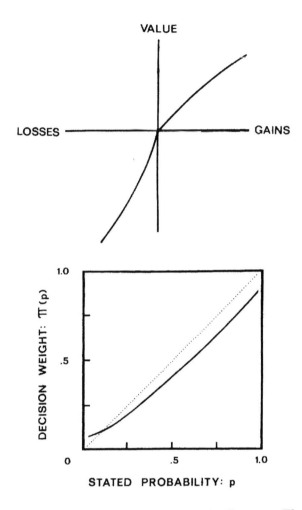

Figure 3.1: Value and Weighting Function under Prospect Theory,
source: (Kahneman and Tversky, 1979, p. 279, 283)

Tversky and Kahneman (1992) developed further the Prospect Theory to the Cumulative Prospect Theory. The Cumulative Prospect Theory can be applied for choices under risk as well as for choices under uncertainty. The transformation of the probabilities into subjective decision weights is the main difference. Rather than transforming each probability into a decision weight, cumulative probabilities for gains and losses are transformed. The transformation of the cumulative probabilities is performed through the cumulative functional proposed by Quiggin (1982) for decisions under risk and by Schmeidler (1989) for decisions under uncertainty. Quiggin (1982) proposes to order the outcomes and the probabilities of each prospect from worst to best and apply a weighting function for probabilities and an utility function to the outcomes ($V = \sum_{i=1}^{n} h_i(p)U(x_i)$, where h is a vector of decision weights and satisfies $\sum_{i=1}^{n} h_i(p) = 1$). The utility function fulfills thereby the same axioms as under the expected utility theory. Schmeidler (1989) weakens the Independece axiom and introduces the maximizing of expected utility with nonadditive probability. Nonadditive probability means that the sum of the (subjective) probabilities of all uncertain events can be less than 1 (Kim, 2011, p. 261). The difference accounts for uncertainty (e.g. Let Ω be a set of states of nature, and the subsets of Ω, $E_1, .., E_K$ are called events. Let σ_i be the nonadditive probability of investor i. Then $1 - \sum_{k=1}^{K} \sigma_i(E_K)$ indicates uncertainty. (Kim, 2011, p. 261)). As the extension of Schmeidler (1989) covers the decision under uncertainty, the probabilities and the utility function provide a description of behavior, but these are not objective probabilities (Dow and Werlang, 1992, p. 197). As explained further below, the theory of Schmeidler (1989) can be used to justify the choice of the Conditional Drawdown at Risk as a risk measure in certain circumstances.

The Cumulative Prospect Theory value for risky prospects (x_i, p_i) is given by (Tversky and Kahneman, 1992, p. 300f)

$$V(f) = V(f^+) + V(f^-)$$

$$V(f^+) = \sum_{i=0}^{n} \pi_i^+ v(x_i), \; V(f^-) = \sum_{i=-m}^{0} \pi_i^- v(x_i) \qquad (3.55)$$

where

$$\pi_n^+ = w^+(p_n), \; \pi_{-m}^- = w^-(p_{-m})$$

$$\pi_i^+ = w^+(p_i + ... + p_n) - w^+(p_{i+1} + ... + p_n), 0 \le i \le n - 1$$

$$\pi_i^- = w^-(p_{-m} + ... + p_i) - w^-(p_{-m} + ... + p_{i-1}), 1 - m \le i \le 0$$

with

f^+ : risky prospect (x_i, p_i) with positive outcomes

f^- : risky prospect (x_i, p_i) with negative outcomes

π_i^+ : decision weight for a positive outcome

π_i^- : decision weight for a negative outcome

w : cumulative weighting function

The value function allows different treatment of weights for gains and weights for losses and can be used for risky or uncertain prospects. An uncertain prospect is characterized by x_i, A_i, where the outcome x_i occurs in scenario A_i. Then, the cumulative weighting function W (instead of w for risky outcomes) assigns a value to each A. As in the Prospect Theory, the value function v is concave for gains or above a reference point ($v''(x) < 0$, for x >0) and convex for losses or below the reference point ($v''(x) > 0$, for x < 0). This characterizes 'diminishing sensitivity': the impact of a change on the value function is the smaller the farther the distance from the reference point (Tversky and Kahneman, 1992, p. 303). Moreover, the value function is steeper for losses than for gains ($v'(x) < v'(-x)$ for $x \geq 0$). That means that losses have a larger impact than gains. In contrast to the Prospect Theory, the Cumulative Prospect Theory satisfies Stochastic Dominance (Tversky and Kahneman, 1992, p. 302).

The cumulative weighting function is usually inversed S-shaped as shown in figure 3.2. It is also characterized through the 'diminishing sensitivity'. This means the farther the change of the probability from the reference point, the lower the impact on the weight. To clarify this property, (Tversky and Kahneman, 1992, p. 303) give the following example: '[...] an increase of 0.1 in the probability of winning a given prize has more impact when it changes the probability of winning from 0.9 to 1 or from 0 to 0.1, than when it changes the probability of winning from 0.3 to 0.4 or from 0.6 to 0.7.' This contains the over- or underweighting of small and high probabilities. It expresses that people will be most sensitive to extreme outcomes and less to intermediate outcomes (Fennema and Wakker, 1997, p. 57).

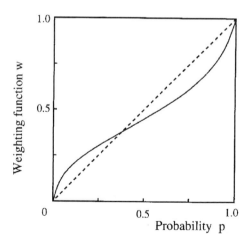

Figure 3.2: Weighting Function under Cumulative Prospect Theory, source: (Fennema and Wakker, 1997, p. 56)

The Dual Theory of Yaari (1987) is another approach that is consistent with the 'Allais Paradox' and considers decisions under risk. Instead of valuing the outcomes by an utility function and multiplying with their probabilities, the probabilities are transformed by a dual utility function and are valued with the amount of the outcome (Hanisch, 2006, p. 152). Thus, the roles of outcomes and probabilities are interchanged by replacing the wealth utility function through a probability distortion function (Hamada et al., 2006, p. 188). Yaari (1987) uses the expected utility's axioms with a modified independence axiom. For the new Independence axiom it is required, that the alternatives A, B and C are pairwise comonotonic (Yaari, 1987, p. 103). Comonotonicity is a distribution-free property and 'an analogue of perfect correlation' (Yaari, 1987, p. 104). This is important to guarantee that the additional alternative is not a hedge of the alternative A or B ('no-hedge condition'). The independence axiom can be represented as follows (Hanisch, 2006, p. 157): For comonotone alternatives A, B and C with probability $p \in [0,1]$ that the alternative occurs, if $A \succeq B$, then $pA + (1-p)C \succeq pB + (1-p)C$.

The value function of the dual theory is given by (Bernard et al., 2013, p. 19):

$$H(X_T) = \int_0^\infty w\left(1 - F(x)\right) dx \qquad (3.56)$$

with

$$X_T : \text{non-negative final wealth}$$
$$w : \text{distortion function}$$
$$F(x) : \text{cumulative distribution function of } x$$

The distortion function $w : [0,1] \to [0,1]$ is non-decreasing with $w(0) = 0$ and $w(1) = 1$. The general approach can be described as follows: The absolute value does not influence the decision, but the relative amount of one outcome compared to another. The probability of a 'poor' outcome is measured different to a probability of a 'good' outcome

(Hanisch, 2006, p. 162). Thus, under the dual theory the probabilities are transformed by a function into subjective decision weights, but the wealth stays linear in the payoffs. This is the opposite to the expected utility, where the wealth is transformed by an utility function and the probabilities are linear. So the Cumulative Prospect Theory can be seen as an 'formal aggregation' of both theories (Hanisch, 2006, p. 206). The dual theory is also the foundation of distortion risk measures (Sereda et al., 2010). The nonadditive expected utility theory of Schmeidler (1989) can be seen as a generalization of the dual theory to uncertain situations, as the axioms are similar (Hanisch, 2006, p. 152).

Implications for Portfolio Models

minCVaR and minCDaR Portfolios

The Prospect Theory gives a behavioral explanation for downside risk measures. Investors seem to treat gains and losses asymmetric. Their aversion to losses seems to be considerably stronger than their liking of gains (Fortin and Hlouskova, 2010, p. 1).

Stracca (2002) studies the optimal allocation among n assets with identical risks and expected returns for an investor under the Cumulative Prospect Theory. The main conclusion is that the optimal allocation results in risk concentration, rather than risk diversification, which is the consequence under the expected utility theory. This is explained with the loss aversion and in particular with the diminishing sensitivity to gains and losses, so that an investor is risk seeking over losses.

As people are more sensitive to losses than to gains, downside risk aversion seems natural. Rather than maximizing the return, the minimizing of downside risk is more important in the sense of Prospect Theory. Thus, downside risk measures such as Conditional Value-at-Risk and Conditional Drawdown-at-Risk are suited to measure loss-averse preferences. The choice of a portfolio which minimizes

the CVaR or the CDaR can thus be seen as an investment alternative, which protects against high losses and is consistent with the
loss-aversion of the Prospect Theory.

As the CVaR measures losses beyond a certain boundary, it can
be interpreted as a risk measure for extreme losses. The drawdown
measure takes instead the subsequent losses into account. Portfolios
based on the CVaR or on the CDaR can therefore be justified through
the implications of the Prospect Theory.

The CVaR measure can also be justified through the dual theory
of Yaari (1987). Hanisch (2006) proofs that the CVaR is consistent
with the dual theory. There are dual utility functions available, under
which the CVaR model and the dual theory attain the same results
(Hanisch, 2006, p. 168ff). This is the case for the 'hybrid-CVaR' as
well as for the minimum CVaR model (Hanisch, 2006, p. 172).

Moreover, Hanisch (2006) argues that the class of rank dependent
utility theories is suitable to justify the CVaR risk measure. As the
CVaR measure takes the worst possible outcomes into account, the
ranking of outcomes is important. The theory of Quiggin (1982), the
dual theory of Yaari (1987), the theory of Schmeidler (1989) as well
as the Cumulative Prospect Theory of Tversky and Kahneman (1992)
belong to this class of utility theories.

The CDaR risk measure is similar to the CVaR risk measure, but
based on the drawdown rather than the return distribution. Thus,
it would be possible to extend the justifications of the CVaR to
the CDaR. However, Kim (2011) gives another justification of the
maximum drawdown (MaxDD) under the nonadditive expected utility
theory of Schmeidler (1989). Nonadditivity means that the sum of
the probabilities can be less than 1 and the difference accounts for
uncertainty. According to Kim (2011), an investor's utility depends
on the maximum drawdown in two cases:

- if the uncertainty of investment timing is extreme or

- if the investor has an extreme uncertainty aversion.

Whereas uncertainty is seen as a characteristic of an act, the uncertainty aversion is seen as a characteristic of the investor. The uncertainty is expressed by the nonadditive probability, whereas uncertainty aversion is expressed by the convexity of the probability.

Kim (2011) describes the situations as follows.The uncertainty of investment timing involves uncertainty over cash flow. It is distinguished between uncertainty over cash flow and uncertainty of returns, which are independent from each other and do not influence one another. The investor assumes that he has cash inflow in the near future, but does not know when exactly. The same applies for cash outflow. Cash outflow follows after cash inflow. It is assumed that an investor buys an asset if there is cash inflow and sells the asset if she needs cash, independent of the returns. Uncertainty of returns is assumed to be smaller than the uncertainty of cash flow, as historical returns are available. If the uncertainty over cash flow is extreme, the probability of the worst cash flow timing is 100%. Thus, the investor supposes the worst case, if she buys when the return is the lowest and sells the asset if the return is the highest. Thus, the decision depends only on the MaxDD (as the MaxDD is realized in the case of worst timing).

The uncertainty aversion can be described as follows. The probability is almost linear (additive) except near the worst possibility, where it exhibits a sudden jump. More detailed, the probability is linear everywhere except near the worst outcome, but does not sum to one. For the linear probability, the expected utility concept is applicable. In the case of uncertainty aversion, the investor's utility is the sum of expected utility and the utility from the worst possibility. Schmeidler (1989) shows that the uncertainty aversion is related to the convexity of a probability function. Thus, the investor is uncertainty averse if the nonadditive probability is convex. In case of extreme uncertainty aversion, the investor's utility is separated into two parts: additive utility of all the possibilities and the expected utility of the worst possibility. The worst possibility is the MaxDD. Thus, if uncertainty aversion is extreme, the maximum drawdown influences the choice of an asset. Kim (2011, p. 278) provides also an extension of the Mean-Variance analysis in case of uncertainty aversion. Following Levy and Markowitz (1979), that an utility function can be approximated by a function of mean and variance, he summarizes the investor's utility under uncertainty aversion as follows (Kim, 2011, p. 278): '[...] *the individual's utility is expressed as the sum of two functions, where the first function is a function of mean and variance of investment returns and the second function is a function of mean and variance of maximum drawdown.*'

Whereas the situation of extreme uncertainty is unlikely, the case of an investor's extreme uncertainty aversion is quite realistic. For example, an individual uses the historical distribution of returns for prediction to select an asset, but to account for uncertainty, she lowers the total probability to the predictive distribution. Instead of relying 100% on the historical returns, she accounts for uncertainty, e.g. by 30%, and reduces the probability of each event by up to 30% (this is perhaps comparable to the idea of Black and Litterman (1992) to use investor specific views). Or if no history is available, the investor uses a uniform distribution as the predictive distribution, but due to uncertainty, she lowers the total probability that she assigns to the uniform distribution (Kim, 2011, p. 277). In both examples, the probability is almost linear everywhere and does not sum up to one. Thus, the decision depends also on the MaxDD. For more formal details see Kim (2011).

The maximum drawdown is a special case of the CDaR or the 'worst case' of the CDaR with $\alpha = 1$. Thus, the CDaR is also connected to the two cases where the MaxDD is chosen. Contrary to the MaxDD, the CDaR risk measure represents not the worst possible outcome, but the average of the α-possible worst outcomes. The investment decision based on the CDaR can then be thought of as a situation where the uncertainty over cash flow or the uncertainty aversion is less extreme than in the case of the MaxDD. The levels of uncertainty can be expressed by the α.

ERC Portfolio

Based on the ideas of (Cumulative) Prospect Theory and behavioral finance, 'verbal' justifications of the ERC portfolio are outlined. Moreover, two approaches with an utility function that yields the ERC portfolio as a special case is illustrated.

As the ERC portfolio is also based on the different risk measures, it can also be regarded as protection against losses or as an investment opportunity for loss-averse investors. Rather than minimizing the portfolio risk, the risk contributions of the assets are equalized. As the minimization of risk induces the concentration of risk budgets, one can argue that an investor who prefers the ERC portfolio has to be less loss-averse. The framework of the Cumulative Prospect Theory allows to define an individual weight function. It can generally be hypothesized that the weight function for losses in the case of the ERC portfolio must differ compared to the minimum risk portfolios. The cumulative probabilities for losses have to be lower than in the case of minimizing the risk, as the equalization of risks creates the investment in all assets. It can be thought of two different situations:

- the investor expects an economic crisis or a 'bear' phase

- the investor has no expectation, she expects either a 'bull' or a 'bear' phase

In the first case, the investor is extreme loss averse and invests in the most riskless assets. This is achieved through the minimum risk portfolios. In the second case, she has no real expectation, but is generally loss-averse. For this case, the ERC portfolio based on the desired risk measure is preferred. Moreover, the investor can be extreme or generally loss-averse on its own, e.g. dependent on the economic situation or personal issues. The level of the loss aversion can be defined through the weight function of the Cumulative Prospect Theory. The weight function allows the definition of uncertain or probable prospects. In the case of the first situation, a loss is more probable than in the second situation. Thus, in the second situation the probabilities for losses have to be lower. The second case leaves open the question why an investor should prefer the ERC portfolio, rather than going upwards the efficient frontier. As the ERC portfolio is not an efficient portfolio, there is another portfolio with the same risk (no matter if it is variance, CVaR or CDaR), but a higher return. The choice of the ERC portfolio implies that the diversification of risks is more important than the higher return. Thus, one could argue that the utility of risk diversification has to be higher than the utility of a higher wealth. Why could it be the case? In the view of the investor, the diversification of individual risks has to be more important than return. This could be the case if the investors thinks that to be invested equally in individual asset risks rather than risk concentration prevents her portfolio from losses. But this would be irrational, which leads to the issues of behavioral finance.

The choice of the ERC portfolio can be derived through anomalies in decision theory or the issue of behavioral finance. According to Byrne and Brooks (2008, p. 1), *'behavioral finance is based on the alternative notion that investors, or at least a significant minority of them, are subject to behavioral biases that mean their financial decisions can be less than fully rational. Evidence of these biases has typically come from cognitive psychology literature and has then been applied in a financial context.'* A known phenomenon in behavioral finance, which is helpful to understand the ERC portfolio's choice, is the 'diversification bias'. That means people tend to spread their choices equally across different possibilities in uncertain situations. Instead of using a model for investment, in uncertain situations people react irrational and use a rule of thumb. As reported by Rubinstein (2002, p. 1376), *'individuals making a 'multiple decision' very often diversify their choices even though the optimal behavior would clearly require them not to diversify.'* This anomaly of investment choice is also reported in Benartzi and Thaler (2001), Fisher and Statman (1997b,a) and Huberman and Jiang (2006).

This observation alone is not sufficient to clarify the choice of the ERC portfolio. It just explains the choice of the naive portfolio. However, if this 'behavioral anomaly' is combined with the loss aversion of the Prospect Theory, a diversification based on the risk is conceivable. Moreover, in light of the recent financial crisis, the diversification of individual asset risks seems a good idea for loss protection, as the experienced loss was painful. The search of alternatives after the financial crisis can be described by the 'availability bias', where investors overstate the probabilities of recently observed or experienced events (Byrne and Brooks, 2008, p. 1). A situation where the ERC portfolio emerges as investor's choice can be summarized as follows. The investor is uncertain about the future and has less knowledge of portfolio theory. However, she knows that an investment in several assets rather then one reduces the total risk. She decides to spread her capital equally across the different assets and uses the well known 1/n rule of thumb. Additionally, she is loss-averse and has recently read that only a diversification in risks is the 'true' diversification and that asset management firms or professional investor propose risk diversification as the solution to invest in crisis periods. As she already wanted to invest equally in all available assets, the 1/n investment in risks seems reasonable, which leads to the ERC portfolio.

Thus, the ERC portfolio can be justified through combining two observed behavioral phenomena of choice under uncertainty: the loss aversion of Kahneman and Tversky (1979) (or the uncertainty aversion described in Schmeidler (1989) and Kim (2011)) and the diversification bias. These two effects could lead together to a diversification of individual risks. However, this illustrates an explanation of investor's behavior rather than a 'rational' explanation in the sense of an utility theory.

Furthermore, Kaya and Lee (2012) offers an utility maximization problem for the general risk budgeting portfolio, in which the ERC portfolio is a special case.

The utility maximization problem can be stated as follows (Kaya and Lee, 2012, p. 15):

$$max \quad \gamma' ln(\boldsymbol{w}) \tag{3.57}$$

$$s.t. \quad \sigma(w) \leq \sigma^T$$

$$w \geq 0, \gamma > 0$$

with

$$\gamma : \text{nx1 vector of risk contributions}$$
$$\boldsymbol{w} : \text{vector of weights}$$
$$\sigma(w) : \text{portfolio volatility}$$
$$\sigma^T : \text{target of portfolio volatility}$$

This utility function allows portfolio assets contributions by different amounts (γ) to the portfolio volatility. The volatility target represents an 'overall risk budget'. Kaya and Lee (2012, p. 15) points out that the utility maximization problem maximizes allocation to those assets that the investor likes but at simultaneously controls the risk of the resulting portfolio. The ERC portfolio is the solution to this utility maximization and yields $\gamma_i = \gamma_j, \forall i, j$. At optimality, the volatility is equal to the volatility target, $\sigma(w) = \sigma^T$. For the proof, see Kaya and Lee (2012, p. 22f).

Kaya and Lee (2012, p. 15) states that the utility function can be interpreted as a constrained maximum likelihood optimization.

There, an investor forms a prior belief on the portfolio weights. The likelihood can be expressed as follows (Kaya and Lee, 2012, p. 15):

$$L(w;\gamma) = \prod_{i=1}^{N} w_i^{\gamma_i} \tag{3.58}$$

According to (Kaya and Lee, 2012, p. 15), *'the maximization objective expressed this way resembles the likelihood function of a multivariate Dirichlet distribution when asset weights sum up to unity'.* The prior on portfolio weights is the so-called 'objective-based prior' (Kaya and Lee, 2012, p. 15). According to Avramov and Zhou (2010, p. 35), priors are usually placed on the portfolio mean and covariance. However, objective based priors are possible. If an investor places a prior on the weights, it can be transformed into a prior on the mean and the covariance matrix.

Without a volatility target, the maximum likelihood solution yields $w = \frac{\gamma}{\sum_{i_1}^{N}\gamma}$ and the $\gamma's$ are interpreted as portfolio weights. If an investors places a prior belief on the weights without a risk constraint, she will invest according to her prior belief. However, if the risk is limited, she will invest with a risk allocation equal to the prior weights belief and the $\gamma's$ are interpreted as risk contributions of the assets. Thus, the general risk budgeting approach (with unequal risk contributions) finds the closest weights to the prior belief under regard of the volatility constraint. If the risk contributions are equal, the portfolio is close to the naive portfolio, but with a risk constraint (Kaya and Lee, 2012, p. 15).

Interesting is the fact that although expected returns appear not directly in the utility function, they can be linked with the prior belief on the weights. Assets with higher expected returns get a higher γ and the resulting weight will be adapted in a risk diversified way (Kaya and Lee, 2012, p. 16).

A similar approach is also proposed in Kaya (2012). He shows that the ERC portfolio can be expressed as a special case of a mean-risk portfolio optimization with a log-regularization constraint on weights. This is called 'the log-regularized mean-risk model'. Regularization techniques are usually used to stabilize the covariance matrix, as the sample covariance often used in practice is nearly singular if the asset universe is large (Ledoit and Wolf, 2004a, p. 366). A singular matrix is not invertible, but this is necessary to optimize the portfolio. Thus, several stabilization techniques were proposed for the covariance matrix (e.g. the shrinking of the covariance by Ledoit and Wolf (2003, 2004b,a), forecasting the covariance with factor models by Chan et al. (1999), or shortsale constraints on the portfolio weights which leads to a shrinking of the extreme elements of the covariance matrix, see Frost and Savarino (1988), Chopra and Ziemba (1993), Jagganathan and Ma (2003)). The shrinking of weights is also an issue in DeMiguel et al. (2009a) and Brodie et al. (2008). Whereas DeMiguel et al. (2009a) use a shrinking constraint to the portfolio-weight vector (1-norm and 2-norm) to diminish the estimation error, Brodie et al. (2008) add a penalty proportional to the sum of the absolute values of the portfolio weights to the objective function. Other applications of regularization techniques in portfolio optimization can be found in Carrasco and Noumon (2012), Fan et al. (2012), Fastrich et al. (2013), Yen (2010).

The log-regularized mean-risk model of Kaya (2012) incorporates a stabilization technique for the portfolio weights as a penalty in the objective function. Instead of constraining the individual weights, the weights are smoothed by using a weighted log function at the total portfolio level. The utility function is given by (Kaya, 2012, p. 3)

$$\arg\max_{w \geq 0} \quad [\mu' w - \lambda \sigma(w) + \kappa \gamma' \ln(w)] \tag{3.59}$$

with

γ : nx1 vector of risk budgets

w : vector of weights

$\mu'w$: portfolio return

$\sigma(w)$: convex risk function: Variance, CVaR or CDaR

κ : regularization parameter

λ : risk aversion parameter

The regularization parameter κ determines the relative importance of the log-regularization constraint. For the case of $\kappa = 0$, the utility function is the same as for the Markowitz optimization (with the variance as risk measure). Thus, this case is disregarded. In the empirical study of Kaya (2012), the κ is set to 0.0005. If $\kappa > 0$, the first order condition yields (for the derivation see (Kaya, 2012, p. 12))

$$\frac{\gamma_i}{\gamma_j} = \frac{\lambda R(w_i) - M(w_i)}{\lambda R(w_j) - M(w_j)} \tag{3.60}$$

with

$R(w_i)$: risk contribution of asset i: $w_i \frac{\partial \sigma(w)}{\partial w_i}$

$M(w_i)$: portfolio return portion of asset i: $\mu_i w_i$

Thus, the $\gamma's$ determine how the mean-risk part of the utility $(\mu'w - \lambda\sigma(w))$ is divided. If the γ of an asset is large, the investor wants to benefit a relatively large part of the utility from this asset. If the $\gamma's$ of all assets are equal, the contribution to the utility of each asset will be the same (Kaya, 2012, p. 3). Thus, γ can be interpreted as the amount to which an asset contributes to the utility function.

Now, two extreme cases can be distinguished for a constant κ. If $\lambda \to 0$, the investor does not care about risk and the $\gamma's$ can then be interpreted as return contributions of the assets. For example, the investor does not want to invest 100% in the asset with the maximum return, but is trying to achieve a diversification in returns. On the other side, if the risk aversion increases, $\lambda \to \infty$, the $\gamma's$ represent the risk contributions. Thus, the $\gamma's$ act as a shrinkage parameter which penalize concentration either in return or in risk contributions. If the $\gamma's$ are equal, the log-regularized mean-risk model yields two extremes: either a mean-variance or a risk budgeting portfolio, depending on the risk aversion.

The ERC portfolio results under this utility formulation through two parameter settings: when the regularization preference of the investor is uniform (the $\gamma's$ are equal) and the risk aversion or equivalently the uncertainty about return expectations increases (a high λ).

This utility function can be again interpreted in a Bayesian setting. It is shown that under exponential utility, Bayesian priors on weights lead to the ERC portfolio. The proof can be found in (Kaya, 2012, p. 12f). At first, the investor has a prior expectation of the optimal weights as well as of the portfolio variance. After investing in the portfolio, the investor observes the portfolio return and its resulting utility. These observations are then incorporated to calculate 'the posterior probability of observing a given set of (potentially inefficient) weights' (Kaya, 2012, p. 5). Through these observations, the prior expectations are 'updated'. This is expressed through the log-regularized mean-risk problem. In the case of the ERC portfolio, no prior preferences between the assets are made ($w_i = w_j = 1/n$).

The log-regularized mean-risk model formulation (with the ERC portfolio as a special case) can be seen as a method of Bayesian shrinkage. Instead of shrinking the return or the covariance, the weights are shrunk towards a portfolio the investor is comfortable with. The comfort is expressed through the utility. Thus, the 'investor-optimal portfolio' is achieved through combining prior weight expectations with the utility. In this sense, the use of risk parity leads also to the argument of robust portfolios outlined in chapter 5.

3.3.3 Summary

At first, this chapter presented downside risk measures as well as risk contributions and the resulting portfolio models. The decision-theoretical foundations of the different risk measures and portfolios has shown that they can be the objective of investor's choice in different situations. As the risk based portfolios are not consistent with the expected utility theory, other utility theories were analyzed.

Moreover, the expected utility is rejected in empirical studies. The Prospect Theory of Kahneman and Tversky (1979) describes the behavior of investors in real situations. Under this theory, downside risk measures can be motivated as investor's mostly experience loss aversion. Thus, downside risk measures like the CVaR and the CDaR serve as a measure for protection against losses. Additionally, the CDaR can be justified in a situation with uncertainty aversion under the theory of Schmeidler (1989).

An interesting conclusion is achieved for the ERC portfolio. Through combining the behavioral investigation of naive diversification and the loss or uncertainty aversion, the choice of the ERC portfolio can be comprehended. The diversification bias is not part of the utility theory, but an observed behavioral bias. However, it is an empirical observation comparable to the experiments of Kahneman and Tversky (1979) which led to the Prospect Theory. Furthermore, an objective function, where the ERC portfolio results in a special case is also available. The ERC portfolio is chosen by an investor with a naive allocation preference, but with a risk constraint. Alternatively, it can be interpreted as a portfolio with the naive allocation as prior weight beliefs and extreme risk aversion or uncertainty about expected return estimates.

All in all, a couple of ideas to justify the different risk measures and portfolio models were outlined. The link to the different portfolio models is established in a situation under risk or uncertainty and the evidence of behavioral finance or the application of the Bayesian theory. However, there are only a few links between the utility theory and the 'statistical' risk measures or portfolio approaches. Especially the ERC portfolio cannot yet be thoroughly motivated through a decision theoretic foundation. Thus, it remains a lot of room for future research.

4 Literature Review

In the following, empirical studies of the presented portfolios are outlined. The literature review justifies the following analysis of the portfolios, from the theoretical as well as from the empirical side.

4.1 Minimum Risk Portfolios

4.1.1 MV/Low Risk Anomaly

Early after the Modern Portfolio Theory of Markowitz, the MV portfolio attracted attention due to the estimation error problems and results concerning the mean-variance or tangency portfolio (Clarke et al., 2006, Behr et al., 2008). The MV portfolio is the single portfolio on the efficient frontier, which requires only the covariance matrix as input and is independent of the forecasted returns. Thus it minimizes risk without an expected return input.

Since then, the performance of the MV portfolio is the objective of many studies. Surprisingly, in most of the studies, the MV portfolio outperforms the corresponding value or market-weighted benchmark. This is remarkable, as the theory (Capital Asset Pricing Model, see chapter 2.2) predicts a positive relationship between risk and return. This relationship should hold for different risk measures, ranging from systematic to specific and total risk measures, and also ranging from volatility-based risk measures to more sophisticated measures (Amenc et al., 2011, p. 8).

As outlined in chapter 2.2, the Capital Asset Pricing Model (CAPM) predicts that the return of an asset depends only on the market excess return $(E(R_M) - R_f)$, the so called market risk premium and the asset's beta. As the model applies the assumption that all investors have the same expectations as well as the same available information, all invest in a combination of the risk-free rate and the tangential portfolio, the portfolio with the highest Sharpe ratio (Tobin, 1958). As all investors hold the tangential portfolio in the CAPM in equilibrium, it is called the 'market portfolio'. The market portfolio consists of all available assets weighted by their market value and is an efficient portfolio (Goltz and Le Sourd, 2010). Thus, the market portfolio provides the best return-risk relationship and should be the best investment. Any other portfolio contains unsystematic risk, which is not rewarded and thus is not an useful investment (Goltz and Le Sourd, 2010). As investing in the whole market is impossible (this would include tradeable, non-tradeable assets, real estate assets and human capital), the value weighted market index is the standard proxy (Amenc et al., 2010). The difficulty to use an value-weighted market index as the market proxy was already outlined in chapter 2.2.2.

Table 4.1 gives an overview about empirical studies on the performance of the MV portfolio or the relationship between volatility and return. In the following, the main results of the studies are summarized.

Haugen and Heins (1972) are the first to claim a negative relationship between risk and return in the U.S. Stock Market and the U.S. Bond market in the period from 1926 - 1971 by sorting the stocks or bonds in 25 portfolios according to their volatility. By exploring the MV portfolio in the period from 1972 - 1989 on 1000 largest U.S. Stocks, Haugen and Baker (1991) state an outperformance vs. the Wilshire 5000 index by higher return and lower standard deviation.

Clarke et al. (2006) extend the study from Haugen and Baker (1991) from 1968 - 2005 and use principal components and Bayesian shrinkage methods to calculate the covariance matrix. They state that the MV strategy has about three-fourths the realized risk of the market with a simultaneously higher return. Thus, the Sharpe ratio of the minimum-variance portfolio (0.55) is much higher than the markets Sharpe ratio (0.36), because of the higher mean and the lower volatility. They control for the three factors of Fama and French (1993) and state that the MV portfolio has a small-cap and a value premium, but is not exposed to the momentum factor.

Blitz and van Vliet (2007) create also decile portfolios based on the historical volatility in the period from 1986 - 2006 and find that portfolios in the lowest volatility decile outperform the portfolios with the highest volatilities by higher Sharpe ratios and statistically significant alphas (up to 12% difference). This result holds not only for the U.S. stocks, but also for the European and Japanese market. Recently, Blitz et al. (2012) examine also the empirical risk-return relationship in 30 emerging equity markets by sorting portfolios and find that this relation is flat, or even negative.

Behr et al. (2008) test the MV portfolio vs. a naive as well as a value weighted market portfolio in the whole U.S. equity universe (CRSP stock database) from the period of 1964 to 2007 by using non-parametric bootstrap performance tests for the Sharpe ratio as well as for the alpha. By applying different maximum weight constraints from 2%-20%, they state that the MV portfolio outperforms significantly the market benchmark over the whole period. The outperformance is greater in the U.S. recession periods and higher for the portfolios with more restrictive weight constraints (a maximum portfolio weight constraint of 4% and less). But in comparison to the naive portfolio, the MV portfolio could not achieve a significant outperformance.

As outlined in van Vliet et al. (2011), methodological choices regarding the sample selection (with/without small caps and look-ahead biases) and performance evaluation (compounded vs. simple average returns) can lead to opposite conclusions about the return-risk relationship. Apart from this, the empirical relationship between volatility and expected returns in an U.S. sample from 1963 - 2009 is negative.

In a study over the time period 1990 to 2011, Baker and Haugen (2012) examine the returns of volatility ranked portfolios in 21 developed countries and 12 emerging markets. The result is that in the Universe and in each individual country low-risk stocks outperform in terms of returns and Sharpe ratios. Thus, they conclude that '*the basic pillar of finance, that greater risk can be expected to produce a greater reward, has fallen.*'

Meanwhile, Amenc et al. (2011) find that the investment horizon has a strong influence on the relation of risk and return. As the negative risk-return relation can be found at short holding periods (but most insignificant), the idiosyncratic-puzzle disappears for holding periods greater than one year and the risk-return trade off over long horizons is exactly what theory predicts - namely positive. This result holds for different risk measures like volatility, semi-deviation and Value at Risk.

Especially the outperformance of the MV portfolio vs. other approaches in recession periods or bear markets seems to be evident (see Clarke et al. (2006), Scherer (2010b), Amenc et al. (2012)). Whereas the outperformance of the MV portfolio seems to be persistent, the reasons for this seems less clear.

However, one reason for the performance seems to be that through minimizing the overall standard deviation, the MV portfolio picks up low beta stocks. Already Haugen and Heins (1972) claim an inverted relationship between beta and return and Blitz and van Vliet (2007) observe that portfolios with low volatility exhibit also a low beta. Moreover, they control the volatility effect for size, value and momentum through the global and local Fama/French regressions (Fama and French, 1992) and a double sorting methodology, but the results indicate that the volatility effect is separated. Clarke et al. (2011) also claim that '*MV portfolios are strictly populated by stocks with betas lower than a specified threshold*' and Carvalho et al. (2012) state that the minimum variance portfolio primarily has an exposure to low-beta stocks. Scherer (2010b) finds out that the MV portfolio implicitly picks up risk based pricing anomalies by investing in low beta stocks. Thus, the results are in line with the 'low-beta' pricing anomaly, meaning that the strong positive relationship between beta and return as stated by the theory is absent. This is reported e.g. by Black et al. (1972), Fama and MacBeth (1973), Fama and French (2004), Baker et al. (2011) and Messikh and Oderda (2010) (see also chapter 2.2.2).

The other reason for outperformance could be the so called 'idiosyncratic puzzle', for gaining a risk-premium for unsystematic risk. However the results of the studies are contradicting. The idiosyncratic or residual risk is the volatility of the residuals of a CAPM or Fama-French three factor model and should not be priced according to the theory, as it can be eliminated through diversification. However, Ang et al. (2006) finds out that low idiosyncratic volatility stocks earn high average returns by a cross-section approach in an U.S. sample (AMEX, NASDAQ and the NYSE stocks) from 1963-2000. They confirm their result in Ang et al. (2009) by an extended study for 23 countries in the period 1963-2003. But other studies claim that the results are sample-specific and do not hold for longer periods (see Amenc et al. (2011)), are driven by small stocks, a liquidity premium or are method specific (Bali et al., 2005, Bali and Cakici, 2008). On the other hand, Scherer (2010b) and Carvalho et al. (2012) state that the MV portfolio is exposed to low residual stocks.

Clarke et al. (2011) derive analytically the weight of an asset in the long-only MV portfolio for a single-index model and state that the weights are determined by beta and idiosyncratic risk. By examining the weights empirically, they find out that the beta has much more impact in the long-only portfolio and 80 to 90 percent of long-only minimum variance portfolio risk is systematic. Thus, the outperformance of MV portfolios is related to the CAPM critique, that the security line is too flat, meaning that the returns on the low beta portfolios are too high, and the returns on the high beta portfolios are too low (low-beta anomaly).

Scherer (2010b) studies the invest strategy of the MV portfolio through different regressions, and state that the three Fama-French factors as well as the low beta and the idiosyncratic factor are responsible for the returns of the MV portfolio. The low beta factor is constructed by holding low beta stocks long and high beta stocks short, whereas the idiosyncratic factor is constructed by holding low idiosyncratic volatility stocks long and high idiosyncratic volatility stocks short. By investing directly in a portfolio consisting of one third of the MSCI US, the beta anomaly portfolio, and the idiosyncratic risk anomaly portfolio, the Sharpe-ratio difference in comparison to the MV portfolio in a bootstrapping test is statistically significant. Thus, it is preferable to directly invest in these anomaly portfolios as in the MV portfolio.

However, Carvalho et al. (2012) state that the beta anomaly, and the idiosyncratic risk anomaly factors from Scherer (2010b) are highly correlated. They examine five risk-based strategies, 1/n, ERB (equal risk budgeting without considering correlations), ERC (Equal Risk Contribution), MV and MD (Maximum Diversification) by the five-factor model of Scherer (2010b), but orthogonalizing the two anomaly factors. They find that all strategies can be almost fully explained by the market, value, small caps, low beta and low idiosyncratic volatility exposure. In a sample from 1997 - 2010, in a global portfolio dataset (MSCI World Index of developed countries) as well as for sub-universes of U.S., EU and Japan, the MV portfolio has the highest Sharpe ratio, the lowest maximum drawdown and the lowest beta of all portfolios, but the highest turnover. By regressing the five factors, it turns out that the MV portfolio is highly exposed to low beta stocks and also to low idiosyncratic stocks.

It is an interesting fact that whereas the 1/n, ERB and ERC portfolio are similar and highly correlated in the investment universe, the MV and MD portfolios are different from the first three, but again similar among each other. The 1/n portfolio is more exposed to small-cap stocks than the ERC and the ERC is additionally exposed to low beta stocks. The MV and MD portfolios are more defensive than the other three strategies and highly exposed to low beta stocks, the MV additionally exposed to low idiosyncratic stocks. Additionally, the authors show that the choice of the model for the covariance (PCA or Bayesian shrinkage) as well as the estimation period (from 2 to 3, 4, 5 years) does not change the results.

Summarizing the empirical tests of the MV portfolio, it seems that the MV portfolio outperforms the capitalized market index across different datasets and countries in almost every study. Goltz and Le Sourd (2010) outline that the capitalization weighted market index is not the 'market portfolio' in the sense of the CAPM, as the market portfolio has to include much more assets and the assumptions of the CAPM do not hold in reality (unlimited borrowing, all assets tradeable, no taxes, no transaction costs). This is already known since the critique of Roll (1977). Goltz and Le Sourd (2010) conclude that: '*In the presence of realistic constraints and frictions, cap-weighted indices cannot, according to the academic literature, be expected to be efficient investments.*' The theory alone does not justify the use of these indices. Similar assumptions were also made in Haugen and Baker (1991). Thus, the results, that the market-cap weighted index is mostly beaten by the MV portfolio, should not be very surprising.

Table 4.1: MV Anomaly/Volatility-Return - Empirical Results

Author (Year)	Period/ Assets/ Benchmark	Calculations/ Constraints	Results
Haugen and Heins (1972, 1975)	NYSE 1926-1971, monthly returns, each portfolio 25 stocks	mean and std over the entire 46-year period and nine shorter periods of five years; regression of means on std	whole period: stock portfolios with lower variance exhibit greater average returns than their riskier counterparts

MV Anomaly - Continued

Author (Year)	Period/ Assets/ Benchmark	Calculations/ Constraints	Results
Haugen and Baker (1991)	1.000 largest U.S. stocks 1972-1989 vs. Wilshire 5000	historical covariance (24-month), quarterly rebalancing, $0 \leq w_i \leq 1,5\%$; $w_{industry} \leq 15\%$, transaction cost of 2%	MV has lower volatility and higher returns (whole period + rolling 5-years) MV = 14.5%/16.5%, Wilshire 5000= 12%/18.5%
Kleeberg (1995)	1. Germany: BARRA-Universe, 1985-1996; 2. UK: FT All Share, 1980-1996; 3. Japan: Nikkei 500 vs. TOPIX, 1978-1996; 4. Canada: TSE 300, 1981-1996; 5. U.S.: S&P 500, 1973-1996;	quarterly rebalancing, BARRA-factor model for covariance	in all markets, MV lower std and higher return than the benchmark; alphas of all markets are statistically significant (return anomaly); after controlling for small firm, earnings/price, book/price and dividend-yield effect, only the alphas of the U.S. and Canada are significant
Ang et al. (2006)	all stocks on AMEX, NASDAQ and the NYSE, 1986-2000	five portfolios sorted on beta loadings to changes in the VIX or idiosyncratic volatility of 1 month, monthly rebalancing	difference in average returns between the highest and lowest quintile portfolios sorted by exposure to VIX loadings is -1.04% per month, and is still statistically significant after controlling for the Fama and French (1993) factors; the portfolio with the highest idiosyncratic risks earns low returns of -0.02% per month, the results are robust to controlling for size, value, size, liquidity, volume and momentum effects and persists in bull and bear markets

MV Anomaly - Continued

Author (Year)	Period/ Assets/ Benchmark	Calculations/ Constraints	Results
Clarke et al. (2006)	1.000 largest U.S. stocks 1968-2005 (monthly) vs. value-weighted	covariance estimation: PCA and Bayesian shrinkage (60 months); $0 \leq w_i \leq 3\%$	Market: 5.6%/15.4% (0.36), MV (Bayesian): lower volatility and higher returns, 6.5%/11.7% (0.55); PCA method slightly better 6.7%/11.6%(0.58); daily returns: improve slightly the risk estimation process, but also lower return 6.1%/11.3% (0.54)
Blitz and van Vliet (2007)	all constituents of the FTSE World Developed index, 1985-2006 (weekly), also US, Europe and Japan markets in isolation	decile portfolios by ranking stocks on the past 3 year volatility, monthly rebalancing; also control for size, value and momentum	stocks with low historical volatility exhibit superior risk adjusted returns (SR and alpha), alpha spread of the top versus bottom decile portfolio amounts to 12% p.a. for the universe of global large-cap stock; volatility effect is a separate effect and of comparable magnitude
Behr et al. (2008)	CRSP stock database from April 1964 to December 2007 (monthly), vs. value-weighted and 1/n	three months rebalancing, historical covariance (60 months); $0 \leq w_i \leq 2\%; 3\%; ...; 20\%$ varied in one percent steps	up to a constraint of 8%: std's below of the value weighted portfolio (up to 19% for the 1/n weighted benchmark); all MV portfolios clearly outperform the value weighted benchmark based on Sharpe ratio and alpha; 1/n portfolio outperform MV on performance metrics except α; U.S. recession periods: MV results in overall higher performance metrics; all MV portfolios with a $w \leq 5\%$ achieved a higher SR than value weighted portfolio

MV Anomaly - Continued

Author (Year)	Period/ Assets/ Benchmark	Calculations/ Constraints	Results
Ang et al. (2009)	1. U.S. 1963 - 2003, 23 developed markets, 2. universe of the MSCI Developed Country Index, 1980-2003 (daily)	portfolios based on idiosyncratic volatility (past month)	stocks with recent past high idiosyncratic volatility have much lower returns than stocks with low idiosyncratic volatility, the difference in alphas adjusting for market, size and book-to-market factors between the highest and the lowest quintile of idiosyncratic volatility stocks is -1.31% per month, high idiosyncratic volatility and low return relation is not just a sample-specific or country-specific effect, but is observed world-wide
Scherer (2010b)	MSCI BARRA minimum volatility index vs. MSCI US equity index, 1998-2009 (monthly)	rebalanced semi-annually using the stocks in the MSCI US equity index, position, sector and BARRA risk factor constraints	whole period: higher excess return and lower std (0.027/3.560 vs. 0.013/4.773), higher SR (0.008 vs. 0.003), bull market: Mkt-cap excess return and SR higher (1.342/0.391 vs. 1.019/0.376), bear market: MV excess return higher (-2.027 vs. -2.738); exposures to five factors: Fama-French three factors, low beta and unsystematic risk: all factors highly significant

MV Anomaly - Continued

Author (Year)	Period/ Assets/ Benchmark	Calculations/ Constraints	Results
Amenc et al. (2011)	all NYSE, AMEX, and NASDAQ stocks, 1963-2009	portfolios/cross-section of portfolios and individual stocks: risk measure based on return observations up to date t (daily data from the past 12 months) and returns for the period t+n	negative risk premium over the period of 1 month (but insignificant), positive premium over 24 month; results are similar for the idiosyncratic volatility, idiosyncratic and total skewness, idiosyncratic and total kurtosis
Baker et al. (2011)	all or the top 1000 CRSP stocks, 1968-2008	five portfolios based on volatility of last 60 months, monthly rebalancing	quintile with the lowest volatility has the highest return over the whole sample, highest SR, lowest std, lowest beta and highest alpha (significant)
Clarke et al. (2011)	1.000 largest U.S. Stocks 1968-2009 vs. value-weighted (monthly)	Bayesian shrinkage covariance (60-month), long only	Bayesian shrinkage leads to maximum weights of 3%-4%, higher excess return (5.37% vs. 4.88%), std is only about three-fourth of the market portfolio risk (11.9% vs. 15.56%), higher SR (0.45 vs. 0.31)
van Vliet et al. (2011)	all stocks from CRSP database, 1963-2009 (monthly and daily)	5 portfolios based on 1-month total/idiosyncratic volatility and 60-month total/idiosyncratic volatility	the average return spread amounts to -3.7% for all stocks and -1.5% for the largest 1,000 stocks with negative and significant alpha spreads varying between -5.9% and -10.6%; about 2% of the negative spread can be explained by small caps, not much difference between idiosyncratic volatility vs. total volatility

MV Anomaly - Continued

Author (Year)	Period/ Assets/ Benchmark	Calculations/ Constraints	Results
Amenc et al. (2012)	MSCI USA Min Volatility Index vs. S&P 500 Equal Weight Index, FTSE EDHEC Risk Efficient U.S. Index, FTSE RAFI U.S. 1000 Index, 2003-2011, weekly	excess return over the S&P 500 Index in half-year periods	MV outperforms the others in the following periods: 2005 (Jan-Jun), 2007 (Jul-Dec), 2008 (Jul-Dec), 2011 (Jan-Jun) and 2011 (Jul-Dec)
Baker and Haugen (2012)	stocks in 21 developed countries and 12 emerging markets 1990-2011	volatility of total return for each company in each country over the previous 24 months, stocks in each country are ranked by volatility and formed into deciles	in the Universe and in each individual country low-risk stocks outperform, negative risk premium
Blitz et al. (2012)	all stocks in the S&P/IFC Investable Emerging Markets Index, 1988-2010 (monthly)	top-minus-bottom quintile portfolio, monthly rebalanced, based on 3 years past volatility	empirical relation between risk and return is negative, return spread of 4.4%, SR of the low-volatility quintile portfolio is over double that of the high-volatility quintile portfolio (0.64 vs 0.29), statistically significant negative alpha spread of -8.8%, spread remains large and significant after controlling for size, value and momentum, results hold also for a holding period up to 5 years

MV Anomaly - Continued

Author (Year)	Period/ Assets/ Benchmark	Calculations/ Constraints	Results
Carvalho et al. (2012)	all stocks of MSCI World Index of developed countries, also sub-universes of U.S., EU and Japan, 1997-2010 (weekly), vs. Mkt-cap, ERC, ERB, MD, 1/n	quarterly re-balancing, $0 \leq w_i \leq 5\%$, PCA covari-ance (past two years)	unconstrained MV: ca. 850 stocks, highest excess return, the lowest volatility, low-est beta, lowest drawdown, the highest tracking error and the highest turnover, long only MV: ca. 120 stocks, lowest return of the strategies (but 3% higher than the market), the other characteristics remain; high correlation (81%/75%) with ERC; strong exposure to low-beta stocks, also exposure to low idiosyncratic risk stocks

4.1.2 Minimum-CVaR Portfolio

Rockafellar and Uryasev (2000) introduce the CVaR for portfolio optimization by using a linear programming approach. In a simulation and an empirical setting, they compare for a large portfolio of options the differences in VaR and the CVaR obtained with the minimum CVaR approach. They show that the minimization of CVaR is efficiently, also results in a near optimal solution to VaR, because CVaR is always greater or equal VaR and that the CVaR is more suitable to capture the risk.

The CVaR minimization approach was applied to credit risk op-timization in Andersson et al. (2001). The portfolio consists of 197 emerging markets bonds, issued by 86 obligors in 29 countries and is also studied in Bucay and Rosen (1999) and Mausser and Rosen (1999). The date of the analysis is October 13, 1998 and the mark-to-market value of the portfolio is 8.8 billion $. They state that the minimization of the CVaR leads simultaneously to a lower VaR, expected loss and standard deviation and therefore is attractive from a bank's perspective. Moreover, the model outperforms the Minimum Expected Regret approach of Mausser and Rosen (1999) in terms of risk-return trade off.

Krokhmal et al. (2002a) extend the minimization of the CVaR and show different equivalent formulations of the mean-CVaR efficient frontiers. In a portfolio model with a CVaR constraint and transaction costs, they examine the comparison with the Mean-Variance Portfolio Optimization of a portfolio consisting of stocks in the S&P 100 index with 10-day returns with different target returns, to construct the efficient frontier. The difference between the Mean-Variance and the Mean-CVaR approach is not very significant, as the dataset was 'close-to-normal'. However, they show that the CVaR approach can handle large set of assets and return scenarios and can be applied with various investment constraints.

Alexander and Baptista (2002) point out that in some cases the mean-VaR portfolio can have a higher standard deviation as the mean-variance portfolio and is thus not a reasonable improvement over the variance as a risk measure. In a further paper, Alexander and Baptista (2004) theoretically compare CVaR and VaR constraints on the mean-variance model and show that a CVaR constraint is more effective than a VaR constraint to control slightly risk averse agents, but highly risk averse agents select through this constraint portfolios with larger standard deviations, if the VaR and CVaR bounds coincide and no risk-free asset exists. However, if the CVaR bound is larger than the VaR bound or a risk-free asset exists, the effect almost disappears and the CVaR-constraint dominates. Then, slightly and highly risk averse investors select portfolios with smaller standard deviations.

Guastaroba et al. (2009) examine the minimization of the CVaR over the whole period as well as in a rebalancing model for a portfolio of 100 securities composed of the XETRA DAX100 from 01.08.1996 - 08.10.2001 divided into four different market trends of in and out-of-sample periods: up-up, up-down, down-up and down-down. In terms of cumulative return, all the portfolios outperform the DAX index and the downside risk is clearly lower especially in the up-down and down-down data sets. The comparison of the static vs. the dynamic strategy shows that the increase of rebalances reduces the downside risk whereas the static approach results in a higher cumulative return.

Sheikh and Qiao (2010) address non-normality in asset returns and state that the mean-variance framework always underestimates the risk. There are nowadays sophisticated statistical tools to model non-normal returns, which should be applied in portfolio optimization. Moreover, if the returns are not normal, the standard deviation is not an adequate risk measure. Thus they use a semi-parametric GPD approach with a Student-t-Copula to model the returns of eight asset classes (monthly return data of 15 years) and estimate then the CVaR efficient frontier and compare it to the mean-variance frontier. The CVaR portfolio incorporates the downside risk much better and is also a more efficient and elegant way to address the problem of real-world return characteristics as it can be applied without constraints (which are often imposed to the mean-variance framework to address the non-normality).

Wang and Zheng (2010) demonstrate in a portfolio with seven asset classes (equities, commodities, benchmark for credit, interest rate, real estate, benchmark for inflation sensitive and cash) in the time range of 1973-2009 with monthly data that the mean-CVaR portfolio is superior to the mean-Variance portfolio in a framework based on a distribution with a t-Copula in a static as well as in a rebalancing period model. Moreover, they state that the variance slightly increases whereas the CVaR largely decreases.

Xiong and Idzorek (2011) examine the impact of fat tails and skewness on the Mean-Variance and the Mean-CVaR allocation by simulating returns with a multivariate L flight distribution. They assume four hypothetical assets and generate four scenarios with different skewness and tails (1: skewness=0, uniform tails; 2: skewness=0, mixed tails, 3: skewness $\neq$ 0, uniform tails and 4: skewness $\neq$ 0, mixed tails) by holding the expected returns and correlations equal. Zero skewness means symmetrical distributions and uniform tails means that the kurtosis for all assets in a universe is the same. If mixed tails are assumed, the kurtosis of the assets varies. Whereas the Mean-Variance portfolio generates similar asset allocations, the Mean-CVaR portfolio leads to different asset allocations. By expectation, scenario 4 has the largest impact. Moreover, they examine the Mean-CVaR portfolio in a setting with 14 asset-classes over the period 1990 - 2010 by bootstrapping from the historical returns. The observations conclude the simulation study: whereas the Mean-CVaR portfolio selects positively skewed (or less negatively skewed) and thin-tailed assets, the Mean-Variance portfolio ignores this information. In the last step, they compare the portfolio in the financial crisis of 2008 by holding the portfolios in an out-of-sample testing period of 6 month (09.2008 - 02.2009, without rebalancing). The Mean-CVaR portfolio outperformes the Mean-Variance portfolio with excess gains from 0.84 percentage point to 1.44 percentage point across the efficient frontier. Therefore the authors suggest that the higher-moment information embedded in historical returns should be considered for the asset allocation process.

Summary of the CVaR Studies
The empirical investigations of the CVaR-portfolio indicate a better performance of the CVaR-portfolio compared to the Mean-Variance and the VaR-portfolio especially by considering fat tails and skewness in the returns. However, most of the studies consider the Mean-CVaR-portfolio with a target return or the CVaR-risk as a constraint in the portfolio optimization and do not study the min-CVaR portfolio in a rebalancing framework. Moreover, it can be observed that the trend is to include non-normality in the returns with different methods (Copula or distributions). In this thesis, the min-CVaR-portfolio will be compared to other asset allocation techniques through a rebalancing approach by modeling the returns with different distributions.

4.1.3 Maximum Drawdown and Drawdown Measures

Due the non-normality of the returns, the interest to a risk measure which does not directly rely on the distribution of the returns, the drawdown risk measures, grows. The drawdown is a less abstract risk measure than the standard deviation (volatility), the Var and CVaR, as it measures the difference between the highest and the lowest point of the sequence of the historical returns. Thus it is an intuitive risk measure and such it is not surprising that the major interest for the 'drawdown-portfolio optimization' arise from the practical side. Moreover, through considering the consecutive returns, it takes through a non-parametric way the serial correlations of the return series into account (Hamelink and Hoesli, 2004).

Grossman and Zhou (1993) are the first to analyze a 2-security-portfolio (one risky and one risk-free asset) with a drawdown constraint and Cvitanic and Karatzas (1994) extend and generalize the approach to a portfolio with different risky investments.

Alexander and Baptista (2006) examine the mean-variance and the mean-tracking error volatility (TEV) portfolio by adding a MaxDD-constraint to the portfolio optimization and allow for short-sales. They conclude that the constrained portfolios (with the MaxDD-constraint) are inefficient as the standard deviation or the TEV increases, respectively, and the loss is larger than those of the unconstrained portfolios. The differences between the both efficient frontiers are the larger, the larger the constrained MaxDD. Thus, the tracking of a benchmark becomes more difficult for a portfolio manager through the MaxDD-constraint.

Burghardt et al. (2003) analyze the impact of different distributions of the drawdown and the MaxDD theoretically and empirically. Through a simulation of log-normal and generalized lambda distributed returns to examine the impact of the mean, volatility, skewness and kurtosis, they show that the investment horizon, the mean expected return and the volatility of the returns affect the distribution, whereas the skewness and kurtosis do not matter much. The higher the mean returns, the lower the expected drawdowns, but the higher the volatility, the higher the drawdowns. The effect of the volatility is thereby more than twice as important as the mean return. Moreover, they emphasize that the expectation of future drawdowns depends on the investment horizon: the longer the investment horizon (1 year vs. 10 years), the higher the possibility to suffer a worse maximum drawdown than the MaxDD to date and the higher the value of the MaxDD.

Harding et al. (2003) point out that the MaxDD-figure should be used with caution if it is used as a criterion for a future performance of an investment or for the choice of a portfolio manager. As the maximum drawdown is a single statistical number derived from a sequence of returns, it contains a large estimation error. If the return generating process is not known, it is dangerous to derive conclusions for future drawdowns. Through averaging, the error could be reduced. Moreover, to compare the MaxDD of different assets, one has to correct for the investment horizon length and the measurement interval, as drawdowns get larger with the frequency of the returns (daily vs. yearly) and with the length of the observed time period.

Krokhmal et al. (2003) integrate the CVaR and CDaR risk measure as a constraint in a portfolio of hedge funds in the period of 1995 - 2001. As the risk measures are included as a constraint to the portfolio optimization, a risk tolerance level has to be set and varies from 0.005 to 0.25 and the risk level α is set to 0.9. Through using all available historical data for estimation, (expanding window approach, 12 month at the beginning), they conclude that the risk tolerance level has a significant impact on the outcome, constraining the risk improves the performance. The best return-risk characteristic is obtained for a portfolio with the tolerance level of 0.005 (high returns, low volatility, low drawdowns). The portfolios were not compared against each other, however, it is outlined that the CVaR- and CDaR-optimal portfolios have quite a similar structure and also similar returns. A comparison against the S&P 500 as a benchmark reveals that both portfolios outperform significantly the market benchmark in returns and risk. Especially in falling market phases the performance of the risk-based portfolios is clearly better.

Hamelink and Hoesli (2004) study the MaxDD-portfolio in an international portfolio with stocks, bonds and real-estate assets (Swiss, UK, USA). They compare the MaxDD-efficient frontier with the mean-variance efficient frontier by considering a dataset from 1980 - 2002. As comparisons of the two portfolios are difficult ('one compares apples with oranges'), they compare the trade-off of the decrease of the MaxDD vs. the increase of the volatility of a portfolio with the same expected return (as portfolios on the MaxDD-frontier have per definition a lower MaxDD than the portfolios on the mean-variance frontier and vice versa). By considering four different samples of returns, they show that the MaxDD-portfolio achieves a substantial decrease in the Max-DD by a slightly rise in the volatility, whereas the mean-variance portfolio trade-off is worse, as the MaxDD is much higher. Moreover, they examine the weights of the assets and figure out that the mean-variance portfolio allocates much more capital to the real estate assets. Thus, the MaxDD-portfolio is more in line with actual allocations by Swiss institutional investors.

Magdon-Ismail and Atiya (2004) introduce the normalized Calmar ratio, to compare the performance based on the maximum drawdown for investments with different time horizons. The Calmar ratio is an adjusted risk measure like the Sharpe ratio, but based on the MaxDD:

$$Calmar\,(T) = \frac{Return\,over\,[0,T]}{MaxDD\,over\,[0,T]} \tag{4.1}$$

The normalization is done by multiplying the Calmar ratio with a scaling factor, which is derived through relating the Calmar ratio with the Sharpe Ratio and removing the dependence of the time interval T. Thus, the MaxDD-performance of the portfolios can be compared through scaling the Calmar ratio to a specific time interval. In the empirical performance studies, the Calmar ratio is also used as one of the performance criteria.

4.1.4 Minimum-CDaR Portfolio

As mentioned above, the MaxDD depends only on a single value and thus is not a statistical reliable number. Thus, recently a new risk measure based on the drawdown distribution, the CDaR, is proposed for the portfolio optimization. The following few studies have compared the CDaR-portfolio with other portfolio approaches.

The CDaR risk measure is at first suggested by Cheklov et al. (2003) and Cheklov et al. (2005), where the authors outline the min-CDaR portfolio as well as a portfolio with drawdown constraints. Both portfolios can be solved by the linear programming approach. In a dataset of 32 assets over a time period of 1988 - 1999, they examine the behavior of the MaxDD-, AvDD and CDaR-portfolio (α=0, 0.2, 0.4, 0.6, 0.8, 0.9, 0.95 and 1). They conclude that the CDaR-portfolio produces more robust results than the MaxDD- or AvDD-portfolios, as the MaxDD-optimization considers only the largest drawdown and the AvDD-optimization is impacted by many small drawdowns. So the MaxDD measure may have a statistical error because it considers only one single observation, wereas the CDaR is the average over the worst $(1 - \alpha) * 100\%$ drawdowns.

Kuutan (2007) studies the linear min-CVaR and min-CDaR portfolio for a portfolio composed of 5 sub-indices of the Goldman Sachs Commodity Index (Agriculture, Energy, Industrial Metals, Livestock, Precious Metal) in the range from 1986-1995 with annual returns. The portfolio is attained by minimizing the CVaR and CDaR with an α of 0.8 and changing the minimum required return to obtain the efficient frontier. The result show that the CDaR has greater values of variance than the CVaR with the same target return and that the CDaR portfolio has a higher cumulative return over the period. Moreover, Kuutan (2007) states that the CDaR portfolio reacts more sensible to changes. However, the results are based on a static portfolio optimization with 20 annual data points, which limits the relevance of this study.

Krokhmal et al. (2002b) test different portfolios by maximizing the expected return subject to various risk constraints: CVaR, CDaR, Mean-Absolute Deviation, Maximum Loss and Market Neutrality. By maximizing the return and constraining the risk, each of the portfolios can be calculated through the linear programming (LP) approach. The dataset consists of 300 hedge funds with monthly data from 12.1995 - 05.2001, the α level of the CVaR and CDaR was set to 0.9 and they examined the risk constraint with varying risk tolerance level from 0.005 - 0.20. By using all the available historical data to optimize the portfolio monthly (instead of a 'rolling window' approach; the first portfolio relies on 12 historical month), they examined the out-of-sample performance of the portfolios. The test show that constraining the risk improves the out-of-sample performance and the higher the risk tolerance level, the higher the volatility of the portfolio. The most attractive return-risk trade-off was obtained for a risk tolerance level of 0.005, that means high returns, low volatility and low drawdowns. Compared to the S&P 500, the CVaR, CDaR and the Maximum-Loss portfolios outperform the index by cumulative returns. The CDaR and CVaR portfolios showed the 'most solid performance', with CVaR having a slightly advantage as the CDaR risk constraint occurs to be more conservative. However, the authors emphasize to combine different risk constraints in the optimization.

The estimation of different risk measures based on Stable Paretrian distributions: Maximum Drawdown, CVaR, CDaR, DaR, AvDD and VaR is the objective of study in Harmantzis and Miao (2005). They use eight major global indices to estimate the risk measures based on daily prices during a period of ten years from 1995 - 2004 and study the impact of skewness, kurtosis as well as the estimation period (tracking time) on the risk levels. The result can be summarized as follows:

- the kurtosis has an impact on the Drawdown and the CVaR (positive correlation), but not on the VaR

- the skewness has only an effect on the CVaR and

- the longer the tracking time, the larger the risk, except for the VaR.

The conclusion of the authors is that the risk measures are different and do not necessarily agree on the risk levels. The different drawdown measures perform similar.

Summary of the CDaR Studies
The CDaR risk measure is the average of the worst drawdowns and thus similar to the CVaR, but considering the distribution of the draw-downs. The few available studies of the CDaR-portfolio indicate that it is a good alternative to the CVaR-portfolio, but a more conservative risk measure. The studies suggest that the CDaR portfolio outper-forms also a value-weighted market benchmark, thus, can also be characterized by the 'low-risk' anomaly. However, the CDaR-portfolio is not compared to the CVaR approach in a realistic out-of sample study with a rolling window portfolio approach. Moreover, the CDaR risk measure is used as a constraint in portfolio optimization and the risk budgets based on the CDaR approach are not yet proposed and examined. Examining the minimization of the CDaR, the min-CDaR portfolio as well as a portfolio with equal risk budgets based on the CDaR will be investigated in this thesis.

4.2 Risk Budgeting Portfolios

4.2.1 Volatility Risk Budgets

In recent times, there is a growing stock of literature concerning risk diversified portfolios. The reason for the popularity of this approach is driven by the dissatisfaction with the realized performance charac-teristics of portfolios in the recent financial crisis or more generally in the recent turbulent or volatile times. Thereby the Mean-Variance

Portfolio is blamed for the known weaknesses and risk diversification seems to be the 'solution'. As (Schachter and Thiagarajan, 2011, p. 87) point out: [The approach] *'strongly appeals to our intuition that risk diversification is the central goal in portfolio decision making, and equalizing estimated risk contributions is probably a good way to try to approach that goal. Risk parity is also appealing in that the resulting portfolio does not depend on the thing we have the least confidence in being able to accurately estimate, namely expected returns.'*

After the proof of Qian (2006) that risk contributions have an economic interpretation and can indeed be seen as expected contributions to potential losses of a portfolio, this idea seems to be 'the solution' for everything what went wrong in the Financial crisis and thus it is not surprising that the interest of the risk diversified portfolio, or 'risk parity', is growing after this drastic event. However, the idea itself is not new and has been used in managing multi-asset portfolios by asset management firms already in the 1990s (e.g. Bridgewater Associates). Booth and Fama (1992) mention already the risk contribution of an asset to the variance in the portfolio.

The idea of risk decomposing is also made in Litterman (1996), who points out: *'To manage risk, you have to understand what the sources of risk are in the portfolio and what trades will provide effective ways to reduce risk. Thus, risk management requires additional analysis, in particular, a decomposition of risk, an ability to find potential hedges, and an ability to find simple representations for complex portfolios.'* However, the risk budgets are seen as additional instruments to detect 'Hot Spots', which have the largest contribution, and 'Hedges', which are trades to reduce the portfolio risk, and not as an objective in portfolio optimization.

Qian (2005b) proposes the risk parity portfolio, but Maillard et al. (2010) are the first to define the 'equal risk contribution' (ERC) portfolio from the academic side and to derive theoretical properties. They provide optimizations to solve the ERC portfolio and also show that a numerical solution exists for a portfolio of two assets. In view of mathematical definitions, the ERC portfolio is located between the naive and the MV portfolio. The naive approach equalizes the weights and the MV equalizes the marginal risk contributions, whereas the ERC equalizes the absolute risk contributions. These results are extended in Bruder and Roncalli (2012), where the authors derive the theoretical properties of the more general 'risk budgeting portfolio', in which the risk budgets are not necessarily equal and are specified to obtain an asset allocation. They show that the risk budgeting portfolio can be seen as the MV portfolio subject to a constraint of risk budgets (an amount of risk measured in dollars), a unique solution exists when the risk budgets are positive and the volatility lies between the MV and the 'weight budgeting' approach. The weight budgeting approach is defined such that the asset weight equals the risk budget, whereas in the risk budgeting approach the risk contribution of an asset equals an amount of risk measured in dollars. Moreover, the weight of an asset increases with the risk budget, decreases with the volatility and is inversely proportional to its beta.

Many studies have examined and discussed the historical performance of the equal risk contribution approach among some asset classes. However, recently, there is also a direction to examine the ERC portfolio in more detail and to justify its use. Table 4.2 gives an overview of empirical studies on the ERC portfolio. In the following, the most important results are summarized.

Maillard et al. (2010) provide comparisons of the ERC portfolio vs. the naive and the MV portfolio with different datasets and show that the ERC portfolio is more balanced in terms of weights and risk contributions than the MV portfolio and the ERC portfolio dominates in terms of return and risk compared to the naive approach. However, in terms of the drawdowns, the ERC portfolio is dominated by the MV portfolio.

Allen (2010) examine the ERC portfolio in a 20-year period from 1989 - 2009 in a policy portfolio with indices as proxies for equities, bonds, real estate, commodities and fixed income. He points out that the portfolio's return would be too low to compete with the mean-variance portfolio (and to satisfy most investors) and analyzes a leveraged ERC portfolio, which has the same expected return as the tangency portfolio. For this, a leverage of 40% - 60% is needed, which causes a higher sensitivity of the portfolio to interest rate movements. However, the leveraged ERC portfolio significantly underperforms the tangency portfolio during the 1990s and outperforms it in the last decade with only half of the volatility of the tangency portfolio. Because of the underperformance in the 'good times' and the leverage, a survival of the ERC portfolio at any major institution would be unlikely.

The underperformance of the ERC portfolio from 1980 - 1989 is also confirmed in Chaves et al. (2011). They compare the ERC portfolio to the naive, the mean-variance, MV and the 60/40 approach by using long-term U.S. Treasury, U.S. investment-grade bonds, global bonds, U.S. high-yield bonds, U.S. equities, international equities, emerging market equities, commodities, and listed real estates with a history of 1980 - 2010 and rebalancing the portfolio yearly. Their comparison focuses mainly on the Sharpe ratio and they find that the ERC portfolio's Sharpe ratio is always higher than those of the Mean-Variance approach, except in the period from 1980 - 1989. But it is not consistently higher than the ratio from the naive and the 60/40 portfolio. By examining the Sharpe ratios in different periods, they conclude that the Sharpe ratio over the last three decades of the ERC portfolio is more stable than those of the other approaches and thus could be a good predictor of the performance for the next 10 years. However, by varying the time periods and assets, Chaves et al. (2011) point out that the choice of the time frame as well as of the dataset can significantly affect the results of the risk parity portfolio.

To sum up table 4.2, the historical results of the ERC portfolio are most times compared to a market-weighted or a 60/40 benchmark index. Thereby, the ERC portfolio clearly outperforms in terms of risk and Sharpe ratio (Qian, 2005b,a, 2010, Little, 2010, Lee, 2012, Bruder and Roncalli, 2012). The superior outperformance vs. the naive portfolio is also evident in all investigated studies (Neukirch, 2008a, Maillard et al., 2010, Demey et al., 2010, Lohre et al., 2011). The outperformance against the tangency portfolio is different: Allen (2010) report a higher Sharpe ratio for the tangency portfolio, and Chaves et al. (2011) report a higher return and Sharpe ratio for the ERC portfolio. Moreover, the outcome vs. the MV portfolio give also divergent results. Whereas Demey et al. (2010), Chaves et al. (2011), Neukirch (2008b) and Maillard et al. (2010) in one dataset state that the ERC portfolio outperforms in return and Sharpe ratio, in the other two examples of Maillard et al. (2010) and in the study of Lohre et al. (2011) the MV portfolio leads to a higher Sharpe ratio, although the return of the ERC portfolio is higher.

As the ERC portfolio outperforms market-weighted indices, like the MV portfolio, one could conclude, that the 'MV anomaly' has also validity for the risk budgeting portfolio. Or in other words, the risk budgeting portfolios can also be seen under the aspect of the low risk anomaly, which would be another argument for the practical application.

Kaya and Lee (2012) investigate the risk parity portfolio more theoretically and examine the assets, which the risk parity portfolio prefers or invests more capital in. According to the studies of Scherer (2010b) and Clarke et al. (2011), they compare the impact of the market beta and the idiosyncratic risk on the weights of the MV and the ERC portfolio. The result is that both portfolios prefer low idiosyncratic and low beta assets, but the ERC portfolio is less concentrated and reacts less sensitive to changes of these characteristics in the assets. Moreover, they compared the out-of-sample risk-reward ratio of the ERC and the MV portfolio by varying the degrees of freedom of a multivariate student-t distribution from 1 - 1000 and the window length to estimate the covariance matrix (as a proxy for estimation noise) from 10 - 800 month. The ERC portfolio overperforms the MV portfolio, the shorter the window length and the more fat tailed the returns. Thus, the ERC portfolio approach dominates the Markowitz approaches when there is uncertainty around the estimates (which always is) and/or there are fat tails in the return series and could be then ex-ante more efficient as the mean-variance and MV approach, although not ex-post on a theoretically basis.

The recent trend in risk diversification is the focus on risk factors instead of assets. Briand et al. (2010) and Page and Taborsky (2010) propose a related approach to the ERC portfolio, based on the diversification on risk premia for a portfolio across asset classes. Page and Taborsky (2010) argue that the risk premia are more robust to 'regime shifts' in asset returns as the correlations across risk factors do not dramatically increase during market crisis. Moreover, the correlations of the risk factors are lower than across the asset classes and thus the diversification should be more efficient. Briand et al. (2010) study the performance of a portfolio with eleven risk premia, which consist of asset-class, style (asset characteristics), and strategy (replicating investment strategies) risk premia. The period spans over May 1995 to October 2008 and the risk premia are captured through long and short positions in different indices. By investing equal weights to each risk premia, they compare the portfolio to an 60/40 equity/bond portfolio by rebalancing monthly. The result show that the realized returns are comparable, whereas the volatility and the MaxDD of the diversificated portfolio is much lower. Also, they examined the losses in recent crisis periods (Asian crisis in 1997, the LTCM debacle of August 1998, the 9/11 attacks in 2001, October 2008) and find out that the losses of the risk premia portfolio is much lower than that of the 60/40 portfolio. However, they did not compare this strategy to the MV or the mean-variance portfolio. Briand et al. (2010) conclude that the risk premia portfolio is a promising approach and should be studied by identifying best combinations of the premia. However, as the diversificated portfolio based on risk premia is not compared to the ERC portfolio, it cannot be concluded which performs better. Moreover, one has to define the risk factors manually/subjectively and it will always remain a part of the returns, which cannot be explained through the risk factors, which makes the approach more difficult than the ERC portfolio.

Related to the risk premia approach, Bhansali et al. (2012) state that the risk parity portfolio can be exposed to only one or two underlying risk factors. By examining nine different asset classes (US equities, international equities, EM equities, real estate investments, commodities, global bonds, US long treasury, investment-grade corporate and high-yield bonds) through a PCA decomposition, they find out that the total variance is in general (68%) explained through two factors. Based on this analysis, they propose a three-factor based framework for examining risk-parity portfolios: one factor accounts for the growth shock (equity markets shock), one for the inflation shock (bond market shocks) and the rest for the 'other' risks, which is not covered of neither of them. They examined the exposure to these three factors of four commercial risk parity products and state that the risk parity strategies have very different factor exposures. Two strategies are dominated by the equity factor, whereas the other two are balanced across the three factors. Thus, following the authors, it is important to assess the true diversification through factor exposures, as equalizing the risk across assets could be dangerous.

Roncalli and Weisang (2012) propose also the risk budgeting approach based on risk factors. They generalize the risk budgeting approach to risk factors, thus, it is possible to apply desired weights to specified risk factors. Moreover, they demonstrate the approach on three different examples: applying risk budgets to Carhart's four factor model, diversifying across PCA factors (each of the first four factors 25%) and strategic asset allocation through diversifying across macroeconomic factors. Unfortunately, they do not report details on the performances of the different approaches vs. the ERC portfolio (except of the PCA factors, whose results are promising), which would be interesting in an additional research. Related to this issue is also the work of Meucci (2009) and Lohre et al. (2011), who address the diversification across principal components of the covariance matrix. However, in a recent research it is shown (Poddig and Unger, 2012) that this approach is highly sensitive to the underlying data and thus delivers undesirable outcomes, as the estimation errors are even larger than those of the Markowitz approaches. Also Roncalli and Weisang (2012) note that *the portfolio construction is very sensitive to these PCA factors, which are not always stable through time.* In this direction it would be interesting to decompose the covariance into the PCA factors (eigenvectors) and diversify not equally across the factors, but set the weight proportional to the eigenvector of the variance.

Criticism of the ERC Portfolio

The problems of the new asset allocation idea arise from different aspects. Lee (2011) emphasize the deficiency of an underlying theory behind the risk parity approach which defines the investment objective and it thus it is not obvious what investment problems these portfolios are built to solve. The risk diversification approach is conceptual and intuitive, rather than theoretical and is therefore considered as a heuristic asset allocation approach (Kaya and Lee, 2012). A theory, which yields the ERC portfolio as the optimal solution would help to understand the performance of the portfolio (Schachter and Thiagarajan, 2011). Asness et al. (2011) try to provide the theoretical link by applying the theory of leverage aversion pioneered by (Black, 1972), which explains the low-beta anomaly (see 2.2.2). Asness et al. (2011, p. 4) argues that contrary to the CAPM, leverage aversion induces that the highest risk-adjusted return (Sharpe ratio) is not achieved by the market portfolio, but by a portfolio that overweights low beta assets (which are the assets with lower risks). An investor, who is less leverage averse than the average investor in the market, profits by leveraging a portfolio that overweights low beta assets and underweights high beta assets. According to Asness et al. (2011), the

ERC portfolio is such a portfolio, as the low beta assets are bonds and the high beta assets are stocks. However, the minimum risk portfolios invest almost entirely only in less riskier assets or low beta assets. Thus, they can also be justified by this theory. Through this argumentation of Asness et al. (2011) it is clear that the ERC portfolio builds also on the low volatility anomaly outlined above (see 4.1.1). The low volatility anomaly seems to be caused by the low beta anomaly which is in turn explained by the theory of leverage aversion. But as the minimum risk portfolios capture even more this anomaly than the ERC portfolio, the leverage aversion alone does not justify the ERC portfolio.

After many studies of the historical performance of the ERC portfolio, the aspect shifts now to the theoretically justification or at least a logical explanation of the investment statement of this approach. The main puzzle seems to be the fact that the ERC portfolio outperforms the mean-variance portfolio without considering the estimates of expected returns. In other words, it *'would represent a profound finding [that] investors who are ignorant of returns are predicted to outperform investors who make an effort to predict returns'* (Lee, 2011). Thus, the circumstances under which an investor should select a portfolio based on risk budgets and ignoring the returns are not clear. A possible explanation could also be deduced from the behavioral finance strand (Schachter and Thiagarajan, 2011).

This aspect is an important part of this thesis. The utility theory is applied to justify the choice of the ERC portfolio. As it is shown in chapter 3.3.1, it can be thought of cases or circumstances in which the ERC portfolio is the 'optimal' choice for the investor.

Related with the aspect of a lacking theory is the argument that the ERC portfolio is not efficient, as there are other portfolios which can achieve the same expected return with a lower risk or a higher expected return with the same risk (see Maillard et al. (2010), Allen (2010), Kaya and Lee (2012)). To be efficient, all assets in the ERC portfolio must have identical Sharpe ratios and the same correlations among the assets, which is not a realistic assumption. Inker (2010) criticizes the use of the volatility as a risk measure and indicates that some assets in the risk parity portfolio could have zero or even a negative risk premium (commodities or government bonds). Moreover, as the return of the risk parity approach is on average lower than of an efficient portfolio, in practice the portfolio is often used with leverage, which creates additional hidden risks (see e.g. Inker (2010), Foresti and Rush (2010)). The aspects of leverage will not be discussed here further, as the focus in this thesis lies on the 'pure' risk contribution portfolios. Another issue is the unclear definition of an 'asset class' in the ERC portfolio, to which the equal contribution of risk is assigned. That is, should all equities taken together and defined as the 'equity class' or be divided in different classes depending on their characteristics (e.g. emerging, domestic, value or growth equities, etc. (Chaves et al., 2011)). This is a subjective task and can have a large impact on the results, however it is not only a problem of the risk parity approach and is a more general problem of the asset selection in the portfolio management process (Ning, 2007, see e.g.).

4.2.2 CVaR Risk Budgets

Although the interest in the risk diversified portfolios is increasing, as one can see from the amount of literature, the risk is mostly defined as the volatility of the portfolio. But the extension to other risk measures, which are convex and satisfy the Euler decomposition, is possible (see Bruder and Roncalli (2012) for a generalization of the risk budgeting approach).

Many authors address the decomposition of the VaR (see for example Hallerbach (1999), Tasche (1999), Rosen and Saunders (2010) and the references therein). Qian (2006) shows that the VaR can also be divided into risk contributions like the standard deviation and these contributions are also linked to losses. However, the calculation of the VaR budgets is not as simple as of the volatility budgets and he proposes to use the Cornish-Fisher expansion method.

Tasche (1999), Stoyanov et al. (2010), Scaillet (2004) and Sarykalin et al. (2008), among others, present the first derivative or the risk decomposition of the CVaR. However, the risk contributions are used for the estimation of risk-adjusted performance measures, as predictors of the asset cash flows given a worst case scenario for the portfolio cash flow (Tasche, 1999) or as an additional information after the portfolio optimization (to rank the asset positions in terms of their contributions, Scaillet (2004)). This additional risk breakdown should help to asses the individual risks of the assets and to adjust the portfolio allocation manually to a desired risk-return profile.

Although the risk contributions of the CVaR are available in the literature, only recently Boudt et al. (2011) propose the equal risk contribution portfolio based on the Conditional Value at Risk. First, Boudt et al. (2008) introduce a new estimator for the CVaR, called modified CVaR which is based on the Cornish-Fisher and Edgeworth approximations of the portfolio return quantile and distribution functions. The definition of this new estimator is consistent with the definition by Zangari (1996) of modified Value at Risk (VaR). Boudt et al. (2008) provide estimation quality tests of the modified CVaR vs. the normal CVaR based on simulated and historical data and conclude that the modified CVaR provide a more accurate estimate than the normal CVaR. However, for levels of above 99%, the estimates get more and more unreliable. Moreover, they calculate the percentage risk contributions to the modified and the normal CVaR in the naive and the tangency (maximum Sharpe ratio) portfolio. Their results illustrate that the weight allocation can be very different from the risk allocation and that the risk dispersion is dependent on the used risk measure.

The implementation of the risk contributions to the modified CVaR is done in Boudt et al. (2011). They study the 'Minimum CVaR Concentration Portfolio (MCC)' by minimizing the largest CVaR contribution as an objective and the minimum CVaR portfolio with an ERC constraint and compare these 'CVaR budget based portfolio allocations' to the minimum CVaR as well as to the naive portfolio. Their first observation is that the two CVaR risk contribution portfolios are quite similar, but the MCC portfolio is easier to solve and can be combined with a target return constraint. In a simple bond/equity portfolio, the minimum CVaR portfolio is highly concentrated in equities, whereas the MCC portfolio delivers a 50/50 risk diversification with a higher average return and only a slight higher CVaR as the minimum CVaR portfolio. In a portfolio with equities, bonds, commodities and real estate with monthly returns over the time period of 1976 - 2010 by rebalancing the portfolio quarterly, they state that the MCC portfolio lies in between the minimum CVaR and the naive portfolio. Whereas the minimum CVaR portfolio has the highest return in bear market periods, the naive portfolio outperforms the other approaches in bull market periods. However, the naive portfolio has a huge CVaR risk and maximum drawdown and the min-CVaR portfolio a high risk concentration and turnover. So the MCC portfolio achieves a balance between the CVaR risk, risk concentration and turnover. As the difference in the annualized returns over the whole period is minimal (0.15%), they recommend to adapt the strategies depending on the market conditions: the minimum CVaR portfolio in bear markets and the MCC portfolio in normal/bull markets.

However, except of the study of Boudt et al. (2011, p. 3), these portfolios are not examined and compared to other portfolios yet. Boudt et al. (2011) mention that the *literature on risk contribution portfolios lacks a detailed study on using downside risk budgets rather than portfolio variance budgets as an ex ante portfolio allocation tool.* This thesis tries to fill this gap by examining portfolios with equal risk contributions to various risk measures as an objective and different calculations of the risk contributions (historical returns vs. analytical formula).

4.2.3 Summary of the Risk Budgeting Studies

The literature review of the risk budgeting approaches has shown that most of the studies focus on the historical performances and comparison of the ERC portfolio based on volatility against other benchmarks, like the 60/40, the value-weighted market index, naive and MV portfolio. Most studies claim thereby an outperformance of the ERC portfolio based on returns or Sharpe ratio against the 60/40, the value-weighted market index and the naive portfolio. The results against the MV portfolio are less clear. Sometimes the returns and the Sharpe ratio of the ERC are higher, but the drawdown of the MV portfolio is always lower. It seems that the ERC portfolio outperforms the MV portfolio, if the naive portfolio is better than the MV portfolio. Thereby it is obvious that the ERC portfolio is located between the two approaches. All studies investigate the ERC portfolio with volatility as the underlying risk measure, except one.

The recent applications of the ERC portfolios focus on the diversification of risk based on risk factors rather than the diversification of individual asset risks. However, which factors should be taken into account is less clear.

Another strand of literature focuses on ideas to confirm the empirical results or the justification of the risk budgeting approach. The concepts encompass leverage aversion as well as fat tails and uncertainty in estimated input parameters.

Based on the analyses, this thesis concentrates on the examination of risk budgets based on different risks and not only the volatility like before. The different risk measures and ERC portfolios are analyzed from the decision theory point of view and the robustness and factor exposures of the risk budgeting portfolios are examined. Moreover, an idea based on hierarchical clustering combined with the risk contribution aspect will also be explored.

Table 4.2: ERC Portfolio - Empirical Results

The following abbreviations are used: 1/n: naive portfolio, MV: minimum variance portfolio, SR: Sharpe ratio, MaxDD: maximum drawdown

Author (Year)	Period/ Assets/ Benchmark	Calculations/ Constraints	Results
Qian (2005b)	S & P 500 Index, Barclays Capital Aggregate Bond Index, 1976-2009, ERC + ERC with leverage (so that same risk as 60/40) vs. 60/40		Unlevered: Lower return than 60/40, but lower Std and higher SR, Levered: higher return and SR, same risk as 60/40; divided into decades, the ERC only outperforms from 2000-2010 in returns
Qian (2005a)	Russell 1000 Index and Lehman Aggregate Bond Index, 1983-2004, ERC + ERC with leverage (so that same risk as 60/40) vs. 60/40		Same result as Qian (2005b)
Neukirch (2008b)	Global equities, European bonds, Global real estate, European Private Equity, Commodities Energy and Commodities Non-Energy	ERC vs. ERC with $\sigma_P \leq 3.25\%$, naive ERC without correlations, MV	all ERC variants have a higher return and SR than MV, MV has the lowest volatility and lowest MaxDD
Neukirch (2008a)	MSCI World Developed Markets Index, 2001-2008, ERC (without correlations) vs. 1/n, Mkt-cap	monthly rebalancing	ERC outperforms the 1/n, both better than the Mkt-cap (more in upward than in downward markets) in return, Std and SR

ERC Portfolio Results - Continued

Author (Year)	Period/ Assets/ Benchmark	Calculations/ Constraints	Results
Allen (2010)	6 assets: Risk-free rate, Real Estate, Fixed Income, US Equity, Non-US Equity and Commodities, 1989-2009, ERC with 8.25% expected return (only attainable with 55% leverage) vs. efficient Mean Variance portfolio with 8.25% return (unlevered + 50% leverage)	quarterly rebalancing	SR of ERC (0.63) greater than mean-variance (0.35), but levered mean-variance portfolio (0.73) higher; levered ERC portfolio underperforms the unlevered mean-variance from 1990-2000 and outperforms from 2000-2009, levered ERC portfolio has half the volatility of an unlevered mean-variance portfolio with the same return since 1990
Demey et al. (2010)	Universe of the DJ Euro Stoxx 50 Index, 1991-2009, ERC vs. DJ Euro Stoxx, 1/n, MV	daily returns, monthly rebalancing, historical covariance (12 month)	ERC has the highest return and SR, MV the lowest volatility and MaxDD, all portfolios outperform the market
Little (2010)	Bond + Equity indices, 1950-2010, ERC vs. 60/40, 70/30, 50/50 Portfolios	monthly returns, historical covariance (3 years), monthly rebalancing	ERC return only higher in the decade of 2000-2010, lowest volatility over the whole period, highest SR in decades of 1970-1980 and 2000-2010
Maillard et al. (2010)	1. 10 US Sectors: 1973-2008; 2. 8 agricultural commodities: 1979-2008; 3. Global portfolio of 13 indices: 1995-2008; ERC vs. 1/n, MV	daily returns, historical covariance (12 months), monthly rebalancing	1.: ERC + 1/n similar return, higher than MV, MV lowest volatility, SR and MaxDD, ERC lower volatility, higher SR and lower drawdowns than 1/n; 2. MV outperforms in all measures, ERC outperforms 1/n; 3. ERC highest return and SR, MV lowest Std and drawdowns, ERC in all datasets lower turnover than MV

ERC Portfolio Results - Continued

Author (Year)	Period/ Assets/ Benchmark	Calculations/ Constraints	Results
Qian (2010)	Commodities (1 index), Fixed Income (4 indices), Equity (4 indices), 1983-2009, ERC vs. individual asset classes	ERC weights are adjusted over time based on forecasted Sharpe ratios	ERC has the highest SR from 1983-1999, from 2000-2009: Commodities have the highest SR, ERC has the same SR as Fixed Income
Boudt et al. (2011)	broad bond, commodity, equity and real estate, 1976-2010, ERC (modCVaR) vs. 1/n and minCVaR	monthly returns, quarterly rebalancing, covariance estimated by DCC-GARCH(1,1) (8 years)	minCVaR highest return, 1/n the lowest, minCVaR much lower Std and CVaR; minCVaR has a large allocation to bonds, outperforms the 1/n and ERC portfolios at times of serious stock market downturn, ERC portfolio lower turnover than the minCVaR
Chaves et al. (2011)	U.S. Treasury, U.S. bonds, global bonds, U.S. high yield bonds, U.S. equities, international equities, emerging market equities, commodities and real estates, 1980-2010, ERC vs. 60/40, 1/n, MV, tangency portfolio	annually rebalancing, tangency portfolio: average return from the past 5 years & shrinkage covariance, $w_i \leq 33\%$	60/40 has the highest return, MV the lowest volatility and return, ERC + 1/n the highest SR; observed ERC performance can be highly dependent on the time period and the asset classes included; the SR's for the 1/n and the ERC portfolios have been more stable over the last three decades

ERC Portfolio Results - Continued

Author (Year)	Period/ Assets/ Benchmark	Calculations/ Constraints	Results
Lohre et al. (2011)	Government bonds, emerging equities, developed equities, commodities and bonds, 1987-2011, ERC vs. 1/n, MV, PCA diversified portfolio (Meucci, 2009)	historical covariance (expanding window and 60 month rolling window), decomposition of portfolio risks by eigenvectors	returns are very similar, but 1/n has the highest return, MV lowest volatility, highest SR and lowest MaxDD, ERC second best by Std, SR and drawdown; decomposing of portfolio risk: 1/n is mostly driven by equity risk, MV mostly by interest rate risk, ERC more diversified in equity and interest rate risk
Bruder and Roncalli (2012)	1. Bonds + Equities, ERC vs. 80/20, 2000-2012; 2. Eurostoxx 50 universe, ERC vs. Eurostoxx, 1993-2011	covariance: past year, monthly rebalancing	1.: ERC has a higher return and a lower volatility than the 80/20 portfolio; 2.: ERC has a higher return, lower volatility and lower MaxDD than the Eurostoxx
Carvalho et al. (2012)	all stocks of MSCI World Index of developed countries, also sub-universes of U.S., EU and Japan, 1997-2010, ERC vs. naive ERC without correlations, 1/n and Mkt-cap	weekly returns, quarterly rebalancing, $0 \leq w_i \leq 5\%$, PCA covariance (past two years)	MV the highest return, lowest volatility, lowest MaxDD and highest SR, ERC second best in volatility, SR and MaxDD; ERC is exposed to low beta and small stocks

ERC Portfolio Results - Continued

Author (Year)	Period/ Assets/ Benchmark	Calculations/ Constraints	Results
Lee (2012)	500 U.S. Stocks at the end of each calendar year, 1979 - 2011, vs. Mkt-cap	covariance: Barra USE3L model, monthly re-balancing	ERC has a higher return and a lower Std than the Mkt-cap, correlation between ERC and the market cap is 0.96, rolling performance: ERC portfolio outperforms the MC portfolio most of the time, except from 1992-2000, higher correlation of assets -> outperformance of the ERC

5 Robustness

Based on the problems of the Markowitz portfolios (see chapter 2.1.4), different solutions to improve the estimation errors or to generate 'robust portfolios' are proposed in the literature. At first, this chapter gives a definition of robustness. Afterwards, a short review of approaches towards robust portfolios is presented. Finally, studies concerning the robustness of the Markowitz as well as of the risk budgeting portfolios are outlined.

5.1 Definition of Robustness

As this issue was already studied in Poddig and Unger (2012), this section follows closely the earlier published work.

Early after the publication of the Mean-Variance portfolio optimization of Markowitz, the high sensitivity to estimation errors in input parameters was recognized in the literature. Since then, there is a large and growing body of literature that deals with estimation errors in order to create more 'robust portfolios', which are less sensitive to unavoidable estimation errors. There are two different literature strands to deal with estimation errors: the robust estimation method, which incorporates uncertainty sets directly in the optimization process, and the Bayesian method, which tries to generate robust inputs by incorporating uncertainty (for an overview, see Fabozzi, 2007; Scutellà and Recchia, 2010 and Fabozzi et al., 2010).

Despite the large amount of literature, the term 'robustness' is not well defined (see Jen, 2001 for at least 17 different definitions of robustness in different contexts and Brinkmann, 2007, p. 18). Tütüncü and Koenig (2004, p. 158) outlines: *'Generally speaking, robust optimization refers to finding solutions to given optimization problems with uncertain input parameters that will achieve good objective values for all, or most, realizations of the uncertain input parameters.'* As the value of the objective function remains stable, this is usually characterized as 'solution robustness'.

In most cases robust portfolios are assumed to provide stable solutions in the case of varying input parameters and most methods in the literature try to reduce the sensitivity of the outcome of the Markowitz-optimal portfolios to input uncertainty or the influences of estimation errors (Goldfarb and Iyengar, 2003, p. 2; Fabozzi, 2007, p. 10). However, there is a difference between the robustness of the solution or stability of portfolio outcomes (influence on the portfolio mean and variance) and the structure robustness (influence on asset weights). Tütüncü and Koenig (2004) state that a robust solution *'has the best performance under its worst case'*. The worst case is thereby specified as an undesirable situation with low returns and high standard deviations of the assets. A portfolio is then more worst-case robust than another, if it provides under the same worst-case scenario a better performance than other portfolios.

In this thesis, robustness is assumed to have two aspects, which will both be examined in the next chapter (Brinkmann, 2007, p. 21):

- Solution robustness: the portfolio return and variance remain stable, although the uncertain input parameters vary;
  - → worst-case robustness: the portfolio provides acceptable outcomes in bad circumstances (low returns and high standard deviations of the assets; obviously, this is simply a special case of solution robustness);
- Structure robustness: the portfolio structure is insensitive to varying input parameters (or, more precisely, the portfolio do not exhibit extreme allocations and sensitive weights).

Brinkmann (2007) states that the two properties are contradictory and 'robustness' depends mainly on the position of the portfolio on the efficient frontier. Portfolios that are near the minimum-variance portfolio display a higher structure robustness, whereas portfolios that lie 'near the investor-optimal mean-variance portfolio' exhibit a better worst-case robustness. But the results vary with the underlying data set and none of the examined approaches show a good worst-case performance (Brinkmann, 2007, p. 281). In this thesis, it is explored whether this is also the case for the minimum risk and the risk budgeting portfolios.

5.2 Approaches to Robust Portfolios: A Short Review

The review in this section is based upon Fabozzi et al. (2007, 2010) and Scutellà and Recchia (2010).

The first step to attain more robust portfolios is to apply robust estimators to the input parameters. After Huber (1981), a robust estimator should have good properties not only for the assumed distribution, but also for distributions in a neighborhood of the assumed distribution. The robust estimators are thus less sensitive to outliers. These techniques like robust covariance matrix estimation (Campbell, 1980), Shrinkage (Jorion, 1986, Ledoit and Wolf, 2004b) and the Black-Litterman approach (Black and Litterman, 1992), which combines the market equilibrium returns with an investor view of the returns, are well known in the literature to obtain more 'robust estimates', which are not so sensitive to a slightly varying data set.

Another common technique is the portfolio resampling (Michaud and Michaud (2008a), Michaud and Michaud (2008b)). The estimators are obtained through a simulation. At first, different samples are drawn from the multivariate normal distribution with the sample mean and covariance as distribution parameters. Then, the portfolios are optimized on each of the samples with the sample estimators. Finally, the portfolio weights result as the average of the weights of the individual portfolios of the sample.

A different strand of the literature, robust optimization, includes the uncertain parameters directly in the portfolio optimization process. The solution remains then 'optimal' or 'good' for all possible realizations of the parameters in a given region. Uncertainty in the expected mean and covariance is modeled by using uncertainty sets, which define possible realizations for the unknown parameters.

It is assumed that the uncertain input parameters vary within the uncertainty set and to solve the optimization problem, a worst-case (max-min) approach is applied: find portfolio weights such that the portfolio return is maximized, even when the vector of realizations for the asset returns takes its 'worst' value over the uncertainty set (Soyster, 1973, Bertsimas and Sim, 2004, Ben-Tal and Nemirovski, 2000).

Most of the models consider uncertainty in the returns and assume that the covariance is known, as the estimation errors of the means have a much larger influence on the portfolio allocation. However, there are also models, which take also the uncertainty in the covariance matrix into account. Soyster (1973) was the first to consider robust optimization techniques in a linear model, where the solution are feasible for all data that belong in a convex set. The resulting model is said to produce solutions, which are too pessimistic and too far from optimality in order to ensure robustness (Bertsimas and Sim, 2004, Ben-Tal and Nemirovski, 2000).

ElGhaoui and Lebret (1997) and Ben-Tal and Nemirovski (1998) took independently of each other important steps toward robust models by considering ellipsoidal uncertainty sets and constructing a 'max-min' or 'min-max' optimization problem, that is, to obtain the maximum value of the objective function (maximize the returns), in the case of minimum values (expected returns) of the uncertain parameters or to obtain the minimum value of the objective function (minimize the risk) for a case of maximum values of the uncertain parameters (covariance). Lobo and Boyd Stephen (2000) considers different uncertainty sets for the mean and the covariance for a portfolio to minimize the worst-case risk. The simplest uncertainty set is the 'interval' or 'box' around the returns (Lobo and Boyd Stephen, 2000) and the mostly used uncertainty set is an ellipsoidal around the returns (ElGhaoui and Lebret, 1997, Ben-Tal and Nemirovski, 1998).

This uncertainty set is an ellipsoid around all the estimated parameters, and not an individual region for each estimate. It implies a protection from the worst possible joint deviation of the estimated returns from the 'true' returns by considering the correlations between the estimation errors through the covariance matrix (Fabozzi, 2007). It is not immediately obvious, how to calculate the covariance of the estimation errors, but Stubbs and Vance (2005) propose different methods to calculate the 'estimation error matrix', including standard approaches like Bayesian statistics or the Black-Litterman model.

The uncertainty of the covariance can also be incorporated through specifying intervals for the individual elements of the covariance matrix (Tütüncü and Koenig, 2004).

It is possible to apply robust optimization techniques without changing the original optimization. In a first step, the worst case parameters are calculated through the uncertainty sets, and in the second step the optimization program is solved with the worst case parameters (Scutellà and Recchia, 2010).

There are also approaches for a worst-case VaR and a worst-case CVaR in the literature. El Ghaoui et al. (2003) propose a robust portfolio optimization for a worst-case VaR, where only partial information on the distribution is available. By defining bounds on the mean and covariance matrix, the worst-case Value-at-Risk is the largest VaR attainable, given the partial information on the distribution of the returns. Natarajan et al. (2006) expand the idea of El Ghaoui et al. (2003) and propose a parametric-VaR based on robust optimization techniques. The resulting risk measure is coherent and approximates also the CVaR. They investigate the approach in a simulation as well as in an empirical study and state that the robust-parametric VaR optimization shows a more robust performance (lower VaR, better efficient frontier and lower maximum loss) than the Normal VaR, the Worst-Case VaR or the sample CVaR optimizations, especially in out-of-sample experiments with skewed distributions for asset returns. Zhu and Fukushima (2009) present the worst-case CVaR minimization problem by using mixture distribution uncertainty, box uncertainty and ellipsoidal uncertainty. They compare the worst-case CVaR with the linear CVaR optimization and conclude that 'the portfolio selection model using the worst-case CVaR as the risk measure performs robustly in practice, and provides more flexibility in portfolio decision analysis' (Zhu and Fukushima, 2009, p. 24).

5.3 Review of the Robustness of the Markowitz Approach

As this issue was already studied in Poddig and Unger (2012), this section follows closely the earlier published work.

The recognition of the estimation errors of the Markowitz approach has been made by many different authors.

Black and Litterman (1992) recognize that a small modification in expected asset returns can result in large changes in the optimal portfolio allocation. The variations in expected returns have a high impact on the resulting estimated asset weights, so that changing the estimation sample by a few observation points may change the complete asset allocation (Jorion, 1985, p. 261). This is also the observation of Best and Grauer (1991). They state that the Mean-Variance optimizer is extremely sensitive to changes in assets means. If only one asset mean is slightly increased, half the assets are excluded from the portfolio. But this dramatic change has only a small influence on the portfolio's expected return and portfolio volatility (Best and Grauer, 1991, p. 339).

Since the true returns or input parameters are unknown in advance, the historical data is used for estimation. However, Merton (1980) and Jorion (1985) show that the historical mean is not a precise estimator for the expected returns. Moreover , the optimizer is more sensible to changes in expected returns than in variances, which leads to a portfolio structure that is far from the true optimal allocation (Jobson and Korkie, 1980; Michaud, 1989; Chopra and Ziemba, 1993; Broadie, 1993 and Jagganathan and Ma, 2003). Michaud (1989) labels the Mean Variance optimizer an 'estimation-error maximizer', as it maximizes the effects of errors in the input parameters (Michaud, 1989, p. 33).

Broadie (1993) distinguishes between the true, the estimated, and the actual efficient frontier and examines the estimation errors in a simulation study. The 'true' efficient frontier is obtained by using the true (but unknown) parameters. The 'estimated' frontier is calculated by using the estimated parameters. By using the estimated portfolio weights, which result through a portfolio optimization with the estimated parameters, and then holding the portfolio in the period, when the true returns and variances appear, the 'actual' frontier is attained. Thus, the estimated frontier is what appears to be the case based on the data and the estimated parameters, but the actual frontier is what actually occurs based on the true parameters (Broadie, 1993, p. 24). Broadie (1993) concludes that the historical estimates should be used with caution as the resulting estimation errors are large.

Brinkmann (2007) compares different 'robust approaches' (input estimation by the Bayesian approach, robust optimization of Tütüncü and Koenig (2004), use of constraints and the sampling approach of

Michaud and Michaud (2008a)) vs. the classical mean-variance optimization as well as the tangency portfolio in a simulation as well as in an
empirical study. As outlined above, he divides robustness as solution
and worst case robustness and examines the approaches according to
these characteristics. He concludes that the two directions of robustness are incompatible, as approaches which are more structure robust
are not the ones which are more worst-case robust. Moreover, none
of the techniques shows a satisfactory solution in a worst case scenario.

It is generally accepted that estimation errors in the estimated expected returns are much larger than those in the estimated covariance
matrix (Chan et al. (1999), Jagganathan and Ma (2003)). This is also a
reason for the risk models without considering the returns. Related to
the high sensitivity to estimation errors in expected returns, DeMiguel
et al. (2009b) show that the naive portfolio allocation outperforms
14 different models (mean-variance model, Bayesian approaches to
estimation error, moment restriction approaches, portfolio constraints
and optimal combinations of portfolios) in terms of Sharpe ratio,
turnover and the certainty equivalent return: $\mu_P - \frac{1}{2}\lambda\sigma_P^2$ in seven
different empirical datasets. Thus, the authors conclude that the gain
from optimal diversification is offset by the sensitivity to estimation
errors. The most effective approaches to reduce the estimation errors
are strategies that combine portfolio constraints with some form of
shrinkage of expected returns or by ignoring expected returns (e.g.
constrained MV portfolio). However, even then, the Sharpe ratios
are not always significantly different from those of the naive portfolio.
Moreover, they study the influence of the number of assets and the
length of the estimation window on the certainty equivalent return of
the portfolios in a simulation. The results is that the largest part of
the estimation errors is attributable to the estimation of the expected
returns and that the mean-variance strategy and its extensions need
an estimation period for a portfolio with 25 assets of ca. 3000 months
and for a portfolio with 50 assets of ca. 6000 months to outperform
the naive portfolio in terms of the Sharpe ratio.

One theoretical explanation for the high sensitivity of the mean-variance portfolio is given in Bruder and Roncalli (2012). The solution structure of the mean-variance portfolio is of the following form:

$$w^* \propto \Sigma^{-1} \mu \tag{5.1}$$

The important variable is Σ^{-1}, called information matrix, which is the inverse of the covariance matrix Σ. The covariance matrix and the information matrix are related through the principal component analysis, which splits the matrix into eigenvalues and eigenvectors, in the following manner: the eigenvectors are the same and the eigenvalues of the information matrix Σ^{-1} are equal to the inverse of the eigenvalues of Σ. But the eigenvalues are decreasingly responsible for the variation in the data set. So through the inverse relation, the weights of the mean-variance portfolio depend on all the eigenvalues of the information matrix, and especially on the less important eigenvalues of the covariance (which are the most important values of the information matrix). As a small a change in the covariance matrix changes the last (less important) eigenvalue of the matrix and such the most important eigenvalue for the solution of the mean-variance portfolio, the weights of the mean-variance portfolio are extremely sensitive to changes in the data input.

5.4 Robustness of the Volatility Risk Budgeting Portfolio

There are a few results concerning the equally risk contribution portfolio based on the volatility, which are summarized in the following. As only one study of risk budgets based on the CVaR exists, results on the robustness are not available. This gap in the literature will be closed in the following.

The motivation behind the equally risk contribution portfolio is often relied on the aspect that the forecasting of returns is 'difficult and noisy' (Schachter and Thiagarajan (2011)). As many studies have demonstrated that estimation errors of the returns have a much higher impact on the portfolio allocation as estimation errors of the risk (Merton, 1980, Chopra and Ziemba, 1993, Jorion, 1985, see), the use of the risk parity portfolio can be based upon this aspect.

However, only a few authors address the estimation error of the ERC portfolio. Kaya and Lee (2012) study the risk parity portfolio sensitivity to changes in the input parameters. In a hypothetical portfolio with three assets and by varying the volatility of an asset from 10% - 20% in 1% steps and holding the others constant, they compare the weights and risk contributions of the ERC portfolio vs. the MV portfolio. They show that the weight changes of the MV portfolio are considerably larger than of the ERC portfolio and the MV portfolio is much more concentrated, no matter if the volatility of the asset is 10% or 20%. In a second step, they examine the impact of the correlation with the same procedure by increasing the correlation between two assets from -0.5 to 1, whereas the others are kept constant. Not surprising, the result is the same as in the case of the volatility: the MV portfolio reacts much more sensitive to the changes in the correlation. Furthermore, the impact on the turnover from the changes in volatility and/or the correlations is always greater in the MV portfolio.

Although the MV portfolio relies also only on the covariance matrix, the risk contribution portfolios tend to be more structure robust and less sensitive to the input parameters, as they are not directly based on optimization techniques (Bruder and Roncalli, 2012). Many different studies demonstrate that the turnover of the ERC portfolio is lower than that of the Markowitz approach (Maillard et al., 2010, Boudt et al., 2011, Bruder and Roncalli, 2012, see e.g.). This aspect indicates that the weights do not change much during the portfolio optimizations and that the ERC portfolio is thus more structure robust.

In an earlier research, Poddig and Unger (2012), the robustness of the ERC portfolio based on the volatility was studied in comparison to the Markowitz efficient portfolio (with a target return equal to the ERC portfolio return), the MV portfolio, the naive portfolio as well as the 'PCA portfolio', which tries to achieve equal risk contributions to uncorrelated principal components. Both aspects of robustness, the structural as well as the solution robustness (and the worst-case robustness) was examined in a simulation as well as in an empirical setting. The main results is that the ERC portfolio is more structure robust and slightly more solution robust than the other portfolios, but in the different worst-case scenarios, there is no real difference. The study of the earlier work will be repeated and expanded in section 6.4 with all the risk based portfolios examined in this thesis to make a general conclusion about the robustness of the equal risk contribution portfolios. Moreover, the extension of the study allows a general statement about the robustness of different risk measures. The earlier study examined the approaches only in an unrealistic simulation, where the naive portfolios is the true asset allocation. Due to this reason, the ERC portfolios have an advantage, as their asset allocation is more similar to the naive diversification than the allocation of the other approaches. Therefore, the simulation is expanded here to a more realistic case, to examine if the higher structure and solution robustness of the ERC portfolios still holds in a different setting. Additionally, significant tests of the actual realized returns are provided to examine the different performances.

Although the motivation behind the risk contribution approaches is often relied upon the sensitivity of the Markowitz approach, there are only a few attempts to study the impact of the estimation errors on the risk contribution portfolio. The available results indicate that the ERC portfolio is more robust than the Markowitz approach regarding the change of the weights. However, as outlined in chapter 5.1, robustness has different aspects. In this thesis, it will be studied how the different approaches react to changes in the input parameters with respect to the weights and portfolio outcomes in a simulation and an empirical study, similar to the earlier work in Poddig and Unger (2012).

5.5 Summary

The high estimation errors of the Markowitz portfolios are the subject
of many studies. However, little is known about the robustness of
risk based portfolios or the risk budgeting portfolios. Only the earlier
work in Poddig and Unger (2012) provides an examination of the
robustness of the ERC portfolio based on the volatility. In this thesis,
the structure as well as the worst case robustness of all minimum risk
as well as risk budgeting portfolios will be tested in a simulation as
well as in an empirical setting close to Poddig and Unger (2012)(see
6.4).

6 Empirical Studies

After the theoretical analysis of the different portfolios, in the following different empirical results of the portfolios are presented.

6.1 Organization of Studies

Figure 6.1 shows the outline of empirical studies. This chapter consists of three main parts. At first, the different risk budgeting portfolios are tested against the minimum risk approaches in three different data sets. The first dataset involves four different European indices from 1996 - 2012, which represent three different asset classes (equities, bonds, real estates) and can be seen as a strategic asset allocation.Therefore the dataset is called 'European Fund'. The next examination of the portfolios takes place on thirteen indices from different countries from 1995 - 2011 and represents a Global portfolio. It is seen as a diversificated asset allocation on different asset classes (equities, bonds, corporate bonds and commodities) with different risks. The last dataset consists of 55 German equities and runs from 1973 - 2012. It is called the Germany 1973 dataset. It is important to examine the different strategies on individual equities, as this is yet omitted in the literature. Moreover, it examines the strategies over a long horizon. The performance studies cover the main performances as well as significance tests of the different returns and volatilities. Additionally, different risk measures, risk ratios and out-of-sample risk contributions of the portfolios are examined. An important part is also the split of the performances into bull and bear periods.

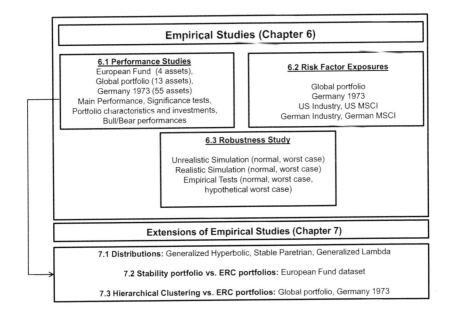

Figure 6.1: Outline of Empirical Studies

The next part examines if the risk budgeting portfolios exhibit abnormal returns. The CAPM, the three and the four factor models are applied to study the exposures to the factors as well as the excess returns. At first, the two datasets from the performance studies are taken to examine the portfolio performances, Global portfolio and German equities. The European Fund dataset is not suited as there are only two equity indices in the universe and the factors are build to explain equity returns. The Global portfolio dataset contains also other asset classes, but nevertheless will be incorporated, as the main part consists of equity indices (nine of thirteen) and it is interesting to explore the results. The factor exposures are also examined on the Germany 1973 dataset. Additionally the following datasets are considered for the investigation of the factors: 32 US equity indices of different sectors, which are constructed by Datastream and run from 1973 - 2012, eight US MSCI style indices, which cover the factors size, value and growth, 16 German equity indices of different factors and eight MSCI style indices for the German market. The style datasets should have a high explanation of the factors and the factor exposures are easier to observe.

The third investigation concerns the investigation of the estimation errors of the different portfolios. The setting includes a simulation as well as an empirical study of the sensitivities to input variations as well as estimation errors in a 'normal' as well as in a 'worst case'. The study is very similar to Poddig and Unger (2012), but has a slightly different setting due to the portfolio approaches, which require a sample of returns as inputs and additionally the simulation study is expanded to a realistic setting.

Chapter 7 contains additionally a few extensions to the performance studies. At first, different fat tailed distributions are considered for the calculation of the 'sample' risk budgeting portfolios. In the performance studies, the calculation of the ERC portfolios is based on the historical returns. It is examined if the simulation of returns has an influence on the portfolio performances. Moreover, an interesting alternative to the ERC portfolios is presented, which focuses on 'stability' as risk. The European Fund dataset is again taken to compare the performance of the 'stable portfolio' to the ERC portfolios. The last extension covers an idea of hierarchical clustering of assets without optimization and is also based on risk contributions. The performance of this approach is compared to the ERC portfolios on the Global portfolio as well as the Germany 1973 dataset.

6.2 Performance Study

In this section, the performance of the different portfolio allocation techniques is outlined by comparing various performance character- istics on different empirical datasets. For each dataset, at first the properties of the assets are demonstrated. Next, the performances of the minimum risk portfolios as well as of the risk budgeting portfolios are shown and compared on different return and risk measures. Following DeMiguel et al. (2009b), the naive portfolio with constant·· weights will serve as a benchmark. After exploring that none of 14 alternative models was better in terms of Sharpe ratio and turnover, DeMiguel et al. (2009b) state that the naive portfolio should serve as a benchmark to compare the performance of more sophisticated models.

6.2.1 Methodology

The performance studies are accomplished as follows. Independent of the data set, **daily logarithmic returns** are used:

$$r_t^S = \ln(\frac{p_t}{p_{t-1}}) = \ln(p_t) - \ln(p_{t-1}) \qquad (6.1)$$

with

$$r_t^S : \text{continuous return in day } t$$
$$p_t : \text{price of the asset in day } t$$
$$p_{t-1} : \text{price of the asset in day } t-1$$

The estimation period of the inputs for the portfolio optimizations consists of 12 months previous daily returns. The portfolios are rebalanced monthly, so that a rolling window approach is applied. At the end of each month (last trading day of the month), the portfolio weights are obtained by optimizing the portfolio with the historical daily returns of the preceding 12 months. Then, the portfolio is hold one month and rebalanced again. Thus, a realistic out-of-sample-backtesting of the portfolios is performed. Depending on the length of the data, a different number of portfolio optimizations is obtained. As described in chapter 3.2, all portfolios are optimized with the full investment constraint and by excluding short sales.

To compare the portfolios, different performance measures are used. The performance measures are all calculated on the out-of-sample portfolio return (estimated portfolio weights * realized asset returns). The total return, the annual mean, the annual standard deviation, the annualized Sharpe ratio and the maximum loss constitute the main criteria. They are displayed in percentage terms and calculated as follows:

Total return:

$$Totalret = \sum_{i=1}^{T} r_{p,i} * 100, \quad r_{p,i} \approx \sum_{j=1}^{N} w_{j,i} \, r_{j,i} \tag{6.2}$$

with

$$r_{p,i} : \text{portfolio return in month } i$$
$$w_{j,i} : \text{weight of asset } j \text{ in month } i$$
$$r_{j,i} : \text{return of asset } j \text{ in month } i$$
$$T : \text{number of months/rebalancing dates}$$
$$N : \text{number of assets}$$

Annual mean:

$$ann.Mean = \frac{1}{T} \sum_{i=1}^{T} r_{p,i} \quad *12* \quad 100$$

The annual standard deviation is calculated through multiplying the standard deviation of the monthly portfolio returns with the factor $\sqrt{12}$. Theoretically, this is is only right if the returns are identically and independent distributed (Poddig et al., 2005, p. 126). However, independent of this, the factor is used simply as a scaling factor to compare the different standard deviations of the portfolios.

Annual standard deviation:

$$ann.Vola = \sqrt{Var(r_p)} \quad *\sqrt{12}* \quad 100$$

with

$$r_p : \text{vector of monthly portfolio returns}$$

Annualized Sharpe ratio (the risk free rate is zero, $r_f = 0$):

$$ann.Sharpe = \frac{ann.Mean}{ann.Vola} * 100$$

Maximum Loss:

$$MaxLoss = \min(r_p) * \quad 100$$

The performance per year is measured as the difference of the cumulative returns of the years and is given as follows:

$$r_i = (rc_{p,i} - rc_{p,i-1}) * \quad 100$$

with

$$r_i : \text{portfolio return in year } i$$

$$rc_{p,i} : \text{cumulative portfolio return up to year } i$$

$$rc_{p,i-1} : \text{cumulative portfolio return up to the preceding year, } i-1$$

Moreover, the different risk measures VaR, CVaR, DaR, CDaR and MaxDD of the portfolios are compared. As the calculations are presented in chapter 3.1.2, they will not be repeated at this point. The risk measures are calculated on the basis of the resulting monthly portfolio returns. For better comparison, they are shown as positive figures (calculation based on the loss distribution).

Moreover, Risk Ratios based on the different risk measures are calculated. They are obtained as follows.

$$Mean = \frac{1}{T} \sum_{i=1}^{T} r_{p,i} \tag{6.3}$$

$$SR\_sigma = \frac{Mean}{\sigma_p} * 100 \qquad (6.4)$$

$$SR\_VaR = \frac{Mean}{VaR} * 100 \qquad (6.5)$$

$$SR\_CVaR = \frac{Mean}{CVaR} * 100 \qquad (6.6)$$

$$SR\_CDaR = \frac{Mean}{CDaR} * 100 \qquad (6.7)$$

$$SR\_avdd = \frac{Mean}{avdd} * 100 \qquad (6.8)$$

$$SR\_maxdd = \frac{Mean}{maxdd} * 100 \qquad (6.9)$$

The turnover is a performance measure for the restructuring of the portfolio through rebalancing and gives a clue about trading costs. The turnover is obtained as follows (Álvarez and Luger (2011), DeMiguel et al. (2009b)):

$$mean\,Turnover = \frac{1}{T}\sum_{t=1}^{T}\sum_{i=1}^{N}\left(|w_{(i)t+1} - w_{(i)t}^{+}|\right) \qquad (6.10)$$

where

$$w_{(i)t}^{+} = \frac{w_{i,t}(1+R_{i,t+1})}{\sum_{i=1}^{n} w_{i,t}(1+R_{i,t+1})}$$

with

$$T : \text{number of rebalances}$$
$$w_{(i)t+1} : \text{weight obtained by optimization in } t+1$$
$$w_{(i)t}^+ : \text{weight at the end of period } t \text{ before}$$
$$\text{rebalancing in } t+1$$
$$i : \text{number of assets}$$
$$R_{i,t+1} : \text{return between times } t \text{ and } t+1 \text{ on asset } i$$

$$total\,Turnover = \sum_{t=1}^{T}\sum_{i=1}^{N} \left(|w_{(i)t+1} - w_{(i)t}^+| \right) \qquad (6.11)$$

Moreover, the number of trades is calculated. A trade is assumed, if the weight before rebalancing does not equal the weight after rebalancing:

$$No.\,of\,Trades = \sum_{t=1}^{T}\sum_{i=1}^{N} w_{(i)t+1} \neq w_{(i)t}^+ \qquad (6.12)$$

Whereas the turnover measures the trade volume, the number of trades show how often the asset weight changes through rebalancing and thus how often the investor needs to act. It depends on the trading system, which of them determines the transaction costs, however, mostly the turnover is the main criterion.

Additionally the weight and the risk allocations of the portfolios are compared. The weight allocations are simply calculated as the average weight of the asset across the whole period. The risk contributions are calculated out-of-sample to show the realized risk budgets due to estimation errors. The calculation is clarified by figure 6.2. The portfolios are optimized in t through the in-sample daily returns of the last 12 months. The portfolio is then held with estimated weights one month until $t+1$ and then optimized again through the returns of the last 12 months. The realized risk budgets are calculated in the month from t until $t+1$ and thus in the out-of-sample period. E.g., if the ERC portfolio is optimized to have equal risk contributions, the risk contributions are only equal in the in-sample period, but in the out-of-sample period the risk contributions are not exactly equal due to different asset returns.

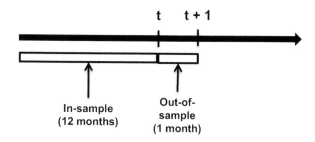

Figure 6.2: In-Sample and Out-of-Sample Periods

Significance Tests

To determine if the performances of the portfolios differ significantly, statistical hypothesis tests will be performed. The first test considers the difference in the means of two portfolios:

$$\Delta r = r_p - r_b \tag{6.13}$$

with

$$\Delta r : \text{vector of return differences}$$
$$r_p : \text{vector of monthly portfolio returns}$$
$$r_b : \text{vector of monthly benchmark returns}$$

The two-sided Student's t-test is considered to identify the significance. The hypotheses of interest are

$$H_0 : \Delta\mu = 0 \quad vs. \quad H_1 : \Delta\mu \neq 0 \tag{6.14}$$

with

$$\Delta\mu : \text{mean of the return differences, } \tfrac{1}{T}\sum_{i=1}^{T}\Delta r_i$$

The t-test is based on the following test statistic:

$$T = \sqrt{n}\,\frac{\Delta\mu - 0}{\sigma(\boldsymbol{\Delta r})} \quad \sim t_{n-1} \tag{6.15}$$

with

$$n : \text{number of observations}$$

$$\sigma(\boldsymbol{\Delta r}) : \text{standard deviation of the return differences}$$

The test statistic is Student's t distributed with n-1 degrees of freedom. The t-test rejects H_0 at significance level α if and only if

$$T < t_{\alpha/2,\,n-1} \quad or \quad T > t_{1-\alpha/2,\,n-1} \tag{6.16}$$

Most softwares offer a p-value for the hypothesis tests. It is the probability of error if H_0 is rejected, but H_0 is true. Thus, if the p-value is smaller than the significance level α, H_0 is rejected.

To examine an outperformance of a portfolio against another, additionally the Jensen's Alpha is used. It is based on the Capital Asset Pricing Model of. For performance measurement, the 'market portfolio' is replaced by the benchmark portfolio. Thus, the outperformance is measured by the following regression:

$$r_{p,t} - r_f = \alpha_p + (r_{b,t} - r_f)\beta_p + \epsilon_{p,t} \tag{6.17}$$

with

$$r_{p,t} : \text{portfolio return in month } t$$

$$r_{b,t} : \text{benchmark return in month } t$$

$$r_f : \text{risk free rate}$$

$$\alpha_p : \text{Jensen's alpha}$$

$$\beta_p : \text{portfolio beta}$$

$$\epsilon_{p,t} : \text{residual return in month } t$$

If the Jensen's alpha is 0, there is no outperformance against the benchmark. Otherwise, if it is positive and statistically significant, the portfolio outperforms the benchmark. Thus, a two-sided t-test is considered on α. The hypotheses are $H_0 : \alpha = 0$ vs. $H_1 : \alpha \neq 0$. If H_0 is rejected and the α is positive, there is an outperformance of the portfolio against the benchmark. However, to obtain reliable parameter estimates, different underlying assumptions for regression analysis have to be true. The most important ones are that the residual returns are uncorrelated and have a constant variance across the observations. The Durbin-Watson test is used to control for autocorrelated residuals and the Breusch-Pagan test as well as the White test to control for constant variance. The Durbin-Watson hypotheses are (Poddig et al., 2003, p. 302f)

$$H_0 : \rho_1 = 0 \quad vs. \quad H_1 : \rho_1 \neq 0 \tag{6.18}$$

where

$$\rho_1 = \frac{Cov(\varepsilon_t, \varepsilon_{t-1})}{Var(\varepsilon_{t-1})} = \frac{Cov(\varepsilon_t, \varepsilon_{t-1})}{Var(\varepsilon_t)} = \frac{\sigma_{t,t-1}}{\sigma^2}$$

with

ρ_1 : first order autocorrelation coefficient

ε_t : residual of the regression in time t

The test statistic of the Durbin-Watson test is

$$DW = \frac{\sum_{t=2}^{n} (\hat{\varepsilon}_t - \hat{\varepsilon_{t-1}})^2}{\sum_{t=1}^{n} \hat{\varepsilon_t^2}} \tag{6.19}$$

with

n : number of observations

The DW test statistic can be approximated as follows:

$$DW \approx 2(1 - \hat{\rho}_1) \tag{6.20}$$

The DW statistic lies between 0 and 4:

- $DW \approx 0 \rightarrow$ first order positive autocorrelation

- $DW \approx 4 \rightarrow$ first order negative autocorrelation

- $DW \approx 2 \rightarrow$ none first order autocorrelation

The exact critical values of the test statistic depend on the number of observations, the number of explanatory variables and the design matrix for a linear regression. The exact critical values are included in softwares, e.g. MATLAB and R and provide p-values for the test statistic.

The Breusch-Pagan (Breusch and Pagan, 1979) and the White (White, 1980) test examine the variance of the residuals. The following regression equation is examined (Poddig et al., 2003, p. 311f):

$$\sigma_t^2 = \alpha_0 + \alpha_1 z_{1t} + \alpha_2 z_{2t} + \ldots + \alpha_l z_{lt} \qquad (6.21)$$

with

$$\sigma_t^2 : \text{variance of the residuals}$$
$$z_t : \text{explanation variable in } t$$
$$l : \text{number of explanatory variables}$$
$$\alpha_0 : \text{regression constant}$$
$$\alpha_j : \text{regression coefficient}$$

The hypotheses of interest are

$$H_0 : \alpha_1 = \alpha_2 = \ldots = \alpha_l = 0 \quad vs. \quad H_1 : \text{at least one} \quad \alpha_j \neq 0 \quad (6.22)$$

The test rejects the null hypothesis if too much of the variance is explained by the explanatory variables. The test statistic is as follows:

$$BP = \frac{RSS}{2\hat{\sigma}^4} \quad \sim \chi_l^2 \quad \text{under} \quad H_0 \qquad (6.23)$$

where

$$RSS = \sum_{t=1}^{n} \left(\hat{\varepsilon}_t^2 - \overline{\hat{\varepsilon}_t^2} \right)^2, \quad \hat{\sigma}^2 = \frac{1}{n} \sum_{t=1}^{n} \hat{\varepsilon}_t^2$$

Under H_0, the BP test statistic is χ^2 distributed with l degrees of freedom. The BP test rejects H_0 at significance level α if

$$BP > \chi_l^2 \tag{6.24}$$

The Breusch-Pagan test requires normal distributed residuals. The White test is closely related to the Breusch-Pagan test, but does not assume a normal distribution for the residuals. If the following regression model is used,

$$y_t = \beta_0 + \beta_1 x_{1t} + \beta_2 x_{2t} + \varepsilon_t \tag{6.25}$$

White (1980) proposes to use the following explanatory variables for the residuals:

$$\varepsilon_t^2 = \alpha_0 + \alpha_1 x_{1t} + \alpha_2 x_{2t} + \alpha_3 x_{1t}^2 + \alpha_4 x_{2t}^2 + \alpha_5 x_{1t} x_{2t} + v_t \tag{6.26}$$

The White test statistic is

$$W = nR^2 \sim \chi_l^2 \quad \text{under} \quad H_0$$

with

$$R^2 : \text{coefficient of determination of the} \\ \text{test regression}$$

The last significance tests concerns the comparison of the variances of the portfolios. The question is whether the variances are statistically different from each other. For this, the F-test is used. The hypotheses of interest are

$$H_0 : \frac{\sigma_p^2}{\sigma_b^2} = 0 \quad vs. \quad H_1 : \frac{\sigma_p^2}{\sigma_b^2} \neq 0 \tag{6.27}$$

with

$$\sigma_p^2 : \text{variance of portfolio}$$
$$\sigma_b^2 : \text{variance of benchmark}$$

The F-test is based on the following test statistic:

$$F = \frac{\sigma_p^2}{\sigma_b^2} \quad \sim F_{n-1,n-1} \tag{6.28}$$

with

$$n : \text{number of observations}$$

The test statistic is F-distributed with n-1 and n-1 degrees of freedom (it is assumed that both portfolios have the same number of observations). The t-test rejects H_0 at significance level α if

$$F < F_{\alpha/2,n-1,n-1} \quad or \quad F > F_{1-\alpha/2,n-1,n-1} \tag{6.29}$$

All the calculations are done in R (R Core Team, 2012) with the following packages: fPortfolio (Würtz et al., 2010), fPortfolioBacktest (Würtz et al., 2010), PerformanceAnalytics (Carl et al., 2012), lmtest (Zeileis and Hothorn, 2002) and Systematic Investor Toolbox (Kapler, 2012). The chosen probability α for the risk measures is 0.95, the h-value for the finite differences is 0.01 and the significance level α for the statistical tests is 0.05.

For reasons of comprehensibility, the following abbreviations of the portfolios will be used in the following to discuss the empirical results:

Table 6.1: Notations of Portfolios

Abbreviation	Portfolio
MV	Minimum Variance Portfolio
minCVaR	Minimum Conditional-Value-at-Risk Portfolio
minCDaR	Minimum Conditional-Drawdown-at-Risk Portfolio
sampleCVaR	Equal Risk Contributions to CVaR - calculated through finite differences
normCVaR	Equal Risk Contributions to CVaR - based on normal distribution
modCVaR	Equal Risk Contributions to CVaR - based on Cornish-Fisher expansion
sampleCOV	Equal Risk Contributions to Volatility
sampleCDaR	Equal Risk Contributions to CDaR - calculated through finite differences

6.2.2 European Fund

At first, the portfolios will be examined on a simple dataset, which consists of four different investable asset classes, namely the STOXX 50 (market-capitalized index of the 50 largest companies in Europe), the STOXX Mid (capitalized index based on 200 mid companies in Europe), the STOXX Europe TMI Real Estate (European Real Estate Index) and the EuroMTS Bond Government index, which is constructed through 1/2 of returns of 3-5 year maturities and 1/2 of returns of 5-7 years. The dataset endures from **01.01.1996 - 31.12.2012.**

The following abbreviations are used in the European Fund dataset:

Table 6.2: Notations of Indices - European Fund

Abbreviation	Index
SX5T	STOXX 50 - 'large cap' (50 companies)
MCXT	STOXX Mid - 'mid cap' (200 companies)
T8600R	SXT600R - real estate
EMTS3A37X	EuroMTS Bond Government Index

Description of the Dataset

Table 6.3 gives the basic statistics of the daily returns of the assets. The annual mean is the highest for the retail index, whereas the bond index displays ca. one fifths of the annual volatility compared to the risky assets. All assets are skewed to the left and display thicker tails as the normal distribution, except the bond index.

Table 6.3: Component Statistics - European Fund
All values are displayed in percent, except the skewness and kurtosis.

	SX5T	SXMCXT	SXT8600R	EMTS3A37X
Observations	4436.00	4436.00	4436.00	4436.00
Minimum	-8.19	-8.24	-7.09	-1.56
Ann. Mean	5.78	6.30	7.15	5.92
Maximum	10.44	9.18	7.57	1.59
Ann. Std	24.22	18.75	18.63	4.10
Skewness	-0.03	-0.37	-0.34	-0.18
Kurtosis	4.37	5.23	6.05	2.17

The correlations of the four assets in table 6.4 show that the three risky assets have a high correlation of 63%, 71% and 91%, whereas the bond index exhibits a negative correlation to all of them.

Table 6.4: Correlations of Indices - European Fund
The values are calculated across the whole period (daily returns) and displayed in percent.

	SX5T	SXMCXT	SXT8600R
SXMCXT	91		
SXT8600R	63	71	
EMTS3A37X	-18	-22	-16

Main Performance

Table 6.5: Portfolio Statistics - European Fund
All values are displayed in percent. For the calculations see section 6.2.1.

	Totalret	ann.Mean	ann.Vola	Sharpe	MaxLoss
MV	92.68	5.79	3.49	165.87	-1.96
minCVaR	96.21	6.01	3.56	168.99	-2.01
minCDaR	93.53	5.85	4.37	133.92	-3.04
Naive	89.12	5.57	12.77	43.60	-14.20
sampleCVaR	105.30	6.58	4.64	141.85	-3.24
normCVaR	104.61	6.54	4.66	140.21	-3.33
modCVaR	104.48	6.53	5.75	113.50	-6.58
sampleCOV	104.26	6.52	4.72	138.00	-3.41
sampleCDaR	99.43	6.21	5.54	112.18	-5.39

Table 6.5 displays the main outcomes of the different portfolios based on the European Fund dataset. It is observable that all risk budgeting models have higher cumulative returns than the minimum risk approaches and the naive portfolio. But the annual standard deviations are also higher, which results in lower Sharpe ratios. Across the risk budgeting models, the sampleCVaR model displays the best Sharpe ratio and the lowest loss. Across the minimum risk models, it is the minCVaR approach. The naive portfolio has in this dataset the

worst outcomes, regardless of whether return, risk or the Sharpe ratio is considered. Table 6.6 displays the returns per calendar year. It is

Table 6.6: Performance per Calender Year - European Fund
The table displays the difference of the cumulative returns of the years. For the calculations see section 6.2.1.

	1997	1998	1999	2000	2001	2002	2003	2004	2005
MV	6.36	9.54	-3.10	7.13	3.41	7.11	7.56	11.09	7.57
minCVaR	6.10	9.82	-3.37	7.14	3.04	8.45	8.35	10.77	7.94
minCDaR	11.04	10.87	5.99	5.45	2.65	4.70	7.12	11.80	8.93
Naive	22.96	11.79	16.52	2.04	-8.20	-17.87	16.84	18.50	18.84
sampleCVaR	17.12	10.83	4.27	5.96	1.73	1.84	9.94	13.57	10.67
normCVaR	16.06	10.41	3.43	5.93	1.40	2.03	9.34	14.26	12.00
modCVaR	16.69	10.25	3.53	6.15	0.87	3.55	9.80	12.45	10.68
sampleCOV	16.17	10.30	3.55	6.03	1.11	1.71	9.52	14.13	12.16
sampleCDaR	15.07	9.51	8.63	4.25	1.04	3.58	8.54	15.35	12.92

	2006	2007	2008	2009	2010	2011	2012	Total
MV	2.27	1.85	6.07	5.61	6.54	3.76	9.91	92.68
minCVaR	2.13	1.29	6.44	5.59	7.30	5.55	9.66	96.21
minCDaR	3.55	1.12	1.18	4.46	7.45	-2.76	9.99	93.53
Naive	21.45	-7.76	-43.05	22.42	7.29	-10.27	17.61	89.12
sampleCVaR	7.28	-0.22	-3.29	8.16	5.70	-0.67	12.40	105.30
normCVaR	8.84	-0.78	-4.51	8.50	5.90	-0.28	12.08	104.61
modCVaR	7.32	-0.35	-4.14	12.57	1.38	1.51	12.20	104.48
sampleCOV	8.75	-0.78	-5.03	8.75	5.95	-0.25	12.19	104.26
sampleCDaR	13.56	-2.34	-8.85	5.76	6.45	-7.53	13.48	99.43

conspicuous that the highest returns are delivered from the naive portfolio, except in down periods, where the minimum risk approaches display the best performance. The risk budgeting portfolios display higher returns than the minimum risk approaches, when the naive portfolio exhibits the highest return. On the opposite, they deliver a worse return than the minimum risk approaches in down periods, but better than the naive portfolio. In sum, the risk budgeting approaches have a higher cumulative return than the naive portfolios, as they do not loose so much in down periods. Based on this split up of returns, it can be supposed that a 'regime switching' approach between the naive and the minimum risk approaches would perform the best.

Significance Tests

Table 6.7 shows the significance tests of the differences in mean returns of the portfolios across the whole period. It is obvious that none of the outperformances of the portfolios is significant. Thus, the higher returns of the risk budgeting portfolios can be random and are within the 'fluctuation noise', as the null hypothesis that the differences are different from 0 cannot be rejected.

Table 6.7: Statistical Significance of Mean Differences - European Fund
For the calculations of the tests see 6.2.1.

	Excess Mean (%)	t-Stat	p-value
sampleCOV vs. MV	0.06	0.88	0.38
sampleCVaR vs. minCVaR	0.05	0.69	0.49
normCVaR vs. minCVaR	0.04	0.63	0.53
modCVaR vs. minCVaR	0.04	0.41	0.68
sampleCDaR vs. minCDaR	0.03	0.50	0.62
sampleCOV vs. Naive	0.08	0.39	0.69
sampleCVaR vs. Naive	0.08	0.41	0.68
normCVaR vs. Naive	0.08	0.40	0.69
modCVaR vs. Naive	0.08	0.40	0.69
sampleCDaR vs. Naive	0.05	0.26	0.79
sampleCOV vs. sampleCVaR	-0.01	-0.48	0.63
sampleCOV vs. normCVaR	-0.00	-0.50	0.62
sampleCOV vs. modCVaR	-0.00	-0.02	0.99
sampleCOV vs. sampleCDaR	0.03	0.51	0.61
sampleCDaR vs. sampleCVaR	-0.03	-0.62	0.54
sampleCDaR vs. normCVaR	-0.03	-0.56	0.58
sampleCDaR vs. modCVaR	-0.03	-0.30	0.77

The calculations of the Jensen's Alpha in table 6.8 show that the α is positive and significant for the outperformances of the risk contribution portfolios vs. the naive portfolio. Moreover, the sampleCOV outperforms the modCVaR and the sampleCDaR portfolio and the normCVaR portfolio outperforms the sampleCOV portfolio.

Table 6.8: Jensen's Alpha - European Fund
For the calculations see 6.2.1.

	Jensen's Alpha (Rf = 0)	t-Stat
sampleCOV vs. MV	0.0008	0.9960
sampleCVaR vs. minCVaR	0.0009	1.0977
normCVaR vs. minCVaR	0.0008	1.0317
modCVaR vs. minCVaR	0.0015	1.2219
sampleCDaR vs. minCDaR	-0.0001	-0.0973
sampleCOV vs. Naive	0.0041	6.5043
sampleCVaR vs. Naive	0.0042	6.4031
normCVaR vs. Naive	0.0042	6.4831
modCVaR vs. Naive	0.0040	4.6331
sampleCDaR vs. Naive	0.0038	4.5195
sampleCOV vs. sampleCVaR	-0.0001	-0.9542
sampleCOV vs. normCVaR	-0.0001	-2.1904
sampleCOV vs. modCVaR	0.0018	2.9805
sampleCOV vs. sampleCDaR	0.0014	3.2528
sampleCDaR vs. sampleCVaR	-0.0008	-1.4343
sampleCDaR vs. normCVaR	-0.0007	-1.3955
sampleCDaR vs. modCVaR	0.0014	1.6593

Table 6.9 shows the regression analyses for the Jensen's Alpha regression. To verify the results of the positive α, all the assumptions of the regression have to be fulfilled. The positive $\alpha's$ of the ERC portfolios against the naive portfolio as benchmark are significant. However, the outperformances of the sampleCOV and the normCVaR portfolios are unclear, as the residuals are autocorrelated or the constant variance is rejected according to the White test. Thus, the positive α is questionable. The values of the F-test in table 6.10 show that nearly all differences in variances are statistically significant. Thus, the risk of the risk budgeting portfolios is lower than the naive portfolio, but higher than of the minimum risk portfolios.

Table 6.9: Analysis of Jensen's Alpha Regression - European Fund
For the calculations see 6.2.1.

	DW statistic	p-value	BP-stat	p-value	White-stat	p-value
sampleCOV vs. MV	1.5741	0.0015	0.0051	0.9433	0.0089	0.9955
sampleCVaR vs. minCVaR	1.5503	0.0009	0.1644	0.6852	0.7728	0.6795
normCVaR vs. minCVaR	1.5279	0.0005	0.1606	0.6886	0.6316	0.7292
modCVaR vs. minCVaR	2.0931	0.7400	1.6794	0.1950	1.7655	0.4136
sampleCDaR vs. minCDaR	1.5499	0.0009	0.8018	0.3706	2.7374	0.2544
sampleCOV vs. Naive	1.8761	0.1892	1.8349	0.1756	2.0825	0.3530
sampleCVaR vs. Naive	1.8540	0.1505	0.8915	0.3451	1.5142	0.4690
normCVaR vs. Naive	1.8705	0.1790	1.9052	0.1675	2.1765	0.3368
modCVaR vs. Naive	2.0146	0.5336	0.3229	0.5699	3.4985	0.1739
sampleCDaR vs. Naive	1.8553	0.1526	0.6094	0.4350	17.6333	0.0001
sampleCOV vs. sampleCVaR	1.5061	0.0003	1.4127	0.2346	21.5584	0.0000
sampleCOV vs. normCVaR	1.5736	0.0014	8.4844	0.0036	20.3150	0.0000
sampleCOV vs. modCVaR	2.0547	0.6489	1.5616	0.2114	139.2978	0.0000
sampleCOV vs. sampleCDaR	1.7456	0.0373	1.4317	0.2315	82.6480	0.0000
sampleCDaR vs. sampleCVaR	1.6182	0.0038	0.0155	0.9008	2.9368	0.2303
sampleCDaR vs. normCVaR	1.6737	0.0113	0.0050	0.9435	1.9184	0.3832
sampleCDaR vs. modCVaR	1.9299	0.3135	1.3756	0.2409	71.7934	0.0000

Table 6.10: Significance of Difference in Variances - European Fund
For the calculations see 6.2.1.

	Ratio of variances	p-value
sampleCOV vs. MV	1.8281	0.0000
sampleCVaR vs. minCVaR	1.7001	0.0003
normCVaR vs. minCVaR	1.7175	0.0002
modCVaR vs. minCVaR	2.6140	0.0000
sampleCDaR vs. minCDaR	1.6102	0.0011
sampleCOV vs. Naive	0.1366	0.0000
sampleCVaR vs. Naive	0.1319	0.0000
normCVaR vs. Naive	0.1333	0.0000
modCVaR vs. Naive	0.2028	0.0000
sampleCDaR vs. Naive	0.1880	0.0000
sampleCOV vs. sampleCVaR	1.0358	0.8084
sampleCOV vs. normCVaR	1.0253	0.8633
sampleCOV vs. modCVaR	0.6736	0.0066
sampleCOV vs. sampleCDaR	0.7266	0.0279
sampleCDaR vs. sampleCVaR	1.4255	0.0147
sampleCDaR vs. normCVaR	1.4110	0.0178
sampleCDaR vs. modCVaR	0.9271	0.6014

Portfolio Characteristics

The risk figures in table 6.11 outline that the MV and the minCVaR portfolio have the lowest risk figures across the whole period.

Table 6.11: Risk Figures - European Fund
All values are displayed in percent. For the calculations of the risk measures see 3.1.2.

	5% VaR	5% CVaR	5% DaR	5% CDaR	MaxDD
MV	1.14	1.49	4.14	5.11	6.78
minCVaR	1.34	1.64	4.01	4.98	6.75
minCDaR	1.48	2.00	4.03	5.10	6.83
Naive	6.25	8.96	37.21	44.38	50.66
sampleCVaR	1.89	2.39	4.48	5.81	7.56
normCVaR	1.90	2.45	5.71	7.41	9.28
modCVaR	2.15	3.26	5.72	7.41	9.49
sampleCOV	1.91	2.51	6.16	7.79	9.89
sampleCDaR	2.01	3.24	11.12	12.77	14.99

Table 6.12: Risk Ratios - European Fund
All values are displayed in percent. For the calculations see 6.2.1.

	SR sigma	SR VaR	SR CVaR	SR CDaR	SR avdd	SR maxdd
MV	47.88	42.35	32.39	9.44	64.33	7.12
minCVaR	48.78	37.38	30.48	10.05	66.19	7.43
minCDaR	38.66	32.84	24.31	9.56	57.29	7.13
Naive	12.59	7.43	5.18	1.05	3.24	0.92
sampleCVaR	40.95	29.05	22.99	9.43	58.58	7.25
normCVaR	40.47	28.71	22.24	7.35	51.03	5.87
modCVaR	32.77	25.27	16.69	7.34	46.17	5.74
sampleCOV	39.84	28.40	21.60	6.97	48.96	5.49
sampleCDaR	32.38	25.70	15.98	4.05	22.58	3.45

Table 6.12 outlines that the best risk ratios are shared by the MV and the minCVaR portfolio. Whereas the MV portfolio generates the best risk ratios based on the VaR and the CVaR, the minCVaR

approach delivers the best risk ratios based on the volatility and the drawdown measures. The sampleCVaR portfolio has the best risk ratios among the risk budgeting approaches, but only the drawdown risk ratios are comparable to the minimum risk approaches, whereas the other lag behind.

Table 6.13: Turnover and Trades - European Fund
The turnover and trades are based on weights before and after the portfolio optimizations. For the calculations see 6.2.1.

	mean Turnover	total Turnover	No. of Trades
MV	0.02	4.54	562
minCVaR	0.05	9.50	535
minCDaR	0.09	16.49	514
Naive	0.02	4.69	768
sampleCVaR	0.04	6.99	768
normCVaR	0.03	4.99	768
modCVaR	0.05	10.42	763
sampleCOV	0.03	4.86	768
sampleCDaR	0.08	15.36	768

The turnover and the total number of trades in table 6.13 show that the MV and the naive portfolio have the lowest turnover, whereas the minCDaR portfolio needs the fewest trades. Some of the risk budgeting approaches display a lower turnover as the minimum risk approaches (sampleCVaR, normCVaR and sampleCDaR compared to their minimum risk counterparts), but therefore more trades (as they are always invested in all assets). What is more expensive, depends on the trading system, whether the investor has to pay for the volume or per trade.

Portfolio Investments

Tables 6.14, 6.15, 6.16 show the average weights and the average out-of sample risk budgets of the portfolios. Based on the estimated weights, all portfolios allocate the most portion in the bond. As the risk budgeting portfolios ensure equal risk contributions, they invest less in the bond and more in the risky assets. Although the weight allocations over the whole period differ not much across the portfolios, the risk budgets between the minimum risk and risk budgeting portfolios are distinct. The average risk contributions of the MV and the sampleCOV portfolio are shown as representatives. Whereas the volatility risk budgets of the MV portfolio and the CVaR risk budgets are mostly allocated in the bond, the CDaR risk budgets in risky assets are on average 30%. The risk budgets of the sampleCOV portfolio to the different risk measures show that the risk contributions do not differ much.

Table 6.14: Weight Allocations - European Fund

These are average estimated weights across the whole period and displayed in percent.

	MV	minCVaR	minCDaR	sampleCVaR	normCVaR	modCVaR	sampleCOV	sampleCDaR
SX5T	1	1	4	7	7	9	8	10
SXMCXT	6	6	9	9	10	10	10	11
SXT8600R	4	4	4	11	11	12	12	12
EMTS3A37X	90	89	83	72	72	69	71	68

Table 6.15: Risk Budget Allocations of the MV Portfolio - European
Fund
The average risk budgets are calculated out-of sample and
displayed in percent. For the calculation see 6.2.1. MVto-
COV: risk contributions to volatility, MVtoCVaR: risk
contributions to CVaR, MVtoCDaR: risk contributions to
CDaR.

	MVweights	MVtoCOV	MVtoCVaR	MVtoCDaR
SX5T	1	1	2	2
SXMCXT	6	8	12	19
SXT8600R	4	4	6	10
EMTS3A37X	90	87	80	70

Table 6.16: Risk Budget Allocations of the sampleCOV Portfolio -
European Fund
The average risk budgets are calculated out-of sample and
displayed in percent. For the calculation see 6.2.1. COV-
toCOV: risk contributions to volatility, COVtoCVaR: risk
contributions to CVaR, COVtoCDaR: risk contributions to
CDaR.

	sampleCOVweights	COVtoCOV	COVtoCVaR	COVtoCDaR
SX5T	8	24	24	22
SXMCXT	10	23	23	22
SXT8600R	12	23	22	24
EMTS3A37X	71	30	30	32

Bull/Bear Market Performance

To examine a better distinction/variation of the performances of the
portfolios, the period is split into bull and bear periods. Put it simply,
bull periods are characterized by periods of time when equity prices
rise and bear markets if the prices fall. The bull phase comes usually
along with a high mean and a low volatility and the bear phase with
a low mean and a high volatility. But despite the common agreement

on the bull and bear market phases existence, it seems difficult to give an exact definition (Gonzalez et al., 2005, p. 470). Many researchers have studied the identification of the phases with different models, also for reasons of forecasting (see e.g Fabozzi and Francis (1979), Harding and Pagan (2002), Pagan and Sossounov (2003), Gonzalez et al. (2005) and Chauvet and Hamilton (2006)). The main point is to identify the 'turning point', that is, the switch from a bull phase to a bear phase and vice versa (Pagan and Sossounov, 2003, p. 24). With their primary work in the business cycle literature, Bry and Boschan (1971) have published an algorithm for the identification of turning points. The points are recognized through local minima or maxima, thus, the turning points are higher or lower than their neighboring points. Other methods focus on the duration of the cycles (Lunde and Timmermann, 2004) or include the Markov-Regime-Switching algorithm (Hamilton, 1989, Gordon and St-Amour, 1999, Maheu and McCurdy, 2000).

As the identification of market phases is not the main object in this thesis, the division in bull and bear market phases follows Bry and Boschan (1971) in a similar fashion. The turning points will be analyzed on the basis of the naive portfolio, as this can be seen as a benchmark for the market. At first, the cumulative sum of the returns is build, and then the turning points are detected through local minima or maxima of a moving window of 8 observations. A local minima or maxima exists, if the surrounding points are higher or lower:

$$\text{local minimum: } (P_{t-n}, ..., P_{t-1}) < P_t > (P_{t+1}, ..., P_{t+n}),$$
$$\text{local maximum: } (P_{t-n}, ..., P_{t-1}) > P_t < (P_{t+1}, ..., P_{t+n}),$$
$$\text{where n=8.}$$

The algorithm of Bry and Boschan (1971) consists of the following steps (Seiler, 2008, p. 141):

- The first and last eight observations are disregarded.

- Through a rolling window of 8 observations, the local minima and maxima are identified.

- The local minima and maxima have to alternate. E.g., if one or several minimum points follow another minimum, the lowest minimum is chosen.

- The identified minima and maxima are turning points. A period, which begins in a local minimum and ends in a local maximum is called a bull-phase, otherwise, if the period starts with a local maxima and ends with a local minimum, it is a bear phase. A cycle consists of a bear and a bull phase.

- The duration of a phase has to be at least 6 months and of a cycle at least 15 months, unless the cumulated price change is more than 20%. Too short phases are eliminated.

This algorithm is used in this thesis to identify the bull and bear phases and to compare the performances of the portfolios in 'up-market' as well as in 'down-market' periods.

The following phases were identified for the Global dataset (the period runs from 01.1997 - 12.2012):

Bull Period	Bear Period
01.1997 - 08.2000	08.2000 - 03.2003
03.2003 - 05.2007	05.2007 - 02.2009
02.2009 - 05.2011	05.2011 - 02.2012

Figure 6.3 demonstrates the identified phases on the basis of the naive portfolio in the European Fund dataset.

Tables 6.17 and 6.18 present the portfolio performances separated into bull and bear phases. It is obvious that the risk budgeting portfolios display higher returns and Sharpe ratios in bull periods than the minimum risk approaches. The best performance among the

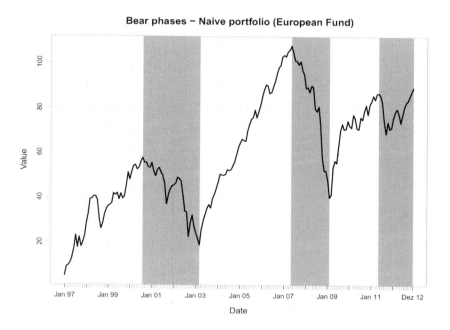

Figure 6.3: Bear Phases - European Fund

risk contribution portfolios offers the sampleCOV portfolio. However, the naive portfolio display a much higher return and Sharpe ratio than the risk budgeting portfolios in the Bull period. According to table 6.19 the underperformances of the ERC portfolios vs. the naive portfolio in the bull period are also statistically significant. Thus, the naive portfolio clearly outperforms the ERC portfolios in up-market periods. The higher return of the sampleCOV portfolio vs. the sampleCVaR as well as the normCVaR portfolio is also significant. Additionally, all the risk contribution portfolios, except the modCVaR portfolio, display a statistically significant higher return vs. their minimum risk counterparts in the bull period. Table 6.21 shows that also almost all the differences in variances are statistically significant.

In the bear market, the opposite picture is shown. The minimum risk portfolios display a positive return by a lower risk, which results

Table 6.17: Bull/Bear Characteristics of Minimum Risk Portfolios -
European Fund

	MV	minCVaR	minCDaR	Naive
Bull Market (%)				
Totalret	85.24	89.70	96.06	241.99
Ann. Mean	6.12	6.45	6.90	17.39
Ann. Std	3.45	3.55	4.40	11.03
Sharpe	177.76	181.57	156.87	157.71
MaxDD	6.78	6.75	6.83	16.87
Bear Market (%)				
Totalret	21.65	22.45	12.23	-106.33
Ann. Mean	5.00	5.18	2.82	-24.54
Ann. Std	3.64	3.63	3.70	14.11
Sharpe	137.30	142.81	76.32	-173.90
MaxDD	3.62	3.64	5.36	67.35

Table 6.18: Bull/Bear Characteristics of Risk Budgeting Portfolios -
European Fund

	sampleCVaR	normCVaR	modCVaR	sampleCOV	sampleCDaR
Bull Market (%)					
Totalret	126.29	129.41	126.90	131.00	125.01
Ann. Mean	9.07	9.30	9.12	9.41	8.98
Ann. Std	4.44	4.44	6.87	4.47	5.29
Sharpe	204.36	209.26	132.76	210.56	169.72
MaxDD	4.56	4.56	9.49	4.49	11.16
Bear Market (%)					
Totalret	-2.68	-5.31	-2.27	-6.78	-9.27
Ann. Mean	-0.62	-1.23	-0.52	-1.56	-2.14
Ann. Std	4.24	4.30	4.15	4.42	4.76
Sharpe	-14.58	-28.53	-12.61	-35.42	-44.97
MaxDD	8.54	10.14	8.99	11.07	15.35

in high positive Sharpe ratios. The risk budgeting portfolios exhibit
negative total returns and show also higher standard deviations and
maximum drawdowns. However, they display a better performance

Table 6.19: Significance in Means in the Bull Period - European Fund

	Excess Mean (%)	t-Stat	p-value
sampleCOV vs. MV	0.27	4.15	0.00
sampleCVaR vs. minCVaR	0.22	3.27	0.00
normCVaR vs. minCVaR	0.24	3.55	0.00
modCVaR vs. minCVaR	0.22	1.50	0.14
sampleCDaR vs. minCDaR	0.17	2.90	0.00
sampleCOV vs. Naive	-0.66	-3.58	0.00
sampleCVaR vs. Naive	-0.69	-3.61	0.00
normCVaR vs. Naive	-0.67	-3.59	0.00
modCVaR vs. Naive	-0.69	-4.08	0.00
sampleCDaR vs. Naive	-0.70	-3.67	0.00
sampleCOV vs. sampleCVaR	0.03	2.37	0.02
sampleCOV vs. normCVaR	0.01	2.93	0.00
sampleCOV vs. modCVaR	0.02	0.21	0.83
sampleCOV vs. sampleCDaR	0.04	0.67	0.51
sampleCDaR vs. sampleCVaR	-0.01	-0.15	0.88
sampleCDaR vs. normCVaR	-0.03	-0.50	0.62
sampleCDaR vs. modCVaR	-0.01	-0.09	0.93

than the naive portfolio, which shows the worst return, volatility and maximum drawdown in the bear period. According to tables 6.20 all the differences in means are again statistically significant. Table 6.22 shows that only the reductions in variances of the risk budgeting portfolios compared to the naive portfolio are statistically significant, but not the higher variances compared to the minimum risk portfolios.

Table 6.20: Significance in Means in the Bear Period - European Fund

	Excess Mean (%)	t Stat	p-value
sampleCOV vs. MV	-0.55	-4.48	0.00
sampleCVaR vs. minCVaR	-0.48	-4.11	0.00
normCVaR vs. minCVaR	-0.53	-4.44	0.00
modCVaR vs. minCVaR	-0.48	-4.37	0.00
sampleCDaR vs. minCDaR	-0.41	-3.90	0.00
sampleCOV vs. Naive	1.91	4.29	0.00
sampleCVaR vs. Naive	1.99	4.34	0.00
normCVaR vs. Naive	1.94	4.27	0.00
modCVaR vs. Naive	2.00	4.28	0.00
sampleCDaR vs. Naive	1.87	3.96	0.00
sampleCOV vs. sampleCVaR	-0.08	-3.78	0.00
sampleCOV vs. normCVaR	-0.03	-3.07	0.00
sampleCOV vs. modCVaR	-0.09	-2.61	0.01
sampleCOV vs. sampleCDaR	0.05	0.61	0.54
sampleCDaR vs. sampleCVaR	-0.13	-1.54	0.13
sampleCDaR vs. normCVaR	-0.08	-1.02	0.31
sampleCDaR vs. modCVaR	-0.13	-1.74	0.09

Table 6.21: Significance in Variances in the Bull Period - European Fund

	Ratio of variances	p-value
sampleCOV vs. MV	1.6835	0.0009
sampleCVaR vs. minCVaR	1.5645	0.0041
normCVaR vs. minCVaR	1.5669	0.0040
modCVaR vs. minCVaR	3.7432	0.0000
sampleCDaR vs. minCDaR	1.4465	0.0179
sampleCOV vs. Naive	0.1644	0.0000
sampleCVaR vs. Naive	0.1622	0.0000
normCVaR vs. Naive	0.1624	0.0000
modCVaR vs. Naive	0.3880	0.0000
sampleCDaR vs. Naive	0.2304	0.0000
sampleCOV vs. sampleCVaR	1.0136	0.9307
sampleCOV vs. normCVaR	1.0121	0.9383
sampleCOV vs. modCVaR	0.4237	0.0000
sampleCOV vs. sampleCDaR	0.7135	0.0303
sampleCDaR vs. sampleCVaR	1.4205	0.0243
sampleCDaR vs. normCVaR	1.4184	0.0249
sampleCDaR vs. modCVaR	0.5937	0.0009

Table 6.22: Significance in Variances in the Bear Period - European
Fund

	Ratio of variances	p-value
sampleCOV vs. MV	1.4730	0.1701
sampleCVaR vs. minCVaR	1.3675	0.2671
normCVaR vs. minCVaR	1.4041	0.2289
modCVaR vs. minCVaR	1.3103	0.3377
sampleCDaR vs. minCDaR	1.6550	0.0750
sampleCOV vs. Naive	0.0980	0.0000
sampleCVaR vs. Naive	0.0904	0.0000
normCVaR vs. Naive	0.0928	0.0000
modCVaR vs. Naive	0.0866	0.0000
sampleCDaR vs. Naive	0.1137	0.0000
sampleCOV vs. sampleCVaR	1.0839	0.7748
sampleCOV vs. normCVaR	1.0556	0.8476
sampleCOV vs. modCVaR	1.1312	0.6615
sampleCOV vs. sampleCDaR	0.8618	0.5974
sampleCDaR vs. sampleCVaR	1.2576	0.4159
sampleCDaR vs. normCVaR	1.2248	0.4716
sampleCDaR vs. modCVaR	1.3125	0.3346

Summary

The examination of the risk budgeting models on an European fund
dataset with four assets can be seen as a strategic asset allocation. The
examination has shown that the risk budgeting models have indeed
higher returns than the minimum risk opposites, but with higher risks,
thereby resulting in lower return-risk proportions. However, the higher
returns are not statistically significant, thus the differences are small
and not distinct. Moreover, the equal risk contribution portfolios
based on different risks do not vary much from each other. The split
into bull and bear periods shows the clear underperformances of the
ERC portfolios: the minimum risk portfolios display higher means
and only slightly higher volatilities.

6.2.3 Global Portfolio

The global portfolio dataset consists of 13 asset classes around the world: S&P 500, Russell 2000, DJ Euro Stoxx 50, FTSE 100, Topix, MSCI Latin America, MSCI Emerging Markets Europe, MSCI AC Asia ex Japan, JP Morgan Global Govt Bond Euro, JP Morgan Govt Bond US, ML US High Yield Master II , JP Morgan EMBI Diversified and S&P GSCI.

Table 6.23 shows the abbreviations used for the assets in the Global portfolio dataset.

Table 6.23: Notations of Indices

Abbreviation	Index
SPCOMP	S&P 500
FRUSSL2	Russell 2000
DJES50I	DJ Euro Stoxx 50
FTSE100	FTSE 100
TOKYOSE	Topix
MSEFLA	MSCI Latin America
MSEEUR	MSCI Emerging Markets Europe
MSASXJ	MSCI AC Asia ex Japan
JPMUSU	JP Morgan Global Govt Bond Euro
JPMEIU	JP Morgan Govt Bond US
MLHMAU	ML US High Yield Master II
JPMGCOC	JP Morgan EMBI Diversified
GSCITOT	S&P GSCI

The dataset was proposed in Maillard et al. (2010) to study the performance of the ERC portfolio, as the indices have different risks and are thus suitable for examining the superior performance of the risk diversification portfolio. However, whereas in the dataset in Maillard et al. (2010) the ERC portfolio has a higher Sharpe ratio than the MV portfolio, the results here indicate the opposite. The dataset in Maillard et al. (2010) spans from 01.1995 - 12.2008, whereas here the dataset is taken from 01.1995 - 06.2011. This could explain the different results. Note that the indices are from different countries and have different currencies. Thus, the currency risk is not considered, which should be hedged in practice. The assumption here is that the currencies are hedged.

Data Analysis

Table 6.24 shows different features of the daily return distributions of the indices: Minimum, Maximum, Annual Mean, Total return, Annual Standard Deviation, Skewness and Kurtosis.

Table 6.24: Component Statistics - Global Portfolio
All values are displayed in percent, except the skewness and kurtosis.

	SPCOMP	FRUSSL2	DJES50I	FTSE100	TOKYOSE	MSEFLA	MSEEUR
Observations	4304	4304	4304	4304	4304	4304	4304
Min	-9.47	-12.61	-8.21	-9.27	-10.01	-15.06	-19.93
Max	10.96	8.86	10.44	9.38	12.86	15.36	18.60
ann. Mean	6.38	7.22	4.64	4.00	-3.67	9.68	9.98
Totalret	105.62	119.54	76.87	66.25	-60.75	160.29	165.23
ann. Vola	20	23.27	23.31	19.32	21.74	29.65	30.35
Skew	-0.21	-0.34	-0.03	-0.15	-0.26	-0.32	-0.53
Kurt	8.41	5.79	5.08	6.36	6.52	9.98	11.45

	MSASXJ	JPMUSU	JPMEIU	MLHMAU	JPMGCOC	GSCITOT	
Observations	4304	4304	4304	4304	4304	4304	
Min	-9.16	-2.01	-3.85	-4.84	-9.30	-9.17	
Max	11.82	2.13	5.35	2.74	8.77	7.22	
ann. Mean	2.84	1.25	7.20	7.81	11.81	5.03	
Totalret	47.01	20.68	119.23	129.22	195.52	83.21	
ann. Vola	22.15	5.01	10.33	4.49	10.31	23.13	
Skew	-0.16	-0.22	0.22	-3.03	-1.78	-0.27	
Kurt	6.23	2.33	3.27	49.78	40.05	2.94	

Through the minimum and maximum returns it is clear that the MSEFLA and the MSEEUR display the highest spread and the JP-MUSU and the MLHMAU the lowest spread of the returns. The JPMGCOC exhibits the highest annual mean and also shows the highest cumulative return. The lowest cumulative return is obtained from the TOKYOSE index, which is a negative performance. The MSEFLA and the MSEEUR indices show the highest annual volatility, whereas the MLHMAU the JPMUSU indices reveal the lowest annual standard deviations. The skewness is for all indices almost negative, which means a skewed distribution to the left. Especially the ML-HMAU and the JPMGCOC indices show a high negative skewness, which signifies that the distribution of the returns is concentrated to the left and negative returns are more likely to occur. The kurtosis is also mostly greater than 3, which is a sign that the returns are not normally distributed and have thick tails. The MLHMAU and the JPMGCOC display the highest kurtosis.

Table 6.25 displays the correlation matrix of the returns. It is obvious that the stock indices have a high positive correlation among each other, whereas the JPMUSU index has low and negative correlations with all other indices. The JPMEIU displays a negative correlation with the stock indices. The examination of the global dataset clarifies that the indices have different properties. In the following, it will be examined how the portfolios react to the different characteristics. This analysis helps to understand the weight allocations of the portfolios.

Table 6.25: Correlation of the Indices - Global Portfolio
The values are calculated across the whole period (daily returns) and displayed in percent.

	SPCOMP	FRUSSL2	DJES50I	FTSE100	TOKYOSE	MSEFLA	MSEEUR	MSASXJ	JPMUSU	JPMEIU	MLHMAU	JPMGCOC
FRUSSL2	86.60											
DJES50I	52.79	49.27										
FTSE100	48.94	44.49	86.40									
TOKYOSE	10.63	10.01	27.51	28.15								
MSEFLA	61.30	57.59	55.08	55.47	22.05							
MSEEUR	31.14	32.24	51.72	52.81	32.48	50.16						
MSASXJ	18.47	20.17	37.61	38.36	55.95	35.76	48.02					
JPMUSU	-22.34	-23.91	-24.73	-22.30	-6.50	-19.13	-17.66	-11.69	100.00			
JPMEIU	-4.84	-5.31	-13.42	-8.41	0.40	4.44	18.78	2.80	25.05			
MLHMAU	20.99	20.22	33.97	35.72	31.66	30.58	36.01	34.84	4.78	6.44		
JPMGCOC	27.75	23.06	28.83	29.00	16.69	57.88	30.30	22.77	9.83	7.44	32.89	
GSCITOT	16.60	17.74	19.50	22.08	12.23	26.92	26.51	16.24	-11.96	12.66	14.14	11.27

Main Performance

In this section, the performance of the minimum risk as well as of the risk budgeting portfolios will be analyzed on the basis of different performance measures on the Global portfolio dataset.

Table 6.26: Portfolio Statistics - Global Portfolio
All values are displayed in percent. For the calculations see section 6.2.1.

	Totalret	ann.Mean	ann.Vola	Sharpe	MaxLoss
MV	64.83	4.18	5.91	70.73	-11.52
minCVaR	63.14	4.07	5.50	74.05	-9.02
minCDaR	68.66	4.43	5.13	86.30	-6.25
Naive	81.62	5.27	13.75	38.31	-21.48
sampleCVaR	79.19	5.11	8.52	59.96	-17.70
normCVaR	72.25	4.66	6.65	70.15	-10.97
modCVaR	78.85	5.09	8.17	62.27	-14.59
sampleCOV	69.25	4.47	6.71	66.61	-11.11
sampleCDaR	89.00	5.74	7.68	74.77	-12.36

Table 6.26 shows the main portfolio performances. Compared to the minimum risk equivalents, the risk budgeting portfolios show greater returns, but also higher standard deviations and losses. Whereas the sampleCDaR model displays the highest return, the minCDaR displays the lowest volatility and loss and also the best Sharpe ratio. The naive portfolio has a much higher return than the minimum risk approaches, however it exhibits also the highest standard deviation and a high maximum loss. This results in the lowest Sharpe ratio. After the naive portfolio, the sampleCVaR and the modCVaR portfolio display the next higher volatilities.

Table 6.27 shows the returns per calendar year. In each year, the highest return is shaded in grey. The results are different. The naive strategy outperforms the other portfolios in the years from 2003 -

2007 and achieves significant gains. However, in 2000, 2002 and 2008 the minCDaR strategy outperforms. It seems that without financial disturbances, the naive portfolio would have been the best strategy to gain significant returns. But when a turbulence appears, the naive strategy suddenly loses the most. For these circumstances, the minCDaR seems to be the best strategy. The sampleCDaR portfolio produces the highest return among the risk budgeting approaches in 1997, 1998, 2002, 2003, and from 2005 - 2007. However, in the periods with losses, other portfolios produced higher returns: the modCVaR was the best in 1999 and 2000, the sampleCVaR in 2001 and the normCVaR portfolio in 2008. Compared to their minimum risk counterpart, the risk budgeting portfolios outperform in 1999, 2000 (except sampleCDaR), 2003, 2005 - 2007 and 2009. Thus, they outperform by returns mostly in the phases where the naive portfolio displays the highest return. In this way it is apparent that the risk budgeting models 'lie' between the minimum risk and naive portfolios (Maillard et al., 2010). However, in the Financial Crisis in 2008, they have a much worse performance. But in 2009 they outperform the minimum risk approaches. That is a sign that the risk budgeting approaches recover more quickly or that they are more sensible to market turbulences.

Figure 6.4 presents the relative performances of the risk budgeting returns vs. their minimum risk counterparts. Additionally, all portfolio performances are illustrated against the naive portfolio returns. The value of the chart is less important than the slope of the line. If the slope is positive, the risk budgeting portfolio is outperforming the minimum risk portfolio, and vice versa. It is observable that the sampleCOV portfolio outperforms the MV portfolio only in the beginning, from 1996 - 1997 1/2 and then from the year 2005 on. The sampleCVaR portfolio can only outperform the minCVaR portfolio during 2005 - beginning of 2008 and second half of 2009 - 2011. The normCVaR portfolio outperforms the minCVaR portfolio without the sacrifice in 2008 from the end of 2003. However, the modCVaR portfolio outperforms the minCVaR from 1999 and is thus the best

Table 6.27: Performance per Calender Year - Global Portfolio
The table displays the difference of the cumulative returns of
the years. For the calculations see section 6.2.1.

	1996	1997	1998	1999	2000	2001	2002	2003	2004
MV	10.23	9.98	2.62	-0.04	-3.89	1.78	3.91	12.94	9.22
minCVaR	9.36	11.45	1.84	-0.19	-2.64	-0.19	3.77	13.33	9.87
minCDaR	12.20	7.56	1.71	-1.63	2.60	-2.86	8.06	14.23	8.85
Naive	13.68	7.17	-5.38	24.44	-8.65	-9.28	-8.64	25.34	13.18
sampleCVaR	10.93	5.47	1.12	4.99	-1.29	-2.11	1.40	16.29	9.31
normCVaR	10.98	6.13	1.70	5.21	-1.61	-2.99	2.64	16.77	9.47
modCVaR	10.25	7.05	-2.43	22.22	0.28	-2.95	2.15	15.26	8.26
sampleCOV	11.01	5.22	1.05	5.17	-1.93	-3.00	2.33	16.61	9.47
sampleCDaR	10.54	9.25	5.48	10.69	0.01	-5.42	5.46	18.77	8.53
	2005	2006	2007	2008	2009	2010	YTD	Total	
MV	1.94	7.92	3.31	-13.25	6.24	8.97	2.94	64.83	
minCVaR	2.39	7.07	3.39	-9.40	1.12	9.00	2.97	63.14	
minCDaR	4.76	3.92	5.94	-3.42	-1.13	7.13	0.78	68.66	
Naive	15.07	12.07	11.10	-46.57	27.12	8.60	2.37	81.62	
sampleCVaR	7.28	6.83	5.78	-25.14	25.04	9.77	3.53	79.19	
normCVaR	8.25	8.16	6.29	-15.02	8.08	5.91	2.26	72.25	
modCVaR	7.44	6.75	6.12	-19.83	5.46	9.04	3.78	78.85	
sampleCOV	8.28	7.98	6.45	-15.41	8.14	5.65	2.23	69.25	
sampleCDaR	10.09	8.38	6.58	-19.97	14.59	4.44	1.60	89.00	

alternative of the CVaR budgeting portfolios in terms of returns. The
sampleCDaR portfolio outperforms the minCDaR obviously from
1999. Concerning the outperformance of the naive portfolio, it is
visible that all the portfolios outperform the naive portfolio only in
crisis periods: in the second half of 1998, from the second half of
2001 - 2005 and from 2008 - 2009. Only the sampleCDaR portfolio
outperforms the naive portfolio from 2000 on.

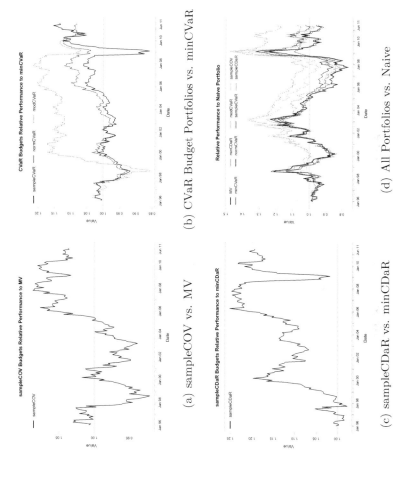

(a) sampleCOV vs. MV

(b) CVaR Budget Portfolios vs. minCVaR

(c) sampleCDaR vs. minCDaR

(d) All Portfolios vs. Naive

Figure 6.4: Relative Performance of Risk Budgeting Portfolios - Global Portfolio

Significance Tests

Table 6.28 shows that also in the Global portfolio dataset the outperformance of the ERC portfolios vs. their minimum risk counterparts
are not statistically significant. Thus, there is no real outperformance
of the ERC portfolios vs. the minimum risk portfolios across the
whole investigation period. Only the sampleCDaR portfolio displays
a significant outperformance against the sampleCOV portfolio.

Table 6.28: Statistical Significance of Mean Differences - Global Portfolio
For the calculations of the tests see 6.2.1.

	Excess Mean (%)	t-Stat	p-value
sampleCOV vs. MV	0.02	0.33	0.74
sampleCVaR vs. minCVaR	0.09	0.76	0.45
normCVaR vs. minCVaR	0.05	0.72	0.47
modCVaR vs. minCVaR	0.08	0.79	0.43
sampleCDaR vs. minCDaR	0.11	1.04	0.30
sampleCOV vs. Naive	-0.07	-0.38	0.70
sampleCVaR vs. Naive	-0.01	-0.09	0.93
normCVaR vs. Naive	-0.05	-0.28	0.78
modCVaR vs. Naive	-0.01	-0.10	0.92
sampleCDaR vs. Naive	0.04	0.23	0.82
sampleCOV vs. sampleCVaR	-0.05	-0.76	0.45
sampleCOV vs. normCVaR	-0.02	-3.23	0.00
sampleCOV vs. modCVaR	-0.05	-0.74	0.46
sampleCOV vs. sampleCDaR	-0.11	-2.11	0.04
sampleCDaR vs. sampleCVaR	0.05	0.70	0.49
sampleCDaR vs. normCVaR	0.09	1.85	0.07
sampleCDaR vs. modCVaR	0.05	0.65	0.51

The Jensen's Alphas in table 6.29 show that the risk contribution
portfolios outperform the naive portfolio. Moreover, the normCVaR
outperforms slightly the sampleCOV portfolio.

Table 6.29: Jensen's Alpha - Global Portfolio
For the calculations see 6.2.1.

	Jensen's Alpha (Rf = 0)	t-value
sampleCOV vs. MV	0.0003	0.4111
sampleCVaR vs. minCVaR	0.0001	0.1147
normCVaR vs. minCVaR	0.0003	0.6716
modCVaR vs. minCVaR	0.0002	0.3901
sampleCDaR vs. minCDaR	0.0005	0.5091
sampleCOV vs. Naive	0.0018	2.8730
sampleCVaR vs. Naive	0.0018	2.2604
normCVaR vs. Naive	0.0020	3.1340
modCVaR vs. Naive	0.0019	2.4839
sampleCDaR vs. Naive	0.0027	3.2630
sampleCOV vs. sampleCVaR	0.0006	1.1440
sampleCOV vs. normCVaR	-0.0002	-3.9398
sampleCOV vs. modCVaR	0.0005	0.9186
sampleCOV vs. sampleCDaR	-0.0003	-0.6124
sampleCDaR vs. sampleCVaR	0.0013	1.8770
sampleCDaR vs. normCVaR	0.0005	1.0163
sampleCDaR vs. modCVaR	0.0013	1.6222

However, the DW test in table 6.30 rejects the null hypotheses of no autocorrelation in the residuals for the regression of sampleCVaR vs. the naive portfolio as well as of sampleCOV vs. normCVaR portfolio. Moreover, the Breusch-Pagan and the White tests show heteroscedasticity in the residual variances. Thus, all the positive α values cannot be verified.

According to table 6.31, the rise in variances is significant for the ERC portfolios vs. the naive portfolio and the reduction for the minimum risk vs. the ERC portfolios (except the MV portfolios vs. the sampleCOV portfolio). Moreover, the sampleCOV portfolio has a significant reduction in risk vs. the sampleCVaR and the modCVaR portfolios.

Table 6.30: Analysis of Jensen's Alpha Regression - Global Portfolio
For the calculations see 6.2.1.

	DW statistic	p-value	BP-stat	p-value	White-stat	p-value
sampleCOV vs. MV	2.1193	0.7889	1.2274	0.2679	4.1697	0.1243
sampleCVaR vs. minCVaR	1.5893	0.0024	7.3266	0.0068	21.2228	0.0000
normCVaR vs. minCVaR	1.9752	0.4280	3.1521	0.0758	3.8683	0.1445
modCVaR vs. minCVaR	1.8987	0.2405	8.2901	0.0040	15.1641	0.0005
sampleCDaR vs. minCDaR	1.6576	0.0094	6.6518	0.0099	22.1593	0.0000
sampleCOV vs. Naive	1.8400	0.1332	3.1618	0.0754	12.5757	0.0019
sampleCVaR vs. Naive	1.7102	0.0227	28.8014	0.0000	131.0768	0.0000
normCVaR vs. Naive	1.8249	0.1123	3.0463	0.0809	11.4241	0.0033
modCVaR vs. Naive	2.0551	0.6419	0.1566	0.6923	48.6441	0.0000
sampleCDaR vs. Naive	1.8492	0.1474	9.1222	0.0025	19.9405	0.0000
sampleCOV vs. sampleCVaR	1.6867	0.0153	0.0189	0.8908	35.8146	0.0000
sampleCOV vs. normCVaR	1.4818	0.0002	0.9952	0.3185	1.3338	0.5133
sampleCOV vs. modCVaR	1.7158	0.0255	0.3469	0.5559	35.0688	0.0000
sampleCOV vs. sampleCDaR	1.7854	0.0695	0.0960	0.7567	7.3751	0.0250
sampleCDaR vs. sampleCVaR	1.8878	0.2164	0.4503	0.5022	11.9192	0.0026
sampleCDaR vs. normCVaR	1.7972	0.0813	0.0045	0.9466	0.5423	0.7625
sampleCDaR vs. modCVaR	1.7922	0.0766	0.0185	0.8918	28.8100	0.0000

Table 6.31: Significance of Difference in Variances - Global Portfolio
For the calculations see 6.2.1.

	Ratio of variances	p-value
sampleCOV vs. MV	1.2867	0.0873
sampleCVaR vs. minCVaR	2.3992	0.0000
normCVaR vs. minCVaR	1.4591	0.0105
modCVaR vs. minCVaR	2.2058	0.0000
sampleCDaR vs. minCDaR	2.2383	0.0000
sampleCOV vs. Naive	0.2381	0.0000
sampleCVaR vs. Naive	0.3843	0.0000
normCVaR vs. Naive	0.2337	0.0000
modCVaR vs. Naive	0.3533	0.0000
sampleCDaR vs. Naive	0.3122	0.0000
sampleCOV vs. sampleCVaR	0.6196	0.0012
sampleCOV vs. normCVaR	1.0187	0.8996
sampleCOV vs. modCVaR	0.6739	0.0075
sampleCOV vs. sampleCDaR	0.7627	0.0662
sampleCDaR vs. sampleCVaR	0.8123	0.1585
sampleCDaR vs. normCVaR	1.3357	0.0497
sampleCDaR vs. modCVaR	0.8836	0.4007

Portfolio Characteristics

Table 6.32 displays the risk figures across the whole period based on monthly portfolio returns. The minCDaR portfolio reveals the lowest risk measures, especially the drawdown risk measures are lower compared to the other approaches. Thus, the minCDaR portfolio is the best portfolio concerning the risk side. The naive portfolio shows much higher values compared to the risk portfolios.

The normCVaR and the sampleCOV portfolio display the lowest risk measures among the risk budgeting approaches. After them, the sampleCDaR shows the second best risk figures. Compared to the minimum risk portfolios, the risk values of the risk budgeting portfolios are all higher, especially concerning the drawdown measures, the minimum risk portfolios outperform.

Table 6.32: Risk Figures - Global Portfolio
All values are displayed in percent. For the calculations of the risk measures see 3.1.2.

	5% VaR	5% CVaR	5% DaR	5% CDaR	MaxDD
MV	2.47	4.43	11.62	15.19	18.04
minCVaR	2.44	4.14	12.31	14.42	16.35
minCDaR	1.60	3.32	7.91	9.42	12.21
Naive	6.26	9.96	31.55	40.67	48.63
sampleCVaR	2.85	5.81	11.54	23.23	31.38
normCVaR	2.74	4.56	12.06	16.81	20.97
modCVaR	2.80	5.76	18.38	21.66	25.36
sampleCOV	2.81	4.65	12.17	17.02	21.23
sampleCDaR	2.94	5.37	12.95	20.01	25.34

Table 6.33 shows Risk Ratios based on the different risk measures. The higher the values, the better the resulting return-risk proportion. Again, the minCDaR portfolio displays the best performance regarding all risk ratios. The sampleCDaR portfolio outperforms the other

risk budgeting portfolios. However, compared to the minimum risk portfolios, the risk budgeting approaches deliver much lower ratio values.

Table 6.33: Risk Ratios - Global Portfolio
All values are displayed in percent. For the calculations see 6.2.1.

	SR sigma	SR VaR	SR CVaR	SR CDaR	SR avdd	SR maxdd
MV	20.42	14.09	7.86	2.29	13.19	1.93
minCVaR	21.38	13.94	8.20	2.35	11.13	2.08
minCDaR	24.91	23.11	11.13	3.92	18.06	3.02
Naive	11.06	7.01	4.41	1.08	3.96	0.90
sampleCVaR	17.31	14.95	7.33	1.83	14.28	1.36
normCVaR	20.25	14.19	8.53	2.31	12.72	1.85
modCVaR	17.97	15.13	7.36	1.96	10.50	1.67
sampleCOV	19.23	13.23	8.01	2.19	11.38	1.75
sampleCDaR	21.58	16.26	8.91	2.39	14.53	1.89

Table 6.34 shows the mean and the total turnover as well as the number of trades for the strategies across the whole sixteen years. The naive portfolio displays the lowest turnover, followed by the sample-COV portfolio. The minCDaR and the minCVaR have the highest mean and total turnover. The turnover of the minCDaR portfolio is twice the total turnover of the MV portfolio. This would diminish the net cumulated outcome of the portfolio. The turnovers of the risk budgeting approaches reveal that the values are all lower than these of the minimum risk portfolios. The sampleCDaR portfolio has thereby the highest rebalancing volume, followed by the modCVaR portfolio. However, a look on the trades turns the picture. There, the minimum risk approaches are better and the minCDaR portfolio needs the lowest trades. Although the estimated weights of the naive portfolio are all equal, the portfolio needs a lot of trades because of the changing asset prices.

Table 6.34: Turnover and Trades - Global Portfolio
The turnover and trades are based on weights before and after the portfolio optimizations. For the calculations see 6.2.1.

	mean Turnover	total Turnover	No. of Trades
MV	0.10	17.78	1173
minCVaR	0.17	30.72	1144
minCDaR	0.21	39.70	975
Naive	0.03	5.87	2418
sampleCVaR	0.08	15.30	2404
normCVaR	0.06	10.51	2418
modCVaR	0.11	20.45	2403
sampleCOV	0.05	9.39	2418
sampleCDaR	0.14	26.29	2418

Portfolio Investments

The matter of this section is to analyze the holdings, that is, the weight proportions and the risk contributions of the different portfolio techniques. Tables 6.35, 6.36, 6.37 show the weights and the risk budgets allocation of the different portfolio techniques across the whole period. As one can easily observe, the MV and minCVaR portfolio have almost equal allocations.

The average holdings of the portfolios through the whole period reveal that the most part of the minimum risk portfolios is invested in the MLHMAU index. The other larger part consists of the JP-MUSU index. The MV and the minCVaR portfolio are thereby more concentrated in the MLHMAU index than the minCDaR portfolio. After that, the JPMEIU and the JPMGCOC have a share of ca. 6%. The other assets are almost disregarded and only invested up to max 2%. The risk budgeting models invests also in these assets the most, but are less concentrated. They invest less in the JPMUSU and the

Table 6.35: Weights Allocations - Global Portfolio
These are average estimated weights across the whole period
and displayed in percent.

	MV	minCVaR	minCDaR	sCVaR	nCVaR	mCVaR	sCOV	sCDaR
SPCOMP	1	1	1	4	4	5	4	5
FRUSSL2	0	1	1	3	3	4	3	3
DJES50I	0	0	1	3	3	3	3	4
FTSE100	1	1	2	4	4	4	4	5
TOKYOSE	0	1	2	4	4	5	4	4
MSEFLA	0	0	0	2	2	2	2	3
MSEEUR	0	1	1	3	3	3	3	3
MSASXJ	0	1	1	4	3	4	3	3
JPMUSU	24	28	39	22	28	24	29	23
JPMEIU	4	6	6	14	12	10	12	12
MLHMAU	62	53	35	21	22	20	20	18
JPMGCOC	6	6	6	11	9	9	8	12
GSCITOT	1	2	5	5	5	6	5	5

MLHMAU index, but therefore relatively more in the JPMEIU and
the JPMGCOC indices. However, from the weights side they are also
concentrated in four assets.

Table 6.36 shows that the weight and the out-of-sample risk contributions of the MV portfolio are quite similar. However, the risk
contributions to the JPMUSU are slightly higher and to the MLH-
MAU slightly lower. As the images are similar for the other portfolios,
they are omitted. Table 6.37 shows exemplary the risk allocations of
the sampleCOV portfolio. It is clear that although the sampleCOV
portfolio is obtained through equalizing the risk contributions to the
variance, the risk budgets to the CVaR and to the CDaR are similar
to the volatility risk contributions. Thus, the table clarifies the similarity of the risk budgeting portfolios. Moreover, the out-of-sample
risk budgets are not equal due to different asset returns. Especially
the JPMUSU, the JPMEIU and the GSCITOT display different risk
contributions. However, the differences are not dramatic and the risk
contributions are almost equal.

Table 6.36: Risk Budget Allocations of the MV Portfolio - Global Portfolio
lio
The average risk budgets are calculated out-of sample and
displayed in percent. For the calculation see 6.2.1. MVto-
COV: risk contributions to volatility, MVtoCVaR: risk
contributions to CVaR, MVtoCDaR: risk contributions to
CDaR.

	MVweights	MVtoCOV	MVtoCVaR	MVtoCDaR
SPCOMP	1	2	3	4
FRUSSL2	0	1	1	1
DJES50I	0	0	1	1
FTSE100	1	1	2	2
TOKYOSE	0	1	2	2
MSEFLA	0	0	0	0
MSEEUR	0	1	1	1
MSASXJ	0	0	1	1
JPMUSU	24	30	30	28
JPMEIU	4	6	8	9
MLHMAU	62	49	42	39
JPMGCOC	6	5	4	5
GSCITOT	1	3	6	7

Table 6.37: Risk Budget Allocations of the sampleCOV Portfolio -
Global Portfolio
The average risk budgets are calculated out-of sample and
displayed in percent. For the calculation see 6.2.1. COV-
toCOV: risk contributions to volatility, COVtoCVaR: risk
contributions to CVaR, COVtoCDaR: risk contributions to
CDaR.

	sampleCOVweights	COVtoCOV	COVtoCVaR	COVtoCDaR
SPCOMP	4	7	7	6
FRUSSL2	3	7	7	7
DJES50I	3	7	7	6
FTSE100	4	7	6	6
TOKYOSE	4	7	8	8
MSEFLA	2	7	6	6
MSEEUR	3	7	7	7
MSASXJ	3	7	7	7
JPMUSU	29	13	14	15
JPMEIU	12	10	10	11
MLHMAU	20	6	6	6
JPMGCOC	8	6	5	4
GSCITOT	5	9	11	11

Bull/Bear Market Performance

The following phases were identified for the Global portfolio dataset (the period runs from 01.1996 - 06.2011):

Table 6.38: Bull and Bear Periods - Global Portfolio
The phases were identified on the naive portfolio by using the method of Bry and Boschan (1971), see 6.2.2.

Bull Period	Bear Period
01.1996 - 09.1997	09.1997 - 08.1998
08.1998 - 03.2000	03.2000 - 09.2001
09.2001 - 10.2007	10.2007 - 02.2009
02.2009 - 06.2011	

Figure 6.5 presents the bear phases based on the naive portfolio for the Global portfolio dataset. Table 6.39 and 6.40 present the characteristics of the portfolio performances split into bull and bear phases.

In the bull market, the MV portfolio presents the highest return with the lowest risk and thus the best Sharpe ratio among the minimum risk approaches. However, all the risk budgeting models have higher returns with a slightly higher standard deviation and feature a higher Sharpe ratio. The highest risk-adjusted performance provide the sampleCDaR and the normCVaR portfolio. The naive portfolio has the highest return, but also the highest volatility (twice as other portfolios) and maximum drawdown (three times higher than other portfolios). It represents a higher Sharpe ratio than the minCVaR and minCDaR portfolio, but lower than the MV portfolio.

The minimum risk approaches are clearly the winner in the bear period. They represent a much better return and much lower drawdowns. The minCDaR portfolio has the lowest standard deviation and maximum drawdown. The naive portfolio has a dramatic low return, the same is the case with the volatility and maximum draw-

Table 6.39: Bull/Bear Characteristics of Minimum Risk Portfolios -
Global Portfolio

	MV	minCVaR	minCDaR	Naive
Bull Market (%)				
Ann. Mean	7.07	6.60	6.61	16.77
Ann. Std	4.22	4.20	4.50	10.10
Sharpe	168	157	147	166
MaxDD	5.40	4	5.21	17.45
Skewness	-0.74	-0.58	-0.14	-0.39
Bear Market (%)				
Ann. Mean	-4.87	-3.85	-2.40	-30.77
Ann. Std	9.01	8.01	6.42	18.0
Sharpe	-54	-48	-37	-171
MaxDD	23.4	20.06	14.55	70.93
Skewness	-1.83	-1.69	-0.78	-1.39

Table 6.40: Bull/Bear Characteristics of Risk Budgeting Portfolios -
Global Portfolio

	sampleCVaR	normCVaR	modCVaR	sampleCOV	sampleCDaR
Bull Market (%)					
Ann. Mean	10.88	9.36	10.60	9.27	11.17
Ann. Std	6.51	5.14	6.21	5.16	6.15
Sharpe	167	182	170	180	182
MaxDD	6.36	5.65	5.76	5.84	4.08
Skewness	0.21	-0.54	0.01	-0.54	-0.34
Bear Market (%)					
Ann. Mean	-12.96	-10.06	-12.16	-12.96	-11.28
Ann. Std	11.57	8.78	11.15	8.89	9.75
Sharpe	-112	-115	-109	-119	-116
MaxDD	40.28	32.53	32.29	33.88	35.86
Skewness	-2.69	-1.52	-2.15	-1.48	-1.68

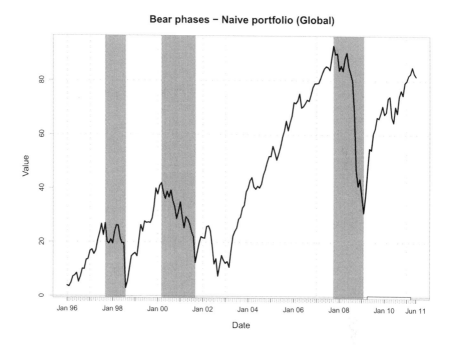

Figure 6.5: Bull/Bear Phases - Global

down compared to the other approaches. Among the risk budgeting approaches, the normCVaR portfolio displays the best performance in the bear period. It is visible that in the crisis period the return distributions are more skewed to the left.

According to table 6.41, the higher returns of the ERC portfolios vs. the minimum risk counterparts are also statistically significant. However, the naive portfolio displays the highest return and is also significant vs. the ERC portfolios. Moreover, the F-test in table 6.43 shows that also the differences in variances are statistically significant. Among the ERC portfolios, the sampleCDaR portfolio shows a significant outperformance against the normCVaR and the sampleCOV portfolio and a significant reduction in the variance vs.

Table 6.41: Significance in Means in the Bull Period - Global Portfolio
For the calculations see 6.2.1.

	Excess Mean (%)	t-Stat	p-value
sampleCOV vs. MV	0.18	2.46	0.02
sampleCVaR vs. minCVaR	0.36	3.07	0.00
normCVaR vs. minCVaR	0.23	3.30	0.00
modCVaR vs. minCVaR	0.33	3.05	0.00
sampleCDaR vs. minCDaR	0.38	3.68	0.00
sampleCOV vs. Naive	-0.62	-4.05	0.00
sampleCVaR vs. Naive	-0.49	-3.81	0.00
normCVaR vs. Naive	-0.62	-3.96	0.00
modCVaR vs. Naive	-0.51	-3.58	0.00
sampleCDaR vs. Naive	-0.47	-3.07	0.00
sampleCOV vs. sampleCVaR	-0.13	-1.88	0.06
sampleCOV vs. normCVaR	-0.01	-1.54	0.13
sampleCOV vs. modCVaR	-0.11	-1.50	0.14
sampleCOV vs. sampleCDaR	-0.16	-2.87	0.00
sampleCDaR vs. sampleCVaR	0.02	0.32	0.75
sampleCDaR vs. normCVaR	0.15	2.83	0.01
sampleCDaR vs. modCVaR	0.05	0.53	0.59

the normCVaR portfolio. The outperformances of the minimum risk
approaches in the bear period are also statistically significant (see
table 6.42). It is also visible that the ERC portfolio outperform
statistically the naive portfolio in the bear period. Among each other,
there is only a slightly outperformance of the normCVaR portfolio vs.
the sampleCOV portfolio. Table 6.44 shows that the risk reduction of
the ERC portfolios compared to the naive portfolio is also statistically
significant in the bear period. The minimum risk approaches display
lower variances, which is significant for all comparisons, except the
sampleCOV vs. the MV and the normCVaR vs. the minCVaR
portfolio.

Table 6.42: Significance in Means in the Bear Period - Global Portfolio For the calculations see 6.2.1.

	Excess Mean (%)	t-Stat	p-value
sampleCOV vs. MV	-0.48	-3.03	0.00
sampleCVaR vs. minCVaR	-0.76	-2.84	0.01
normCVaR vs. minCVaR	-0.52	-3.38	0.00
modCVaR vs. minCVaR	-0.69	-2.77	0.01
sampleCDaR vs. minCDaR	-0.74	-2.90	0.01
sampleCOV vs. Naive	1.68	3.76	0.00
sampleCVaR vs. Naive	1.48	3.63	0.00
normCVaR vs. Naive	1.73	3.81	0.00
modCVaR vs. Naive	1.55	4.18	0.00
sampleCDaR vs. Naive	1.62	3.66	0.00
sampleCOV vs. sampleCVaR	0.20	1.08	0.29
sampleCOV vs. normCVaR	-0.04	-3.24	0.00
sampleCOV vs. modCVaR	0.13	0.77	0.45
sampleCOV vs. sampleCDaR	0.06	0.52	0.61
sampleCDaR vs. sampleCVaR	0.14	0.72	0.47
sampleCDaR vs. normCVaR	-0.10	-0.95	0.35
sampleCDaR vs. modCVaR	0.07	0.37	0.71

Table 6.43: Significance in Variances in the Bull Period - Global Portfolio

	Ratio of variances	p-value
sampleCOV vs. MV	1.4976	0.0174
sampleCVaR vs. minCVaR	2.4008	0.0000
normCVaR vs. minCVaR	1.5016	0.0167
modCVaR vs. minCVaR	2.1904	0.0000
sampleCDaR vs. minCDaR	1.8707	0.0002
sampleCOV vs. Naive	0.2610	0.0000
sampleCVaR vs. Naive	0.4152	0.0000
normCVaR vs. Naive	0.2597	0.0000
modCVaR vs. Naive	0.3788	0.0000
sampleCDaR vs. Naive	0.3712	0.0000
sampleCOV vs. sampleCVaR	0.6287	0.0064
sampleCOV vs. normCVaR	1.0052	0.9757
sampleCOV vs. modCVaR	0.6891	0.0283
sampleCOV vs. sampleCDaR	0.7032	0.0380
sampleCDaR vs. sampleCVaR	0.8941	0.5086
sampleCDaR vs. normCVaR	1.4295	0.0353
sampleCDaR vs. modCVaR	0.9800	0.9050

Table 6.44: Significance in Variances in the Bear Period - Global Portfolio

	Ratio of variances	p-value
sampleCOV vs. MV	0.9726	0.9269
sampleCVaR vs. minCVaR	2.0892	0.0163
normCVaR vs. minCVaR	1.2026	0.5432
modCVaR vs. minCVaR	1.9405	0.0302
sampleCDaR vs. minCDaR	2.3071	0.0066
sampleCOV vs. Naive	0.2439	0.0000
sampleCVaR vs. Naive	0.4132	0.0041
normCVaR vs. Naive	0.2378	0.0000
modCVaR vs. Naive	0.3838	0.0019
sampleCDaR vs. Naive	0.2932	0.0001
sampleCOV vs. sampleCVaR	0.5902	0.0838
sampleCOV vs. normCVaR	1.0253	0.9345
sampleCOV vs. modCVaR	0.6354	0.1364
sampleCOV vs. sampleCDaR	0.8316	0.5435
sampleCDaR vs. sampleCVaR	0.7096	0.2592
sampleCDaR vs. normCVaR	1.2328	0.4905
sampleCDaR vs. modCVaR	0.7640	0.3754

Summary

In the Global portfolio dataset, the sampleCDaR portfolio has the best risk ratios among the risk budgeting portfolios. It delivers the highest total return and low drawdowns. However, the standard deviation and the maximum loss are higher than of the normCVaR and the sampleCOV portfolio. All the risk budgeting approaches deliver higher returns than the minimum risk counterparts, but hence higher risk measures. Thus, they cannot reach the risk ratios of the minimum risk portfolios. The significant tests show that all the outperformances in returns are not significant. Thus, the higher returns could be accidentally. The behavior in financial turbulences (like 1999 - 2001 and 2007 - 2009) reveal that the minimum risk portfolios, and especially the minimum Conditional Drawdown-at-risk portfolio, perform much better than the risk budgeting portfolios, although they were designed for sudden crisis periods. The split into bull and bear periods outlines the significant underperformance of the risk budgeting models in trough market periods. If the market phase changes, the risk budgeting models seem not to be more robust than the minimum risk approaches, as the risk statistics in these turnrounds are worse.

Table 6.45: Correlations of Portfolio Returns - Global Portfolio

	Naive	MV	minCVaR	minCDaR	nCVaR	mCVaR	sCVaR	sCOV	sCDaR
Naive	100.00	70.11	66.50	53.34	89.46	89.95	89.71	89.96	86.80
MV		100.00	95.89	75.73	87.01	79.29	82.38	86.61	79.33
minCVaR			100.00	83.84	87.52	79.47	78.64	86.78	80.66
minCDaR				100.00	76.89	68.90	63.88	75.78	76.70
normCVaR					100.00	92.01	93.03	99.94	95.86
modCVaR						100.00	89.12	92.08	87.79
sampleCVaR							100.00	93.15	90.81
sampleCOV								100.00	95.45
sampleCDaR									100.00

The correlation of the portfolio returns in table 6.45 show that all the risk budgeting approaches are similar as the correlations among the portfolios are 90% or more. The correlations with the MV and the minCVaR portfolios lie around 80%, the least correlations of the risk budgeting portfolios are with the minCDaR portfolio, which are in the interval from 63% - 76%. The correlation with the naive portfolio amounts to ca. 90%. The minimum risk approaches have not such a high correlation with the naive portfolio, as the values are 53%, 66% and 70%, with the minCDaR portfolio displaying the lowest and the MV portfolio the highest correlation.

6.2.4 German Market

In this section, the portfolios will be tested on a long equity dataset of the German market. The dataset spans from **01.1973 - 09.2012**. On the one hand, the stability of the portfolios across a long period can be observed and on the other hand the benefits to apply the risk budgeting portfolios on individual equities. For this, all still active assets (in 09.2012) from 1973 are used, which results in an investment universe of 55 available equities. For reasons of clarity and comprehensibility, the assets will be named A1,..,A55. The asset names can be found in the appendix.

It is clear that through choosing the assets, which survive since 1973, the so called 'survivorship bias' arises (Elton et al., 1996, Brown et al., 1995, Boynton and Oppenheimer, 2006). That means that the performance results of the portfolios could be too positive, as the equities which disappear are mostly the ones with a worse performance. However, the examination and the comparison of the portfolios on individual assets has priority and for convenience, the practical ability to invest will be ignored for this study. As the underlying dataset is similar for all portfolios, the comparison of the portfolio outcomes is justified under the given circumstances.

Data Analysis

As there is an investment universe of 55 equities available, the asset statistics cannot be given in detail. Instead the asset means and standard deviations are shown in a chart, sorted increasingly by value.

Figure 6.6 shows the annualized asset means. A spread of -20% till +10% is observable. Most of the assets have positive annualized returns. The assets with the lowest returns are (from left to right): A2, A7, A14, A8, A39 and the assets with the highest returns (from right to left): A38, A46, A21, A18, A15. Figure 6.7 shows the annualized asset volatilities. There exists also a huge difference of ca. 130 points, from 17% - up to extreme 150%. The assets with the extreme high annualized volatilites are (from highest to lower): A39 (150%), A32 (125%), A2 (116%), A7 (84%) and A8 (59%). On the opposite, the assets with the lowest annualized standard deviations are: A6 (17%), A43 (20%), A47 (21%), A34 (22%) and A49 (23%).

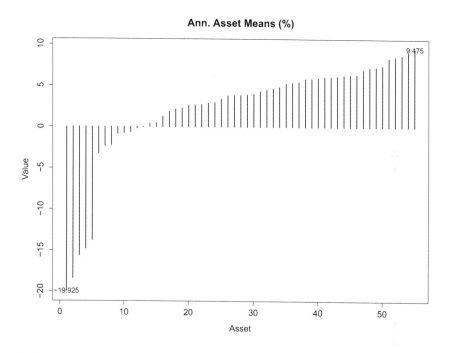

Figure 6.6: Annualized Asset Means - Germany 1973
The asset means are calculated on the basis of daily returns
over the whole investigation period.

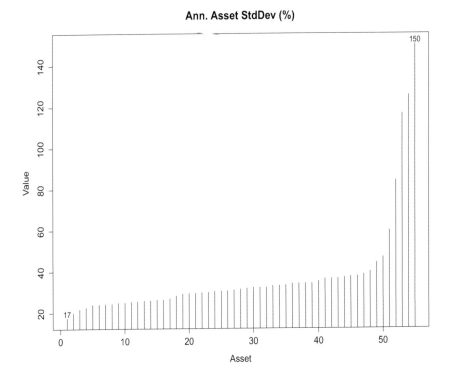

Figure 6.7: Annualized Standard Deviations - Germany 1973
The asset volatilities are calculated on the basis of daily
returns over the whole investigation period.

Main Performance

Table 6.46 displays the main portfolio outcomes. The minCVaR and the sampleCDaR have the highest cumulative and annualized return of the portfolios. The minCVaR portfolio has additionally a low annual volatility, which results in the highest Sharpe ratio of the portfolios. The sampleCDaR has a high annual standard deviation, that is why the risk-return proportion is not the highest, however it is the highest among the risk budgeting approaches. The Naive portfolio has the lowest cumulative and annualized return and also the highest volatility, which emerges in the lowest Sharpe ratio. Surprisingly, the highest loss arises from the minCDaR portfolio. Except the minCDaR portfolio, the minimum risk portfolios display a higher return and a lower risk than the risk budgeting portfolios (except the mentioned sampleCDaR portfolio). The risk budgeting approaches have also a higher maximum loss than the MV and minCVaR portfolio. Only the sampleCDaR portfolio outperforms the minimum risk counterpart, the minCDaR portfolio, in each feature except the volatility.

Table 6.46: Main Performance Statistics - Germany 1973

	Totalret	ann.Mean	ann.Vola	Sharpe	MaxLoss
MV	152.94	3.95	8.77	45.02	-10.01
minCVaR	181.53	4.68	9.95	47.09	-13.14
minCDaR	132.41	3.42	12.03	28.40	-41.26
Naive	98.88	2.55	16.07	15.87	-23.01
sampleCVaR	133.14	3.44	12.80	26.84	-19.22
normCVaR	129.50	3.34	12.34	27.07	-18.67
modCVaR	109.45	2.82	12.88	21.92	-19.73
sampleCOV	119.31	3.08	12.43	24.77	-18.42
sampleCDaR	170.90	4.41	13.95	31.62	-20.95

Table 6.47 shows the returns of the portfolios in 5 year periods. It is obvious that the examination period has started with a recession period, as all portfolios exhibit negative returns in 1974. There, the

minCDaR portfolio has the most difficulties, as it shows a return of
-57% during the first year. The minCVaR portfolio displays also a
high loss. In this year, the naive and the risk budgeting approaches
outperform, this could be coherent with the estimation errors, as these
portfolios don't need much time to adapt (see chapter 9.3). From 1980
- 2005 all portfolios display positive returns, except the naive and the
modCVaR portfolio. From 1974 - 1980 the risk budgeting portfolios
display higher returns than the minimum risk portfolios, from 1980-
1985 the sampleCDaR portfolio outperforms, but beyond the minimum
risk approaches have higher returns. From 1985 - 2005 the minimum
risk portfolios have higher returns than the risk contribution portfolios
and the minCDaR portfolio displays the highest returns from 1985 -
1995. Surprisingly, from 1990 - 1995 it has a much higher return than
the other approaches. But it exposes the lowest return from 2005 -
2010. In this period, the minCVaR and the sampleCDaR have the
only positive returns. Thus, the table reveals, that the risk budgeting
approaches have outperformed their minimum risk counterpart only
in the period from 1973 - 1985. Figure 9.25 at the end of this section
illustrates the relative performances of the risk budgeting portfolios
vs. their counterpart.

Table 6.47: Performance per 5 Calender Years - Germany1973
The table displays the difference of the cumulative returns
between the years. For the calculations see section 6.2.1.
YTD: Year-to-Date, as the investigation period ends in
09.2012.

	1974	1980	1985	1990	1995	2000	2005	2010	YTD	Total
MV	-16.61	16.00	51.62	59.67	4.31	38.53	8.09	-3.35	-5.32	152.94
minCVaR	-25.37	20.60	67.05	59.74	1.97	35.54	19.84	3.39	-1.23	181.53
minCDaR	-57.43	16.72	64.88	67.09	25.47	39.38	9.40	-23.97	-9.13	132.41
Naive	-11.87	22.72	67.62	34.79	-2.22	24.72	-9.75	-9.80	-17.32	98.88
sampleCVaR	-14.86	22.02	63.84	42.28	0.76	34.64	5.41	-11.78	-9.18	133.14
normCVaR	-13.65	21.04	62.38	45.23	1.77	32.03	8.76	-16.42	-11.64	129.50
modCVaR	-17.14	25.22	58.97	49.93	-8.02	26.92	2.33	-19.83	-8.94	109.45
sampleCOV	-15.53	20.36	61.19	44.99	0.02	30.64	6.63	-17.10	-11.89	119.31
sampleCDaR	-13.29	25.89	72.44	38.57	4.32	41.47	8.40	2.02	-8.93	170.90

Figure 6.8 summarizes the relative performances of the risk budget models vs. their minimum risk counterpart. It is obvious that the risk contribution portfolios based on volatility and CVaR outperform the minimum risk portfolios only till the year 1986, then falling backwards. Only the sampleCDaR portfolio has beaten its minimum risk counterpart almost during the whole investment period in terms of returns. Compared to the naive portfolio, the returns of the risk based portfolios were all higher from 1994 on.

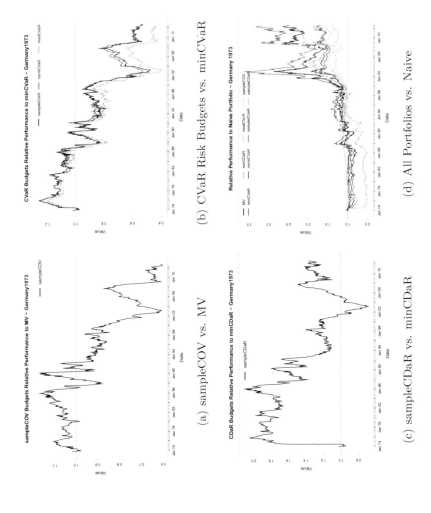

(a) sampleCOV vs. MV

(b) CVaR Risk Budgets vs. minCVaR

(c) sampleCDaR vs. minCDaR

(d) All Portfolios vs. Naive

Figure 6.8: Relative Performance of Risk Budgeting Portfolios - Germany 1973

Significance Tests

Table 6.48 shows that the performances of the portfolios lie close together and the outperformances of the minimum risk portfolios vs. the ERC portfolios as well as the outperformances of the ERC portfolios vs. the naive portfolio are not significant. Only the differences of the sampleCDaR portfolio to the other ERC portfolios are statistically significant.

Table 6.48: Statistical Significance of Mean Differences - Germany 1973
For the calculations of the tests see 6.2.1.

	Excess Mean (%)	t-Stat	p-value
sampleCOV vs. MV	-0.07	-0.77	0.44
sampleCVaR vs. minCVaR	-0.10	-0.91	0.36
normCVaR vs. minCVaR	-0.11	-1.05	0.29
modCVaR vs. minCVaR	-0.16	-1.33	0.18
sampleCDaR vs. minCDaR	0.08	0.51	0.61
sampleCOV vs. Naive	0.04	0.61	0.54
sampleCVaR vs. Naive	0.07	1.20	0.23
normCVaR vs. Naive	0.07	0.90	0.37
modCVaR vs. Naive	0.02	0.32	0.75
sampleCDaR vs. Naive	0.15	3.22	0.00
sampleCOV vs. sampleCVaR	-0.03	-1.31	0.19
sampleCOV vs. normCVaR	-0.02	-2.92	0.00
sampleCOV vs. modCVaR	0.02	0.58	0.56
sampleCOV vs. sampleCDaR	-0.11	-2.55	0.01
sampleCDaR vs. sampleCVaR	0.08	2.51	0.01
sampleCDaR vs. normCVaR	0.09	2.06	0.04
sampleCDaR vs. modCVaR	0.13	2.54	0.01

The Jensen's Alpha shows an outperformance of almost all ERC portfolios vs. the naive portfolio, except the modCVaR portfolio. Moreover, the sampleCDaR portfolio outperforms the modCVaR portfolio according to the positive and significant α. However, again the regressions show heteroscedastic variances according to the White test

Table 6.49: Jensen's Alpha - Germany 1973
For the calculations see 6.2.1.

	Jensen's Alpha (Rf = 0)	t-value
sampleCOV vs. MV	-0.0013	-1.4246
sampleCVaR vs. minCVaR	-0.0009	-1.0309
normCVaR vs. minCVaR	-0.0009	-1.1803
modCVaR vs. minCVaR	-0.0014	-1.4859
sampleCDaR vs. minCDaR	0.0018	1.1586
sampleCOV vs. Naive	0.0010	2.1419
sampleCVaR vs. Naive	0.0012	3.1918
normCVaR vs. Naive	0.0012	2.6063
modCVaR vs. Naive	0.0007	1.4493
sampleCDaR vs. Naive	0.0019	5.1717
sampleCOV vs. sampleCVaR	-0.0002	-0.8629
sampleCOV vs. normCVaR	-0.0002	-3.1379
sampleCOV vs. modCVaR	0.0003	0.9781
sampleCOV vs. sampleCDaR	-0.0006	-1.7414
sampleCDaR vs. sampleCVaR	0.0006	1.9998
sampleCDaR vs. normCVaR	0.0006	1.5066
sampleCDaR vs. modCVaR	0.0012	2.3690

and some also to the Breusch-Pagan test. Thus, the positive alpha value is unclear.

The F-test in table 6.51 shows that the minimum risk portfolios have a statistically lower variance compared to the ERC portfolios, whereas the naive portfolio exhibits a statistically higher variance compared to the risk budgeting portfolios.

Table 6.50: Analysis of Jensen's Alpha Regression - Germany 1973
For the calculations see 6.2.1.

	DW statistic	p-value	BP-stat	p-value	White-stat	p-value
sampleCOV vs. MV	1.8470	0.0481	0.7826	0.3763	84.6446	0.0000
sampleCVaR vs. minCVaR	1.9010	0.1405	7.3784	0.0066	125.6918	0.0000
normCVaR vs. minCVaR	1.8505	0.0522	10.8998	0.0010	165.1380	0.0000
modCVaR vs. minCVaR	1.7730	0.0069	3.5989	0.0578	111.1818	0.0000
sampleCDaR vs. minCDaR	1.8488	0.0501	147.8944	0.0000	304.0787	0.0000
sampleCOV vs. Naive	2.0930	0.8403	0.9585	0.3276	76.6933	0.0000
sampleCVaR vs. Naive	2.0969	0.8504	2.3268	0.1272	38.6967	0.0000
normCVaR vs. Naive	2.0978	0.8528	1.8442	0.1745	87.5008	0.0000
modCVaR vs. Naive	2.0210	0.5866	10.7437	0.0010	61.4130	0.0000
sampleCDaR vs. Naive	2.0730	0.7825	7.6702	0.0056	69.5521	0.0000
sampleCOV vs. sampleCVaR	2.1616	0.9587	0.0009	0.9765	13.7778	0.0010
sampleCOV vs. normCVaR	2.1281	0.9152	4.4762	0.0344	6.4769	0.0392
sampleCOV vs. modCVaR	1.9452	0.2730	14.8163	0.0001	37.2047	0.0000
sampleCOV vs. sampleCDaR	2.0858	0.8207	3.4083	0.0649	13.8644	0.0010
sampleCDaR vs. sampleCVaR	2.1127	0.8863	0.0747	0.7846	2.7440	0.2536
sampleCDaR vs. normCVaR	2.2060	0.9866	0.0286	0.8658	9.4585	0.0088
sampleCDaR vs. modCVaR	2.0863	0.8213	18.0151	0.0000	47.7035	0.0000

Table 6.51: Significance of Difference in Variances - Germany 1973
For the calculations see 6.2.1.

	Ratio of variances	p-value
sampleCOV vs. MV	2.0095	0.0000
sampleCVaR vs. minCVaR	1.6564	0.0000
normCVaR vs. minCVaR	1.5399	0.0000
modCVaR vs. minCVaR	1.6771	0.0000
sampleCDaR vs. minCDaR	1.3437	0.0015
sampleCOV vs. Naive	0.5977	0.0000
sampleCVaR vs. Naive	0.6345	0.0000
normCVaR vs. Naive	0.5898	0.0000
modCVaR vs. Naive	0.6424	0.0000
sampleCDaR vs. Naive	0.7528	0.0023
sampleCOV vs. sampleCVaR	0.9421	0.5210
sampleCOV vs. normCVaR	1.0134	0.8859
sampleCOV vs. modCVaR	0.9305	0.4383
sampleCOV vs. sampleCDaR	0.7941	0.0132
sampleCDaR vs. sampleCVaR	1.1865	0.0659
sampleCDaR vs. normCVaR	1.2763	0.0087
sampleCDaR vs. modCVaR	1.1719	0.0879

Portfolio Characteristics

Table 6.52 summarizes different risk figures of the portfolios. The
Naive portfolio has the highest risk values among all risk measures.
The minimum risk portfolios display lower values than the risk budgeting portfolios, except the CDaR and the MaxDD of the minCDaR
portfolio, which is similar to the risk budgeting models. Among the
risk budgeting models, the sampleCDaR portfolio shows the highest
VaR and CVaR, but the lowest Drawdown values. The modCVaR
has the highest values among the Drawdown values, however, there is
only a small difference between the other approaches.

The Risk ratios in table 6.53 reveal that the minCVaR portfolio
has the best resulting return-risk rewards. The second best is the MV
portfolio, then follows the sampleCDaR portfolio and the minCDaR
portfolio. Among the CVaR and Variance risk budgets portfolios
there are barely variations, however, the modCVaR and the Variance
risk budgets portfolio have the lowest figures. The Naive portfolio has
the lowest ratios of all portfolios, thus it is the 'loser' in this dataset,
as all portfolios outperform the naive portfolio in all characteristics.

Table 6.52: Risk Figures - Germany 1973
All values are displayed in percent. For the calculations of
the risk measures see 3.1.2.

	5% VaR	5% CVaR	5% DaR	5% CDaR	MaxDD
MV	3.60	5.29	33.13	36.05	39.17
minCVaR	3.76	5.91	29.65	32.35	35.39
minCDaR	4.10	8.00	47.69	49.70	54.98
Naive	7.20	12.03	56.95	59.56	63.65
sampleCVaR	5.51	9.16	46.15	48.88	54.09
normCVaR	5.37	8.60	48.01	50.30	54.09
modCVaR	5.56	9.19	48.96	51.54	56.35
sampleCOV	5.38	8.74	48.64	50.87	54.56
sampleCDaR	6.30	10.01	41.85	45.49	52.89

Table 6.53: Risk Ratios - Germany 1973
All values are displayed in percent. For the calculations see
6.2.1.

	SR	SR_VaR	SR_CVaR	SR_CDaR	SR_avdd	SR_maxdd
MV	13.00	9.14	6.22	0.91	3.20	0.84
minCVaR	13.59	10.39	6.60	1.21	3.47	1.10
minCDaR	8.20	6.95	3.56	0.57	1.46	0.52
Naive	4.58	2.95	1.77	0.36	0.94	0.33
sampleCVaR	7.75	5.20	3.13	0.59	1.82	0.53
normCVaR	7.82	5.18	3.24	0.55	1.82	0.51
modCVaR	6.33	4.24	2.56	0.46	1.40	0.42
sampleCOV	7.15	4.77	2.94	0.50	1.59	0.47
sampleCDaR	9.13	5.83	3.67	0.81	2.34	0.69

Table 6.54: Turnover and Trades - Germany 1973
The turnover and trades are based on weights before and
after the portfolio optimizations. For the calculations see
6.2.1.

	mean Turnover	total Turnover	No. of Trades
MV	0.22	99.45	13034
minCVaR	0.38	178.89	10612
minCDaR	0.39	182.22	7570
Naive	0.05	25.54	25575
sampleCVaR	0.08	38.39	25575
normCVaR	0.08	36.97	25572
modCVaR	0.16	72.68	25477
sampleCOV	0.08	37.46	25564
sampleCDaR	0.09	43.05	25575

Table 6.54 shows the turnover and the number of trades of the approaches. The naive portfolio displays again the lowest turnover. It is noticeable that the risk budgeting approaches display much lower turnover than the minimum risk approaches. However, the modCVaR portfolio has twice the turnover of the other risk budgeting approaches. The minCDaR portfolio has the highest turnover of all approaches and the MV portfolio the lowest among the minimum risk portfolios, it is approximately the half of the turnover of the minCVaR or minCDaR approaches. The number of trades is again the lowest for the minCDaR portfolio. On the opposite, the naive portfolio and the ERC portfolios need the most trades.

Portfolio Investments

The tables 6.55, 6.56, 6.57 display the average portfolio weights across the examination period and the average out-of-sample holdings of the risk contributions for the MV and the sampleCOV portfolio as substitutes for the minimum risk and risk budgeting group.

It is visible that the minimum risk portfolios are invested by ca. 20% in A6, ca. 14% in A43 and ca. 6% in A25. Thus, 40% of the asset allocation account for 3 out of 55 assets. Additional 10% are invested in the assets A34 and A47. The risk budgeting approaches invest in all assets and are not concentrated in certain assets. They display in average a maximum holding of only 5%. The sampleCDaR portfolio is even more diversified, as it displays a maximum average holding of 3% in one asset.

The risk budgets of the MV portfolio show that the weights and the risk budgets are quite similar to the Variance and the CVaR. The risk allocations to the CDaR risk measure are slightly more diversified. That the weights and risk contributions are similar in this dataset could lie in the fact that all assets are equities with similar characteristics, as analyzed above. Moreover, the portfolio consists of 55 assets and the minimum risk portfolios depicts only assets which minimizes the portfolio variance. The most differences arise between the weights and the risk allocations, if the assets have huge different risks, but the weights are equal.

The risk budgets of the sampleCOV portfolio show that the risk allocations are mostly equally distributed among the assets with only slight differences. The most variations can be observed from the risk budgets to the CDaR risk measure. However, due to the amount of assets the differences are very small.

Table 6.55: Weights Allocations - Germany 1973
These are average estimated weights across the whole period
and displayed in percent.

Asset	MV	minCVaR	minCDaR	sampleCVaR	normCVaR	modCVaR	sampleCOV	sampleCDaR
A1	2	1	1	2	2	2	2	2
A2	0	0	0	1	1	1	1	1
A3	1	1	1	2	2	3	2	2
A4	2	2	1	2	2	2	2	2
A5	4	4	4	3	3	3	3	2
A6	21	22	19	5	6	4	5	3
A7	1	1	1	1	1	1	1	1
A8	2	2	1	2	2	2	2	2
A9	3	3	5	2	2	3	2	3
A10	2	1	1	2	2	3	2	2
A11	2	2	1	2	2	3	3	1
A12	0	1	0	1	1	1	1	2
A13	2	3	3	2	2	3	2	2
A14	0	0	1	1	1	1	1	1
A15	1	1	1	2	2	2	2	2
A16	0	0	0	1	1	1	1	2
A17	0	0	0	1	1	1	1	2
A18	3	2	1	2	2	2	2	2
A19	2	2	3	2	3	2	3	2
A20	1	0	0	1	1	1	1	2
A21	0	0	0	1	1	1	1	2
A22	1	1	1	2	2	2	2	2
A23	0	0	0	1	1	1	1	2
A24	0	0	0	1	1	1	1	1
A25	6	7	6	3	4	3	4	2
A26	0	0	0	1	1	1	1	2
A27	0	0	0	1	1	1	1	2
A28	0	0	0	1	1	1	1	1
A29	1	1	2	2	2	2	2	1
A30	1	1	1	2	1	2	1	2
A31	0	0	1	1	1	1	1	2
A32	1	1	1	2	2	3	2	1
A33	0	0	0	1	1	1	1	1
A34	5	5	7	3	4	4	4	3
A35	0	1	0	1	1	1	1	1
A36	1	1	1	2	2	2	2	2
A37	1	1	2	1	2	2	1	2
A38	0	0	1	1	1	1	1	2
A39	2	2	3	2	2	2	2	1
A40	1	1	0	2	2	2	2	2
A41	0	0	0	1	1	1	1	1
A42	3	3	3	3	3	3	3	2
A43	14	13	14	5	5	4	5	3
A44	0	0	0	1	1	1	1	2
A45	0	0	0	1	1	1	1	2
A46	1	1	1	2	1	1	1	2
A47	6	5	5	4	4	3	4	3
A48	0	0	0	1	1	1	1	1
A49	1	1	1	2	1	1	1	2
A50	0	0	0	1	1	1	1	2
A51	2	2	2	2	2	2	2	2
A52	0	0	0	1	1	1	1	2
A53	0	0	1	1	1	1	1	2
A54	0	0	1	1	1	1	1	1
A55	3	2	2	3	3	3	3	2

Table 6.56: Risk Budget Allocations of the MV Portfolio - Germany 1973

The average risk budgets are calculated out-of sample and displayed in percent. For the calculation see 6.2.1. MVto-COV: risk contributions to volatility, MVtoCVaR: risk contributions to CVaR, MVtoCDaR: risk contributions to CDaR.

Asset	MVweights	MVtoCOV	MVtoCVaR	MVtoCDaR	Asset	MVweights	MVtoCOV	MVtoCVaR	MVtoCDaR
A1	2	2	2	2	A29	1	2	2	2
A2	0	0	1	1	A30	1	1	1	1
A3	1	1	1	2	A31	0	0	0	0
A4	2	2	2	2	A32	1	2	3	3
A5	4	4	4	4	A33	0	0	0	0
A6	21	15	12	10	A34	5	5	5	5
A7	1	1	1	1	A35	0	1	1	1
A8	2	2	3	3	A36	1	1	1	1
A9	3	2	2	2	A37	1	1	1	1
A10	2	2	3	3	A38	0	0	0	0
A11	2	3	3	3	A39	2	2	3	3
A12	0	0	0	0	A40	1	1	1	1
A13	2	3	4	4	A41	0	0	0	0
A14	0	0	1	1	A42	3	3	3	4
A15	1	1	2	2	A43	14	10	9	8
A16	0	0	0	0	A44	0	0	0	0
A17	0	0	0	0	A45	0	0	0	0
A18	3	3	3	3	A46	1	1	1	1
A19	2	2	2	3	A47	6	5	5	4
A20	1	1	1	1	A48	0	0	0	0
A21	0	0	0	0	A49	1	1	1	1
A22	1	1	2	2	A50	0	0	0	0
A23	0	0	0	0	A51	2	2	2	2
A24	0	0	0	0	A52	0	0	0	0
A25	6	6	6	6	A53	0	0	0	0
A26	0	0	0	0	A54	0	0	0	0
A27	0	0	0	0	A55	3	3	3	3
A28	0	0	0	0					

Table 6.57: Risk Budget Allocations of the sampleCOV Portfolio - Germany 1973
The average risk budgets are calculated out of sample and displayed in percent. For the calculation see 6.2.1. COVtoCOV: risk contributions to volatility, COVtoCVaR: risk contributions to CVaR, COVtoCDaR: risk contributions to CDaR.

	sampleCOVweights	COVtoCOV	COVtoCVaR	COVtoCDaR
A1	2	2	2	2
A2	1	2	3	2
A3	2	2	2	2
A4	2	2	2	2
A5	3	2	2	2
A6	5	2	1	2
A7	1	2	2	2
A8	2	2	2	3
A9	2	2	2	2
A10	2	2	2	2
A11	3	3	3	3
A12	1	2	1	1
A13	2	2	3	3
A14	1	2	1	2
A15	2	2	2	2
A16	1	2	1	1
A17	1	2	1	1
A18	2	2	2	2
A19	3	2	3	3
A20	1	2	1	2
A21	1	2	1	1
A22	2	2	2	2
A23	1	2	1	1
A24	1	2	1	1
A25	4	3	3	3
A26	1	2	1	1
A27	1	2	1	1
A28	1	2	2	1
A29	2	2	3	3
A30	1	2	1	1
A31	1	2	1	1
A32	2	3	3	3
A33	1	2	1	1
A34	4	2	2	2
A35	1	2	2	2
A36	2	2	2	2
A37	1	2	2	2
A38	1	2	1	1
A39	2	3	4	3
A40	2	2	2	2
A41	1	2	1	1
A42	3	2	2	2
A43	5	2	2	2
A44	1	1	1	1
A45	1	2	1	1
A46	1	2	2	1
A47	4	2	2	2
A48	1	2	2	2
A49	1	2	1	1
A50	1	2	1	1
A51	2	2	2	2
A52	1	2	1	1
A53	1	2	1	1
A54	1	2	1	1
A55	3	2	2	2

Bull/Bear Market Performance

Table 6.58 and figure 6.9 present the identified bul and bear phases based on the naive portfolio for the German dataset (the period runs from 01.1974 - 09.2012).

Table 6.58: Bull and Bear Periods - Germany 1973
The phases were identified on the naive portfolio by using the method of Bry and Boschan (1971), see 6.2.2.

Bear Period	Bull Period
01.1974 - 10.1974	10.1974 - 11.1975
11.1975 - 10.1976	10.1976 - 09.1978
09.1978 - 03.1980	03.1980 - 06.1981
06.1981 - 08.1982	08.1982 - 01.1984
01.1984 - 07.1984	07.1984 - 04.1986
04.1986 - 01.1988	01.1988 - 05.1991
05.1991 - 09.1992	09.1992 - 04.1994
04.1994 - 07.1996	07.1996 - 08.1999
08.1999 - 03.2003	03.2003 - 02.2004
02.2004 - 09.2004	09.2004 - 05.2007
05.2007 - 02.2009	02.2009 - 02.2011
02.2011 - 09.2011	09.2011 - 09.2012

Table 6.59 and 6.60 present the characteristics of the portfolio performances split into bull and bear phases.

The minCVaR portfolio displays the highest return in the bull period among the minimum risk approaches. However, the standard deviation of the MV portfolio is lower, thus, the MV portfolio presents the highest Sharpe ratio. The risk budgeting approaches present much higher returns in the bull period with only a minor increase in the volatility, accordingly they have better return-risk ratios. The minCDaR has the worst performance in the bull period by returns and Sharpe ratio and the naive and the sampleCDaR portfolio the best in returns. It is noticeable that the sampleCDaR portfolio achieves the same return as the naive portfolio with a lower standard

deviation. However, both have high maximum drawdown values and
the modCVaR portfolio displays the highest Sharpe ratio.

Table 6.59: Bull/Bear Germany1973 - Minimum Risk Portfolios

	MV	minCVaR	minCDaR	Naive
Bull Market (%)				
Ann. Mean	13.71	14.21	13.19	21.90
Ann. Std	8.47	9.31	9.62	13.69
Sharpe	162	153	137	160
MaxDD	12.13	15.35	14.51	30.14
Skewness	0.56	0.27	0.46	-0.92
Bear Market (%)				
Ann. Mean	-8.88	-7.83	-9.42	-22.86
Ann. Std	7.72	9.62	13.78	16.05
Sharpe	-115	-81	-68	-142
MaxDD	79.08	75.67	83.65	98.41
Skewness	-0.68	0.45	-5.40	-1.19

Table 6.60: Bull/Bear Germany1973 - Risk Budgeting Portfolios

	sampleCVaR	normCVaR	modCVaR	sampleCOV	sampleCDaR
Bull Market (%)					
Ann. Mean	19.20	18.62	19.75	18.48	21.04
Ann. Std	11.20	11.08	10.90	11.13	12.26
Sharpe	171	168	181	166	172
MaxDD	26.37	26.17	22.76	26.72	28.27
Skewness	-0.91	-0.88	-0.38	-0.91	-1.08
Bear Market (%)					
Ann. Mean	-17.27	-16.73	-19.40	-17.15	-17.43
Ann. Std	12.34	11.51	12.49	11.62	13.54
Sharpe	-140	-145	-155	-147	-129
MaxDD	95.44	94.91	96.83	95.26	95.70
Skewness	-1.15	-1.16	-1.08	-1.14	-1.11

In the bear period the minimum risk approaches display much better performances than the risk budgeting models, as they achieve a higher return by a lower fluctuation. The returns of the risk budgeting models are twice as low as those of the minimum risk portfolios. The drawdowns of the minimum risk portfolios are also smaller, with the minCVaR portfolio experiencing the smallest maximum drawdown. The naive portfolio has the lowest returns and also the highest risks, thus, it is not suited for the bear market.

In the bear period the lower returns of the ERC portfolios compared to the minimum risk approaches and the outperformances vs. the naive portfolio are also significant as displayed in table 6.62. Moreover, the sampleCOV portfolio as well as the sampleCDaR portfolio have a significant higher return than the modCVaR portfolio. The differences in the variances are also statistically significant. The lower variance of the sampleCDaR portfolio compared to the minCDaR portfolio is not significant.

Table 6.61: Significance in Means in the Bull Period - Germany 1973
For the calculations see 6.2.1.

	Excess Mean (%)	t-Stat	p-value
sampleCOV vs. MV	0.40	3.35	0.00
sampleCVaR vs. minCVaR	0.42	3.21	0.00
normCVaR vs. minCVaR	0.37	2.94	0.00
modCVaR vs. minCVaR	0.46	3.62	0.00
sampleCDaR vs. minCDaR	0.65	3.72	0.00
sampleCOV vs. Naive	-0.29	-3.50	0.00
sampleCVaR vs. Naive	-0.22	-3.14	0.00
normCVaR vs. Naive	-0.27	-3.30	0.00
modCVaR vs. Naive	-0.18	-2.09	0.04
sampleCDaR vs. Naive	-0.07	-1.33	0.18
sampleCOV vs. sampleCVaR	-0.06	-2.06	0.04
sampleCOV vs. normCVaR	-0.01	-1.46	0.15
sampleCOV vs. modCVaR	-0.11	-2.17	0.03
sampleCOV vs. sampleCDaR	-0.21	-3.97	0.00
sampleCDaR vs. sampleCVaR	0.15	3.69	0.00
sampleCDaR vs. normCVaR	0.20	3.81	0.00
sampleCDaR vs. modCVaR	0.11	1.56	0.12

Table 6.61 shows that the higher returns of the ERC portfolios compared to the minimum risk portfolios in the bull period are all significant. Moreover, the sampleCDaR exhibits a significant outperformance vs. the other ERC portfolios, except the modCVaR portfolio. But compared to the naive portfolio, the risk budgeting portfolios display a significant lower return, except the sampleCDaR portfolio. The F-test in table 6.62 shows an opposite picture: the variances of the ERC portfolios are statistically higher compared to the minimum risk counterparts and statistically lower compared to the naive portfolio. Among each other, there is no statistical difference in variances.

Table 6.62: Significance in Means in the Bear Period - Global Portfolio
For the calculations see 6.2.1.

	Excess Mean (%)	t-Stat	p-value
sampleCOV vs. MV	-0.69	-4.86	0.00
sampleCVaR vs. minCVaR	-0.79	-4.08	0.00
normCVaR vs. minCVaR	-0.74	-4.24	0.00
modCVaR vs. minCVaR	-0.96	-4.90	0.00
sampleCDaR vs. minCDaR	-0.67	-2.33	0.02
sampleCOV vs. Naive	0.48	3.94	0.00
sampleCVaR vs. Naive	0.47	4.69	0.00
normCVaR vs. Naive	0.51	4.12	0.00
modCVaR vs. Naive	0.29	2.50	0.01
sampleCDaR vs. Naive	0.45	5.54	0.00
sampleCOV vs. sampleCVaR	0.01	0.28	0.78
sampleCOV vs. normCVaR	-0.03	-2.58	0.01
sampleCOV vs. modCVaR	0.19	3.49	0.00
sampleCOV vs. sampleCDaR	0.02	0.34	0.74
sampleCDaR vs. sampleCVaR	-0.01	-0.27	0.79
sampleCDaR vs. normCVaR	-0.06	-0.82	0.41
sampleCDaR vs. modCVaR	0.16	2.07	0.04

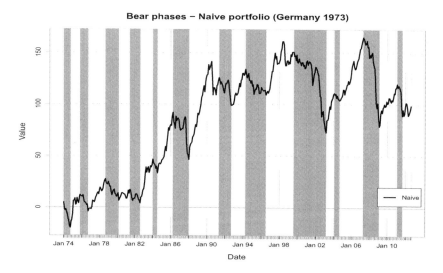

Figure 6.9: Bull/Bear Phases - Germany 1973

Table 6.63: Significance in Variances in the Bull Period - Germany 1973

	Ratio of variances	p-value
sampleCOV vs. MV	1.7240	0.0000
sampleCVaR vs. minCVaR	1.4460	0.0029
normCVaR vs. minCVaR	1.4170	0.0049
modCVaR vs. minCVaR	1.3706	0.0108
sampleCDaR vs. minCDaR	1.6241	0.0001
sampleCOV vs. Naive	0.6604	0.0008
sampleCVaR vs. Naive	0.6686	0.0012
normCVaR vs. Naive	0.6552	0.0006
modCVaR vs. Naive	0.6337	0.0002
sampleCDaR vs. Naive	0.8016	0.0736
sampleCOV vs. sampleCVaR	0.9878	0.9209
sampleCOV vs. normCVaR	1.0080	0.9483
sampleCOV vs. modCVaR	1.0421	0.7381
sampleCOV vs. sampleCDaR	0.8238	0.1167
sampleCDaR vs. sampleCVaR	1.1991	0.1417
sampleCDaR vs. normCVaR	1.2236	0.1024
sampleCDaR vs. modCVaR	1.2650	0.0572

Table 6.64: Significance in Variances in the Bear Period - Germany 1973

	Ratio of variances	p-value
sampleCOV vs. MV	2.2680	0.0000
sampleCVaR vs. minCVaR	1.6459	0.0005
normCVaR vs. minCVaR	1.4335	0.0112
modCVaR vs. minCVaR	1.6859	0.0002
sampleCDaR vs. minCDaR	0.9653	0.8029
sampleCOV vs. Naive	0.5246	0.0000
sampleCVaR vs. Naive	0.5910	0.0002
normCVaR vs. Naive	0.5147	0.0000
modCVaR vs. Naive	0.6053	0.0004
sampleCDaR vs. Naive	0.7112	0.0163
sampleCOV vs. sampleCVaR	0.8876	0.4000
sampleCOV vs. normCVaR	1.0192	0.8934
sampleCOV vs. modCVaR	0.8666	0.3121
sampleCOV vs. sampleCDaR	0.7376	0.0319
sampleCDaR vs. sampleCVaR	1.2034	0.1914
sampleCDaR vs. normCVaR	1.3817	0.0227
sampleCDaR vs. modCVaR	1.1748	0.2554

Summary

The results show that the risk budgeting portfolios are not useful in an investment universe of one asset class, namely only equities. The returns of the risk budgeting portfolios based on the volatility and the CVaR are behind the minimum risk approaches. The portfolio based on the risk measure CDaR displays higher returns than its counterpart, the minCDaR portfolio. However, the higher return is not statistically significant. The sampleCDaR portfolio shows only a significant higher return compared to all the other risk contribution portfolios. Surprisingly, the minCDaR portfolio presents the highest loss and the lowest Sharpe ratio among the risk-based asset allocations. The Naive portfolio is not suited for this dataset, as it displays the worst performances in terms of returns, risk figures, drawdowns and risk ratios. The minCVaR portfolio shows the highest return and risk-return relationship, having a slightly higher volatility than the MV portfolio, but is neither statistically significant.

Table 6.65: Correlations of Portfolio Returns - Germany 1973

	Naive	MV	minCVaR	minCDaR	nCVaR	mCVaR	sCVaR	sCOV	sCDaR
Naive	100.00	72.42	65.96	51.33	95.93	95.76	97.53	96.11	98.12
MV		100.00	90.26	75.27	83.52	80.47	81.25	83.37	77.10
minCVaR			100.00	80.34	76.48	73.94	74.56	76.44	70.22
minCDaR				100.00	61.49	59.40	60.20	61.80	57.49
normCVaR					100.00	97.59	99.13	99.90	97.71
modCVaR						100.00	97.77	97.71	96.10
sampleCVaR							100.00	99.13	98.73
sampleCOV								100.00	97.62
sampleCDaR									100.00

The correlations in table 6.65 show that the risk budgeting portfolios are highly correlated among each other with 96% and higher. They are also highly correlated with the naive portfolio by values of 95% - 98%. The MV portfolio presents a correlation of ca. 80%, the minCVaR of ca. 75% and the minCDaR of ca. 60% with the risk budget portfolios. The least correlations come from the minCDaR with the risk budget portfolios and the sampleCDaR with the minimum risk approaches.

The lowest correlation presents the minCDaR portfolio with the naive portfolio of 51%. The minCVaR and the MV portfolio are by 65% and 72% correlated with the naive portfolio.

6.2.5 Summary of the Performance Studies

The risk budgeting models were tested on three different datasets vs. their minimum risk counterpart. Whereas in the European Fund and in the Global portfolio dataset (which consist of different asset classes) the risk budgeting models display higher total returns, in the German equities dataset the returns are lower as the minimum risk portfolios. Only the equal risk contribution portfolio based on the CDaR exhibit a higher total return as its opponent, the minCDaR portfolio. The fact that the investment universe is different can also be seen at the cumulative return of the naive portfolio: where it is higher as the minimum risk approaches in the global dataset, which is usual, in the equities dataset the benchmark displays the lowest cumulative return. Independent of the datasets, the risk budgeting portfolios do not show a significant outperformance compared to the minimum risk or the naive portfolio.

On the risk side, the risk budgeting models display higher risk levels in all datasets. The higher variance is statistically significant in all datasets. Thus, the minimum risk models result in much better risk-return relationships.

The split into bull and bear periods proves that the minimum risk approaches are much better suited for crisis periods than the risk contribution models. The minimum risk portfolios offer higher significant returns and lower volatilities.

Based on the results in all datasets as well as in the bull/bear periods, the risk budgeting models seem to be not a competitive to the minimum risk models, but to the naive portfolio. Compared to the naive portfolio, the models achieve higher returns with much lower risk measures and thus much better risk ratios and the results are statistically significant. However, in the bull period the naive portfolio outperforms significantly the ERC portfolios and offers a much higher return.

As the risk budgeting models are calculated on sample historical returns, the question is if the performances differ if other return distributions are applied. In the next chapter the ERC portfolios are calculated by using simulated returns from different underlying return distributions. It can be summarized that the return distributions increase the returns, but also the risks. However, the risk ratios of the sampleCVaR and the sampleCDaR portfolios can be substantially improved. Concerning the sampleCOV portfolio, in the global dataset it is not useful to make use of the different heavy tailed return distributions. Thus, it has to be individually proved if it is useful to apply a heavy-tailed distribution to the risk budgeting models. However, the return distributions do not change the general conclusion of the performance results.

6.3 Exploring Risk-Based Pricing Anomalies

As outlined above (see chapter 4.1.1 and 4.2), Scherer (2010b) and Carvalho et al. (2012) point out that the performance of the Minimum Variance as well as the risk budgeting portfolio based on the variance can be explained through exposures to known pricing factors, like the three Fama-French factors (Fama and French, 1992). Scherer (2010b) reports an explanation of 73% of the variation of the MV returns through the Fama-French factors and Carvalho et al. (2012) state 75% - 87% with two additional factors for the US equity universe. Also Clarke et al. (2006) report a small-cap and value bias and Clarke et al. (2011) a low-beta anomaly of the MV portfolio. However, the whole universe of stocks in the U.S. market was used and own factors were constructed by Scherer (2010b) and Carvalho et al. (2012). In this section, it will be studied on two of the aformentioned datasets, if the returns of the minimum risk portfolios as well as of the risk budgeting portfolios can be attributed to the known factors. Moreover, four other datasets will be used to examine the exposures and the α: The first one consists of 32 equity indices of the U.S. market and runs from 01.1973 - 09.2012. These are value-weighted subsector equity indices constructed by Datastream[1]. Subsector means that the sectors are divided into subsectors, e.g. the sector Telecommunications is divided into Fixed Line and Mobile Communications. The names of the indices can be found in the Appendix. The second one consists of the eight MSCI style indices for the U.S. market [2]: Investable Growth, Large Growth, Mid Growth, Small Growth, Investable Value, Large Value, Mid Value and Small Value. As these indices are constructed through the methodology of risk factors, the regressions are supposed to have a high explanation. Thus, it is interesting to observe the exposures as well as the $\alpha's$ of the portfolios and if they can produce a positive α in such a dataset. Moreover, the same two datasets are taken for the German market. However, there are not so many subindices for the German market with a long dataset available. Therefore the dataset consits of 16 subsector indices. The names of the indices can also be found in the appendix. The sector datasets run from 01.1973 - 09.2012 and the two MSCI style datasets from 01.1994 - 09.2012. Thus, through investigating the portfolio exposures and $\alpha's$ on 6 different datasets (one Global, two for the U.S. and three for the German market), a general conclusion of the characteristics of the portfolios can be made.

6.3.1 Methodology

The CAPM as well as the Fama-French three factor model is used to explain the variation of the excess returns of the risk portfolios over the risk-free return. The approach of (Fama and French, 1992, 1993) is well known for explaining stock asset returns as contradiction to

---

[1] http://thomsonreuters.com/global-equity-indices/?subsector=
market-indices

[2] http://www.msci.com/products/indices/style/

the CAPM (see chapter 2.2.3). Through cross-section and time-series regressions, Fama and French (1992) find out that the size and book-to-market factors can explain the differences in average returns across stocks. The factors are build through sorting the stocks according to different characteristics (size and book-to-market ratio) into portfolios and building return differences across the portfolios.

The return of the assets can be explained through three main factors, the market return, the size and the book-to-market factors. As the focus lies on the portfolio performances, the asset return is substituted through the portfolio return:

$$R_p - R_f = \alpha + \beta_{MKT}(R_M - R_f) + \beta_{SMB}SMB + \beta_{HML}HML + \varepsilon_p, \tag{6.30}$$

with

$$R_p : \text{return of portfolio } p$$
$$R_f : \text{Risk-free return}$$
$$\alpha : \text{intercept / excess return}$$
$$SMB : \text{return of small minus big stocks}$$
$$HML : \text{return of high minus low stocks}$$
$$\beta : \text{factor coefficients}$$
$$\varepsilon_p : \text{residual return}$$

The α can be interpreted as the excess return of the portfolio, which cannot be explained through the exposures to the three factors. If α is positive (so-called abnormal return), it can be seen as an outperformance of the portfolio over the three-factor portfolio, and is therefore used for the performance measurement of portfolio managers or funds (Carhart, 1997, Davis, 2001, Kothari and Warner, 2001, Fama and French, 2010).

The factors are available for download at the Kenneth French website [3]. The US factors are constructed using all NYSE, AMEX, and NASDAQ stocks and forming 6 value-weight portfolios on size and book-to-market. SMB (Small Minus Big) is the average return on the three small portfolios minus the average return on the three big portfolios,

$$SMB = 1/3 \text{ (Small Value + Small Neutral + Small Growth)}$$
$$- 1/3 \text{ (Big Value + Big Neutral + Big Growth)}.$$

HML (High Minus Low) is the average return on the two value portfolios minus the average return on the two growth portfolios,

$$HML = 1/2 \text{ (Small Value + Big Value)}$$
$$- 1/2 \text{ (Small Growth + Big Growth)}.$$

$R_M - R_f$, the excess return on the market, is the value-weight return on all NYSE, AMEX, and NASDAQ stocks (from CRSP) minus the one-month Treasury bill rate [4].

The global factors will be used for the first dataset, as the Global portfolio dataset consists of major asset classes around the world. The global Fama-French factors are constructed through including stocks from 23 countries: Australia, Austria, Belgium, Canada, Denmark, Finland, France, Germany, Greece, Hong Kong, Ireland, Italy, Japan, Netherlands, New Zealand, Norway, Portugal, Singapore, Spain, Switzerland, Sweden, United Kingdom, United States [5]. The methodology is the same as for the US factors, but the factors are constructed by using international equities. The global factors are updated versions of those used in Fama and French (2012).

---

[3] http://mba.tuck.dartmouth.edu/pages/faculty/ken.french/data_library.html

[4] from Ibbotson Associates, http://mba.tuck.dartmouth.edu/pages/faculty/ken.french/Data_Library/f-f_factors.html

[5] http://mba.tuck.dartmouth.edu/pages/faculty/ken.french/Data_Library/details_global.html

For the German datasets, German factors are used. The factors are available from the website of the Centre for Financial Research at the University of Cologne [6]. For the construction of the factors and the empirical study for the German market see Artmann et al. (2012). The factors are build from more than 900 stocks listed at the Frankfurt Stock Exchange during the period 1960-2010. Moreover, Hanauer et al. (2013) constructed factors for the German market from equities which are listed in the CDAX. They are available for download from the website of the Technical University of Munich [7] and run from 1996 - 2012. These factors will also additionally be used to examine the differences.

As the portfolios are rebalanced monthly, the monthly returns and monthly factors are used for the analysis. Table 6.66 gives an overview of the data sets and regression periods.

Table 6.66: Overview of Regressions

Notation	Dataset	Regression period
Global portfolio	13 global indices (9 equity indices)	01.1996 - 06.2011
Germany 1973 (Artmann et al., 2012)	55 German equities	01.1974 - 12.2010
Germany 1973 (Hanauer et al., 2013)	55 German equities	08.1996 - 01.2012
US Industry	32 US sector indices	01.1974 - 09.2012
US MSCI	8 US style indices	06.1995 - 06.2013
German Industry (Artmann et al., 2012)	16 German sector indices	01.1974 - 12.2010
German Industry (Hanauer et al., 2013)	16 German sector indices	08.1996 - 01.2012
German MSCI (Artmann et al., 2012)	8 German style indices	06.1995 - 12.2010
German MSCI (Hanauer et al., 2013)	8 German style indices	08.1996 - 01.2012

At first, the portfolio excess returns will be regressed only on the excess market return (this will be called the 'CAPM regression' although it is a market model, as the CAPM is only valid in equilibrium and is an ex-ante model, whereas the market model is not an equilibrium model and can also be used ex-post (Poddig et al., 2003, p. 257)). After this, the two additional Fama-French factors, size and

---

[6]http://www.cfr-cologne.de/version06/html/research.php?topic=paper&auswahl=data&v=dl

[7]http://www.fm.wi.tum.de/en/research/data

value, are used (this will be called 'Fama-French regressions', whereas
the factors are meant and not the methodology of Fama and French
(1992)). Thus, it is explored which explanation power is provided
by the additional two factors and the CAPM regression is compared
to the Fama-French three-factor model regression. Additionally, the
four-factor model of Carhart (1997) is applied and the detailed results
can be found in the appendix.

6.3.2 Global Portfolio

The Global portfolio dataset consists of equity and bond indices as
well as one commodity index. As the Fama-French factors are constructed from equities and serve for the explanation of equity returns,
the Global dataset is not perfect for testing the risk-based pricing
anomalies. However, as the dataset consists mainly of equity indices
(nine out of thirteen), the exposures will nevertheless be examined.
It is expected that the minimum risk approaches have a lower explanation through the factors than the ERC portfolios, as they are
concentrated only on bonds. The ERC portfolios allocate their capital
equally by risk into all indices and thus have in sum more risk in the
equities, as the equities have a larger proportion in this dataset.

At first, table 6.67 provides a summary of the factors data used
for the study of the excess returns. The HML factor has the highest
return and a much lower volatility than the market. Thus, it displays
the highest Sharpe ratio whereas the size factor presents a much
lower Sharpe ratio than the market. While the market and the size
factor are skewed to the left, the value factor has a positive skewness.
Moreover, the minimum returns of the two factor portfolios are much
lower than those of the market, although they achieve almost the
maximum return of the market. The values in table 6.68 show that all
the factors have small correlations. Whereas the size factor correlation
with the market is near 0%, the value factor is slightly negatively
correlated with the market. The size and the value factors also display
a slightly negative correlation among each other.

Table 6.67: Fama-French Global Factors - Statistics
The period is 01.1996 - 06.2011. All values are displayed in %, except the skewness and kurtosis. The mean and the volatility are annualized by the factor 12, as the factors consist of monthly returns.

Name	Mkt-RF	SMB	HML
Symbol	R_{MKT}	R_{SMB}	R_{HML}
annual Mean	4.86	0.94	5.77
annual Volatility	16.12	8.12	9.31
annual Sharpe ratio	30.16	11.6	62.0
Maximum	11.42	10.30	11.23
Minimum	-19.46	-9.65	-9.62
Skewness	-0.78	-0.13	0.35
Kurtosis	1.56	2.66	3.80

Table 6.68: Correlations of the Global Factor Returns

	SMB	HML
Mkt-RF	1.78	-17.82
SMB		-22.44
HML		

At first, the portfolio excess returns are regressed only on the international excess market return. This can be seen as an ex post CAPM test, as the only explanation variable is the market return. As visible from tables 6.69 and 6.70, the portfolios cannot display a significant positive alpha. However, as stated above, this dataset is influenced by bond indices and one commodity index and the results should be treated with caution.

Table 6.71 displays the regression results of the excess returns (portfolio return - risk-free rate) of the minimum risk portfolios against the Fama-French factors. The factor regressions explain the variation

Table 6.69: CAPM Regression Results for the Minimum Risk Portfolios -
Global Portfolio
Signification codes: ***: ≤ 0.01, **: ≤ 0.05, *: ≤ 0.1
If the null hypothesis of the Durbin-Watson test is rejected,
the test statistic is shaded in grey.

Excess return	MV	minCVaR	minCDaR	Naive
α	0.0000269	0.0000525	0.0005833	-0.0013806
β_{MKT}	0.2301229***	0.2013908***	0.1437344***	0.8001555***
R^2	0.3881	0.3435	0.2002	0.8774
DW	1.7716	1.7936	1.9137	1.7775

Table 6.70: CAPM Regression Results for the Risk Budgeting Portfolios
- Global Portfolio
Signification codes: ***: ≤ 0.01, **: ≤ 0.05, *: ≤ 0.1
If the null hypothesis of the Durbin-Watson test is rejected,
the test statistic is shaded in grey.

Excess return	sampleCVaR	normCVaR	modCVaR	sampleCOV	sampleCDaR
α	-0.0000714	-0.0000171	0.0000535	-0.0001983	0.0007277
β_{MKT}	0.4449229***	0.3394996***	0.4096399***	0.3443160***	0.3779121***
R^2	0.6997	0.6712	0.6516	0.6775	0.6256
DW	1.6207	1.8949	2.0378	1.8877	1.9834

of the excess returns of the Naive portfolio with 89%, but of the
minimum risk approaches only with 22%, 37% and 42% in descending
order for the MV, the minCVaR and the minCDaR portfolio. Compared to the CAPM regressions, the factors have a low additional
explanation power. Moreover, the DW nullhypothesis is rejected fot
the MV portfolio, which is a sign for missing variables. Whereas the
naive portfolio has a market beta of 0.8 and thus moves in general
with the market, which is not surprising, the other approaches display
a low beta with 23%, 20% and 14%. The naive portfolio loads on small
caps, which is also the result in Carvalho et al. (2012). The value
factor coefficients are low and not significant for the minimum risk approaches. The alpha values are all negative, except for the minCDaR

Table 6.71: Fama-French Regression Results for the Minimum Risk Portfolios - Global Portfolio
Signification codes: ***: ≤ 0.01, **: ≤ 0.05, *: ≤ 0.1
If the null hypothesis of the Durbin-Watson test is rejected,
the test statistic is shaded in grey.

Excess return	MV	minCVaR	minCDaR	Naive
α	-0.0002460	-0.0002121	0.0004923	-0.0018699*
β_{MKT}	0.2324577***	0.2039251***	0.1435074***	0.8051114***
β_{SMB}	0.1280569***	0.1127464***	0.0850367**	0.1971129***
β_{HML}	0.0338950	0.0344955	0.0052278	0.0654140*
R^2	0.4172	0.3698	0.2175	0.8905
DW	1.743	1.7788	1.884	1.8291

portfolio, but the excess return is statistically not significant. All
in all, the explanation of the minimum risk approaches through the
Fama factors is insufficient. The portfolios seem to have additional
exposures to other, nonincluded factors. This is not surprising due to
the underlying dataset, as explained above. Under this circumstances,
the factors have an unexpected high explanation.

Table 6.72: Fama-French Regression Results for the Risk Budgeting
Portfolios - Global Portfolio
Signification codes: ***: ≤ 0.01, **: ≤ 0.05, *: ≤ 0.1
If the null hypothesis of the Durbin-Watson test is rejected,
the test statistic is shaded in grey.

Excess return	sampleCVaR	normCVaR	modCVaR	sampleCOV	sampleCDaR
α	-0.0009412	-0.0002478	-0.0004023	-0.0004341	0.0005414
β_{MKT}	0.4576315***	0.3408569***	0.4148849***	0.3457798***	0.3784757***
β_{SMB}	0.1860796***	0.1342579***	0.1571592***	0.1339212***	0.1308262***
β_{HML}	0.1398215***	0.0249333	0.0647319*	0.0259398	0.0169168
R^2	0.7412	0.6964	0.6761	0.7022	0.6437
DW	1.6194	1.9169	2.0453	1.9194	2.0026

For completeness, table 6.72 displays the regression results for the risk budgeting portfolios. The explanation of the risk budgeting portfolio returns are higher in the range from 64% for the sampleCDaR portfolio to 74% for the sampleCVaR portfolio. However, the high R^2 of the sampleCVaR portfolio could result through autocorrelated residuals, as the DW test identificates autocorrelation. Only the sampleCDaR portfolio displays a positive alpha, but it is insignificant. All the risk budgeting models exhibit a beta around 0.4, which is higher than of the minimum risk approaches, but also low. The size factor is highly significant and the exposure lie around 13%, the mod-CVaR and the sampleCVaR portfolio show higher exposure with 15% and 18%. The exposure to the value factor is only highly significant for the sampleCVaR portfolio with 13%. Thus, the portfolio displays also the highest R^2 with 74%. All the other risk budgeting portfolios show low values, which are insignificant, except of the modCVaR portfolio, which is yet slightly significant at the 10% level.

All the values are higher compared to the minimum risk portfolios and the Fama-French three factor model explains the returns of the risk budgeting portfolios quite well. The reason lies in the fact that the risk budgeting portfolios are more diversified and thus include more equity exposures in this dataset, whereas the minimum risk portfolios are more concentrated in bonds. The loadings on the factors have also large values. Moreover, the loadings for the SMB factor are higher than those of the value factor. This was also the result in the study of Carvalho et al. (2012). However, as the value factor is practically insignificant, there could be another exposures to other factors, like in the study of Scherer (2010b) and Carvalho et al. (2012) to low beta and low idiosyncratic risk assets.

6.3.3 Germany 1973

In this section, the German dataset of section 6.2.4 will be tested on the Fama-French factors.

Artmann Factors

Table 6.73 summarizes the characteristics of the German factors of Artmann et al. (2012). The value factor has again the highest return and the highest Sharpe ratio. The size factor has a low return and a low Sharpe ratio. However, the two factors display a much lower standard deviation and also a much lower maximum loss of the returns.

Table 6.73: Fama-French German Factors (Artmann et al., 2012) - Statistics
The period is 01.1974 - 12.2010. All values are displayed in %, except the skewness and kurtosis.

Name	Mkt-RF	SMB	HML
Symbol	R_{MKT}	R_{SMB}	R_{HML}
Mean	0.41	0.08	0.48
Volatility	4.65	2.34	2.69
Sharpe ratio	8.71	3.35	17.90
Maximum	11.42	10.30	11.23
Minimum	-19.46	-9.65	-9.62
Skewness	-0.78	-0.13	0.35
Kurtosis	1.56	2.66	3.80

Table 6.74: Correlations of the German Factor Returns

	SMB	HML
Mkt-RF	-51.32	4.70
SMB		-4.72

The correlations of the factors in the German market display a high negative correlation of the SMB factor with the market factor. The value factor has a slightly negative correlation to the size factor and a slightly positive correlation to the market factor.

Tables 6.75 and 6.76 show the regression results of the excess portfolio returns on the excess market return. It is obvious that the portfolios display negative alphas and thus underperform the market. The exposures to the market factor are highly significant, however, the minimum risk portfolios display a low beta of 0.3. The naive portfolio has a high market beta of 0.8 and the ERC portfolios of ca. 0.6. The explanations of the returns are low for the minimum risk portfolios, but for the naive and the ERC portfolios the R^2 is relative high with 82% and ca. 70%.

Table 6.75: CAPM Regression Results for the Minimum Risk Portfolios - Germany 1973 (Artmann et al., 2012)
Signification codes: ***: ≤ 0.01, **: ≤ 0.05, *: ≤ 0.1
If the null hypothesis of the Durbin-Watson test is rejected, the test statistic is shaded in grey.

Excess return	MV	minCVaR	minCDaR	Naive
α	-0.0020568*	-0.0015697	-0.0024350	-0.0054444***
β_{MKT}	0.2995634***	0.3131580***	0.2998451***	0.8127880***
R^2	0.3692	0.3143	0.1943	0.8264
DW	1.7709	1.7677	1.6886	1.6047

Table 6.76: CAPM Regression Results for the Risk Budgeting Portfolios - Germany 1973 (Artmann et al., 2012)
Signification codes: ***: ≤ 0.01, **: ≤ 0.05, *: ≤ 0.1
If the null hypothesis of the Durbin-Watson test is rejected, the test statistic is shaded in grey.

Excess return	sampleCVaR	normCVaR	modCVaR	sampleCOV	sampleCDaR
α	-0.0039795***	-0.0037964***	-0.0044447***	-0.0040332***	-0.0035022***
β_{MKT}	0.6284341***	0.5843552***	0.6129077***	0.5870722***	0.7057095***
R^2	0.7662	0.7128	0.7138	0.7104	0.822
DW	1.6586	1.7049	1.5971	1.6823	1.7036

As presented in tables6.77 and 6.78, the explanations of the Fama-French factor regressions in the German equities dataset is similar to

Table 6.77: Fama-French Regression Results for the Minimum Risk Portfolios - Germany 1973 (Artmann et al., 2012)
Signification codes: ***: ≤ 0.01, **: ≤ 0.05, *: ≤ 0.1
If the null hypothesis of the Durbin-Watson test is rejected,
the test statistic is shaded in grey.

Excess return	MV	minCVaR	minCDaR	Naive
α	-0.0019910**	-0.001371	-0.002361	-0.0059063***
β_{MKT}	0.3814226***	0.385072***	0.358033***	0.9095551***
β_{SMB}	0.2640492***	0.229971***	0.187308***	0.3197986***
β_{HML}	0.0691143***	0.038094	0.044754	0.1684078***
R^2	0.4557	0.3632	0.2169	0.8739
DW	1.8058	1.7989	1.7124	1.7385

the Global dataset with 45%, 36% and 22% for the minimum risk and
87% for the naive portfolio. However, all Durbin Watson test statistics indicate autocorrelated residuals, thus the coefficients should be
treated with caution and the R^2 could be too high. This is surprising,
as this dataset should be more suited to measure the exposures to the
Fama-factors than the Global dataset. It is an indication that factors
are missing to explain the performances on individual equities. The
missing factors could be the low-beta or the unsystematic risk factor
as examined by Scherer (2010b) and Carvalho et al. (2012). Compared to the regressions with only the market factor as explanatory
variable, the two Fama-French factors deliver additional explanation
power. The explanation of the MV portfolio return is increased by
9%, whereas the explanation of the ERC returns is increased by ca.
6%. The minCDaR portfolio has not a high exposure to the factors,
as the explanation is only increased by 2%.

All $\alpha's$ are negative and the minimum risk approaches move about
38% with the market, but the naive with high 91%. The size factor
is highly significant for all portfolios. Again, the naive portfolio has
the highest exposure to small-cap stocks. Whereas the naive portfolio
displays also a high significant exposure to value stocks (stocks with

high book-to-market value), the value stocks do not have a significant impact on the other portfolios.

Table 6.78: Fama-French Regression Results for the Risk Budgeting
Portfolios - Germany 1973 (Artmann et al., 2012)
Signification codes: ***: ≤ 0.01, **: ≤ 0.05, *: ≤ 0.1
If the null hypothesis of the Durbin-Watson test is rejected,
the test statistic is shaded in grey.

Excess return	sampleCVaR	normCVaR	modCVaR	sampleCOV	sampleCDaR
α	-0.0042807***	-0.0039639***	-0.0045868***	-0.0041757***	-0.0040638***
β_{MKT}	0.7181703***	0.6773562***	0.7208895***	0.6828971***	0.7776248***
β_{SMB}	0.2947572***	0.3034291***	0.3515619***	0.3122147***	0.2407669***
β_{HML}	0.1357404***	0.1174555***	0.1279512***	0.1161770***	0.1602305***
R^2	0.8251	0.7759	0.7896	0.7756	0.8629
DW	1.7822	1.807	1.6968	1.7853	1.8262

The factor regressions of the risk budgeting portfolios show high explanations from 78% for the normCVaR, the modCVaR and the sampleCOV portfolios to 83% and 87% for the sampleCVaR and the sampleCDaR portfolios. But again, all regressions display autocorrelated residuals and the $R^{2'}s$ could be too high. All the intercepts are negative and significant. Thus, the portfolios do not display an excessive return above the three factor exposures. In this dataset, all the three factors are highly significant for all portfolios. The portfolios move with the market of around 70% and display exposures to small caps with approximately 30% and to value stocks with approximately 13%. The sampleCDaR portfolio shows the highest market and value exposure, but the lowest size exposure. The regressions reveal a high similarity between the ERC portfolios as well as to the naive portfolio.

Hanauer Factors
Table 6.79 displays the statistics of the German factors constructed by Hanauer et al. (2013). The factors of Hanauer et al. (2013) are available for the period of 08.1996 - 01.2012. In this period, the size factor displays a high negative mean return.

Table 6.79: Fama-French German Factors of Hanauer et al. (2013) -
Statistics

The period is 08.1996 - 01.2012. All values are displayed in
%, except the skewness and kurtosis.

Name	Mkt-RF	SMB	HML
Symbol	R_{MKT}	R_{SMB}	R_{HML}
Mean	0.55	-0.71	0.74
Volatility	5.92	4.14	3.49
Sharpe ratio	9.35	-17.05	21.04
Maximum	13.83	10.36	11.91
Minimum	-15.49	-14.30	-10.36
Skewness	-0.53	-0.23	0.32
Kurtosis	0.14	0.002	0.75

As visible from table 6.80, the correlation of the SMB factor with
the market factor as well as with the value factor is negative. The
HML factor is slightly positive correlated with the market factor, but
the factors are almost independent of each other.

Table 6.80: Correlations of the German Factor Returns of Hanauer et al.
(2013)

	SMB	HML
Mkt-RF	-55.04	4.39
SMB		-19.40

Table 6.81 and 6.82 show the Fama-French regression results for the
Germany 1973 portfolios with the Hanauer et al. (2013) factors. Also
in these regressions, the DW statistics show autocorrelated residuals,
except for the Naive, the sampleCVaR and the sampleCDaR portfolios.
The explanation of the portfolio returns is lower than in the regressions
above. This is not surprising, as the data period of the Artmann et al.
(2012)'s factors is longer. The market factor has here a lower value

in all regressions. As above, the explanation of the factors are the
lowest for the minimum risk portfolios and the highest for the naive
portfolio. All the factors are highly significant for the ERC portfolios.
For the minimum risk portfolios, the HML factor has no explanation
power.

Table 6.81: Fama-French Regression Results for the Minimum Risk Portfolios - Germany 1973 Hanauer et al. (2013)
Signification codes: ***: ≤ 0.01, **: ≤ 0.05, *: ≤ 0.1
If the null hypothesis of the Durbin-Watson test is rejected,
the test statistic is shaded in grey.

Excess return	MV	minCVaR	minCDaR	Naive
α	-0.0011687	-0.0004694	-0.0020224	-0.0075633***
β_{MKT}	0.2550475***	0.2463982***	0.2223306***	0.8467441***
β_{SMB}	0.1959201***	0.1366516**	0.1048580**	0.4796510***
β_{HML}	0.0507117	0.0390712	-0.0052568	0.3708593***
R^2	0.3239	0.1989	0.1872	0.7533
DW	1.5175	1.699	1.7612	2.1063

Table 6.82: Fama-French Regression Results for the Risk Budgeting
Portfolios - Germany 1973 Hanauer et al. (2013)
Signification codes: ***: ≤ 0.01, **: ≤ 0.05, *: ≤ 0.1
If the null hypothesis of the Durbin-Watson test is rejected,
the test statistic is shaded in grey.

Excess return	sampleCVaR	normCVaR	modCVaR	sampleCOV	sampleCDaR
α	-0.0044103***	-0.0038760**	-0.0048583***	-0.0040584**	-0.0043285***
β_{MKT}	0.6014646***	0.5346320***	0.5973608***	0.5408349***	0.6528404***
β_{SMB}	0.3663982***	0.3430119***	0.4141836***	0.3516086***	0.3142710***
β_{HML}	0.2322858***	0.1701043***	0.2349730***	0.1716844***	0.2641794***
R^2	0.7044	0.6372	0.6667	0.6321	0.7264
DW	1.8162	1.7003	1.7619	1.7107	2.0342

6.3.4 Rolling Regressions

Interestingly to observe is the significance of the factors in different periods. This can be done through rolling regressions. For reasons of clarity, only the rolling alpha values of all the portfolios are shown here and all the rolling values only of the MV portfolio as representative. The rolling values of all the portfolios can be found in the appendix A.2.3. The rolling regression window consists of 36 months.

Figure 6.10 show the rolling alpha values for the portfolios in the global dataset. It is observable that all the alpha values vary around 0 and the mean is also around 0, except for the naive portfolio. Positive α is exhibited approximately in the period of 2003-2006 and after 2010. Clearly visible are the negative alpha values from the beginning of the examination period until 2003. The positive alpha of the risk budgeting models in the period of 2003-2006 is weaker compared to the minimum risk approaches. The modCVaR portfolio displays a positive alpha only around 2002. Moreover, it is visible that the naive portfolio displays a negative alpha almost across the whole period, independent of the market phase.

The rolling factor values in figure 6.11 show that the market beta lies around 0.25 during the whole period, except at the end in the period of 2008 - 2011, where it shortly increases to 0.4 and then falls to 0.3. The size factor varies around 0.15, being higher in the period from 2001 - 2005 and lower from 2005 - 2010. The HML factor displays low values near 0 from the beginning until 2004, then slightly increasing to 0.2, but drops from 2004 - 2011 from 0.2 to -0.4.

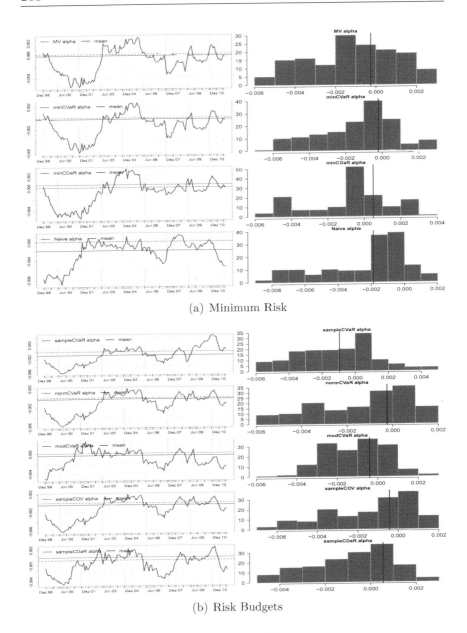

(a) Minimum Risk

(b) Risk Budgets

Figure 6.10: Rolling Alpha - Global Portfolio

The explanation power of the three factor model varies around 0.4 from the beginning until 2008, but then suddenly increases to 0.7. Thus, it seems that at the beginning of the financial crisis a 'regime switching' took place, as the MKT, the HML and the R^2 values display sudden changes. This changes can be observed more or less in all portfolios.

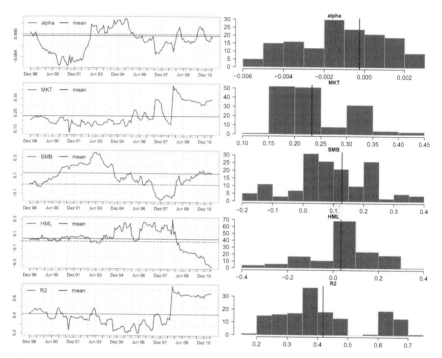

Figure 6.11: Rolling Regressions of the MV Portfolio - Global Portfolio

The rolling alphas of the portfolios in the German dataset (factors of Artmann et al. (2012)) in figure 6.12 show that the mean of the minimum risk approaches lies around 0, wheras the mean of the risk budgeting approaches is negative. A slightly positive alpha is displayed around 1988 - 1990, 1999 - 2000 and 2001 - 2002 of the MV, minCVaR and the minCDaR approach.

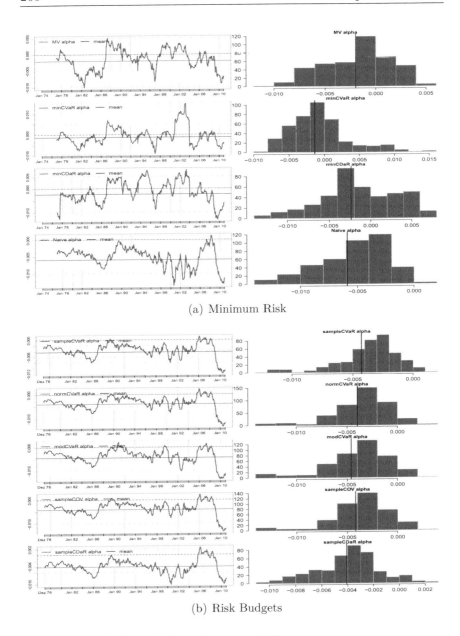

(a) Minimum Risk

(b) Risk Budgets

Figure 6.12: Rolling Alpha - Germany 1973

The minCDaR portfolio exhibits also a positive alpha around 1993 - 1995. The naive as well as the risk budgeting portfolios show at all times negative alphas. Thus, the risk budgeting approaches cannot outperform the minimum risk approaches based on factor returns in the German equities dataset.

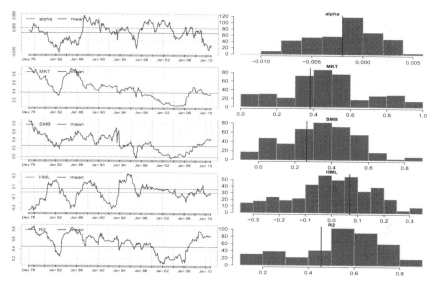

Figure 6.13: Rolling Regressions of the MV Portfolio - Germany 1973

The values of the MV portfolio in the German dataset in figure 6.13 show that the market factor is above the mean of 0.4 at the beginning of the examination period to 1995 shortly with values of 0.8 in 1975 and 1985, but during 2001 - 2008 drops to 0.2 and then rises to 0.4. The size factor is more or less stable with values of around 0.4, again higher in the first half until 1995. The opposite is the case with the value factor, which is in average negative in the first half and then around 0 from 1998. The explanatory power of the factors is at the beginning higher, even with values around 0.8, then slightly falls to 0.4 until 1995, then drops to 0.2 and rises again to around 0.6. It can be observed from the behavior of the curve that the explanation power is correlated to the market as well as to the size factor.

6.3.5 US Industry Indices

As outlined above, this dataset consists of 32 value-weighted sector indices of the U.S. market and lasts from 01.1973 - 09.2012 (Thus, the portfolio returns are from 01.1974 - 09.2012).

Tables 6.83 and 6.84 show at first the regression results for the excess market return. All the portfolios exhibit a high exposure to the market factor and the explanation power is high, except for the minimum risk portfolios. However, in some regressions there are autocorrelated residuals. Thus, the R^2 could be higher due to the autocorrelation of residuals.

Table 6.83: CAPM Regression Results for the Minimum Risk Portfolios - US Industry
Signification codes: ***: ≤ 0.01, **: ≤ 0.05, *: ≤ 0.1
If the null hypothesis of the Durbin-Watson test is rejected, the test statistic is shaded in grey.

Excess return	MV	minCVaR	minCDaR	Naive
α	-0.0021388*	-0.0027273**	-0.0033322***	-0.0030019***
β_{MKT}	0.5472384***	0.5754820***	0.6906102***	0.9670471***
R^2	0.5006	0.4803	0.608	0.9256
DW	1.8885	1.9304	2.0206	1.7177

Table 6.84: CAPM Regression Results for the Risk Budgeting Portfolios - US Industry
Signification codes: ***: ≤ 0.01, **: ≤ 0.05, *: ≤ 0.1
If the null hypothesis of the Durbin-Watson test is rejected, the test statistic is shaded in grey.

Excess return	sampleCVaR	normCVaR	modCVaR	sampleCOV	sampleCDaR
α	-0.0027229***	-0.0027250***	-0.0027230***	-0.0027721***	-0.0023414***
β_{MKT}	0.8961065***	0.8940809***	0.8870543***	0.8910800***	0.9115564***
R^2	0.8928	0.8925	0.8788	0.8939	0.9117
DW	1.7987	1.7995	1.7503	1.7776	1.9025

Tables 6.85 and 6.86 give the results of the Fama-French regressions for the US Industry portfolios. All the portfolios exhibit a high significant negative α and thus are behind the performance of the three factor portfolios. The explanation power of the factors is very high for the naive as well as the risk budgeting approaches. Thus, it is obvious that they have a high similarity between each other as well as to the naive portfolio. The minimum risk approaches display a coefficient of determination of ca. 60%. It is an indicate that there are missing factors for the explanation. Moreover, it is interesting that in this dataset the size factor is negative. In case of the risk budgeting portfolios, all factors deliver a significant explanation. For the minimum risk portfolios, the size factor is not significant. The HML factor has a higher value for the minimum risk portfolios than for the risk budgeting portfolios. Compared to the CAPM regressions, the explanation is especially enhanced for the MV and the minCVaR portfolios by 8% and 7%. To all the other portfolios, the two additional factors add only 2% - 3% to the R^2. However, as there are autocorrelated residulas in the CAPM regressions, this should be treated with caution.

Table 6.85: Fama-French Regression Results for the Minimum Risk Portfolios - US Industry
Signification codes: ***: ≤ 0.01, **: ≤ 0.05, *: ≤ 0.1
If the null hypothesis of the Durbin-Watson test is rejected, the test statistic is shaded in grey.

Excess return	MV	minCVaR	minCDaR	Naive
α	-0.0037296***	-0.0043973***	-0.0043374***	-0.0036528***
β_{MKT}	0.6288404***	0.6604862***	0.7508079***	1.0156254***
β_{SMB}	-0.0429140	-0.0424670	-0.0609467	-0.0770739***
β_{HML}	0.3538177***	0.3703657***	0.2374815***	0.1692370***
R^2	0.5841	0.5594	0.6393	0.9403
DW	1.8877	1.9287	2.0384	1.7919

Table 6.86: Fama-French Regression Results for the Risk Budgeting
Portfolios - US Industry
Signification codes: ***: ≤ 0.01, **: ≤ 0.05, *: ≤ 0.1
If the null hypothesis of the Durbin-Watson test is rejected,
the test statistic is shaded in grey.

Excess return	sampleCVaR	normCVaR	modCVaR	sampleCOV	sampleCDaR
α	-0.0035260***	-0.0035731***	-0.0035625***	-0.0036248***	-0.0029437***
β_{MKT}	0.9515009***	0.9477474***	0.9462200***	0.9455518***	0.9570736***
β_{SMB}	-0.0772970***	-0.0626916**	-0.0857409***	-0.0650434**	-0.0735459***
β_{HML}	0.2014909***	0.2050018***	0.2126526***	0.2069445***	0.1575048***
R^2	0.9146	0.9137	0.9037	0.9159	0.9259
DW	1.855	1.8683	1.809	1.8407	1.9364

6.3.6 US MSCI

Additionally, a dataset of eight MSCI style indices, which are constructed to capture exposures to the size and value factors in different combinations is examined for the US market. This dataset lasts from 06.1994 - 06.2013 (thus, the regressions are from 06.1995 - 06.2013).

Tables 6.87 and 6.88 show the results for the market factor regressions. It is visible that also in this dataset the alphas are negative. Moreover, the market factor has a high explanation power in all portfolios, which is not surprising in this dataset. The minimum risk approaches display a lower exposure than the naive portfolio and the ERC portfolios. Again, a few regressions display autocorrelated residuals and indicate missing factors or that the R^2 could be too high.

The regression results for the Fama-French factors in tables 6.89 and 6.90 show also significant negative alphas for all portfolios. As expected by construction, all factors have a high explanation power of the portfolio returns. However, also in this dataset, the minimum risk approaches have the lowest $R^{2'}s$ and the naive the highest. Moreover, the regressions for the MV and the minCVaR portfolio display autocorrelated residuals. The differences between the naive and the ERC

Table 6.87: CAPM Regression Results for the Minimum Risk Portfolios -
US MSCI
Signification codes: ***: ≤ 0.01, **: ≤ 0.05, *: ≤ 0.1
If the null hypothesis of the Durbin-Watson test is rejected,
the test statistic is shaded in grey.

Excess return	MV	minCVaR	minCDaR	Naive
α	-0.0012429	-0.0013457	-0.0004744	-0.0025681***
β_{MKT}	0.8421940***	0.8523391***	0.9036424***	1.0878730***
R^2	0.8348	0.8416	0.8365	0.9652
DW	1.4782	1.511	1.87	2.0386

Table 6.88: CAPM Regression Results for the Risk Budgeting Portfolios
- US MSCI
Signification codes: ***: ≤ 0.01, **: ≤ 0.05, *: ≤ 0.1
If the null hypothesis of the Durbin-Watson test is rejected,
the test statistic is shaded in grey.

Excess return	sampleCVaR	normCVaR	modCVaR	sampleCOV	sampleCDaR
α	-0.0020365***	-0.0020137***	-0.0021860***	-0.0020529***	-0.0009518
β_{MKT}	1.0301549***	1.0265774***	1.0355735***	1.0268294***	1.0169402***
R^2	0.96	0.9591	0.9623	0.9593	0.9389
DW	1.8096	1.7597	1.8052	1.7562	1.8785

portfolios concerning the R^2 are very small. However, the risk budgeting portfolios load more on the value factor and less on the SMB
factor compared to the naive portfolio. The SMB factor is positive
in this dataset. All the approaches have a market beta of approx.
1, except the minimum risk approaches, where it is slightly lower at
ca. 0.9. The two additional Fama-French factors add 6% and 5% to
the explanation power of the MV and the minCVaR excess portfolio
return regression. But for the naive and the ERC portfolios, the
inclusion accounts only for ca. 2% more.

Table 6.89: Fama-French Regression Results for the Minimum Risk Portfolios - US MSCI
Signification codes: ***: ≤ 0.01, **: ≤ 0.05, *: ≤ 0.1
If the null hypothesis of the Durbin-Watson test is rejected, the test statistic is shaded in grey.

Excess return	MV	minCVaR	minCDaR	Naive
α	-0.0025272*	-0.0025556*	-0.0011375	-0.0030771***
β_{MKT}	0.8778661***	0.8860072***	0.8764459***	1.0588364***
β_{SMB}	0.1026619***	0.0964792**	0.2263232***	0.2047299***
β_{HML}	0.3168939***	0.2986296***	0.0965609*	0.0621208***
R^2	0.8877	0.8879	0.8628	0.9822
DW	1.4626	1.4923	1.8404	2.0051

Table 6.90: Fama-French Regression Results for the Risk Budgeting Portfolios - US MSCI
Signification codes: ***: ≤ 0.01, **: ≤ 0.05, *: ≤ 0.1
If the null hypothesis of the Durbin-Watson test is rejected, the test statistic is shaded in grey.

Excess return	sampleCVaR	normCVaR	modCVaR	sampleCOV	sampleCDaR
α	-0.0028773***	-0.0028818***	-0.0029817***	-0.0029199***	-0.0018670**
β_{MKT}	1.0277968***	1.0255905***	1.0321918***	1.0271024***	1.0041352***
β_{SMB}	0.1649146***	0.1647714***	0.1604487***	0.1597885***	0.2183986***
β_{HML}	0.1696759***	0.1773161***	0.1588946***	0.1789512***	0.1696279***
R^2	0.9782	0.9782	0.9787	0.978	0.9646
DW	1.8966	1.8281	1.8907	1.8318	1.9292

6.3.7 German Industry Indices

Like for the US market, a dataset of value-weighted sector indices is examined for the German market. Contrary to the US market, there are only 16 sector indices with a long enough history available. The dataset runs also from 01.1973 - 09.2012. As the Germany 1973 datasets, the German regressions will be examined with the Fama-French factors constructed by Artmann et al. (2012) as well as by Hanauer et al. (2013).

Artmann Factors

At first, tables 6.91 and 6.92 present the CAPM regression results for the German industry sector indices dataset. The alphas are negative and significant, except for the minimum risk portfolios. The coefficients of determination are high for the naive and the ERC portfolios and show also in the German dataset a high similarity. The market factor accounts for ca. 40% of the explanation of the minimum risk portfolio excess returns and 83% and ca. 75% of the naive and the ERC portfolios.

Table 6.91: CAPM Regression Results for the Minimum Risk Portfolios - German Industry (Artmann et al., 2012)
Signification codes: ***: ≤ 0.01, **: ≤ 0.05, *: ≤ 0.1
If the null hypothesis of the Durbin-Watson test is rejected, the test statistic is shaded in grey.

Excess return	MV	minCVaR	minCDaR	Naive
α	-0.0005073	-0.0003238	0.0006718	-0.0030138***
β_{MKT}	0.3906578***	0.3831162***	0.3654156***	0.7710990***
R^2	0.447	0.4202	0.3634	0.8311
DW	1.909	1.949	2.0127	1.9139

Table 6.92: CAPM Regression Results for the Risk Budgeting Portfolios - German Industry (Artmann et al., 2012)
Signification codes: ***: ≤ 0.01, **: ≤ 0.05, *: ≤ 0.1
If the null hypothesis of the Durbin-Watson test is rejected, the test statistic is shaded in grey.

Excess return	sampleCVaR	normCVaR	modCVaR	sampleCOV	sampleCDaR
α	-0.0022724**	-0.0022285**	-0.0024746**	-0.0023455**	-0.0016860*
β_{MKT}	0.6336616***	0.6386410***	0.6612717***	0.6417338***	0.6389596***
R^2	0.749	0.7513	0.7345	0.752	0.7557
DW	1.8845	1.8874	1.8954	1.8836	1.995

The tables 6.93 and 6.94 show the results of the Fama-French factor regressions for the portfolios build on the German sector indices of Datastream. Again, the alphas are negative and significant, except for the minimum risk portfolios. All the factors are highly significant in explaining the portfolio returns. The explanation power is ca. 50% for the MV and the minCVaR portfolios, whereas the minCDaR displays the lowest explanation with 41%. The returns of the naive and the ERC portfolios are explained by ca. 80%. This is mainly due to the lower market beta of the minimum risk approaches, thus, similar to the literature the low beta anomaly can be observed. Compared to the CAPM regressions, the explanatory power is increased by ca. 7% for the minimum risk portfolios and by ca. 4% for the ERC portfolios.

Table 6.93: Fama-French Regression Results for the Minimum Risk Portfolios - German Industry (Artmann et al., 2012)
Signification codes: ***: ≤ 0.01, **: ≤ 0.05, *: ≤ 0.1
If the null hypothesis of the Durbin-Watson test is rejected, the test statistic is shaded in grey.

Excess return	MV	minCVaR	minCDaR	Naive
α	-0.0009703	-0.0008156	0.0001750	-0.0036529***
β_{MKT}	0.4645352***	0.4562653***	0.4269970***	0.8337014***
β_{SMB}	0.2457182***	0.2437703***	0.2063944***	0.2117191***
β_{HML}	0.1462975***	0.1502235***	0.1397488***	0.1636000***
R^2	0.5173	0.4893	0.4135	0.8612
DW	1.9132	1.9443	2.0301	2.0117

Table 6.94: Fama-French Regression Results for the Risk Budgeting Portfolios - German Industry (Artmann et al., 2012)
Signification codes: ***: ≤ 0.01, **: ≤ 0.05, *: ≤ 0.1
If the null hypothesis of the Durbin-Watson test is rejected, the test statistic is shaded in grey.

Excess return	sampleCVaR	normCVaR	modCVaR	sampleCOV	sampleCDaR
α	-0.0028868***	-0.0028142***	-0.0030944***	-0.0029267***	-0.0023313**
β_{MKT}	0.7023595***	0.7067159***	0.7336352***	0.7103035***	0.6930968***
β_{SMB}	0.2311005***	0.2286765***	0.2430435***	0.2302144***	0.1844045***
β_{HML}	0.1655731***	0.1603536***	0.1700135***	0.1601154***	0.1563546***
R^2	0.794	0.7941	0.7785	0.7947	0.7886
DW	1.9511	1.9489	1.951	1.9449	2.0589

Hanauer Factors

The tables 6.95 and 6.96 show the results of the Fama-French factors of Hanauer et al. (2013) for the German industry indices in the period from 08.1996 - 01.2012. Again, the factors have a lower explanatory power than in the regressions with the Artmann et al. (2012) factors. However, all factors are highly significant and all portfolios display negative alphas, except the MV and the minCDaR portfolio. However, the positive alphas are not significant. As the explanatory power of the factors is the lowest for the minimum risk portfolios, the positive alpha results through missing factors in the regressions. Again, the minimum risk approaches have the lowest market β with ca. 0.30. The naive portfolio displays a market beta of 0.72 and the ERC portfolios lie in between with a market beta of ca. 0.55. The size factor has in these regression higher values than in the regressions with the other factors and thus the portfolios have a higher exposure to the SMB factor in this period.

Table 6.95: Fama-French Regression Results for the Minimum Risk Portfolios - German Industry (Hanauer et al., 2013)
Signification codes: ***: ≤ 0.01, **: ≤ 0.05, *: ≤ 0.1
If the null hypothesis of the Durbin-Watson test is rejected, the test statistic is shaded in grey.

Excess return	MV	minCVaR	minCDaR	Naive
α	0.0003391	-0.0000222	0.0024346	-0.0032719*
β_{MKT}	0.3066283***	0.2910619***	0.2923646***	0.7275946***
β_{SMB}	0.2682460***	0.2566911***	0.1920829***	0.3197606***
β_{HML}	0.2073622***	0.2032588***	0.1272362**	0.3136995***
R^2	0.3809	0.34	0.2795	0.723
DW	1.7577	1.7735	1.9082	2.0023

Table 6.96: Fama-French Regression Results for the Risk Budgeting
Portfolios - German Industry (Hanauer et al., 2013)
Signification codes: ***: ≤ 0.01, **: ≤ 0.05, *: ≤ 0.1
If the null hypothesis of the Durbin-Watson test is rejected,
the test statistic is shaded in grey.

Excess return	sampleCVaR	normCVaR	modCVaR	sampleCOV	sampleCDaR
α	-0.0021850	-0.0020150	-0.0022363	-0.0021219	-0.0011937
β_{MKT}	0.5469765***	0.5471155***	0.5805560***	0.5518754***	0.5459271***
β_{SMB}	0.3045601***	0.2971879***	0.2987057***	0.3008483***	0.2503969***
β_{HML}	0.2655695***	0.2536441***	0.2682840***	0.2572876***	0.2193514***
R^2	0.6432	0.6395	0.6316	0.6426	0.6301
DW	1.8289	1.8064	1.8289	1.8043	1.9223

6.3.8 German MSCI

The German MSCI dataset consists as above for the US market of
eight MSCI style indices. It runs also from 05.1994 - 06.2013. But
the German factors of Artmann et al. (2012) are only available until
12.2010and the factors of Hanauer et al. (2013) until 01.2012.

The tables 6.97 and 6.98 show the exposures as well as the explanation power of the market factor for the German MSCI dataset.
The alphas are also negative and significant, except for the minimum
risk portfolios. As in the US MSCI dataset, all portfolios exhibit
a high exposure to the market factor and the explanation power is
high. The minimum risk approaches, and especially the minCDaR
portfolio, display again the lowest R^2. As visible from tables 6.99
and 6.100, the Fama-French regressions for the German style indices
show also a high explanation power for all portfolio returns with
the highest explanations for the naive and the ERC portfolios. The
Fama-French factors provide a higher explanation of 5% for the MV
and the minCVaR portfolio and 3% for the minCDaR portfolio. For
the naive portfolio and the ERC portfolios the increase is only max.
2%. In this dataset, the HML factor is not highly significant and some
portfolios show an insignificant exposure to the value factor. The
minimum risk approaches load more on the size factor than the risk

budgeting portfolios. The alphas are also in this dataset negative and significant, except for the minimum risk approaches.

Table 6.97: CAPM Regression Results for the Minimum Risk Portfolios - German MSCI (Artmann et al., 2012)
Signification codes: ***: ≤ 0.01, **: ≤ 0.05, *: ≤ 0.1
If the null hypothesis of the Durbin-Watson test is rejected, the test statistic is shaded in grey.

Excess return	MV	minCVaR	minCDaR	Naive
α	-0.0011270	-0.0010021	-0.0017424	-0.0060505***
β_{MKT}	0.7244590***	0.7288375***	0.6819021***	1.0295511***
R^2	0.7225	0.7296	0.6744	0.9223
DW	1.9144	1.9755	2.1352	1.9773

Table 6.98: CAPM Regression Results for the Risk Budgeting Portfolios - German MSCI (Artmann et al., 2012)
Signification codes: ***: ≤ 0.01, **: ≤ 0.05, *: ≤ 0.1
If the null hypothesis of the Durbin-Watson test is rejected, the test statistic is shaded in grey.

Excess return	sampleCVaR	normCVaR	modCVaR	sampleCOV	sampleCDaR
α	-0.0049767***	-0.0050034***	-0.0049922***	-0.0050653***	-0.0041940***
β_{MKT}	0.9396132***	0.9373855***	0.9486476***	0.9384984***	0.9524378***
R^2	0.9024	0.899	0.9055	0.8992	0.918
DW	1.9377	1.9381	1.9826	1.9387	1.8856

Hanauer Factors

The regressions with the Hanauer et al. (2013) factors show a similar picture. The explanation power of the factors is very large and the portfolios display negative alphas. After the market return, the size factor has the highest influence on the portfolio returns. In this period, the value factor is also highly significant and the portfolios display positive exposures to this factor. The minimum risk approaches exhibit higher exposures to the size as well as to the value factor.

Table 6.99: Fama-French Regression Results for the Minimum Risk Portfolios - German MSCI (Artmann et al., 2012)
Signification codes: ***: ≤ 0.01, **: ≤ 0.05, *: ≤ 0.1
If the null hypothesis of the Durbin-Watson test is rejected,
the test statistic is shaded in grey.

Excess return	MV	minCVaR	minCDaR	Naive
α	-0.0003821	-0.0003622	-0.0016994	-0.0050421***
β_{MKT}	0.8227460***	0.8207154***	0.7408415***	1.0794001***
β_{SMB}	0.3236754***	0.3016708***	0.1876705***	0.1742016***
β_{HML}	0.0995198*	0.0990702*	0.1028925*	-0.0170450
R^2	0.7796	0.7797	0.6987	0.9324
DW	2.1819	2.2681	2.3335	2.0459

Table 6.100: Fama-French Regression Results for the Risk Budgeting
Portfolios - German MSCI (Artmann et al., 2012)
Signification codes: ***: ≤ 0.01, **: ≤ 0.05, *: ≤ 0.1
If the null hypothesis of the Durbin-Watson test is rejected,
the test statistic is shaded in grey.

Excess return	sampleCVaR	normCVaR	modCVaR	sampleCOV	sampleCDaR
α	-0.0042931***	-0.0043102***	-0.0042344***	-0.0043672***	-0.0037600**
β_{MKT}	1.0101898***	1.0112464***	1.0180410***	1.0125297***	1.0117223***
β_{SMB}	0.2347873***	0.2453600***	0.2322169***	0.2459790***	0.1949903***
β_{HML}	0.0555465*	0.0605059*	0.0454298	0.0602897*	0.0616636*
R^2	0.9239	0.9226	0.926	0.9228	0.9333
DW	2.1151	2.1182	2.1495	2.1197	2.0233

Table 6.101: Fama-French Regression Results for the Minimum Risk
Portfolios - German MSCI(Hanauer et al., 2013)
Signification codes: ***: ≤ 0.01, **: ≤ 0.05, *: ≤ 0.1
If the null hypothesis of the Durbin-Watson test is rejected,
the test statistic is shaded in grey.

Excess return	MV	minCVaR	minCDaR	Naive
α	-0.0014061	-0.0012693	-0.0022425	-0.0055068***
β_{MKT}	0.8753271***	0.8820709***	0.8375408***	1.1107443***
β_{SMB}	0.4868978***	0.4767988***	0.4176372***	0.3956951***
β_{HML}	0.3821528***	0.3835704***	0.3023226***	0.2176439***
R^2	0.7832	0.7915	0.731	0.8556
DW	2.157	2.193	2.1612	2.3517

Table 6.102: Fama-French Regression Results for the Risk Budgeting
Portfolios - German MSCI (Hanauer et al., 2013)
Signification codes: ***: ≤ 0.01, **: ≤ 0.05, *: ≤ 0.1
If the null hypothesis of the Durbin-Watson test is rejected,
the test statistic is shaded in grey.

Excess return	sampleCVaR	normCVaR	modCVaR	sampleCOV	sampleCDaR
α	-0.0047156***	-0.0047333***	-0.0047130***	-0.0047739***	-0.0042420**
β_{MKT}	1.0438653***	1.0424558***	1.0499595***	1.0431766***	1.0395448***
β_{SMB}	0.4408559***	0.4485774***	0.4324086***	0.4482605***	0.4084053***
β_{HML}	0.2956643***	0.3008465***	0.2881781***	0.3003324***	0.2927035***
R^2	0.8614	0.8578	0.8617	0.8574	0.8594
DW	2.2917	2.2615	2.3227	2.264	2.2777

6.3.9 Four-Factor Model

Additionally to the Fama-French three-factor model, the four factor model of Carhart (1997) was also applied for all datasets. The results can be found in the Appendix A.2. The momentum factor has no additional explanation power for all the portfolios in the global dataset and is insignificant, except for the strategies based on the CDaR: the minCDaR and the sampleCDaR portfolio. Surprisingly, the momentum factor is highly significant and increases the explanation of the factors. Thus, the CDaR approaches pick implicitly this pricing anomaly. However, the explanation is increased by 5% for the minCDaR and by 3% for the sampleCDaR portfolio. Especially for the minCDaR portfolio the exposures to the factors in total is still very low. For the Germany 1973 dataset, the factor is admittely significant for the most of the portfolios. The momentum factor does not add to the explanatory power of the other factors considering the risk based strategies. In the US Industry dataset, again only the minCDaR portfolio displays a significant increase of 5% of the explanation power due to the momentum factor. In all the other portfolios, the momentum factor does not considerable increase the determinant of coefficient. In the US MSCI, the German Industry as well as the German MSCI datasets, the momentum does not have a high additional explanation power. In the US MSCI it is 1% for the minCDaR portfolio, in the German Industry dataset it is 1% for the MV portfolio and ca. 2% for the minCVaR and minCDaR portfolio and in the German MSCI dataset it increases the R^2 by ca. 1% for the MV and the minCVaR portfolio. Generally, the momentum factor displays more significance in all German datasets, as the risk budgeting show also a significant exposure. But the increase in the explanation power can be disregarded. That the momentum factor does not significantly increase the explanatory power of the ERC portfolio is also the result in Carvalho et al. (2012) and for the MV portfolio in Clarke et al. (2006).

6.3.10 Summary of the Factor Regressions

The factor analyses have shown that the ERC portfolios do not show a risk adjusted outperformance, as the alphas in all datasets are negative and highly significant. All risk budgeting portfolios display high exposures to all three factors. Whereas the minimum risk portfolios have the lowest explanations of the returns, the naive portfolio return displays a high coefficient of determination. The ERC portfolios display also a high R^2 and the similarity to the naive portfolio is obvious. Moreover, as observed through separate regressions, the main part of the exposures of the ERC portfolios as well as the naive portfolio is due to the market factor. The two additional factors, size and value, account in most regressions only for additional 2% (except in the German Industry dataset for additional 4%). The size and the value factors add the most to the explanation of the MV and the minCVaR portfolio returns (up to 9%). This leads to the conclusion that the performances of the ERC portfolios can simple be explained through exposures to the market performance and thus by a shift of the beta. The minimum risk approaches, and especially the minCDaR portfolio, seem to build on additional risk factors. In this regard, it would be interesting to study the influence of other known factors in the asset pricing literature, like exposures to beta, volatility, idiosyncratic volatility, liquidity or dividend yield (see Amenc et al. (2012), Subrahmanyam (2010)). Moreover, it is observed that the minimum risk approaches have the lowest market beta and thus the results are conform with the suggestions in the literature that the 'low volatility anomaly' is driven by exposures to 'low beta' stocks (see chapter 4.1.1).

Concerning the risk budgeting portfolios, Carvalho et al. (2012) state that the portfolios are exposed to five factors: the three Fama-French factors, a low beta factor as well as an unsystematic risk factor. However, as examined by the regressions, the $\alpha's$ are even for the three Fama-French factors negative and the highest explanatory power provides the market return. By adding two additional factors, the outperformance of the ERC portfolios can only get worse. A difficulty consists in the matter of fact that the factors are all constructed for equities. However, as examined by the performance studies in chapter 6.2, the ERC portfolios are not suited for individual equities, but more for the diversification across different asset classes. In a further research it would be interesting to construct factors to explain the portfolio returns in case of a diversificated asset class portfolio. However, as the results indicate the ERC portfolios do not display a significant outperformance and thus are more a 'promotion campaign' of the asset pricing industry than a new innovative asset allocation approach. To put it in the words of Carvalho et al. (2012), they are nothing more than 'a *simple alpha plus beta description*'.

6.4 Robustness Study

As outlined above, the robustness of the ERC portfolio based on the volatility, the MV and the naive portfolio is already studied in an earlier work, see Poddig and Unger (2012). In this section, the study is repeated and exactly the same methodology is used, as the setting is well suited to study the robustness of the approaches. However, this study encompasses more portfolios, minimum risk and the risk budgeting portfolios, which are based on different risk measures. Moreover, the simulation is expanded. Thus, it is going to be explored if the use of the risk measure influences the estimation errors of the portfolios. Whereas in Poddig and Unger (2012) it was enough to determine true asset means and the covariance matrix for obtaining the portfolios, here, additionally a 'true dataset' has to be given. This is necessary to obtain the true asset weights for the minCVaR, minCDaR, sampleCDaR and sampleCVaR portfolios, as they rely on a sample of returns and not simply on input parameters. Because of this reason, the resampling in each simulation run consists of drawing 250 points instead of 60 as in Poddig and Unger (2012), to have enough points to estimate the weights of the mentioned portfolios.

The effect of the estimation errors on the portfolio allocations is compared by calculating different performance measures. First, the portfolios are studied in a simulation approach with unrealistic simple true parameters of the assets (constant true returns as well as constant true correlations). This is done to examine in a first step the pure effect of the estimation errors on the portfolio allocations. Next, a simulation with realistic parameters is done and then, the portfolio approaches are examined on the Global portfolio dataset to observe the real outcomes.

6.4.1 Methodology

The main idea of the robustness study follows Broadie (1993) and Brinkmann (2007). It is distinguished between a true portfolio, where the true input parameters are given, the estimated portfolio, where the portfolio is optimized by using estimated input parameters and the actual portfolio, which results through multiplying the estimated weights with the true mean returns. The true and actual portfolio means and portfolio volatilities are calculated as follows:

$$\mu_{estimated} = \boldsymbol{w}'_{estimated}\hat{\boldsymbol{r}}_{estimated} \tag{6.31}$$

$$\mu_{actual} = \boldsymbol{w}'_{estimated}\boldsymbol{r}_{true} \tag{6.32}$$

$$\sigma_{estimated} = \boldsymbol{w}'_{estimated}V_{estimated}\boldsymbol{w}_{estimated} \tag{6.33}$$

$$\sigma_{actual} = \boldsymbol{w}'_{estimated}V_{true}\boldsymbol{w}_{estimated} \tag{6.34}$$

with

$$\hat{\boldsymbol{r}}_{estimated} : \text{vector of estimated asset means}$$

$$\boldsymbol{r}_{true} : \text{vector of true asset means}$$

$$\boldsymbol{V}_{true} : \text{true covariance matrix}$$

$$\boldsymbol{V}_{estimated} : \text{estimated covariance matrix}$$

The sensitivity of the asset weights to changes in input parameters are examined by computing the minimum, the maximum, and the standard deviation of each portfolio estimated asset weight across the simulation runs.

The (unnormalized) Euclidean distance of the weight vectors for each simulation run is calculated to examine the distance of the estimated portfolio asset weights to the true portfolio asset weights. The standard deviation of the weight distances serves for the measurement of the robustness of the portfolio weights. The index k represents either a simulation run in the simulation study or the month of the optimization in the empirical study. These measures are given by

$$Mean \quad Distance(MD_w) =$$

$$\frac{1}{NumSim} \sum_{k=1}^{NumSim} \sqrt{(\boldsymbol{w}_{estimated}(k) - \boldsymbol{w}_{true})'(\boldsymbol{w}_{estimated}(k) - \boldsymbol{w}_{true})}$$

$$(6.35)$$

$$Standard \quad Deviation(SD_w) =$$

$$\sqrt{\frac{1}{NumSim} \sum_{k=1}^{NumSim} (d_k - MD_w)^2}, \qquad (6.36)$$

with

$$d_k : \text{distance in period } k$$
$$\boldsymbol{w}_{estimated} : \text{vector of estimated weights}$$
$$\boldsymbol{w}_{true} : \text{vector of true weights}$$

The differences between the estimated portfolio return and volatility and the actual portfolio return and volatility are measured by the the average differences of the μ- and σ-values between the estimated and the actual portfolios. They are calculated by

$$AV\mu = \frac{1}{NumSim} \sum_{k=1}^{NumSim} (\mu_{estimated}(k) - \mu_{actual}(k)) \qquad (6.37)$$

$$AV\sigma = \frac{1}{NumSim} \sum_{k=1}^{NumSim} (\sigma_{estimated}(k) - \sigma_{actual}(k)). \qquad (6.38)$$

Generally the $AV\mu$ is positive whereas the $AV\sigma$ is negative as the mean is overestimated and the risk underestimated. Moreover, different performance measures are compared: the Sharpe ratio, the turnover, the Herfindahl index for the weights and the risk contributions, as well as the Value at Risk (VaR) and the maximum drawdown (MaxDD).The Sharpe Ratio and the Herfindahl indices are given by

$$SharpeRatio = \frac{1}{NumSim} \sum_{k=1}^{NumSim} \frac{\mu_{actual}(k)}{\sigma_{actual}(k)} \qquad (6.39)$$

$$h_k = \sum_{i=1}^{n} w^2_{estimated,k,i} \;\; or \;\; h_k = \sum_{i=1}^{n} CR^2_{actual,k,i}, \qquad (6.40)$$

with

$w_{estimated,k,i}$: estimated weight in run k for asset i

$CR_{actual,k,i}$: actual percental risk contribution
in run k for asset i: $CR_i = \frac{ARC_i}{\sigma_{actual}}$
and $\sum_{i=1}^{n} CR = 1$

This index takes the value 1 for a portfolio invested in only one asset and $1/n$ for a portfolio with equal weights. To scale the statistics onto [0,1], the modified Herfindahl index is observed (Maillard et al. (2010), p. 22):

$$Herfindahl_{w \; or \; rc} = \frac{1}{NumSim} \frac{h_k - 1/n}{1 - 1/n}. \qquad (6.41)$$

Moreover, the turnover, the VaR and the MaxDD of the portfolios are obtained on actual parameters. Different to the performance studies, the turnover is simply calculated on the estimated weights and does not account for shifts in asset prices. Thus, per definition the naive portfolio has a turnover of 0%. The turnover is calculated as follows (Maillard et al., 2010, p. 70):

$$mean\,Turnover = \frac{1}{T}\sum_{t=1}^{T}\sum_{i=1}^{N}|w_{(i)t+1} - w_{(i)t}| \qquad (6.42)$$

with

$$T : \text{number of rebalances}$$
$$w_{(i)t} : \text{estimated weight of asset } i \text{ in period } t$$
$$N : \text{number of assets}$$

6.4.2 Simulation Study

Structure Robustness

The effect of the estimation errors on the different portfolio approaches is studied in a simulation study similar to Michaud (1998) and Broadie (1993). At first, true mean returns and a true variance-covariance matrix are defined, then returns are simulated which are statistically equal to the true returns and the resulting portfolio weights are estimated for every simulation run. After the simulation, the estimation errors of the portfolios are compared.

The simulation study involves the following steps.

1) The following parameters are defined:

• n - the number of securities,

• r_{true} - the vector of true mean asset returns, i.e., $r_{true} = (\mu_1, ..., \mu_n)$,

- σ - the vector of true standard deviations of returns, i.e., $\sigma = (\sigma_1, ..., \sigma_n)$,

- ρ - the matrix of true correlations of returns of the securities, i.e., ρ_{ij} is the true correlation of returns of securities j and i, for $j, i = 1, ..., n$,

- the true dataset (draw from a multivariate normal distribution with 10.000 draws with the true mean vector and covariance) for the portfolio, which need a sample as input.

2) The true portfolio compositions $w = (w_1, ..., w_n)$ from the inputs of 1) are computed. The true variance-covariance matrix $\Sigma = \sigma^T \rho \sigma$ is also obtained.

3) 250 draws (1 year of daily returns) from a multivariate normal distribution $\Phi(\mu, \Sigma)$ are taken by resampling from the inputs of 1) and new input parameters $\hat{\mu}$ and $\hat{\Sigma}$ are estimated.

4) Step 3) is repeated $NumSim$ times and the estimated parameters are saved.

5) The estimated portfolio compositions $\hat{w} = ((\hat{w}_1), ..., (\hat{w}_n))$ with the estimators $\hat{\mu}$ and $\hat{\Sigma}$ or the dataset (250 returns) from step 4) are computed. This gives $NumSim$ different portfolio optimizations and parameters.

6) The estimation errors of the approaches are compared with the presented performance measures.

To compare the estimation errors, the portfolios need to have the same data sample as inputs. Therefore, the samples are drawn and the estimated parameters as well as the samples are saved, as the approaches of the minCVaR, minCDaR, sampleCVaR and sampleCDaR budgets need a scenario of returns as input. After this, the portfolio optimization for the different approaches is performed.

Unrealistic Simulation
The first simulation consists of a simple setting with

- 10 assets with

- multivariate normal distributed returns,

- each asset with a return of 1% and a standard deviation of 8%,

- a correlation of 0,5 among all assets, and

- $NumSim = 10.000$.

The naive portfolio is the true asset allocation according to the predetermined dataset. Thus, the results of the naive allocation are not really comparable. Table 6.103 and 6.104 show the minimum and the maximum of the weights across the 10.000 runs for each asset of the minimum risk (MV, minCVaR, minCDaR) portfolios and of the risk contribution portfolios.

As table 6.103 unveils, the minimum risk portfolios have all high spreads between the minimum and the maximum asset weights. Whereas the MV portfolio has at least an average spread of 35%, the minCVaR and the minCDaR portfolios record a spread of the weights of 59% and 98%. All the minimum risk portfolios take zero weights as minimum positions across the simulation. The minCDaR portfolio takes the largest possible position in almost each asset. This is an indication of the concentration of the asset allocation on a few assets.

As it is obvious from Table 6.104, the risk budgeting portfolios display an opposite picture compared to the minimum risk portfolios. None of the risk contribution approaches allocates an asset weight of 0%, the minimum asset weight is 4% from the sampleCDaR budget portfolio. The spreads are all much lower than the minimum risk portfolios, in the range of 10% - 27%, with the largest spread from the

Table 6.103: Minimum and Maximum Portfolio Weights for the Minimum Risk Portfolios in the Simulation (%)
These are the minimum and maximum estimated portfolio weights across 10.000 simulation runs per asset.

Asset	weights	MV	minCVaR	minCDaR
Asset 1	max	33	59	100
	min	0	0	0
Asset 2	max	35	64	100
	min	0	0	0
Asset 3	max	37	56	100
	min	0	0	0
Asset 4	max	35	59	100
	min	0	0	0
Asset 5	max	34	62	100
	min	0	0	0
Asset 6	max	35	63	89
	min	0	0	0
Asset 7	max	35	61	91
	min	0	0	0
Asset 8	max	37	57	100
	min	0	0	0
Asset 9	max	33	55	100
	min	0	0	0
Asset 10	max	37	58	100
	min	0	0	0
Average	max	35	59	98
	min	0	0	0

sampleCDaR and the smallest from the normCVaR and the sample-COV portfolios. Thus, the portfolios based on the CDaR risk measure seem to be the most concentrated.

Moreover, the sampleCVaR and the modCVaR portfolio provide a similar picture among each other of the estimated weights, as well as the normCVaR and the sampleCOV portfolios between themselves, which is not surprising in this normal-distributed dataset. The naive weights do not change by construction, as the naive portfolio is always

Table 6.104: Minimum and Maximum Portfolio Weights for the Risk
Budgeting Portfolios in the Simulation (%)
These are calculated as the minimum and maximum estimated portfolio weights across 10.000 simulation runs per
asset.

Asset	weights	sampleCVaR	sampleCDaR	normCVaR	modCVaR	sampleCOV	Naive
Asset 1	max	17	29	13	17	13	10
	min	7	4	8	6	8	10
Asset 2	max	16	33	13	15	13	10
	min	7	4	8	7	8	10
Asset 3	max	16	32	13	15	13	10
	min	7	4	8	7	8	10
Asset 4	max	16	38	13	17	12	10
	min	7	4	8	7	8	10
Asset 5	max	16	30	13	17	12	10
	min	6	4	8	7	8	10
Asset 6	max	17	30	13	15	12	10
	min	7	4	8	7	8	10
Asset 7	max	16	32	13	16	13	10
	min	7	5	8	6	8	10
Asset 8	max	18	29	14	16	13	10
	min	7	4	8	6	8	10
Asset 9	max	17	32	13	16	13	10
	min	6	4	8	7	8	10
Asset 10	max	17	28	13	16	12	10
	min	7	4	8	5	8	10
Average	max	17	31	13	16	13	10
	min	7	4	8	6	8	10

equally invested in all assets. The maximum weights of the risk budgeting portfolios range between 12% and 32%, with the sampleCDaR
providing the highest maximum weights and the normCVaR and
sampleCOV providing the lowest maximum weights. However, all the
risk budgeting models invest always in all available assets and are
thus more diversified than the minimum risk portfolios.

To assess the stability of the asset weights across the 10.000 portfolio formations, the standard deviation of the asset weights is observed.
This value is indicative of the redeployment of the portfolio. The
higher the variation of the asset weights, the higher the investors
transaction costs. Thus, this is an important indicator of structure

Table 6.105: Standard Deviations of Minimum Risk Portfolio Weights
These are the standard deviations of the estimated weights
across 10.000 simulation runs for each asset.

	A1	A2	A3	A4	A5	A6	A7	A8	A9	A10
MV	6.09	6.11	6.07	5.99	5.99	6.11	5.99	6.02	6.05	6.07
minCVaR	10.04	10.23	10.13	10.14	10.24	10.16	10.10	10.11	10.13	10.17
minCDaR	13.84	14.43	14.06	14.27	14.14	14.39	14.15	14.04	14.45	14.42

Table 6.106: Standard Deviations of Risk Budgeting Portfolio Weights
These are the standard deviations of the estimated weights
across 10.000 simulation runs for each assets.

	A1	A2	A3	A4	A5	A6	A7	A8	A9	A10
sampleCVaR	1.17	1.19	1.17	1.18	1.18	1.17	1.17	1.15	1.18	1.17
sampleCDaR	2.76	2.88	2.83	2.87	2.84	2.88	2.87	2.84	2.90	2.88
normCVaR	0.64	0.65	0.64	0.64	0.63	0.64	0.64	0.64	0.64	0.64
modCVaR	0.98	0.99	0.98	0.99	0.99	0.99	1.00	0.97	0.99	0.98
sampleCOV	0.54	0.54	0.53	0.53	0.52	0.53	0.52	0.53	0.53	0.53
Naive	0.00	0.00	0.00	0.00	0.00	0.00	0.00	0.00	0.00	0.00

robustness. Table 6.105 and 6.106 show the standard deviations of
the weights across 10.000 simulation runs per asset.

Contrary to the observed spread of the portfolio weights, the MV
and the minCVaR portfolio have lower standard deviations of the
portfolio weights as the sampleCVaR budgeting portfolio. Beside the
sampleCVaR budgeting portfolio, the variability of the weights of the
risk budgeting approaches are much lower than the minimum risk
portfolios. The lowest standard deviations are displayed from the mod-
CVaR and the sampleCOV portfolio. Surprisingly, the sampleCDaR
budget portfolio has small standard deviations of the weights compared to the weights spread. However, the weights spread can result
through outliers in the simulation. The minCDaR portfolio denotes
an average standard deviation of 14%. Although the spreads of the
normCVaR and the sampleCOV portfolio are similar, the average
standard deviation of the normCVaR portfolio is much higher with
6,4% compared to the 0,5% of the sample COV portfolio.

Table 6.107 displays the performance measures for comparison of portfolio robustness as well as performance statistics for the minimum risk portfolios. In this special setting, the estimation error $(AV\mu)$ of the return should be near 0%, but the minCVaR as well as the minCDaR portfolio overestimate the return with 0.081% and 0.180%. The portfolio standard deviation is underestimated the most from the MV portfolio with 0.205% and the minCVaR portfolio with 0.0149%, whereas the minCDaR portfolio displays the lowest value with 0.1%. However, the minCDaR portfolio has a higher standard deviation than the other approaches. As suspected from the spread and the standard deviations of the weights, the minCDaR portfolio is the most concentrated in terms of weights $(Herfindahl_w$ of 22.5%) as well as in terms of risk $(Herfindahl_{rc}$ of 25%), which is correlated in this setting. The concentration is also obvious from the turnover, which is the highest from the minCDaR portfolio with ca. 70%. The MV portfolio is the most diversified of the minimum risk portfolios due to the Herfindahl indices and has the highest Sharpe ratio. The distance measures $(MD_w$ and $SD_w)$ show that the estimated weights of the minCDaR portfolio are the farthest from the true weights.

Table 6.108 summarizes the results for the risk budgeting portfolios. The estimation error $(AV\mu)$ of the returns is near 0% for all approaches, which is not surprising in this special setting, except the sampleCVaR budget portfolio, which overestimates the return of about 0.014%. The difference between the estimated and the actual risk $(AV\sigma)$ is only 0.004% for all approaches, except for the sampleCVaR budget portfolio, which underestimates the standard deviation by about 0.02%. The standard deviations of the risk budgeting approaches are similar and lie by about 5.9%. This is lower than the actual standard deviations of the minimum risk portfolios with values of 6%, 6.2% and 6.4%. This is surprising for the MV portfolio, as it is constructed to minimize the standard deviation. The volatility is the lowest in the estimation period, but due to the estimation error not any more in the 'true' period.

Table 6.107: Performance Statistics for the Simulation - Minimum Risk
Portfolios
The statistics are all given as means across 10.000 portfolio
optimizations and are based on the actual parameters. For
better comparison they are all shown in percent.

	MV	minCVaR	minCDaR
μ estimated	1.005%	1.081%	1.180%
μ actual	1.000%	1.000%	1.000%
σ estimated	5.826%	6.054%	6.351%
σ actual	6.031%	6.203%	6.450%
MD_w	18.719%	31.490%	43.664%
SD_w	3.955%	6.129%	10.782%
AV μ	0.005%	0.081%	0.180%
AV σ	-0.205%	-0.149%	-0.100%
Sharpe Ratio	16.582%	16.124%	15.525%
$Herfindahl_w$	4.067%	11.435%	22.476%
$Herfindahl_{rc}$	4.622%	12.919%	25.373%
Turnover	34.364%	55.254%	69.309%
VaR	10.920%	11.204%	11.610%
MaxDD	0.000%	0.000%	0.000%

The distance measures (MD_w and SD_w) show that the sampleCDaR
budget portfolio has the highest deviation from the true portfolio
weights with 8.5%, followed by the sampleCVaR and the modCVaR
portfolio with 3.5% and 3%. The sampleCOV portfolio shows the
smallest distance on average and the smallest standard deviation of
the distances (except for the naive portfolio, by construction). The
mean Sharpe ratios (based on actual parameters) are all similar and
lie with a value of about 16.85% above the minimum risk portfolios.
All the approaches are diversified in terms of weights as well as in
terms of risk contributions to the true standard deviation as they
display Herfindahl indices of about 0.1% (except the sampleCDaR
$Herfindahl_{rc}$ of 1%). The turnover is the highest for the sampleCDaR
portfolio with 15%, which is considerably higher than the turnovers
of the other approaches with 3% - 6%. However, the turnovers are

Table 6.108: Performance Statistics for the Simulation - Risk Budgeting
Portfolios
The statistics are all given as means across 10.000 portfolio
optimizations and are based on actual parameters. For
better comparison they are all shown in percent.

	sampleCVaR	sampleCDaR	normCVaR	modCVaR	sampleCOV	Naive
μ estimated	1.014%	0.998%	0.998%	0.998%	0.998%	1.005%
μ actual	1.000%	1.000%	1.000%	1.000%	1.000%	1.000%
σ estimated	5.917%	5.951%	5.930%	5.931%	5.930%	5.932%
σ actual	5.937%	5.955%	5.934%	5.936%	5.934%	5.933%
MD_w	3.584%	8.535%	1.962%	3.006%	1.630%	0.000%
SD_w	0.942%	2.952%	0.493%	0.820%	0.399%	0.000%
AV μ	0.014%	-0.002%	-0.002%	-0.002%	-0.002%	0.005%
AV σ	-0.020%	-0.004%	-0.004%	-0.004%	-0.004%	-0.001%
Sharpe Ratio	16.844%	16.793%	16.852%	16.848%	16.853%	16.855%
$Herfindahl_w$	0.153%	0.906%	0.045%	0.108%	0.031%	0.000%
$Herfindahl_{rc}$	0.183%	1.126%	0.054%	0.129%	0.037%	0.000%
Turnover	6.518%	15.169%	3.587%	5.497%	2.981%	0.000%
VaR	10.765%	10.795%	10.761%	10.763%	10.760%	10.759%
MaxDD	0.000%	0.000%	0.000%	0.000%	0.000%	0.000%

lower than those of the minimum risk approaches. The VaR and the
MaxDD are not different from each another in this simulated dataset.

All in all, the risk budgeting portfolios are more structure robust
than the minimum risk portfolios in the simulation setting. This is not
surprising in this setting, as the risk budgeting portfolios are closer
to the 'true' naive portfolio. The portfolios based on the CDaR risk
measure exhibit the highest turnover and distances of the true weights.
However, the estimation error of the return and risk is the highest for
the sampleCVaR portfolio among the risk budgeting approaches.

Worst-Case Performance

As outlined above, robustness has generally two aspects. To analyze
the outcomes in a worst-case scenario, the simulation is altered, so
that the portfolio is held in a sudden crash. For this, the estimated
parameters are all very optimistic (high expected returns and low
volatilities), but the true parameters poor (low returns and high
volatilities).

1) The same parameters as in the structure robustness study above are defined.

2) 250 draws from a multivariate normal distribution $\Phi(\mu, \Sigma)$ are taken.

3) A bootstrap sample by taking 1000 data samples (each data sample has 250 returns for each asset) from the data in step 2) is generated and the mean returns of each bootstrap sample μ =mean (Bootstrap sample returns) as well as the covariance matrices are defined. Thus, it results a 1000 x 10 matrix of mean returns and an 10 x 10 x 1000 array of covariance matrices of the 1000 bootstrap samples.

4) The estimated parameters (best values) are obtained by taking the maximum means of the mean vector of step 3) and the lowest entries of the covariance matrix array. This is done by components. On the opposite, the true parameters are obtained by taking the minimum means of the mean vector and the highest entries of the covariance matrix array of step 3). To ensure that the covariance matrices are positive definite (which is a requirement to obtain the portfolios), the eigenvalues of the covariances are calculated. If any of the eigenvalues are negative, the diagonal of the covariance matrix is increased until the eigenvalues are positive and the covariance matrix positive definite. As some of the portfolios need a sample of returns as input, the 'best samples' are obtained by taking the one bootstrap sample of the 1000, where the sum of the means is the highest. The 'worst samples are by contrary the ones, where the sum of the means is the lowest.

5) The steps 2), 3) and 4) are repeated 10.000 ($NumSim$) times and the input parameters as well as the best and the worst samples are saved. Thus, there are 10.000 best means, best covariances, best samples as well as worst means, worst covariances and worst samples.

6) The portfolio optimizations with the input parameters from step 5) are performed by taking the worst means and the worst variance-covariances as the true and the best means and the best variance-covariances as the estimated input parameters.

7) The portfolio outcomes are compared with the presented performance measures.

This setting can be thought as a case in which the market is in a bull phase and the portfolio is estimated with the best parameters and then the situation changes to a bear market and the true parameters are the worst. Table 6.109 summarizes the results for the minimum risk portfolios in the worst-case simulation. As intended by the worst-case setting, the estimated portfolio returns are positive, but the actual returns negative. The returns are overestimated and the portfolio standard deviation is underestimated by all the approaches. There is no difference of the estimation error statistics (AV μ and AV σ) between the minimum risk portfolios. The turnover and the distances are again the highest for the minCDaR portfolio. According to the downside risk statistics, the minCDaR displays the lowest value of the MaxDD, but not of the VaR.

Table 6.110 shows the worst-case results for the risk budgeting portfolios. The actual portfolio returns of the risk budgeting portfolios in the worst case are lower than the actual minimum risk portfolio returns, but the risk budgeting portfolios display a slightly lower standard deviation. However, the estimation errors concerning the portfolio mean and standard deviation of the risk budgeting approaches are not different from the minimum risk portfolios.

The mean, the standard deviations of the distances, as well as the Herfindahl indices demonstrate again that the risk budgeting models display the best stability in terms of weights and are thus much more structure robust than the minimum risk equivalents. Moreover, the risk budgeting approaches show a much lower turnover. The Sharpe

Table 6.109: Performance Statistics for the Worst Case Simulation - Minimum Risk Portfolios

The statistics are given as means across 10.000 portfolio optimizations and are based on actual parameters. The worst case is seen as a situation, in which the portfolio is estimated with the 'best' parameters, but the 'worst' parameters are the 'true' parameters.

	MV	minCVaR	minCDaR
$\mu_{estimated}$	2.609%	2.696%	2.761%
μ_{actual}	-0.613%	-0.546%	-0.502%
$\sigma_{estimated}$	4.488%	4.871%	5.001%
σ_{actual}	7.041%	7.320%	7.455%
MD_w	13.350%	56.447%	77.290%
SD_w	3.653%	13.447%	16.458%
AV μ	3.222%	3.242%	3.263%
AV σ	-2.553%	-2.449%	-2.454%
Sharpe Ratio	-8.696%	-7.457%	-6.713%
$Herfindahl_w$	3.612%	14.504%	18.946%
$Herfindahl_{rc}$	3.605%	15.867%	20.842%
Turnover	32.397%	60.424%	66.080%
VaR	10.968%	11.494%	11.760%
MaxDD	6128.430%	5461.389%	5016.463%

ratio is negative and thus not informative (in this case, a large negative portfolio return with a large portfolio standard deviation results in a better Sharpe ratio than only a slightly negative portfolio return with a small portfolio standard deviation (see, e.g., Brinkmann (2007), p. 185)). With view to the risk figures, the risk budgeting approaches exhibit higher drawdowns than the minimum risk approaches.

The estimation errors of all portfolios are huge and similar. The minimum risk portfolios display slightly higher actual returns and lower drawdowns, but the differences are small. The best portfolio regarding these characteristics is the minCDaR portfolio with the low-

Table 6.110: Performance Statistics for the Worst Case Simulation -
Risk Budgeting Portfolios
The statistics are given as means across 10.000 portfolio
optimizations and are based on actual parameters. The
worst case is seen here as a situation, in which the portfolio
is estimated with the 'best' parameters, but the 'worst'
parameters are the 'true' parameters.

	sampleCVaR	sampleCDaR	normCVaR	modCVaR	sampleCOV	Naive
$\mu_{estimated}$	2.641%	2.675%	2.642%	2.643%	2.630%	2.633%
μ_{actual}	-0.624%	-0.594%	-0.623%	-0.622%	-0.634%	-0.636%
$\sigma_{estimated}$	4.586%	4.609%	4.575%	4.578%	4.575%	4.591%
σ_{actual}	7.123%	7.143%	7.116%	7.118%	7.117%	7.135%
MD_w	6.049%	10.784%	3.002%	4.380%	2.473%	0.000%
SD_w	2.082%	3.765%	0.794%	1.558%	0.643%	0.000%
AV μ	3.266%	3.270%	3.265%	3.265%	3.264%	3.269%
AV σ	-2.538%	-2.534%	-2.541%	-2.539%	-2.541%	-2.544%
Sharpe Ratio	-8.755%	-8.309%	-8.745%	-8.733%	-8.897%	-8.911%
$Herfindahl_w$	0.331%	1.144%	0.109%	0.223%	0.065%	0.000%
$Herfindahl_{rc}$	0.353%	1.323%	0.087%	0.217%	0.043%	0.033%
Turnover	9.432%	17.194%	5.537%	7.772%	4.298%	0.000%
VaR	11.092%	11.155%	11.082%	11.086%	11.072%	11.099%
MaxDD	6242.111%	5944.138%	6229.417%	6222.069%	6337.862%	6363.875%

est drawdown and the highest return. Also among the risk budgeting
portfolios, the sampleCDaR portfolio has the best outcomes. However,
the turnover of the CDaR approaches is the highest, which reduces
the net return and diminishes the difference.

Expanding the Simulation Study to a More Realistic Case

The simulation study so far has shown that the risk budgeting
portfolios are more structure robust. But this can be related to the
case, that the naive portfolio is the true portfolio allocation in the
unrealistic simulation study and the ERC portfolios have an advantage as their allocations are closer to the naive portfolio than the
minimum risk approaches. Thus, the simulation study is expanded to
a realistic example, where the assets have different expected returns
and correlations.

The setting of the realistic simulation is in general the same as above, but similar to Brinkmann (2007, p. 197), the true means and correlations are calculated through historical estimates of real assets. For this, daily returns of 10 German assets are taken in the period of 01.1973 - 09.2012. The 10 assets are the first ten assets of the Germany 1973 dataset of section 6.2.4. The true mean returns and the true correlation matrix are visible from tables 6.111 and 6.112. The asset characteristics are very different and display different mean returns and correlations. Some assets display negative true returns. Thus, the naive allocation is not the true allocation in this dataset and the structure robustness as well as the worst case robustness of the portfolios will be observed in a more realistic simulation. The methodology of the simulation study remains the same as above. Thus, the estimated parameters are obtained by simulating multivariate normal distributed returns with the true parameters and estimate the estimated parameters through the simulated samples. For the 'sample' portfolios, the sample of simulated returns are saved and forwarded as inputs for the optimizations.

Table 6.111: True Means of the Assets in the Realistic Simulation
The values are calculated from daily returns in the period from 01.1973 - 09.2012.

Asset	μ_{true}
A1	0.00060446
A2	-0.0095597
A3	0.0012914
A4	0.00087117
A5	-0.00037588
A6	0.0010198
A7	-0.0088229
A8	-0.0071017
A9	0.0029069
A10	0.0019071

Table 6.112: True Correlations of the Assets in the Realistic Simulation
The values are calculated from daily returns in the period
from 01.1973 - 09.2012 and are all shown in percent.

	A1	A2	A3	A4	A5	A6	A7	A8	A9	A10
A1	100	2.22	5.44	5.92	4.27	2.87	4.44	0.91	9.20	4.85
A2		100	3.37	1.73	0.69	0.43	4.35	0.75	6.41	2.16
A3			100	5.15	4.94	2.13	2.36	1.38	6.89	5.61
A4				100	4.41	5.51	2.06	1.11	10.97	4.22
A5					100	3.79	1.42	2.46	5.38	2.36
A6						100	2.56	-0.47	4.75	3.11
A7							100	-0.57	5.84	3.5
A8								100	6.10	3.35
A9									100	10.45
A10										100

Table 6.113 shows the resulting true weights of the different portfolio
approaches. It is visible that the asset 6 gets the highest proportion in
all approaches. After this, the assets 9 and 10 have also relative large
proportions. Not surprising, these are the assets with the highest mean
returns. The minCDaR portfolio displays the highest concentration.

Table 6.113: True Asset Weights of the Portfolios in the Realistic Simulation
The values are all shown in percent.

Asset	MV	minCVaR	minCDaR	sampleCVaR	normCVaR	modCVaR	sampleCOV	sampleCDaR
A1	10.44	9.61	0.33	11.87	11.61	10.88	11.37	8.63
A2	0.42	0.05	0	2.31	2.97	0	3.09	6.34
A3	6.38	7.58	11.10	9.49	9.29	10.29	9.25	7.07
A4	14.19	13.09	31.14	13.18	13.11	13	13.16	15.24
A5	6.37	6.34	0	8.95	9.17	9.55	9.39	6.36
A6	36.27	36.60	26.45	21.41	20.31	19.97	20.34	14.59
A7	0.83	0.06	0	3.21	3.88	3.94	4.21	6.34
A8	2.73	1.30	0	5.09	5.55	6.03	6.22	6.34
A9	12.08	14.44	19.28	12.88	12.55	12.41	11.70	16.84
A10	10.28	10.93	11.69	11.62	11.55	13.93	11.28	12.25

Tables 6.114 and 6.115 show the minimum and maximum estimated
weights across the 10.000 optimizations for the minimum risk as well
as for the risk budgeting portfolios. As in the unrealistic simulation

above, the minimum risk portfolios display the highest spreads and
the largest concentrations in terms of maximum weights. Especially
the minCDaR portfolio displays the highest maximum weights. It
is interesting that the MV portfolio is always invested in the asset
6, as the minimum asset weight is ca. 30%. The ERC portfolios
display lower spreads and as above, the sampleCDaR portfolio has
the largest maximum weights as well as the average spread of the
weight allocations among the risk budgeting portfolios.

Tables 6.116 and 6.117 display the standard deviations of the weights
across the 10.000 simulations for each asset. Surprisingly, the MV
portfolio displays very low standard deviations of the weights. Thus,
the asset allocation does not change much. The volatilities are comparable to the sampleCOV portfolio. The minCDaR displays the
highest values, especially for the asset 6 and asset 9. Among the ERC
portfolios, the sampleCDaR portfolio has the highest values.

Tables 6.118 and 6.119 show the performances of the different portfolios in the 'normal case' in the realistic simulation. In this simulation,
the actual means are underestimated, as the simulation delivers lower
estimated means due to the negative returns of some assets. Thus,
all approaches underestimate the return by 0.002%. The volatility is
also underestimated, as in the unrealistic simulation. There, the MV
portfolio displays the highest estimation error. The estimation errors
of the other minimum risk approaches do not differ from the ERC
portfolios. The minimum risk approaches show higher actual means
as the risk budgeting portfolios and the minCDaR portfolio shows the
highest actual mean. The MD_w and SD_w values indicate that the
minimum risk portfolios and especially the minCDaR portfolio display
the highest distances to the true weights. The Herfindahl values show
that the minimum risk approaches are more concentrated in terms of
weights as well as risks. However, in this setting, the concentration of
the minimum risk portfolios, and especially of the minCDaR portfolio
results in the highest mean, as the ERC portfolios are invested in all
assets, but some of the asset have negative returns. The sampleCOV

Table 6.114: Minimum and Maximum Portfolio Weights for the Minimum Risk Portfolios in the Realistic Simulation
These are average minimum and maximum estimated portfolio weights across 10.000 simulation runs per asset. The
values are shown in percent.

Asset	weights	MV	minCVaR	minCDaR
Asset 1	max	16	31	54
	min	6	0	0
Asset 2	max	2	6	12
	min	0	0	0
Asset 3	max	10	26	74
	min	3	0	0
Asset 4	max	19	40	76
	min	8	0	0
Asset 5	max	10	20	48
	min	3	0	0
Asset 6	max	42	66	97
	min	30	4	0
Asset 7	max	2	8	16
	min	0	0	0
Asset 8	max	5	11	29
	min	1	0	0
Asset 9	max	17	41	87
	min	6	0	0
Asset 10	max	14	30	66
	min	6	0	0
Average	max	14	28	53
	min	6	0	0

portfolio shows the highest MaxDD, as the portfolio return is always
negative and this represents the (cumulative) drop from the beginning
until the end of the 10.000 optimizations.

Table 6.120 displays additionally the t-test of the differences in
actual portfolio returns across the 10.000 simulations. It is obvious
that all differences are significant. Thus, the minimum risk portfolios
have a much higher actual return than the ERC portfolios. As in

Table 6.115: Minimum and Maximum Portfolio Weights for the Risk
Budgeting Portfolios in the Realistic Simulation
These are average minimum and maximum estimated portfolio weights across 10.000 simulation runs per asset. The
values are shown in percent.

Asset	weights	sampleCVaR	sampleCDaR	normCVaR	modCVaR	sampleCOV	Naive
Asset 1	max	22	42	17	22	16	10
	min	0	2	8	6	8	10
Asset 2	max	4	10	5	6	5	10
	min	1	1	0	0	0	10
Asset 3	max	17	42	13	20	14	10
	min	5	2	6	0	7	10
Asset 4	max	23	45	20	26	18	10
	min	0	3	9	0	9	10
Asset 5	max	17	37	14	18	13	10
	min	5	2	6	5	6	10
Asset 6	max	35	63	30	31	27	10
	min	0	0	0	0	4	10
Asset 7	max	7	10	7	7	6	10
	min	2	2	0	0	0	10
Asset 8	max	10	16	9	11	9	10
	min	2	1	0	0	0	10
Asset 9	max	25	51	18	23	17	10
	min	7	4	8	0	8	10
Asset 10	max	22	48	17	22	16	10
	min	0	3	8	0	8	10
Average	max	18	36	15	19	14	10
	min	2	3	5	1	5	10

Table 6.116: Standard Deviations of the Minimum Risk Weights across
10.000 Simulations in the Realistic Simulation for each
Asset
The values are displayed in percent.

	A1	A2	A3	A4	A5	A6	A7	A8	A9	A10
MV	1	0	1	1	1	2	0	1	1	1
minCVaR	5	1	4	6	4	7	1	2	6	5
minCDaR	9	1	7	11	6	15	1	2	12	10

the performance studies, the ERC portfolios can only outperform the
naive portfolio. Among the risk budgeting portfolios, the sampleCDaR
portfolio shows a significant outperformance against the other ap-

Table 6.117: Standard Deviations of the Risk Budgeting Weights across
10.000 Simulations in the Realistic Simulation for each
Asset
The values are displayed in percent.

	A1	A2	A3	A4	A5	A6	A7	A8	A9	A10
sampleCVaR	2	0	1	2	1	4	1	1	2	2
sampleCDaR	5	1	4	6	3	9	1	1	7	6
normCVaR	1	0	1	1	1	2	0	1	1	1
modCVaR	2	1	2	2	2	4	1	1	2	2
sampleCOV	1	1	1	1	1	2	1	1	1	1
Naive	0	0	0	0	0	0	0	0	0	0

Table 6.118: Performance Statistics for the Realistic Simulation - Minimum Risk Portfolios
The statistics are all given as means across 10.000 portfolio
optimizations and are based on the actual parameters. For
better comparison they are all shown in percent.

	MV	minCVaR	minCDaR
μ estimated	0.082%	0.093%	0.114%
μ actual	0.084%	0.095%	0.116%
σ estimated	1.278%	1.389%	1.563%
σ actual	1.325%	1.390%	1.565%
MD_w	6.550%	13.965%	33.786%
SD_w	1.965%	4.193%	9.891%
AV μ	-0.002%	-0.002%	-0.002%
AV σ	-0.047%	-0.001%	-0.002%
Sharpe Ratio	6.321%	6.820%	7.453%
$Herfindahl_w$	11.215%	13.153%	17.999%
$Herfindahl_{rc}$	11.355%	14.319%	22.800%
Turnover	11.124%	22.850%	40.024%
VaR	2.263%	2.381%	2.689%
MaxDD	0.000%	0.023%	0.131%

Table 6.119: Performance Statistics for the Realistic Simulation - Risk Budgeting Portfolios

The statistics are all given as means across 10.000 portfolio optimizations and are based on the actual parameters. For better comparison they are all shown in percent.

	sampleCVaR	sampleCDaR	normCVaR	modCVaR	sampleCOV	Naive
μ estimated	0.023%	0.033%	0.003%	0.004%	-0.008%	-0.1740%
μ actual	0.025%	0.034%	0.005%	0.006%	-0.006%	-0.1726%
σ estimated	1.415%	1.517%	1.449%	1.459%	1.470%	2.2225%
σ actual	1.416%	1.519%	1.451%	1.460%	1.471%	2.2248%
MD_w	5.421%	16.757%	3.496%	6.642%	3.096%	0%
SD_w	2.210%	5.387%	1.296%	2.511%	1.027%	0%
AV μ	-0.002%	-0.002%	-0.002%	-0.002%	-0.002%	-0.002%
AV σ	-0.001%	-0.002%	-0.001%	-0.001%	-0.002%	-0.002%
Sharpe Ratio	1.750%	2.295%	0.360%	0.432%	-0.422%	-7.7576%
$Herfindahl_w$	3.663%	6.111%	2.875%	3.067%	2.594%	0%
$Herfindahl_{rc}$	1.460%	7.642%	0.465%	0.984%	0.346%	15.67%
Turnover	8.835%	22.417%	5.901%	9.141%	5.351%	0%
VaR	2.354%	2.533%	2.391%	2.408%	2.414%	3.487%
MaxDD	0.045%	0.100%	0.076%	0.142%	63.436%	0%

proaches.

Table 6.120: Significance in Actual Means (μ actual) in the Realistic
Simulation across the 10 000 Simulations
For the calculation of the t-test see 6.2.1.

	Excess Mean (%)	t-Stat
sampleCOV vs. MV	-0.09	-491.42
sampleCVaR vs. minCVaR	-0.07	-300.29
normCVaR vs. minCVaR	-0.09	-363.79
modCVaR vs. minCVaR	-0.09	-353.11
sampleCDaR vs. minCDaR	-0.06	-174.83
sampleCOV vs. Naive	0.17	1545.21
sampleCVaR vs. Naive	0.20	1717.73
normCVaR vs. Naive	0.18	1834.93
modCVaR vs. Naive	0.18	1179.50
sampleCDaR vs. Naive	0.21	774.59
sampleCOV vs. sampleCVaR	-0.03	-244.33
sampleCOV vs. normCVaR	-0.01	-124.89
sampleCOV vs. modCVaR	-0.01	-80.89
sampleCOV vs. sampleCDaR	-0.04	-145.16
sampleCDaR vs. sampleCVaR	0.01	36.77
sampleCDaR vs. normCVaR	0.03	113.73
sampleCDaR vs. modCVaR	0.03	100.58

For completeness, tables 6.121 and 6.122 present the performance
for the worst case in the realistic simulation. The general results
are similar to the unrealistic simulation, but the differences are smaller. The estimated returns are positive and the actual negative, as
intended by the worst case setting. The minCVaR and minCDaR
portfolios display the highest actual mean returns and the lowest
volatilities, thus they have the best performances in the wort case.
The ERC portfolios display again lower actual returns as well as
higher actual portfolio volatilities. The ERC portfolios have still the
lowest distances to the true weights, but this does not help in terms
of performances. They display also the highest VaR and MaxDD.

The minCVaR and the minCDaR portfolio have the lowest estimation errors. Thus, they are best suited for the worst case scenario. The performances of the MV portfolio is in this simulation comparable to the ERC portfolios due to estimation errors, the actual mean and actual volatility and thus behind the minCVaR and minCDaR portfolios.

Table 6.121: Performance Statistics for the Worst Case Simulation in the Realistic Simulation - Minimum Risk Portfolios
The statistics are given as means across 10.000 portfolio optimizations and are based on actual parameters. The worst case is seen as a situation, in which the portfolio is estimated with the 'best' parameters, but the 'worst' parameters are the 'true' parameters.

	MV	minCVaR	minCDaR
μ estimated	0.900	0.761	0.821
μ actual	-1.181	-0.554	-0.548
σ estimated	1.744	1.796	1.887
σ actual	3.074	2.062	2.203
MD_w	44.441	23.987	47.937
SD_w	4.139	6.915	12.513
AV μ	2.081	1.315	1.369
AV σ	-1.33	-0.267	-0.316
Sharpe Ratio	-38.389	-26.779	-24.747
$Herfindahl_w$	0.476	12.949	14.173
$Herfindahl_{rc}$	4.453	10.148	12.891
Turnover	8.074	28.248	38.341
VaR	3.876	2.839	3.075
MaxDD	11806.379	5535.719	5477.094

Table 6.122: Performance Statistics for the Worst Case Simulation in
the Realistic Simulation - Risk Budgeting Portfolios
The statistics are given as means across 10.000 portfolio
optimizations and are based on actual parameters. The
worst case is seen as a situation, in which the portfolio
is estimated with the 'best' parameters, but the 'worst'
parameters are the 'true' parameters.

	sampleCVaR	sampleCDaR	normCVaR	modCVaR	sampleCOV	Naive
μ estimated	0.871	0.884	0.821	0.824	0.811	0.937
μ actual	-0.994	-0.711	-0.794	-0.798	-0.823	-1.282
σ estimated	0.819	1.335	0.940	0.979	0.890	0.565
σ actual	2.801	2.404	2.340	2.360	2.360	3.379
MD_w	12.598	20.104	5.686	8.899	4.823	0.000
SD_w	10.441	7.231	3.318	5.997	2.062	0.000
AV μ	1.865	1.595	1.615	1.621	1.634	2.219
AV σ	-1.981	-1.069	-1.400	-1.382	-1.470	-2.814
Sharpe Ratio	-35.494	-29.522	-33.922	-33.772	-34.863	-37.967
$Herfindahl_w$	2.062	6.451	2.959	3.243	2.730	0.000
$Herfindahl_{rc}$	4.416	5.395	0.504	0.999	0.333	9.163
Turnover	15.455	26.377	9.104	12.997	7.707	0.000
VaR	3.613	3.243	3.055	3.085	3.059	4.276
MaxDD	9939.923	7113.740	7942.138	7976.682	8230.206	12822.519

Table 6.123 shows additionally the t-test of the actual mean differences in the worst case of the realistic simulation. As in the normal
simulated case, the minimum risk portfolios display a significant higher
actual return, except the MV portfolio compared to the sampleCOV
portfolio. Among each other, the sampleCDaR has again the highest
actual return.

Table 6.123: Significance in Actual Means (μ actual) in the Worst Case of the Realistic Simulation across the 10.000 Simulations For the calculation of the t-test see 6.2.1.

	Excess Mean (%)	t-Stat
sampleCOV vs. MV	0.36	391.72
sampleCVaR vs. minCVaR	-0.44	-150.42
normCVaR vs. minCVaR	-0.24	-240.33
modCVaR vs. minCVaR	-0.24	-231.39
sampleCDaR vs. minCDaR	-0.16	-155.33
sampleCOV vs. Naive	0.46	502.34
sampleCVaR vs. Naive	0.29	101.36
normCVaR vs. Naive	0.49	490.69
modCVaR vs. Naive	0.48	446.89
sampleCDaR vs. Naive	0.57	405.78
sampleCOV vs. sampleCVaR	0.17	61.53
sampleCOV vs. normCVaR	-0.03	-59.57
sampleCOV vs. modCVaR	-0.03	-36.71
sampleCOV vs. sampleCDaR	-0.11	-110.02
sampleCDaR vs. sampleCVaR	0.28	96.22
sampleCDaR vs. normCVaR	0.08	86.98
sampleCDaR vs. modCVaR	0.09	81.52

Results of the Simulation Study

The results show that the risk budgeting models are more structure robust than the minimum risk portfolios according to the lower change of the weights, the lower turnover and the lower estimation error of the actual return and risk in the unrealistic simulation setting. They are less concentrated in terms of weights and in terms of risk contributions than the minimum risk portfolios and also have a higher Sharpe ratio due to a slightly lower standard deviation. However, in the setting of the simulation, this is not a surprising result. The risk budgeting models have in this setting an advance, as the naive portfolio is the 'true allocation' and the risk budgeting models are more similar to the naive portfolio as the minimum risk approaches. In the more realistic simulation it is obvious that the estimation errors of the ERC portfolios are similar to the minimum risk approaches. The only advantage of the ERC portfolios is the lower change of the weights and thus a lower turnover as well as lower distances. However, this does not help in terms of actual returns and volatilities, as the minimum risk portfolios display significant higher returns in the realistic simulation.

In both simulated worst cases, there is no real difference between the estimation errors of the portfolios. But the minimum risk approaches exhibit a lower drawdown and have significant higher actual returns in the realistic simulation (except the MV portfolio). Thus, it seems that risk concentration rather than risk diversification performs better in a worst case. In the next section, the performances of the portfolios will be examined under real circumstances based on an empirical dataset.

6.4.3 Empirical Study

The empirical simulation study of robustness is based on the global portfolio of section 6.2.3. The first estimated parameters are the mean and the covariance matrix based on the first 12-month daily returns (31.01.1995 - 31.01.1996). The true portfolio parameters are constructed by using the return vector from the following month and the true covariance matrix from the following 12-month. The samples for the portfolios, which require returns as inputs consist of the 12 month of daily returns, from which the estimated or true parameters are obtained. By rolling the dataset one month further, the portfolio optimization is performed 175 times and the robustness is compared across the 175 months.

Structure Robustness

The average maximum and minimum estimated asset weights across the 175 optimizations across all assets are summarized in Table 6.124

and 6.125. (The results for every asset in detail are given in the Appendix.)

Table 6.124: MMinimum and Maximum Portfolio Weights for the Minimum Risk Portfolios in the Global Dataset
These are averages of the 13 maximum and minimum values after the 175 optimizations. The values are shown in percent.

	weights (%)	MV	minCVaR	minCDaR
Average	max	21	26	35
	min	1	0	0

The average spread between the minimum and the maximum asset weights is higher for the minimum risk portfolios than the risk budgeting portfolios, however, the difference is not that large. As it can be observed from the table in the appendix, the highest asset weights result from the allocation in the bonds, which is up to 98% for the MV portfolio. All assets exhibit a minimum asset weight of 0%. The risk budgeting models also invest the most in the three bonds, with maximum values by the sampleCVaR budgeting portfolio of 68%, the sampleCDaR of 63%, the modCVaR of 72% and the normCVaR and the sampleCOV of 55% and 52%.

Table 6.125: Minimum and Maximum Portfolio Weights for the Risk Budget Portfolios in the Global Dataset
These are averages of the 13 maximum and minimum values after the 175 optimizations. The values are shown in percent.

	weights (%)	sampleCVaR	sampleCDaR	normCVaR	modCVaR	sampleCOV	Naive
Average	max	20	24	17	23	16	8
	min	2	1	3	1	3	8

Table 6.126 and 6.127 display the average standard deviation of the weights for the different portfolios across the whole 175 months of portfolio optimizations. The standard deviations of the risk budgeting

models are lower and the minCVaR and the minCDaR show the highest values. Among the risk budgeting models, the normCVaR as well as the sampleCOV portfolio exhibit the lowest standard deviations.

Table 6.126: Average Standard Deviations of Minimum Risk Portfolio Weights
The values are calculated as average of the standard deviations of the weights across 175 months and assets.

	Average σ_w
MV	5,4%
minCVaR	6,2%
minCDaR	8,3%

Table 6.127: Std Deviations of Risk Budgeting Weights
The values are calculated as average of the std of the weights across 175 months and assets.

	Average σ_w
CVaR	4,2%
CDaR	4,8%
normCVaR	3,6%
modCVaR	4,9%
sampleCOV	3,6%
Naive	0%

Results of the solution robustness as well as of the historical performance of the minimum risk portfolios are summarized in table 6.128. The return is overestimated (AV μ) and the standard deviation is underestimated (AV σ) by all approaches, but the actual return is quite similar (0.015% and 0.017%). The minCDaR portfolio shows the highest estimation error in the mean, but the MV and the minCVaR show the highest estimation error in the standard deviation. The minCDaR approach has again high distances and the highest turnover, but exhibits the highest return and the lowest drawdown and Value-at-Risk. With regard to the cumulative return, the minCDaR outperforms the other approaches. But the Sharpe ratio is the highest of the MV portfolio, due to the lowest actual standard deviation.

Table 6.128: Performance Statistics of the Minimum Risk Portfolios for the Global Dataset
The statistics are given as means across 175 month of portfolio optimizations. For better comparison they are all shown in percent. The annual (and cumulative) return, standard deviation and Sharpe Ratio are based on the actual parameters and are calculated as follows: $\mu_{annual} = \mu_{actual} * 250$, $\sigma_{annual} = \sigma_{actual} * \sqrt{250}$, $SharpeRatio_{annual} = \frac{\mu_{annual}}{\sigma_{annual}}$, as 250 trading days in a year are assumed.

	MV	minCVaR	minCDaR
$\mu_{estimated}$	0.024%	0.027%	0.033%
μ_{actual}	0.015%	0.015%	0.017%
$\sigma_{estimated}$	0.167%	0.179%	0.231%
σ_{actual}	0.205%	0.218%	0.263%
MD_w	37.144%	45.116%	54.679%
SD_w	18.319%	19.039%	25.061%
AV μ	0.009%	0.012%	0.016%
AV σ	-0.038%	-0.039%	-0.032%
Sharpe Ratio	11.405%	9.531%	8.077%
$Herfindahl_w$	53.712%	47.140%	45.095%
$Herfindahl_{rc}$	56.231%	45.978%	44.315%
Turnover	4.653%	8.281%	10.846%
VaR	11.515%	9.024%	6.251%
MaxDD	18.954%	16.901%	12.617%
μ_{annual}	3.836%	3.731%	4.327%
$\mu_{cumulative}$	58.158%	56.573%	63.501%
σ_{annual}	3.243%	3.452%	4.153%
$SharpeRatio_{annual}$	118.275%	108.082%	104.194%

Table 6.129 summarizes the empirical results for the risk budgeting

Table 6.129: Performance Statistics of the Risk Budgeting Portfolios for the Global Dataset
The statistics are given as means across 175 month of portfolio optimizations. For better comparison they are all shown in percent. The annual (and cumulative) return, standard deviation and Sharpe Ratio are based on the actual parameters and are calculated as follows: $\mu_{annual} = \mu_{actual} * 250$, $\sigma_{annual} = \sigma_{actual} * \sqrt{250}$, $SharpeRatio_{annual} = \frac{\mu_{annual}}{\sigma_{annual}}$, as 250 trading days in a year are assumed.

	sampleCVaR	sampleCDaR	normCVaR	modCVaR	sampleCOV	Naive
$\mu_{estimated}$	0.020%	0.037%	0.022%	0.023%	0.020%	0.021%
μ_{actual}	0.020%	0.022%	0.021%	0.025%	0.020%	0.017%
$\sigma_{estimated}$	0.387%	0.328%	0.383%	0.409%	0.388%	0.647%
σ_{actual}	0.398%	0.368%	0.399%	0.427%	0.403%	0.676%
MD_w	22.740%	29.518%	19.111%	29.678%	18.364%	0.000%
SD_w	10.915%	11.388%	10.036%	13.020%	11.252%	0.000%
AV μ	0.000%	0.015%	0.001%	-0.002%	0.000%	0.003%
AV σ	-0.011%	-0.040%	-0.016%	-0.018%	-0.015%	-0.029%
Sharpe Ratio	7.460%	7.810%	7.934%	7.817%	7.592%	5.536%
$Herfindahl_w$	10.010%	10.816%	9.796%	10.250%	8.856%	0.000%
$Herfindahl_{rc}$	2.692%	7.998%	2.365%	4.001%	2.098%	4.498%
Turnover	6.500%	7.086%	4.121%	7.842%	3.248%	0.000%
VaR	17.702%	12.357%	18.926%	14.568%	17.724%	21.478%
MaxDD	36.775%	27.498%	39.734%	32.738%	38.901%	58.571%
μ_{annual}	5.122%	5.506%	5.157%	6.352%	4.949%	4.358%
$\mu_{cumulative}$	76.170%	82.153%	70.285%	95.592%	74.272%	64.218%
σ_{annual}	6.300%	5.817%	6.309%	6.753%	6.378%	10.690%
$SharpeRatio_{annual}$	81.303%	94.645%	81.736%	94.072%	77.599%	40.767%

portfolios. The return is only overestimated by the sampleCDaR approach, but the standard deviation is underestimated by all approaches, with the highest estimation error of the sampleCDaR and the naive approach. However, the estimation errors of the actual standard deviation are lower than these of the minimum risk approaches (except of the sampleCDaR approach). The actual returns of the risk budgeting portfolios are all slightly higher than those of the minimum risk approaches, with the highest actual return of the modCVaR portfolio. However, the actual standard deviations are all higher than those of the minimum risk approaches. The highest standard deviation is shown from the naive and the modCVaR portfolio.

Thus, the Sharpe ratios of all risk budgeting approaches are lower than those of the minimum risk counterparts.

The distances, the Herfindahl indices and the turnover values show again the outperformance based on the structure robustness by the risk budgeting portfolios. But this is not an advantage according to the downside risk measures: all approaches exhibit higher drawdowns and show a higher Value-at-Risk.

The cumulative return of all approaches is higher than that of the minimum risk counterpart, with the highest cumulative return of the modCVaR portfolio, followed by the sampleCDaR portfolio. However, as the annual standard deviation is approximately twice as high as the volatility of the minimum risk approaches, the annual Sharpe ratio is much lower. Table 6.130 shows the significance tests of the differences in actual returns of the portfolios. In the empirical case, the performances are very close and none of the portfolios displays a significant higher return.

Table 6.130: Significance in Actual Means (μ actual) in the Empirical
Dataset
For the calculation of the t-test see 6.2.1.

	Excess Mean (%)	t-Stat
sampleCOV vs. MV	0.0045	0.724
sampleCVaR vs. minCVaR	0.0056	0.85
normCVaR vs. minCVaR	0.0057	0.85
modCVaR vs. minCVaR	0.0105	1.59
sampleCDaR vs. minCDaR	0.0047	0.92
sampleCOV vs. Naive	0.0024	0.42
sampleCVaR vs. Naive	0.0031	0.50
normCVaR vs. Naive	0.0032	0.57
modCVaR vs. Naive	0.0080	1.39
sampleCDaR vs. Naive	0.0046	0.56
sampleCOV vs. sampleCVaR	-0.0007	-0.63
sampleCOV vs. normCVaR	-0.0008	-0.94
sampleCOV vs. modCVaR	-0.0056	-1.99
sampleCOV vs. sampleCDaR	-0.0022	-0.48
sampleCDaR vs. sampleCVaR	0.0015	0.33
sampleCDaR vs. normCVaR	0.0014	0.30
sampleCDaR vs. modCVaR	-0.0034	-0.78

Worst-Case Performance

The first worst-case scenario consists of the returns of the recent financial crisis. The 12 months returns from 30.05.2008 - 30.04.2009 are
taken to compare the portfolio outcomes. Although there are different
definitions of the financial crisis period, the peak of the crisis is defin-
itely included in this time frame (see e.g. Chong (2011), Campello
(2010)). The estimated and the true parameters are obtained as in
the normal empirical case. Table 6.131 shows that the annualized
returns are all negative and the volatilities as well as the correlations
are all higher than in the whole data sample. This characterizes a
typical crisis period.

Table 6.131: Annualized Returns, Annualized Volatilities and Correlations of the Assets in the Crisis Period

	Return	Volatility	Correlation matrix(%)											
SPCOMP	-38.8%	45.6%	100	93.6	61.8	56.8	12.8	73.5	44	32.3	-38.9	5.6	24	34.5	40.6
FRUSSL2	-35.8%	53.5%		100	51.2	45.1	3.8	65.4	38.7	25.4	-34.7	5.3	19.9	26.9	33.5
DJES50I	-37.9%	42.1%			100	94.4	43.9	79	70.8	56.1	-35.7	24.3	50.2	55.9	51.1
FTSE100	-31.1%	39.4%				100	44.8	77	71.5	54.7	-36.4	22.9	52.3	56.8	53.6
TOKYOSE	-40.6%	41.5%					100	38.4	56.5	74	-7.4	29	54.6	57.2	24.9
MSEFLA	-51.6%	62.6%						100	70.3	56.1	-40.5	24.5	43.7	59.3	58.4
MSEEUR	-65.1%	68.6%							100	66.6	-37.1	39.5	46.8	60.3	50.2
MSASXJ	-39.8%	42.1%								100	-18.6	26.5	52.5	56.9	36.1
JPMUSU	5.4%	7.7%									100	12.8	-14.3	-13.8	-36.2
JPMEIU	-7%	16.7%										100	14.5	31	25.3
MLHMAU	-15.6%	12.6%											100	64.8	28.9
JPMGCOC	-5.2%	14.7%												100	38.1
GSCITOT	-64.7%	45.3%													100

As shown in table 6.132, all estimated and actual returns are negative, however the estimation error is large. Concerning the estimation error of the actual standard deviation, the minCDaR shows the lowest value. The minCDaR has the best performance according to the actual and the cumulative return, the VaR and the maximum drawdown. Thus, it is the best suited for a crisis period. According to table 6.133, the estimation errors of the actual return and the actual standard deviation of the risk budgeting approaches are lower than these of the minimum risk portfolios. The highest estimation errors display the sampleCDaR and the naive approach.

Table 6.134 shows additionally the test of the mean differences for the crisis period. It is obvious that the performances of the minimum risk as well as of the ERC portfolios are similar and not significant. However, the ERC portfolios (except the sampleCDaR portfolio) display a significant higher return than the naive portfolio.

The first worst-case assumes negative estimated returns. However, this is unrealistic, as none investor would invest in such a portfolio. Therefore, a second, 'hypothetical' worst case is constructed, which is similar to the worst-case in the simulation study. The estimated parameters are positive, but the true parameters are negative and the

Table 6.132: Performance Statistics of the Minimum Risk Portfolios in
the Empirical Worst Case
The statistics are given as means across 12 month of portfolio optimizations (30.05.2008 - 30.04.2009). For better
comparison, they are all shown in percent.

	MV	minCVaR	minCDaR
$\mu_{estimated}$	-0.012%	-0.005%	0.015%
μ_{actual}	-0.049%	-0.053%	-0.034%
$\sigma_{estimated}$	0.261%	0.287%	0.352%
σ_{actual}	0.392%	0.401%	0.414%
MD_w	53.473%	65.514%	61.673%
SD_w	13.021%	16.387%	30.338%
AV μ	0.037%	0.048%	0.049%
AV σ	-0.131%	-0.114%	-0.063%
Sharpe Ratio	-4.663%	-9.491%	-6.232%
$Herfindahl_w$	38.902%	48.271%	68.996%
$Herfindahl_{rc}$	54.372%	54.740%	73.887%
Turnover	10.135%	17.206%	15.009%
VaR	7.178%	5.237%	3.730%
MaxDD	12.969%	10.541%	4.788%
μ_{annual}	-12.208%	-13.194%	-8.610%
$\mu_{cumulative}$	-9.413%	-6.733%	-0.466%
σ_{annual}	6.205%	6.342%	6.553%
$SharpeRatio_{annual}$	-196.748%	-208.063%	-131.388%

market 'crashes' (sudden, unexpected decline of the prices). Different
to the simulation study above, the best and worst parameters are
not constructed artificially, but through obtaining them through the
empirical returns. The samples are chosen by examining the vector
of means of the asset means of the samples (175 x 1 vector). The
best samples are obtained from the highest average means (above the
0.9 quantile) and the worst samples from the lowest average means
(below the 0.2 quantile). In sum, 17 best and worst samples are taken.
Thus, the historical time periods are shifted and it is assumed that the

Table 6.133: Performance Statistics of the Risk Budgeting Portfolios in the Empirical Worst Case
The statistics are given as means across 12 month of portfolio optimizations (30.05.2008 - 30.04.2009). For better comparison, they are all shown in percent.

	sampleCVaR	sampleCDaR	normCVaR	modCVaR	sampleCOV	Naive
$\mu_{estimated}$	-0.075%	-0.031%	-0.074%	-0.070%	-0.075%	-0.111%
μ_{actual}	-0.067%	-0.060%	-0.074%	-0.052%	-0.074%	-0.136%
$\sigma_{estimated}$	0.781%	0.481%	0.789%	0.771%	0.790%	1.221%
σ_{actual}	0.835%	0.591%	0.857%	0.839%	0.860%	1.313%
MD_w	20.270%	36.984%	16.444%	28.458%	13.622%	0.000%
SD_w	6.394%	13.194%	3.787%	13.418%	2.621%	0.000%
AV μ	-0.008%	0.029%	-0.001%	-0.018%	-0.002%	0.025%
AV σ	-0.054%	-0.111%	-0.068%	-0.069%	-0.070%	-0.092%
Sharpe Ratio	-3.057%	-3.650%	-2.510%	-2.095%	-2.468%	-4.644%
$Herfindahl_w$	8.638%	18.573%	8.391%	10.764%	8.165%	0.000%
$Herfindahl_{rc}$	2.676%	4.183%	2.194%	4.907%	2.025%	4.013%
Turnover	8.729%	10.833%	3.956%	15.421%	3.577%	0.000%
VaR	18.119%	9.866%	18.078%	9.965%	18.048%	21.478%
MaxDD	38.162%	21.009%	38.804%	30.148%	39.139%	58.171%
μ_{annual}	-16.769%	-14.982%	-18.377%	-13.013%	-18.450%	-33.885%
$\mu_{cumulative}$	-24.488%	-12.619%	-24.868%	-16.658%	-25.186%	-40.286%
σ_{annual}	13.201%	9.352%	13.551%	13.269%	13.592%	20.760%
$SharpeRatio_{annual}$	-127.025%	-160.197%	-135.617%	-98.075%	-135.735%	-163.223%

worst parameters follow after the best parameters, as in the worst-case construction above.

Tables 6.135 and 6.136 show the result for the hypothetical, but possible, market crash for the minimum risk and the risk budgeting portfolios. As desired by construction, the estimated returns are positive and the actual are negative, as the market crashes. The estimation error of the actual return is the highest for the minCDaR portfolio. The actual standard deviation is also greater than the estimated one and the estimation error is also the highest for the minCDaR portfolio. Due to these special conditions, the MV portfolio performs the best according to the actual mean and risk, but also according to the VaR and the maximum drawdown.

The risk budgeting portfolios display a much lower actual return than the minimum risk portfolios and a higher actual standard de-

Table 6.134: Significance in Actual Means (μ actual) in the Empirical
Worst Case
For the calculation of the t-test see 6.2.1.

	Excess Mean (%)	t-Stat
sampleCOV vs. MV	-0.025	-0.48
sampleCVaR vs. minCVaR	-0.014	-0.23
normCVaR vs. minCVaR	-0.02	-0.32
modCVaR vs. minCVaR	0.00072	0.01
sampleCDaR vs. minCDaR	-0.026	-0.57
sampleCOV vs. Naive	0.062	2.86
sampleCVaR vs. Naive	0.069	2.59
normCVaR vs. Naive	0.062	2.82
modCVaR vs. Naive	0.084	2.37
sampleCDaR vs. Naive	0.076	1.36
sampleCOV vs. sampleCVaR	-0.0067	-0.76
sampleCOV vs. normCVaR	-0.0003	-0.31
sampleCOV vs. modCVaR	-0.02	-1.10
sampleCOV vs. sampleCDaR	-0.014	-0.38
sampleCDaR vs. sampleCVaR	0.0071	0.20
sampleCDaR vs. normCVaR	0.0136	0.37
sampleCDaR vs. modCVaR	-0.008	-0.32

viation. The estimation errors of the actual mean are larger, but as for the standard deviation, the estimation errors are much lower. However, the downside risks are larger and the cumulative return is lower. Table 6.137 shows the t-test of the differences in means in the hypothetical worst case scenario. All the minimum risk portfolios outperform the risk budgeting counterparts. Moreover, the ERC portfolios display a significant higher actual mean than the naive portfolio. So when the market crashes, the risk budgeting approaches display worse performance statistics and a higher loss than the minimum risk approaches do. In such circumstances, the risk budgeting approaches are not suited.

Table 6.135: Performance Statistics of the Minimum Risk Portfolios in the Hypothetical Worst Case
The statistics are given as means across the portfolio optimizations. For better comparison, they are all shown in percent. The hypothetical worst case is seen as a situation, where the market is in a bull period and high positive returns are expected, but then the market crashes in a bear period with high negative returns.

	MV	minCVaR	minCDaR
$\mu_{estimated}$	0.052%	0.061%	0.066%
μ_{actual}	-0.050%	-0.064%	-0.077%
$\sigma_{estimated}$	0.169%	0.179%	0.230%
σ_{actual}	0.217%	0.236%	0.306%
MD_w	35.702%	46.456%	73.202%
SD_w	14.829%	11.299%	27.868%
AV μ	0.103%	0.124%	0.143%
AV σ	-0.048%	-0.057%	-0.076%
Sharpe Ratio	-21.713%	-26.424%	-26.487%
$Herfindahl_w$	54.087%	48.577%	43.425%
$Herfindahl_{rc}$	60.619%	45.552%	37.199%
Turnover	12.127%	14.640%	20.915%
VaR	0.854%	0.874%	2.650%
MaxDD	0.878%	1.246%	3.292%
μ_{annual}	-12.579%	-15.906%	-19.225%
$\mu_{cumulative}$	12.889%	12.751%	12.796%
σ_{annual}	3.436%	3.735%	4.839%
$SharpeRatio_{annual}$	-366.127%	-425.820%	-397.278%

Table 6.136: Performance Statistics of the Risk Budgeting Portfolios in
the Hypothetical Worst Case
The statistics are given as means across 17 portfolio optimizations. For better comparison, they are all shown in
percent. The hypothetical worst case is seen as a situation,
where the market is in a bull period and high positive returns are expected, but then the market crashes in a bear
period with high negative returns.

	sampleCVaR	sampleCDaR	normCVaR	modCVaR	sampleCOV	Naive
$\mu_{estimated}$	0.082%	0.095%	0.084%	0.086%	0.082%	0.104%
μ_{actual}	-0.133%	-0.174%	-0.141%	-0.145%	-0.144%	-0.239%
$\sigma_{estimated}$	0.345%	0.416%	0.364%	0.362%	0.385%	0.645%
σ_{actual}	0.342%	0.470%	0.361%	0.370%	0.376%	0.645%
MD_w	26.685%	37.430%	23.303%	26.028%	20.691%	0.000%
SD_w	9.023%	9.949%	8.342%	7.624%	10.137%	0.000%
AV μ	0.215%	0.270%	0.225%	0.231%	0.226%	0.343%
AV σ	0.003%	-0.054%	0.003%	-0.009%	0.010%	0.000%
Sharpe Ratio	-38.392%	-36.605%	-38.401%	-38.485%	-37.868%	-36.268%
$Herfindahl_w$	10.868%	6.095%	9.805%	10.722%	8.141%	0.000%
$Herfindahl_{rc}$	3.766%	6.097%	3.110%	4.235%	2.838%	5.016%
Turnover	11.010%	12.577%	10.368%	11.935%	10.820%	0.000%
VaR	2.176%	2.544%	3.072%	2.645%	3.518%	4.318%
MaxDD	4.755%	4.979%	5.284%	4.799%	5.929%	10.805%
μ_{annual}	-33.208%	-43.570%	-35.192%	-36.315%	-35.901%	-59.703%
$\mu_{cumulative}$	6.879%	8.738%	6.043%	5.181%	4.654%	2.929%
σ_{annual}	5.411%	7.433%	5.703%	5.853%	5.939%	10.203%
$SharpeRatio_{annual}$	-613.675%	-586.174%	-617.102%	-620.412%	-604.546%	-585.138%

Table 6.137: Significance in Actual Means (μ actual) in the Hypothetical
Worst Case
For the calculation of the t-test see 6.2.1.

	Excess Mean (%)	t-Stat
sampleCOV vs. MV	-0.093	-6.22
sampleCVaR vs. minCVaR	-0.0692	-5.35
normCVaR vs. minCVaR	-0.077	-5.58
modCVaR vs. minCVaR	-0.082	-4.72
sampleCDaR vs. minCDaR	-0.097	-4.43
sampleCOV vs. Naive	0.095	4.74
sampleCVaR vs. Naive	0.106	5.37
normCVaR vs. Naive	0.098	5.08
modCVaR vs. Naive	0.094	5.81
sampleCDaR vs. Naive	0.065	5.52
sampleCOV vs. sampleCVaR	-0.0108	-2.58
sampleCOV vs. normCVaR	-0.0028	-0.96
sampleCOV vs. modCVaR	0.0017	0.16
sampleCOV vs. sampleCDaR	0.0307	1.88
sampleCDaR vs. sampleCVaR	-0.0414	-2.85
sampleCDaR vs. normCVaR	-0.034	-2.22
sampleCDaR vs. modCVaR	-0.029	-2.95

Results of the Empirical Study

In the empirical 'normal' case the risk budgeting portfolios show better results concerning the estimation errors of the actual means and standard deviations. Moreover, the distances are smaller. However, the actual standard deviations are much higher, which results in a lower Sharpe ratio. Additionally they display higher tail risks (VaR and MaxDD).

In the crisis period, the minimum risk portfolios are more resistant due to higher actual mean and cumulative return and downside risk measures.

Concerning the hypothetical worst case, the risk-budgeting portfolios are worse than the minimum risk portfolios and cannot prevent loss. The estimation errors and drawdowns are higher and the cumulative returns lower.

6.4.4 Results of the Robustness Study

The simulation study has shown that the risk budgeting approaches are more structure and solution robust than the minimum risk portfolios. They obtain lower distances, are more diversified in terms of weights and risk, the weights or the portfolio composition does not change much (due to the standard deviations of the weights and the turnover). However, they exhibit lower estimation errors of the portfolio actual mean and risk only in the unrealistic simulation, due to the advantage that the naive portfolio is the true allocation. In the more realistic simulation with an unknown true allocation, the estimation errors are similar. The higher structure robustness of the risk budgeting portfolios does not result in better performance measures, like the Sharpe ratio nor in a lower downside risk.

In both simulated worst cases, if the estimated returns are positive, and the true returns are negative, the estimation errors of all approaches are large. The minimum risk portfolios outperform due to higher actual returns (which are significant in the realistic simulation) and less downside risk, but the differences are small.

Concerning the empirical study, the risk budgeting approaches have less estimation errors concerning the actual standard deviation and obtain higher actual mean return. But the higher returns are not significant and they exhibit an approximately twice higher actual standard deviation, so that they cannot beat the Sharpe ratio of the minimum risk approaches. Regarding the empirical worst case, the crisis period and the hypothetical market crash, the risk budgeting models underperform the minimum risk approaches concerning the actual mean and cumulative return and the downside risk measures. In the hypothetical worst case, the minimum risk portfolios display significant higher actual returns. Thus, they are neither suited for crisis periods nor for sudden market crashes, as in such circumstances the estimation errors are not different to the minimum risk approaches, and the performance is worse.

The results are similar to Poddig and Unger (2012). The expansion of the study to more minimum risk approaches and ERC portfolios based on the risk measures CVaR and CDaR does not change the general conclusion. Comparing the risk measures among the minimum risk portfolios, in the 'normal case' of the simulation and empirical case, the estimation errors of the minCVaR and the minCDaR portfolios are larger than the MV portfolio. This concerns the standard deviations of the weights, the distances of the weights and the estimation errors of the actual means (AV μ). Moreover, the actual standard deviations are higher, which results in lower Sharpe ratios compared to the MV portfolio. Among the ERC portfolios, the choice of the risk measures has not a high impact and the differences between the portfolios are small. But it is observable that the sampleCVaR and sampleCDaR portfolios display higher distances and slightly higher estimation errors (AV μ and AV σ). In the worst cases (except the hypothetical worst case), the minCDaR and minCVaR portfolios display higher actual returns and lower drawdowns vs. the MV portfolio, but the estimation errors are similar. Also among the risk budgeting portfolios, the sampleCDaR displays a better actual return, actual standard deviation and drawdowns in the worst cases, except the hypothetical worst case.

So combining the results of the earlier study in Poddig and Unger (2012) and this extension, it can be concluded that the ERC portfolios are more structure and solution robust in the 'normal' case as the minimum risk approaches, independent of the underlying risk measure. Moreover, there are no real differences between the ERC portfolios on different risk measures. But these characteristics do not help in terms of performance measures and also they do not held in uncertain market conditions, when these properties are needed the most. Thus, the benefit of the risk budgeting models is questionable.

7 Extensions of Empirical Studies

7.1 Fat Tailed Distributions

As described in cestion 3.1.3, the 'sample' models are based on the historical distribution. However, as the historical values are sparsely, especially in the tails, which are used for the risk calculation, there are many possibilities to extend the distribution assumption. The risk budgets can also be calculated through fitting a desired distribution and then simulating the returns based on the fitted parameters.

Generalized Hyperbolic as well as Stable Paretian distributions seem to capture the return distribution quite well and are used to calculate different risk measures in the literature (see Kassberger and Kiesel (2007), Harmantzis and Miao (2005), Harmantzis et al. (2006), Hellmich and Kassberger (2011), Aas et al. (2005), McNeil and P. (2005), Mittnik and Rachev (1993), Ortobelli et al. (2002), Stoyanov et al. (2005)). Already Fama (1965b) has claimed the use of the stable Paretian distribution in modeling asset returns. Thus, these distributions are applied to the calculation of the sampleCVaR, sampleCDaR as well as of the sampleCOV portfolio, to study the impact of the distribution assumption. For this, the distributions are first shortly described and then applied to the risk budgeting framework. This extension can be seen as a robustness test of the different performance results of section 6.2.

Generalized Hyperbolic Distributions

The presentation about the generalized hyperbolic distributions is cited according to McNeil and P. (2005), Hellmich and Kassberger (2011) and Breymann and Lüthi (2011).

The multivariate generalized hyperbolic (mGH) distribution is a normal mean-variance mixture. A randomness in the covariance matrix as well as in the mean vector of a multivariate normal distribution is included via a positive mixing variable. Normal mixture distributions are constructed by mixing normal distributions with different means as well as different variances (McNeil and P., 2005).

To introduce the mGH distribution, at first, the normal multivariate distribution and the normal variance mixture distribution is presented. The multivariate normal distribution is defined as follows (McNeil and P., 2005, p. 66):

$$X = \mu + AZ,$$

with

$$X : X = (X_1, ..., X_d)'$$

$A \in \mathbb{R}^{d \times k}$: d x k matrix of constants

$\mu \in \mathbb{R}^d$: vector of constants

Z : vector of iid univariate standard normal random variables, $Z = (Z_1, ..., Z_k)'$, $Z \sim N_k(0, I_k)$, where I_k is the identity matrix of dimension k

The mean of this distribution is $E(X) = \mu$ and the covariance matrix is $cov(X) = \Sigma$, where $\Sigma = AA'$. As the distribution is characterized by its mean vector and covariance matrix, the standard notation is $X \sim N_d(\mu, \Sigma)$. A multivariate normal variance mixture distribution is defined as follows (McNeil and P., 2005, p. 73):

$$X = \mu + \sqrt{W} AZ,$$

with

$$\boldsymbol{Z} \sim N_k(0, I_k)$$

$A \in \mathbb{R}^{d \times k} : d \times k \text{ matrix of constants}$

$\mu \in \mathbb{R}^d : \text{vector of constants}$

$W \geq 0 : \text{non-negative, scalar-valued random}$
$\qquad \text{variable, which is independent of } \boldsymbol{Z}$

These distributions are known as variance mixtures, because if it is conditioned on the random variable W, $\boldsymbol{X}|W = w \sim N_d(\mu, w\Sigma)$, where $\Sigma = AA'$. The variance mixture distribution can be seen as a combination of multivariate normal distributions with the same mean vectors and covariance matrices up to a multiplicative constant w. The distribution is constructed by sampling from this combined distribution according to a set of 'weights', which are defined by the distribution of W.

Now, from the definition of the normal variance mixture distribution, if W is a random variable with a generalized inverse Gaussian (GIG) distribution, then the normal variance mixture distribution is called a generalized hyperbolic distribution. W has a GIG distribution, $W \sim GIG(\lambda, \chi, \psi)$, if the density of W is (McNeil and P., 2005, p. 497):

$$f(x) = \frac{\chi^{-\lambda}\left(\sqrt{(\chi,\psi)}\right)^{\lambda}}{2K_\lambda\left(\sqrt{(\chi,\psi)}\right)} x^{\lambda-1} exp(-\frac{1}{2}(\chi x^{-1} + \psi x)), \quad x > 0$$

with

$K : \text{modified Bessel function of the third kind with index } \lambda.$

The parameters satisfy

$$\chi > 0, \psi \geq 0, if \lambda < 0$$
$$\chi > 0, \psi > 0, if \lambda = 0$$
$$\chi \geq 0, \psi > 0, if \lambda > 0$$

The vector $\boldsymbol{X}$ is said to have a multivariate generalized hyperbolic distribution if (McNeil and P., 2005, p. 77f)

$$\boldsymbol{X} = \mu + W\gamma + \sqrt{W}A\boldsymbol{Z},$$

with

$$Z \sim N_k(0, I_k)$$

$A \in \mathbb{R}^{d \, x \, k}$: matrix

$\mu, \gamma \in \mathbb{R}^d$: vector of constants

$W \geq 0$: non-negative, scalar-valued random variable, which is independent of Z and has a Generalized Inverse Gaussian (GIG (λ, χ, ψ)) distribution

The parameters can be interpreted as follows. The GIG parameters define the shape and the fat tails of the distribution. μ is the location parameter and γ defines the symmetry of the distribution (0 if the distribution is symmetrical). The mGH distribution has different subclasses:

- Hyperbolic distribution: if $\lambda = \frac{d+1}{2}$. The marginals are GH distributed.

- Normal Inverse Gaussian (NIG) distribution: if $\lambda = -\frac{1}{2}$.

- Variance Gamma (VG) distribution: if $\chi = 0$ and $\lambda > 0$.

- Skew Student's t distribution: if $\psi = 0$ and $\lambda < 0$

The different GH distributions are implemented in R in the ghyp package (Breymann and Lüthi, 2011).

Stable Paretian Distribution

The presentation about the stable distributions is cited according to Fama (1965a) and Harmantzis et al. (2006).

Stable Paretian distributions are usually characterized by their characteristic function, as densities and distribution functions are not known analytically. A random variable X is said to have a Stable distribution $(St(\alpha, \beta, \gamma, \delta))$ if its characteristic function has the form (Harmantzis et al., 2006, p. 123):

$$\phi(t) = E\,exp(i, t\,X) =$$
$$\begin{cases} exp(-\gamma^\alpha |t|^\alpha (1 - i\beta sign(t)tan(\frac{\pi}{2})\alpha) + i\delta t), \alpha \neq 1 \\ exp(-\gamma |t|(1 + i\beta sign(t)(2/\pi)ln|t|) + i\delta t), \alpha = 1 \end{cases}$$

with

t : any real number

i : $\sqrt{-1}$

$\alpha \in [0,2]$, characteristic exponent

$\beta \in [-1,1]$, skewness parameter

$\gamma > 0$, scale parameter

$\delta \in \mathbb{R}$, location parameter

The parameters can be interpreted as follows. The α value determines the heavy tails of the distribution. It takes values between $0 < \alpha \leq 2$. If it equals 2, the tails are equal to the normal distribution. Otherwise, the distribution displays heavy tails. β is the skewness parameter and is 0, if the distribution is symmetric. The δ parameter defines the location of the distribution, whereas γ specifies the scale or the expansion of the distribution around the position of the distribution.

The fitting and simulation algorithms will be used from the R package portes (Mahdi and McLeod, 2011). There, the quantile estimation method of McCulloch (1986) is used for fitting the parameters.

Generalized Lambda Distribution

The generalized lambda distribution (GLD) is an alternative to the stable distribution, as it offers analytic formulas for the density and can create distributions with a large range of different shapes (Chalabi and Würtz, 2012a). Thus, the GLD can cover a lot of other known distributions (like the students-t, the generalized hyperbolic and the stable distributions). However, the distribution is not widely spread, as the estimation of the parameters is difficult.

Chalabi and Würtz (2012a) introduce a new parametrization of the GLD, which is available in R through the package gldist (Chalabi and Würtz, 2012b).

The known parametrization of the GLD of Freimer et al. (1988) is as follows (Chalabi and Würtz, 2012a, p. 5):

$$Q(u) = \lambda_1 + \frac{1}{\lambda_2}[\frac{u^{\lambda_3} - 1}{\lambda_3} - \frac{(1-u)^{\lambda_4} - 1}{\lambda_4}],$$

with

$$Q(u) : \text{quantile function}$$
$$\lambda_1 : \text{location parameter}$$
$$\lambda_2 : \text{scale parameter}$$
$$\lambda_3, \lambda_4 : \text{tail index parameters}$$

The tail indices define the shape and the symmetry of the distribution. If the indices are equal, the distribution is symmetric. The size of the indices defines the tails: if both indices are small, the distribution has fat tails.

Chalabi and Würtz (2012a) defines an asymmetry parameter χ as well as a steepness parameter ξ instead of the two shape parameters λ_3 and λ_4, which allows a more intuitive interpretation. The asymmetry parameter takes values in the interval of (-1,1) and is proportional to the difference between the two shape indices, whereas the steepness parameter can display values between (0,1) and is proportional to the sum of both shape indices. As the quantile function with the two knew parameters includes a set of formulas, the elaboration is omitted here. For further details see Chalabi and Würtz (2012a).

Results

To examine the influences of the different distributions on the calculation of risk contributions and thus the portfolio performances, the distributions are applied for fitting the historical returns to the sampleCOV, sampleCVaR as well as the sampleCDaR model. In each estimation period (12 months of daily returns), the historical returns are fitted to a distribution and then returns with a sample size of 10.000 aree simulated. Based on this simulated returns, the risk budgeting models are calculated. To examine the results, the Global portfolio dataset of section 6.2.3 is used for the following examination. The different models based on the distributions are compared to the 'sample' portfolio, which is calculated on the historical sample of returns, as in the performances studies in chapter 6.2. For the fitting and simulation of the different distributed returns, the afro mentioned R packages are used.

Table 7.1 shows the abbreviations used for the different models based on simulated returns on the afro mentioned distributions. The tables 7.2, 7.4 and 7.6 show the main performance figures of the sample risk budgeting models calculated through the different distributions. The sampleCVaR portfolio displays the highest returns based on the generalized lambda distribution. However, it displays also the highest annual volatility. The highest Sharpe ratio is exhibited from the hyperbolic distribution, whereas the portfolio based on the stable distribution has the lowest standard deviation as well as the lowest loss. Table 7.3 shows the differences in means of the different models. It is obvious that the return differences are not significant and thus not different from the returns of the sampleCVaR portfolio.

Table 7.1: Notations of Portfolios with Simulated Returns

Abbreviation	Portfolio
sampleCOV	Equal Risk Contributions to Volatility based on historical returns
NIGCOV	based on simulated returns of the Normal Inverse Gaussian distribution
ghypCOV	based on simulated returns of the Generalized Hyperbolic distribution
hypCOV	based on simulated returns of the Hyperbolic distribution
tCOV	based on simulated returns of the Skewed Student t distribution
VGCOV	based on simulated returns of the Variance Gamma distribution
stableCOV	based on simulated returns of the Stable Paretian distribution
lambdaCOV	based on simulated returns of the Generalized Lambda distribution

Table 7.2: Main Statistics - sampleCVaR with Distributions

	Total Return	Ann. Return	Ann. StDev	Sharpe	Max Loss
sampleCVaR	79.19	5.11	8.52	60	-17.70
NIGCVaR	77.57	5.00	10.55	47.46	-19.01
ghypCVaR	91.90	5.93	9.40	63.04	-18.17
hypCVaR	95.70	6.17	9.36	65.98	-18.03
tCVaR	94.14	6.07	9.40	64.64	-18.08
VGCVaR	80.21	5.18	10.51	49.24	-18.99
stableCVaR	66.89	4.32	8.15	52.97	-14.69
lambdaCVaR	97.58	6.30	11.16	56.44	-16.11

Table 7.3: Differences in Mean Returns - sampleCVaR with Distributions

	Excess Mean (%)	t-Stat	p-value
NIGCVaR vs. sampleCVaR	-0.01	-0.09	0.93
ghypCVaR vs. sampleCVaR	0.07	1.27	0.21
hypCVaR vs. sampleCVaR	0.09	1.66	0.10
tCVaR vs. sampleCVaR	0.08	1.39	0.17
VGCVaR vs. sampleCVaR	0.01	0.06	0.95
stableCVaR vs. sampleCVaR	-0.07	-1.02	0.31
lambdaCVaR vs. sampleCVaR	0.10	0.90	0.37

The sampleCOV portfolio has the highest returns based on the hyperbolic as well as on the VG distribution. Noticeable is the fact that all the portfolios based on the distributions display higher returns than the sampleCOV portfolio based on the historical distribution. On the other side, they display also higher risk figures, so that the Sharpe ratio and the lowest loss of the sampleCOV portfolio cannot be out-competed. However, as table 7.5 reveals, the higher returns of applying a different distribution to the calculation of the sampleCOV portfolio are not statistically significant.

Table 7.4: Main Statistics - sampleCOV with Distributions

	Total Return	Ann. Return	Ann. StDev	Sharpe	Max Loss
sampleCOV	69.25	4.47	6.71	67	-11.11
NIGCOV	88.98	5.74	9.62	59.67	-18.07
ghypCOV	87.59	5.65	9.64	58.61	-18.13
hypCOV	89.49	5.77	9.61	60.11	-18.02
tCOV	88.37	5.70	9.64	59.12	-18.14
VGCOV	89.36	5.77	9.57	60.24	-18.07
stableCOV	75.55	4.87	8.62	56.53	-14.30
lambdaCOV	88.71	5.72	9.60	59.63	-16.40

Table 7.5: Differences in Mean Returns - sampleCOV with Distributions

	Excess Mean (%)	t-Stat	p-value
NIGCOV vs. sampleCOV	0.11	1.18	0.24
ghypCOV vs. sampleCOV	0.10	1.09	0.28
hypCOV vs. sampleCOV	0.11	1.21	0.23
tCOV vs. sampleCOV	0.10	1.14	0.26
VGCOV vs. sampleCOV	0.11	1.21	0.23
stableCOV vs. sampleCOV	0.03	0.56	0.58
lambdaCOV vs. sampleCOV	0.10	1.16	0.25

A look on table 7.6 reveals that the CDaR risk budgets based on the different generalized hyperbolic distributions outperform the historical distribution based on returns as well as on the Sharpe ratio. But the annual volatility as well as the loss are higher than those of the sampleCDaR portfolio. It seems that the stable as well as the lambda distribution are not suited for the CDaR risk budgets, as the returns are lower, but the risk figures much higher. Through applying the NIG, hyp or VG distribution, the sampleCDaR approach has higher returns and a higher Sharpe ratio than the minCDaR portfolio. But the higher returns of the different distributions to calculate the CDaR risk budgests are either statistically significant, as obvious from table 7.7.

Table 7.6: Main Statistics - sampleCDaR with Distributions

	Total Return	Ann. Return	Ann. StDev	Sharpe	Max Loss
sampleCDaR	89.00	5.74	7.68	75	-12.36
NIGCDaR	111.43	7.19	8.21	87.52	-16.18
ghypCDaR	105.38	6.80	8.16	83.27	-14.63
hypCDaR	110.25	7.11	7.82	90.92	-12.95
tCDaR	106.54	6.87	8.44	81.42	-16.48
VGCDaR	109.94	7.09	7.93	89.50	-13.65
stableCDaR	69.83	4.51	12.61	35.73	-21.48
lambdaCDaR	74.42	4.80	10.43	46.04	-20.53

Table 7.7: Differences in Mean Returns - sampleCDaR with Distributions

	Excess Mean (%)	t-Stat	p-value
NIGCDaR vs. sampleCDaR	0.12	1.81	0.07
ghypCDaR vs. sampleCDaR	0.09	1.31	0.19
hypCDaR vs. sampleCDaR	0.11	1.85	0.07
tCDaR vs. sampleCDaR	0.09	1.33	0.19
VGCDaR vs. sampleCDaR	0.11	1.74	0.08
stableCDaR vs. sampleCDaR	-0.10	-0.67	0.50
lambdaCDaR vs. sampleCDaR	-0.08	-0.57	0.57

The following tables show the risk figures for the different portfolios. The tables 7.8, 7.9 and 7.10 outline the outperformance of the 'sample' portfolios, thus the historical distribution, as they display the lowest

risk measures. Especially the sampleCOV portfolio displays much
lower risk figures than the counterparts based on the different return
distributions. However, in the case of the sampleCDaR portfolio, the
risk measures are not far apart from each other (except of the stable
distribution) and the VaR and the CVaR are even lower from the
portfolio based on the NIG and the hyperbolic distribution.

Table 7.8: Risk Figures - sampleCVaR with Distributions

	5% VaR	5% CVaR	5% DaR	5% CDaR	MaxDD
sampleCVaR	2.85	5.81	11.54	23.23	31.38
NIGCVaR	3.82	8.12	19.39	27.14	34.14
ghypCVaR	4.05	6.76	15.79	26.98	34.50
hypCVaR	4.06	6.56	15.25	26.46	34.11
tCVaR	4.23	7.09	14.79	25.44	33.08
VGCVaR	3.66	8.05	19.22	26.87	33.85
stableCVaR	2.94	6.20	17.74	23.39	28.07
lambdaCVaR	3.98	7.73	16.81	26.78	34.46

Table 7.9: Risk Figures - sampleCOV with Distributions

	5% VaR	5% CVaR	5% DaR	5% CDaR	MaxDD
sampleCOV	2.81	4.65	12.17	17.02	21.23
NIGCOV	3.79	6.96	17.28	26.79	34.05
ghypCOV	3.93	6.98	17.19	27.09	34.42
hypCOV	3.99	6.87	17.42	26.99	34.41
tCOV	4.18	7.34	17.08	27.44	34.95
VGCOV	3.76	6.83	17.27	27.03	34.30
stableCOV	3.33	6.49	15.98	22.67	28.63
lambdaCOV	3.94	6.64	15.48	24.80	32.77

For completeness, the tables 7.11, 7.12 and 7.13 present the risk
ratios based on the different risk measures. The risk ratios of the
different CVaR risk budgeting portfolios show that the skewed t-

distribution provides the best risk-return relationships based on the drawdown risk figures. The Sharpe ratio as well as the CVaR risk ratio are the highest based on the hyperbolic distribution. Only the VaR risk ratio of the sampleCVaR portfolio is the best. Thus, although the risk figures are all higher, the portfolios display a better risk-return relationship. This is not the case in the COV risk budgeting portfolio. There, the sampleCOV portfolio displays the best risk figures as well as the best risk ratios. The CDaR risk budget portfolio profits from the distributions, as the risk ratios are much higher compared to the historical distribution.

Table 7.10: Risk Figures - sampleCDaR with Distributions

	5% VaR	5% CVaR	5% DaR	5% CDaR	MaxDD
sampleCDaR	2.94	5.37	12.95	20.01	25.34
NIGCDaR	2.75	5.52	14.35	23.81	32.18
ghypCDaR	3.14	5.56	15.23	24.18	32.63
hypCDaR	2.96	5.34	13.56	22.50	30.61
tCDaR	3.18	5.81	15.85	25.31	33.83
VGCDaR	2.92	5.39	13.95	23.07	31.49
stableCDaR	5.58	9.56	25.69	35.42	42.27
lambdaCDaR	4.25	7.34	18.64	30.16	38.52

Table 7.11: Risk Ratios - sampleCVaR with Distributions

	SR	SR VaR	SR CVaR	SR CDaR	SR avdd	SR maxdd
sampleCVaR	59.96	51.79	25.39	6.35	12.49	1.36
NIGCVaR	47.46	37.78	17.80	5.32	8.17	1.22
ghypCVaR	63.04	42.25	25.30	6.34	13.03	1.43
hypCVaR	65.98	43.93	27.16	6.74	13.88	1.51
tCVaR	64.64	41.43	24.72	6.89	14.11	1.53
VGCVaR	49.24	40.83	18.56	5.56	8.53	1.27
stableCVaR	52.97	42.34	20.09	5.33	7.54	1.28
lambdaCVaR	56.44	45.71	23.52	6.79	11.11	

Table 7.12: Risk Ratios - sampleCOV with Distributions

	SR	SR_VaR	SR_CVaR	SR_CDaR	SR_avdd	SR_maxdd
sampleCOV	66.61	45.84	27.76	7.58	9.89	1.75
NIGCOV	59.67	43.68	23.82	6.19	11.40	1.41
ghypCOV	58.61	41.54	23.37	6.02	11.00	1.37
hypCOV	60.11	41.78	24.27	6.17	11.39	1.40
tCOV	59.12	39.38	22.43	6.00	11.00	1.36
VGCOV	60.24	44.23	24.38	6.16	11.39	1.40
stableCOV	56.53	42.20	21.68	6.21	8.93	1.42
lambdaCOV	59.63	41.93	24.88	6.66	11.14	1.46

Table 7.13: Risk Ratios - sampleCDaR with Distributions

	SR	SR_VaR	SR_CVaR	SR_CDaR	SR_avdd	SR_maxdd
sampleCDaR	74.77	56.32	30.86	8.28	12.14	1.89
NIGCDaR	87.52	75.48	37.62	8.72	23.19	1.86
ghypCDaR	83.27	62.56	35.29	8.12	18.98	1.74
hypCDaR	90.92	69.41	38.44	9.13	23.43	1.94
tCDaR	81.42	62.42	34.15	7.84	19.64	1.69
VGCDaR	89.50	70.19	38.01	8.87	22.78	1.88
stableCDaR	35.73	23.31	13.61	3.67	4.44	0.89
lambdaCDaR	46.04	32.64	18.89	4.60	7.19	1.04

Table 7.14: Turnover - sampleCVaR with Distributions

	mean Turnover	total Turnover	No. of Trades
sampleCVaR	0.08	14.78	2391
NIGCVaR	0.10	17.95	2371
ghypCVaR	0.09	17.62	2388
hypCVaR	0.09	16.11	2378
tCVaR	0.10	19.01	2376
VGCVaR	0.10	18.33	2390
stableCVaR	0.24	44.06	2405
lambdaCVaR	0.59	108.91	2395

Table 7.15: Turnover - sampleCOV with Distributions

	mean Turnover	total Turnover	No. of Trades
sampleCOV	0.05	8.84	2405
NIGCOV	0.07	12.41	2382
ghypCOV	0.07	13.12	2384
hypCOV	0.07	12.57	2379
tCOV	0.08	15.43	2376
VGCOV	0.07	13.40	2376
stableCOV	0.37	69.39	2405
lambdaCOV	0.27	49.99	2405

Table 7.16: Turnover - sampleCDaR with Distributions

	mean Turnover	total Turnover	No. of Trades
sampleCDaR	0.14	26.21	2405
NIGCDaR	0.27	51.04	2405
ghypCDaR	0.28	51.18	2405
hypCDaR	0.27	50.51	2405
tCDaR	0.28	51.99	2405
VGCDaR	0.26	49.16	2405
stableCDaR	0.79	146.26	2379
lambdaCDaR	1.17	216.74	2353

The turnovers of the different portfolios are presented in the tables 7.14, 7.15 and 7.16. It is clearly observable that the historical distribution causes the lowest turnover for all risk budgeting portfolios. Moreover, the turnover of the stable and the lambda distribution is much higher than of the other ones, especially in the case of the CDaR risk contributions portfolio. The choice of the distribution has a low impact on the number of trades. The number of trades remains approximately the same or is slightly lower.

Summary
In this section it was shown that the different 'sample' portfolios, which rely on a sample of returns to calculate the equal risk contribution portfolios can also be obtained by using different distributions. The applied distributions capture common observed characteristics of returns, as fat tails and skewness (asymmetry). The results show that in some cases the returns and the Sharpe ratios are higher compared to the historical distribution. However, the return differences are not significantly different from each other. Thus, this section can be seen as a robustness check of the performances of the risk budgeting portfolios and approves the conclusion that the performance results of chapter 6 are valid and independent of the underlying return distribution.

7.2 Binary Stability Portfolio

Although the datasets of the performances are different, the results concerning the risk budgeting portfolios do not differ much. The risk budgeting portfolios have higher drawdowns in crisis periods as the minimum risk approaches and according to the CAPM and Fama-French regressions, the higher return is not high enough to compensate for this. Based on this sober results of the risk diversified portfolios, the question is what alternatives exist in the literature or which 'new directions in portfolio management' are available. Thus, an interesting approach, the so called stable portfolio, is going to be presented and compared to the ERC portfolios.

Description of the Approach
An interesting new approach in portfolio optimization is the Binary Stability Portfolio of Chalabi et al. (2011). They propose to focus on stability to quantify risk rather than well known risk measures. Stability is thereby generally defined as *'a steady increase in the cumulated returns that goes with a low volatility, small drawdowns and short recovery times.'* (Würtz et al., 2012b) The stability or instability of a time series is detected through a Bayesian Analysis for Change Points

of Barry and Hartigan (1993). Thereby it is assumed that a time series can be divided in different blocks. The beginning of a block is a 'change point' and the data of different blocks are independent of each other. The observations within a block have constant parameters, that is, equal means. Moreover, it is assumed that a parameter sequence in one block forms a Markov chain. The identification of a change point in a time series takes place through a Markov Chain Monte Carlo (MCMC) method where in each iteration, each observation is drawn from the conditional distribution of the observation given the data and the current block and the transition probability of a change point is calculated Erdman and Emerson (2007). Thus, the number of change points is considered as a random variable and obtained through a simulation (Loschi et al., 2005).

The method is implemented in the R package bpc of Erdman and Emerson (2007, 2008). For further mathematical details of the method the reader is referred to Barry and Hartigan (1993) and Erdman and Emerson (2008). Thus, the model can determine in each point from the sequence if the observation is a change point. The result of the model is a posterior probability of each observation being a change point. The probability can take values of [0,1] and the higher the value, the higher the possibility of a change in the next observation. The posterior mean and the posterior variance can also be calculated.

Based on this method, Chalabi et al. (2011), Würtz et al. (2012b) go a step further and apply a spline smoother on the sequence of the posterior probabilities. The smoothing rate of the smoother can be thereby defined differently in the interval of [0,1]. Then, the difference between the strongest smoothed curve (rate=0.8) and the lowest smoothed curve (rate=0.3) of the posterior probabilities of the Bayesian Change Model equals a stability indicator of the time series. This procedure can be best clarified in figures.

Figure 7.1 shows the Bayesian change point analysis of the SX5T. The chart shows the posterior mean, the posterior variance, the pos-

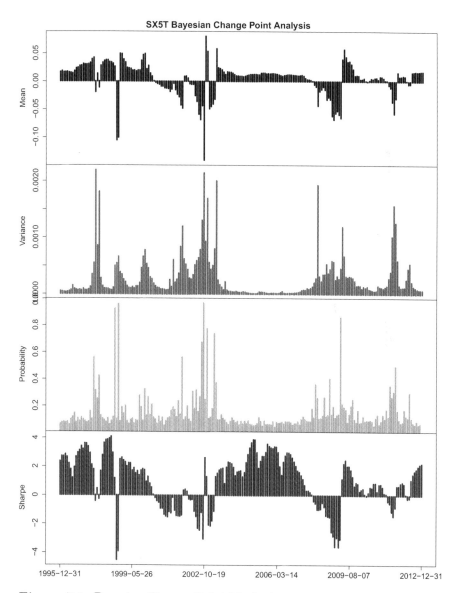

Figure 7.1: Bayesian Change Point Method

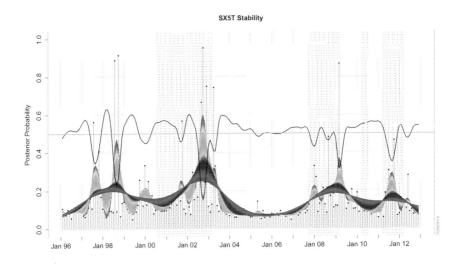

Figure 7.2: SX5T Stability

terior probability and the Sharpe ratio (mean/std). It is visible that in crisis periods, the mean is negative, the variance and the probability of a change gets higher and the Sharpe ratio is negative. Thus, the method identifies instable phases of a time series. The density of the posterior probabilities and the number of change points in a series can also serve as stability indicator (Chalabi et al., 2011). Rather than to take the pure posterior probabilities, the difference between the strongest and the weakest smoothed probabilities is taken for calculating the stability indicators. This is visible in figure 7.2. The small dots are the posterior probabilities and the rainbow colors show the different smooth grades of the probabilities in small steps (0.005). The black curve around 0.5 is the difference between the strongest and the weakest smoothed curves, which represents the stability indicator. If it is above 0.5, the time series is stable, otherwise the more the line is under 0.5, the more unstable.

Now, for forecasting the stability of a time series, the described stability indicator can be extrapolated or an average over the estimating period can be taken. The binary switching stability portfolio takes the stability indicator of each series in the portfolio as a criterion for investment in an asset. If the asset is stable, the portfolio invests in it, otherwise the portion is allocated in a more stable asset. The following investigation will illustrate the technique.

Furthermore, stability can also be assessed through a principal component outliers analysis or through a wavelet analysis (Chalabi et al., 2011). The PCA extreme value analysis takes place through dissecting the time series by robust principal components. As the PCA factors explain the variance and the variance increases, if outliers are present, the technique is suitable to detect them. The outliers are then identified through a Mahalanobis distance. This method is described in (Filzmoser et al., 2008) and implemented in the R package mvoutlier (Filzmoser and Gschwandtner, 2013). The wavelet analysis allows to detect the non-stationary behavior in the time series, which is a sign for a break. Chalabi et al. (2011) use the Morlet wavelet and the square of the absolute value as the transform value to identify instabilities in time series as formulated by Torrence and Compo (1998). The method is implemented in the R package dplR of Bunn et al. (2012). In the following, the stable portfolio based on the Bayesian Analysis for Change Points will be examined.

Comparison of the Binary Stability Portfolio

Because of the problems described above with two datasets, namely not included currency risk and survivorship bias, the first dataset of the European Fund will be used again to compare the risk budgeting models to the described alternatives.

The binary switching portfolio explores the stability of the time series on a rolling window period and decides whether or not to invest in the assets. At first, the risky assets are studied. If they are stable, an amount of 25% is invested. The rest is left for the bond. If the bond is unstable, the money is invested in the money market. Whereas the risky assets can have a max. weight of 25%, the bond and the libor can account for 100%.

Figure 7.3 shows the Indices of the European Fund dataset, from which the portfolios are constructed. The thin curves display the 'stabilized indices': If the Stability portfolio is invested in the asset, the return of the index is taken, otherwise it is 0. It is obvious that only through not investing in unstable periods, the cumulated returns are much higher. Only the cumulated returns of the bond gets lower.

Table 7.17: Main Statistics - Binary Stability Portfolio

	Totalret	ann.Mean	ann.Vola	Sharpe	MaxLoss
MV	92.68	5.79	3.49	165.87	-1.96
minCVaR	96.21	6.01	3.56	168.99	-2.01
minCDaR	93.53	5.85	4.37	133.92	-3.04
Naive	89.12	5.57	12.77	43.60	-14.20
sampleCVaR	105.30	6.58	4.64	141.85	-3.24
normCVaR	104.61	6.54	4.66	140.21	-3.33
modCVaR	104.48	6.53	5.75	113.50	-6.58
sampleCOV	104.26	6.52	4.72	138.00	-3.41
sampleCDaR	99.43	6.21	5.54	112.18	-5.39
Stability	178.78	11.17	7.88	141.88	-6.73

Table 7.17 summarizes the results of the different risk based portfolios compared to the Binary Stability Portfolio. The returns of the Binary Stability strategy are higher than of the portfolios studied before. However, the volatilities are also all higher, as the risk portfolios are more invested in the bond. Thus, the Sharpe ratio is lower than of the MV and the minCVaR portfolio and comparable to some of the ERC portfolios.

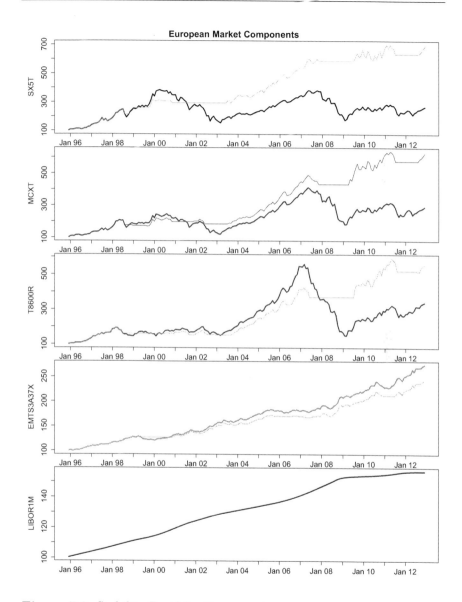

Figure 7.3: Stability Portfolio Components

As presented in tables 7.18 and 7.19, the higher returns as well as the higher volatilities of the Binary Stability approach are both statistically significant compared to all portfolios.

Table 7.18: Statistical Significance of Mean Differences - Binary Stability Portfolio
For the calculations of the tests see 6.2.1.

	Excess Mean (%)	t-Stat	p-value
Stability vs. MV	0.45	2.84	0.01
Stability vs. minCVaR	0.43	2.74	0.01
Stability vs. minCDaR	0.44	3.10	0.00
Stability vs. Naive	0.47	2.08	0.04
Stability vs. sampleCVaR	0.38	3.01	0.00
Stability vs. normCVaR	0.39	3.06	0.00
Stability vs. modCVaR	0.39	3.36	0.00
Stability vs. sampleCOV	0.39	3.06	0.00
Stability vs. sampleCDaR	0.41	3.37	0.00

Table 7.19: Significance of Difference in Variances - Binary Stability Portfolio
For the calculations see 6.2.1.

	Ratio of variances	p-value
Stability vs. MV	5.0855	0.0000
Stability vs. minCVaR	4.8985	0.0000
Stability vs. minCDaR	3.2547	0.0000
Stability vs. Naive	0.3801	0.0000
Stability vs. sampleCVaR	2.8813	0.0000
Stability vs. normCVaR	2.8521	0.0000
Stability vs. modCVaR	1.8739	0.0000
Stability vs. sampleCOV	2.7818	0.0000
Stability vs. sampleCDaR	2.0213	0.0000

Table 7.20: Returns per Calendar Year - Binary Stability Portfolio

	1997	1998	1999	2000	2001	2002	2003	2004	2005
MV	6.36	9.54	-3.10	7.13	3.41	7.11	7.56	11.09	7.57
minCVaR	6.10	9.82	-3.37	7.14	3.04	8.45	8.35	10.77	7.94
minCDaR	11.04	10.87	5.99	5.45	2.65	4.70	7.12	11.80	8.93
Naive	22.96	11.79	16.52	2.04	-8.20	-17.87	16.84	18.50	18.84
sampleCVaR	17.12	10.83	4.27	5.96	1.73	1.84	9.94	13.57	10.67
normCVaR	16.06	10.41	3.43	5.93	1.40	2.03	9.34	14.26	12.00
modCVaR	16.69	10.25	3.53	6.15	0.87	3.55	9.80	12.45	10.68
sampleCOV	16.17	10.30	3.55	6.03	1.11	1.71	9.52	14.13	12.16
sampleCDaR	15.07	9.51	8.63	4.25	1.04	3.58	8.54	15.35	12.92
Stability	22.99	15.06	11.39	1.22	5.41	2.78	11.72	18.95	18.21

	2006	2007	2008	2009	2010	2011	2012	Total
MV	2.27	1.85	6.07	5.61	6.54	3.76	9.91	
minCVaR	2.13	1.29	6.44	5.59	7.30	5.55	9.66	
minCDaR	3.55	1.12	1.18	4.46	7.45	-2.76	9.99	
Naive	21.45	-7.76	-43.05	22.42	7.29	-10.27	17.61	
sampleCVaR	7.28	-0.22	-3.29	8.16	5.70	-0.67	12.40	
normCVaR	8.84	-0.78	-4.51	8.50	5.90	-0.28	12.08	
modCVaR	7.32	-0.35	-4.14	12.57	1.38	1.51	12.20	
sampleCOV	8.75	-0.78	-5.03	8.75	5.95	-0.25	12.19	
sampleCDaR	13.56	-2.34	-8.85	5.76	6.45	-7.53	13.48	
Stability	21.02	-0.87	12.77	15.09	8.67	0.89	13.47	

The returns per year in table 7.20 outline that the Stability Portfolio delivers in 6 out of 16 years the highest return. In all other years, the portfolio is outperformed by the naive or the MV or the minCVaR portfolio. Impressive is the performance in 2008, where it receives 12%, where the risk budgeting and the naive portfolio exhibit high losses. The tables 7.21 and 7.22 outline again the risk measures and the risk ratios of the portfolios based on the European dataset together with the Binary Stability Portfolio. The minimum risk portfolios display still the lowest risk measures. Compared to the risk budgeting portfolios, Binary Stability shows a higher VaR and CVaR, but lower drawdown risks. The risk ratios based on the drawdown measures are by contrast the highest for the Stability portfolio, except the SR_avdd.

Table 7.21: Risk Figures - Binary Stability Portfolio

	5% VaR	5% CVaR	5% DaR	5% CDaR	MaxDD
MV	1.14	1.49	4.14	5.11	6.78
minCVaR	1.34	1.64	4.01	4.98	6.75
minCDaR	1.48	2.00	4.03	5.10	6.83
Naive	6.25	8.96	37.21	44.38	50.66
sampleCVaR	1.89	2.39	4.48	5.81	7.56
normCVaR	1.90	2.45	5.71	7.41	9.28
modCVaR	2.15	3.26	5.72	7.41	9.49
sampleCOV	1.91	2.51	6.16	7.79	9.89
sampleCDaR	2.01	3.24	11.12	12.77	14.99
Stability	2.71	4.17	5.30	6.40	8.30

Table 7.22: Risk Ratios - Binary Stability Portfolio

	SR sigma	SR VaR	SR CVaR	SR CDaR	SR avdd	SR maxdd
MV	165.87	146.72	112.22	32.71	64.33	7.12
minCVaR	168.99	129.50	105.58	34.82	66.19	7.43
minCDaR	133.92	113.76	84.22	33.11	57.29	7.13
Naive	43.60	25.72	17.95	3.62	3.24	0.92
sampleCVaR	141.85	100.65	79.63	32.68	58.58	7.25
normCVaR	140.21	99.45	77.05	25.47	51.03	5.87
modCVaR	113.50	87.54	57.80	25.44	46.17	5.74
sampleCOV	138.00	98.39	74.81	24.16	48.96	5.49
sampleCDaR	112.18	89.04	55.37	14.04	22.58	3.45
Stability	141.88	119.22	77.27	50.43	61.58	11.21

Figure 7.4 shows the weights of the Stability portfolio through time
and the average allocation of each asset. It is visible that in the risky
assets, the portfolio is either invested with 25% or not at all. The
Libor and the bond positions are taken by contrast in some periods
with 100%. During 1999 - half of 2000, the libor position is taken as
the bond is unstable. This is also the case between 2006 - 2007. From
the end of 2008 - the beginning of 2009 and from the end of 2012
- 06.2012, only the bond position is taken. Thus, the crisis periods
are clearly identified and losses are avoided through investment in

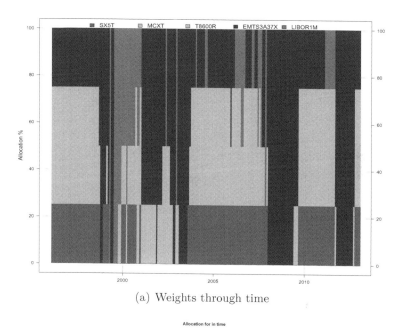

(a) Weights through time

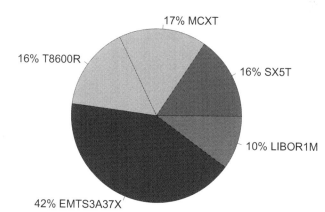

(b) Average Allocation

Figure 7.4: Binary Stability Portfolio Weights

the safer investment. In other periods, 1996 - 1999, 06.2003 - 2008 and 06.2009 - 06.2011, the Stability portfolio is equal to the naive portfolio to benefit from the increasing returns of the assets. The average allocation shows that throughout the whole period the Stability portfolio results in a 50/40 allocation of stocks and bonds or 50/50 in risky and non-risky assets.

Stabilizing the Assets

Based on the exploration of the steadiness of the time series is another possibility to stabilize the assets first through the binary switching method and then use these stabilized assets as inputs for the portfolios. This works in the following way. At first the bond is stabilized: if the stable portfolio is invested in the bond, the return of the bond is taken, otherwise that of the Libor. Then for the three risky assets applies: if the stable portfolio is invested in the asset, the return of the asset is taken, otherwise that of the stabilized bond.

$$stablebond = r_{bond} * sgn(w_{bond}) + r_{libor} * (1 - sgn(w_{bond})) \qquad (7.1)$$

$$stableasset = r_{asset} * sgn(w_{asset}) + r_{stablebond} * (1 - sgn(w_{asset})) \qquad (7.2)$$

with

$$r : \text{return}$$

$$w : \text{weight in the Binary Stability Portfolio}$$

$$sgn(x) : \text{signum function of x, 1 if x > 0, -1 if x < 0}$$

Table 7.23 displays the results of the portfolios with the stabilized assets. The results show that the portfolio returns can be lifted and the risk reduced, except of the MV portfolio. However, the Stability portfolio remains still the best in terms of cumulated returns. The naive portfolio with the stabilized asset series is almost equally to the Stable portfolio, which is not surprising as at first the weights of the Stable portfolio are taken to obtain the stable asset series and then it is equally invested in the stabilized assets. Moreover, it can be observed that the stabilizing of the assets shifts the relation of the risk budgeting models compared to the minimum risk counterparts in the case of the sampleCOV and the sampleCDaR portfolios, as they display now higher Sharpe ratios than the corresponding minimum risk models.

Table 7.23: Statistics - Portfolios with Stabilized Assets

	Totalret	ann.Mean	ann.Vola	Sharpe	MaxLoss
MV	91.78	5.74	3.74	153.44	-1.70
minCVaR	114.80	7.18	3.81	188.47	-2.01
minCDaR	113.47	7.09	4.52	156.86	-4.52
Naive	178.03	11.13	7.82	142.23	-6.61
sampleCVaR	135.56	8.47	5.17	164.02	-6.20
normCVaR	138.74	8.67	5.13	169.03	-6.18
modCVaR	131.97	8.25	5.26	156.90	-6.18
sampleCOV	139.70	8.73	4.76	183.26	-3.04
sampleCDaR	137.33	8.58	5.04	170.30	-3.54
Stability	178.78	11.17	7.88	141.88	-6.73

Summary
The comparison of the risk based portfolios to the Binary Stability Portfolio has shown that the Stability Portfolio can deliver higher returns. However, it cannot outperform the minimum risk portfolios in terms of Sharpe ratio and risk measures. The Sharpe ratio as well as the risk measures are comparable to the ERC portfolios, except the drawdown risks, where the Stability portfolio displays better results. Through this method, it is possible to detect unstable periods and to invest in safer assets like bonds or the money market, if the market goes down. Thus, as already observed in section 6.2, the diversification of risk seems not to be the key to success in crisis

periods, but on the contrary, to invest in more safer assets. As the MV or the minCVaR portfolio show the best Sharpe ratios and also the lowest risk measures, another possibility is to leverage the MV portfolio to get higher returns.

7.3 Hierarchical Clustering

In this section, alternative techniques to form a portfolio will be explained and tested, as the following techniques are also heuristic, related with the idea of the risk budgeting approach and also worth of mention and inspection.

Related with the idea of the risk budgets is the technique of the hierarchical asset clustering, in which the assets are clustered according to their individual characteristics. The idea of the hierarchical clustering is differently used in finance. It is either used as an heuristic search to select an asset universe out of many assets before the optimization (Da Costa et al., 2005, Dose and Cincotti, 2005) or to cluster assets into groups by similarity. In this thesis, the latter is of further importance. The clustering of equities can improve economic forecasting and modeling (Bonanno et al., 2001). In this scope, the principal component analysis is the most popular technique. However, the clustering allows to define different asset characteristics, such as correlation or risk, by which the assets are arranged into groups.

Common to all sorts of clustering is that the technique is part of the multivariate data analysis (Kaufman and Rousseeuw, 1990). The aim of the clustering analysis is to group different objects in similar groups according to their characteristics (Tola et al., 2008). The characteristic, upon which the clustering is done, can be very different and depends on the target of the clustering. Two basic methods have been proposed in the literature: hierarchical clustering (Ward, 1963, Duda et al., 2001) and k-means clustering (Hartigan and Wong, 1979, Das et al., 1997).

Many studies have applied the clustering analysis techniques to financial portfolios. However, the idea used here and the ones examined in the literature are different. Some studies applied the clustering technique before the portfolio optimization (see Tola et al. (2008) for obtaining a correlation matrix with the clustering technique; Zhang and Maringer (2009) and Zhang and Maringer (2011) for a clustering technique to improve Sharpe ratios). Several authors used the analysis to explore the hierarchical correlation structure of the financial market (see Onnela et al. (2002, 2003), Miccichè et al. (2003), Bonanno et al. (2003, 2004), Di Matteo et al. (2004), Mizuno et al. (2006), Guillermo and Matesanz (2006), Brida and Risso (2010)). Another field of application is the categorization of Funds (see Das (2003) for Hedge Fund Classification using K-means, Marathe and Shawky (1999) for Mutual Funds, Lisi and Otranto (2009) for Clustering Mutual Funds by return and risk, Shawky and Marathe (2010) for hierarchical and k-means clustering of Hedge Funds). In this thesis the cluster analysis will be used to obtain directly a portfolio without further optimization, through simply combining assets pairwise according to their individual risk levels.

The assets are clustered pairwise according to their risk measure. The used risk measures are the standard deviation, the normal CVaR, the modified CVaR, the sample CVaR as well as the sample CDaR. At first, the risk measures are calculated and the assets are sorted in increasing order by the amount of the risk. Then, the first and the second, the third and the forth asset, and so on, are combined together to an index through applying the analytical formula of the equal risk contribution portfolio for the two-asset case (Maillard et al., 2010):

$$w_1 = \frac{risk_1^{-1}}{risk_1^{-1} + risk_2^{-1}}, \tag{7.3}$$

with

$$w_1 : \text{weight of asset 1}$$
$$risk_1 : \text{risk measure of asset 1}$$
$$risk_2 : \text{risk measure of asset 2}$$

$$(7.4)$$

The weight of the second asset is obtained through subtract the weight from 1: $w_2 = 1 - w_1$, as the portfolios weights sum up to one. Next, the procedure is repeated. By applying iteratively this algorithm, a portfolio is attained without 'real optimization'. The weights are then recursively obtained by going the 'cluster chain' backwards. Figure 7.5 clarifies the strategy. The assets are combined according to their individual risk measures. Thus, an estimation of the returns are not needed.

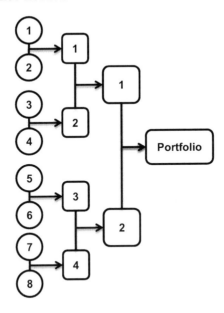

Figure 7.5: Hierarchical Clustering Algorithm

The portfolio allocation, or better the individual asset weight, depends only on the amount of the risk from the individual asset, like it is the case of the risk budgeting approaches. However, the assets are iteratively clustered by two into indices (or to a portfolio consisting of two assets). Through this method, the assets with the lowest risks get the highest weights in the portfolio, as the assets are sorted increasing by risks and combined through their risk budgets, and the assets with the highest risks the lowest weights (or zero weights). E.g., if there are more than 8 assets in the portfolios and less than 16, these assets are disregarded. Thus, the assets with the highest risks get a weight of zero in the portfolio. This could also be a disadvantage, if the asset risks change from period to period, as then the turnover increases. However, through this method, the investor can intuitively understand which assets contribute the most to the portfolio risk and use the risk contributions of the assets to build her asset allocation. The objective of this approach is comparable to the ERC portfolio with the difference that the assets with the lowest risks get the highest risk contributions and the risk contributions are not equal. Thus, it is interesting to explore the risk budgets and the performance of the hierarchical applied portfolios in comparison to the ERC portfolios.

Five different portfolios based on the risk measures used for the risk budgeting approach are obtained. The Global portfolio and Germany 1973 dataset from sections 6.2.3 and 6.2.4 are used for the examination of the hierarchical optimization, to investigate the properties and similarities of the hierarchical approach vs. the risk budgeting techniques. The first dataset, the European Fund, is not suited for this examination, as there are only 4 assets available and this is inadequate for the hierarchical clustering algorithm.

For reasons of comprehensibility, the following abbreviations of the portfolios will be used in the following to discuss the results of the hierarchical obtained portfolios.

Table 7.24: Abbreviations of Hierarchical portfolios

Abbreviation	Portfolio
HSds	Hierarchical Optimization based on standard deviation
HCVaRgaussian	Hierarchical Optimization based on normal CVaR
HCVaRmodified	Hierarchical Optimization based on modified CVaR
HCVaRsample	Hierarchical Optimization based on historical CVaR
HCDaR	Hierarchical Optimization based on CDaR

7.3.1 Global Portfolio

Table 7.25 shows the general characteristics of the hierarchical portfolios together with the minimum risk and risk budgeting portfolios for the Global portfolio dataset. The HCDaR portfolio offers the highest return and the highest Sharpe ratio of all approaches. But the minimum risk portfolios display a lower volatility and maximum loss. Compared to the risk budgeting portfolios, the hierarchical portfolios display higher returns and higher Sharpe ratios, except the HCVaRmodified vs. the modCVaR portfolio. Thus, the hierarchical clustering method seem to be the better alternative compared to the ERC portfolios in this dataset. However, as outlined in table 7.26, the higher returns are not statistically significant vs. the minimum risk and the risk budgeting counterparts.

The risk figures and risk ratios in table 7.27 and 7.28 show that the minimum risk portfolios have still the lowest risk measures and the risks of the hierarchical portfolios are similar to the ERC portfolios, but slightly lower. The risk ratios stay also the highest for the minCDaR portfolio, except the Sharpe ratio and the SR_avdd. However, in general the risk ratios are lower than of the minimum risk portfolios and slightly higher compared to the risk budgeting portfolios. The turnover of the hierarchical portfolios is comparable to the minimum risk approaches. This is not surprising, as the hierarchical portfolios concentrate also on the assets with the lowest risks.

Table 7.25: Statistics of the Hierarchical portfolios - Global portfolio

	Total Return	Ann. Return	Ann. StDev	Sharpe	Max Loss
MV	64.83	4.18	5.91	70.73	-11.52
minCVaR	63.14	4.07	5.50	74.05	-9.02
minCDaR	68.66	4.43	5.13	86.30	-6.25
Naive	81.62	5.27	13.75	38.31	-21.48
sampleCVaR	79.19	5.11	8.52	59.96	-17.70
normCVaR	72.25	4.66	6.65	70.15	-10.97
modCVaR	78.85	5.09	8.17	62.27	-14.59
sampleCOV	69.25	4.47	6.71	66.61	-11.11
sampleCDaR	89.00	5.74	7.68	74.77	-12.36
HSds	76.69	4.95	7.07	70.01	-13.90
HCVaRgaussian	83.89	5.41	6.98	77.58	-14.04
HCVaRmodified	69.82	4.50	7.49	60.14	-17.79
HCVaRsample	80.41	5.19	6.73	77.05	-13.23
HCDaR	98.03	6.32	7.10	89.06	-12.81

Table 7.26: Statistical Significance of Mean Differences of the Hierarchical Portfolios - Global Portfolio

	Excess Mean (%)	t-Stat	p-value
HSds vs. MV	0.06	0.97	0.33
HSds vs. sampleCOV	0.04	1.00	0.32
HCVaRgaussian vs. minCVaR	0.11	1.55	0.12
HCVaRgaussian vs. normCVaR	0.06	1.53	0.13
HCVaRmodified vs. minCVaR	0.04	0.43	0.66
HCVaRmodified vs. modCVaR	-0.05	-0.60	0.55
HCVaRsample vs. minCVaR	0.09	1.40	0.16
HCVaRsample vs. sampleCVaR	0.01	0.11	0.92
HCDaR vs. minCDaR	0.16	1.78	0.08
HCDaR vs. sampleCDaR	0.05	1.12	0.26

Table 7.27: Risk Figures of the Hierarchical Portfolios - Global Portfolio

	5% VaR	5% CVaR	5% DaR	5% CDaR	MaxDD
MV	2.47	4.43	11.62	15.19	18.04
minCVaR	2.44	4.14	12.31	14.42	16.35
minCDaR	1.60	3.32	7.91	9.42	12.21
Naive	6.26	9.96	31.55	40.67	48.63
sampleCVaR	2.85	5.81	11.54	23.23	31.38
normCVaR	2.74	4.56	12.06	16.81	20.97
modCVaR	2.80	5.76	18.38	21.66	25.36
sampleCOV	2.81	4.65	12.17	17.02	21.23
sampleCDaR	2.94	5.37	12.95	20.01	25.34
HSds	2.72	4.98	10.65	18.59	23.45
HCVaRgaussian	2.62	4.79	10.47	18.30	23.09
HCVaRmodified	2.65	5.09	17.63	22.87	26.85
HCVaRsample	2.41	4.59	10.17	17.36	21.93
HCDaR	2.81	4.80	15.19	19.32	22.80

Table 7.28: Risk Ratios of the Hierarchical Models - Global Portfolio

	SR	SR VaR	SR CVaR	SR CDaR	SR avdd	SR maxdd
MV	20.42	14.09	7.86	2.29	13.19	1.93
minCVaR	21.38	13.94	8.20	2.35	11.13	2.08
minCDaR	24.91	23.11	11.13	3.92	18.06	3.02
Naive	11.06	7.01	4.41	1.08	3.96	0.90
sampleCVaR	17.31	14.95	7.33	1.83	14.28	1.36
normCVaR	20.25	14.19	8.53	2.31	12.72	1.85
modCVaR	17.97	15.13	7.36	1.96	10.50	1.67
sampleCOV	19.23	13.23	8.01	2.19	11.38	1.75
sampleCDaR	21.58	16.26	8.91	2.39	14.53	1.89
HSds	20.21	15.14	8.28	2.22	16.01	1.76
HCVaRgaussian	22.39	17.24	9.41	2.46	19.53	1.95
HCVaRmodified	17.36	14.19	7.37	1.64	10.47	1.40
HCVaRsample	22.24	17.93	9.41	2.49	19.14	1.97
HCDaR	25.71	18.73	10.97	2.73	19.21	2.31

Table 7.29: Turnover of the Hierarchical Portfolios - Global Portfolio

	mean Turnover	total Turnover
MV	0.10	17.78
minCVaR	0.17	30.72
minCDaR	0.21	39.70
Naive	0.03	5.87
sampleCVaR	0.08	15.30
normCVaR	0.06	10.51
modCVaR	0.11	20.45
sampleCOV	0.05	9.39
sampleCDaR	0.14	26.29
meanHSds	0.09	17.07
meanHCVaRgaussian	0.10	17.80
meanHCVaRmodified	0.22	41.42
meanHCVaRsample	0.14	25.26
meanHCDaR	0.22	40.22

7.3.2 German Market

Table 7.30 shows the major characteristics of the hierarchical portfolios based on the German equities asset universe. In the German dataset with 55 equities, the hierarchical portfolio based on the CDaR exhibits also the highest total return. However, the Sharpe ratio is similar to the MV portfolio, but lower than of the minCVaR portfolio. Nevertheless, the hierarchical portfolios seem to be the better alternative compared to the risk budgeting portfolios if it comes to similar assets, like equities in this dataset. The returns are higher with a slightly lower standard deviation as of the risk budgeting portfolios.

Table 7.31 shows that the returns of three hierarchical portfolios are significantly higher than of the risk budgeting counterparts. Thus, in the equities dataset, the hierarchical clustering method delivers significantly higher returns than the risk budgeting models with a similar standard deviation and are better suited for an investment in individual equities. However, they do not display a significant higher return compared to the minimum risk portfolios.

Table 7.30: Statistics of the Hierarchical Portfolios - Germany 1973

	Total Return	Ann. Return	Ann. StDev	Sharpe	Max Loss
MV	152.94	3.95	8.77	45.02	-10.01
minCVaR	181.53	4.68	9.95	47.09	-13.14
minCDaR	132.41	3.42	12.03	28.40	-41.26
Naive	98.88	2.55	16.07	15.87	-23.01
sampleCVaR	133.14	3.44	12.80	26.84	-19.22
normCVaR	129.50	3.34	12.34	27.07	-18.67
modCVaR	109.45	2.82	12.88	21.92	-19.73
sampleCOV	119.31	3.08	12.43	24.77	-18.42
sampleCDaR	170.90	4.41	13.95	31.62	-20.95
HSds	190.59	4.92	12.61	39.02	-18.74
HCVaRgaussian	213.66	5.51	12.49	44.15	-17.98
HCVaRmodified	185.93	4.80	14.83	32.35	-15.58
HCVaRsample	179.96	4.64	12.76	36.39	-17.13
HCDaR	216.67	5.59	12.35	45.27	-17.38

Table 7.31: Statistical Significance of Mean Differences of the Hierarchical Portfolios - Germany 1973

	Excess Mean (%)	t-Stat	p-value
HSds vs. MV	0.08	0.78	0.44
HSds vs. sampleCOV	0.15	3.09	0.00
HCVaRgaussian vs. minCVaR	0.07	0.58	0.56
HCVaRgaussian vs. normCVaR	0.18	3.57	0.00
HCVaRmodified vs. minCVaR	0.01	0.06	0.95
HCVaRmodified vs. modCVaR	0.16	1.40	0.16
HCVaRsample vs. minCVaR	-0.00	-0.03	0.98
HCVaRsample vs. sampleCVaR	0.10	2.56	0.01
HCDaR vs. minCDaR	0.18	1.31	0.19
HCDaR vs. sampleCDaR	0.10	1.83	0.07

Table 7.32: Risk Figures of the Hierarchical Portfolios - Germany 1973

	5% VaR	5% CVaR	5% DaR	5% CDaR	MaxDD
MV	3.60	5.29	33.13	36.05	39.17
minCVaR	3.76	5.91	29.65	32.35	35.39
minCDaR	4.10	8.00	47.69	49.70	54.98
Naive	7.20	12.03	56.95	59.56	63.65
sampleCVaR	5.51	9.16	46.15	48.88	54.09
normCVaR	5.37	8.60	48.01	50.30	54.09
modCVaR	5.56	9.19	48.96	51.54	56.35
sampleCOV	5.38	8.74	48.64	50.87	54.56
sampleCDaR	6.30	10.01	41.85	45.49	52.89
HSds	5.40	8.63	33.29	37.74	44.48
HCVaRgaussian	5.51	8.58	31.71	36.50	43.30
HCVaRmodified	6.85	9.39	41.94	45.09	49.33
HCVaRsample	5.78	8.89	36.31	40.04	47.04
HCDaR	5.82	8.45	31.73	36.91	44.41

The risk figures in table 7.32 present still the lowest values for the MV and minCVaR portfolios. Compared to the risk budgeting approaches, the hierarchical portfolios exhibit similar VaR and CVaR, but lower drawdown risks. The lower drawdown risk figures are also expressed by the highest risk ratios SR_CDaR and SR_avdd for the HCDaR portfolio. Moreover, all the risk ratios of the hierarchical portfolios are higher than of the ERC portfolios.

The turnovers, displayed in table 7.34, show the highest redeployment for the HCVaRmodified portfolio and the lowest for the HCVaR-gaussian portfolio among the hierarchical portfolio. The turnovers are again higher than those of the risk budgeting portfolios.

Table 7.33: Risk Ratios of the Hierarchical Portfolios - Germany 1973

	SR SR	VaR SR	CVaR SR	CDaR SR	avdd SR	maxdd
MV	13.00	9.14	6.22	0.91	3.20	0.84
minCVaR	13.59	10.39	6.60	1.21	3.47	1.10
minCDaR	8.20	6.95	3.56	0.57	1.46	0.52
Naive	4.58	2.95	1.77	0.36	0.94	0.33
sampleCVaR	7.75	5.20	3.13	0.59	1.82	0.53
normCVaR	7.82	5.18	3.24	0.55	1.82	0.51
modCVaR	6.33	4.24	2.56	0.46	1.40	0.42
sampleCOV	7.15	4.77	2.94	0.50	1.59	0.47
sampleCDaR	9.13	5.83	3.67	0.81	2.34	0.69
HSds	11.26	7.59	4.75	1.09	3.17	0.92
HCVaRgaussian	12.74	8.34	5.36	1.26	4.02	1.06
HCVaRmodified	9.34	5.84	4.26	0.89	2.42	0.81
HCVaRsample	10.51	6.70	4.35	0.97	2.89	0.82
HCDaR	13.07	8.00	5.51	1.26	4.14	1.05

Table 7.34: Turnover of the Hierarchical Portfolios - Germany 1973

	mean Turnover	total Turnover
MV	0.22	99.45
minCVaR	0.38	178.89
minCDaR	0.39	182.22
Naive	0.05	25.54
sampleCVaR	0.08	38.39
normCVaR	0.08	36.97
modCVaR	0.16	72.68
sampleCOV	0.08	37.46
sampleCDaR	0.09	43.05
HSds	0.35	162.46
HCVaRgaussian	0.35	162.65
HCVaRmodified	1.02	475.79
HCVaRsample	0.42	194.35
HCDaR	0.37	170.43

7.3.3 Different Clustering Algorithm

As outlined above, the clustering method excludes some assets, as the assets are always combined sequentially by two in a portfolio. This could be inefficient due to a higher volatility and turnover. Another possibility is to cluster two assets and sequentially include another asset. This strategy is displayed in figure 7.6. The main results of this clustering method is compared to the first clustering technique above.

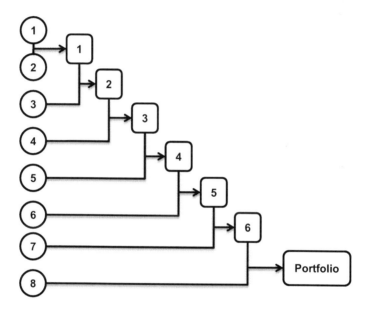

Figure 7.6: Different Hierarchical Clustering Algorithm

As the assets are combined step-by-step to a portfolio, they have to be ordered decreasingly by risks, because the last asset gets the highest weight in the portfolio.

The main results of this clustering order are shown in tables 7.35 for the Global portfolio as well as in table 7.36 for the Germany 1973 dataset. In the Global portfolio dataset, the returns are lower, but as expected, also the volatilities. These effects lead in sum to higher

Table 7.35: Statistics of the Hierarchical Portfolios with an Alternative
Clustering Technique - Global Portfolio

	Total Return	Ann. Return	Ann. StDev	Sharpe	Max Loss
MV	64.83	4.18	5.91	70.73	-11.52
minCVaR	63.14	4.07	5.50	74.05	-9.02
minCDaR	68.66	4.43	5.13	86.30	-6.25
Naive	81.62	5.27	13.75	38.31	-21.48
sampleCVaR	79.19	5.11	8.52	59.96	-17.70
normCVaR	72.25	4.66	6.65	70.15	-10.97
modCVaR	78.85	5.09	8.17	62.27	-14.59
sampleCOV	69.25	4.47	6.71	66.61	-11.11
sampleCDaR	89.00	5.74	7.68	74.77	-12.36
HSds	76.51	4.94	6.42	76.88	-14.53
HCVaRgaussian	78.82	5.09	6.46	78.72	-14.56
HCVaRmodified	63.92	4.12	5.81	71.01	-10.18
HCVaRsample	74.62	4.81	6.39	75.31	-14.56
HCDaR	92.84	5.99	6.21	96.47	-11.68

Sharpe ratios of all portfolios, as the decrease of the volatility is higher than the decrease in returns, except in the case of the HCVaRsample portfolio.

In the German equities dataset, this clustering order does not decrease the volatilities, as they are higher than in the clustering technique above, except for the HSds and the HCVaRgaussian portfolios. Moreover, the returns are also all lower, which leads to lower or similar Sharpe ratios and the losses are dramatically increased. Thus, in a universe of many equities it does not make sense to invest in all equities, as this leads to worse outcomes. Interesting is the observation that in both datasets the returns are lower if all assets are included, but higher if only low risk assets are in the portfolio. This is an indication of the low beta or low risk anomaly described in chapter 4.1.1 and 2.2.2.

Table 7.36: Statistics of the Hierarchical Portfolios with an Alternative
Clustering Technique - Germany 1973

	Total Return	Ann. Return	Ann. StDev	Sharpe	Max Loss
MV	152.94	3.95	8.77	45.02	-10.01
minCVaR	181.53	4.68	9.95	47.09	-13.14
minCDaR	132.41	3.42	12.03	28.40	-41.26
Naive	98.88	2.55	16.07	15.87	-23.01
sampleCVaR	133.14	3.44	12.80	26.84	-19.22
normCVaR	129.50	3.34	12.34	27.07	-18.67
modCVaR	109.45	2.82	12.88	21.92	-19.73
sampleCOV	119.31	3.08	12.43	24.77	-18.42
sampleCDaR	170.90	4.41	13.95	31.62	-20.95
HSds	205.24	5.30	11.57	45.78	-23.04
HCVaRgaussian	205.29	5.30	11.87	44.63	-23.60
HCVaRmodified	194.36	5.02	15.32	32.74	-37.53
HCVaRsample	197.77	5.10	13.86	36.83	-42.41
HCDaR	199.71	5.15	14.70	35.05	-47.76

7.3.4 Summary

The investigation of the pairwise hierarchical clustering technique
based on the risk contributions of different risks has shown that the
hierarchical portfolios outperform the risk budgeting portfolios in both
investigated datasets. The hierarchical portfolios have a higher return
by a similar volatility and maximum loss and thus higher Sharpe
ratios in both datasets compared to the ERC portfolios. In the Global
dataset, the Sharpe ratios are even slightly higher than of the minimum
risk portfolios. However, the higher returns are only significant in the
Germany 1973 dataset vs. the risk budgeting portfolios. By including
all assets in the portfolio with a different clustering technique, in the
Global dataset, the volatilities are lowered such that the Sharpe ratios
are all higher than of the minimum risk approaches. However, in the
German dataset, it increases the volatility of the most portfolios and
this leads to a lower Sharpe ratio. As the returns are lower in the
second clustering technique, they are either statistically significant
higher compared to the minimum risk and risk budgeting approaches.

Whereas the risk budgeting models are not suited for an investment across individual assets of an asset class, the hierarchical portfolio models seem to be more similar to the minimum risk portfolios. However, they do not need an optimizer and are thus more intuitively understandable for an investor, how the portfolio is build and which assets contribute the most to his portfolio risk. It is also generally possible that the assets are ordered by a characteristic which is defined by the investor. Thus, it is an alternative technique to the risk budgeting portfolios, where the assets with the lowest risks have the highest risk contribution instead of equalizing the risk contributions. Which feature is seen as risk can then be individually defined by an investor. In this way, the idea of the ERC portfolios can be used in an alternative and 'reasonable' way, as the examinations have shown that the equalization of the risk contributions seems to not make a great sense.

8 Conclusion

This thesis outlined the use of equal risk contribution models in portfolio management based on different risk measures and calculation methods.

At first, it was shown that the modern portfolio theory has two main weaknesses: variance as a risk measure and estimation error. Based on this, the thesis presented downside risk measures and the corresponding risk contributions. As only coherent risk measures are suited for the task of risk decomposition, the Volatility, the CVaR as well as the CDaR risk measures were applied for risk contributions. It was shown that different methods of calculations exist for obtaining the risk budgets and the risk contributions based on the CDaR were introduced. After this, the portfolio models based on the risk measures as well as on equalizing the risk contributions were presented.

The review of studies concerning the minimum risk portfolios outlined that the most studies exist for the MV portfolio, thereby observing an outperformance of the MV portfolio vs. a capitalization weighted index. The reasons for the outperformance are different: On the one hand, the MV portfolio holds low beta and low idiosyncratic assets, thus implicitly picking up known asset pricing anomalies. On the other hand, the capitalized weighted index is not the 'efficient market portfolio' and thus not principally efficient in the sense of the CAPM. The investigation of the CVaR portfolio has shown that the CVaR risk measure is similar to the VaR, but is more effective (results also in a smaller VaR and variance) and can better capture the risk. It is especially superior to the mean-variance portfolio in the presence of non-normal returns (fat tails and skewness). The drawdown risk measures are intuitive, but are the subject of only a few empirical studies. It is revealed that, opposite to the CVaR, the mean and especially the volatility are important for drawdown measures, whereas the skewness and kurtosis do not matter much. One study outlines the improved trade-off of the MaxDD portfolio vs. the mean-variance in terms of slightly higher volatility, but a much lower MaxDD. As the MaxDD has a large estimation error, because it depends on only one value, and the AvDD is disturbed by small drawdowns, the CDaR risk measure is better suited for portfolio optimizations. The few studies concerning the CDaR in portfolio optimization indicate that the risk measure is more robust than the AvDD or the MaxDD, but more conservative than the CVaR.

The literature review of the ERC portfolio has shown that at first the idea of risk decomposition was used as an additional instrument to the portfolio process. Nowadays, risk budgeting portfolios have gained popularity in different and broad areas: they are used for allocating capital in asset management, as a benchmark for the capital market (index), or for institutional investors as strategic asset allocation. Thereby diversification across different risks is applied: individual asset risks, statistical factors (PCA), macroeconomic factors and also factors from asset pricing. The risk contributions need not to be equal, but can be individually defined to asset or risk factors. The studies reveal that theoretically, the ERC portfolio is located between the naive and the MV portfolio. Historical results show that the ERC portfolio outperforms the market, 60/40 benchmarks and the naive portfolio, while the results vs. the tangency and the MV portfolio are different.

Whereas there are a lot of studies on portfolio downside risk measures, the opposite is the case with the equal risk contribution portfolio. Almost all studies focus on the volatility as a risk measure and examine the performance based on return and risk in different periods. However, studies based on different risk measures as well as on the examination of other characteristics (especially the robustness, which is presented in chapter 7) are missing. The results of chapter 6 represent the main part of the thesis. The compared portfolios have all the risk as objective, whether minimization or diversification, but the outcomes differ much. Based on the research questions in the beginning, the answers resting upon the empirical results are as follows:

1. *Can the ERC portfolio be justified through the utility or decision theory?* Some ideas, which are based on the utility theory, behavioral finance or regularization techniques were outlined, in which the ERC portfolio could be the resulting investment decision. However, the ideas present more an explanation of investor's behavior rather than a 'rational' explanation in the sense of an utility theory. The decision theoretical justification of the ERC portfolio is a difficult task, as the Expected Utility Theory is not suited and alternative utility theories have to be applied. As there is a gap in the literature concerning this issue, it would be interesting to establish a compatibility or to show an incompatibility of the ERC approach to the outlined descriptive utility theories (this would include a mathematical derivation, similar to the approach of Hanisch (2006) for the CVaR).

2. *Does the use of other risk measures improve the asset allocation compared to the volatility (minimum risk and risk budgeting models)?*
   In all three datasets, the minCVaR (European Fund and Germany) or the minCDaR (Global, European Fund) portfolio display higher returns and/or a higher Sharpe ratio compared to the MV portfolio. Moreover, some risk figures are lower and the Risk ratios can be improved. However, the differences are small and very likely statistically insignificant. Among the risk budgeting models, only the sampleCDaR portfolio shows a significantly higher return compared to the sampleCOV portfolio in the Global as well as in the Germany 1973 dataset. But in the European Fund dataset the sampleCDaR portfolio shows the lowest return and Sharpe ratio among the ERC portfolios. Thus, a general conclusion is difficult, as the differences are not that large.

3. *Does the use of risk budgets in the portfolio optimization process improve the risk-return balance compared to the downside risk optimization?*

   The results reveal that the risk budgeting models have admittedly higher returns than the minimum risk approaches, but throughout higher risk figures. In all three datasets, the higher returns are not statistically significant. However, the ERC portfolios display all significant higher volatilities than the minimum risk approaches. As all risk ratios are lower, the ERC portfolios do not improve the risk-return balance compared to the minimum risk approaches.

4. *How is the performance of the approaches considering the estimation error or how robust are the asset allocations based on risk budgets?*

   As the risk budgeting models are always invested in all assets, they display a lower concentration of the allocation and thus lower maximum weights than the minimum risk approaches. The standard deviations of the weights are also lower, which means that the portfolio structure does not change so dramatically. They display also lower estimation errors for the mean and the standard deviation in the unrealistic simulation in the 'normal case'. However, in the realistic simulation the estimation errors are similar to the minimum risk approaches. In both worst case, they achieve the same poor results as the minimum risk counterparts, namely huge estimation errors and even higher drawdowns. Thus, they cannot protect from sudden market crashes.

5. *Can the performance of the risk budgeting models be explained through exposures to known factors?*

   The investigation of exposures to the Fama-French factors has shown that the risk budgeting models display in all datasets a negative alpha, which is mostly significant. Thus, the performances can in general be attributed to the factors, whereas the market factor contributes the most to the explanation of the portfolio returns. The strategies can be simply explained through a shift in the betas.

All in all, risk budgeting portfolios do not what they should or what one expects from them through the intuitive idea of risk diversification. The use of these risk diversified portfolios is not really clear. They provide perhaps an alternative to naive portfolios, but they are not a safe alternative from losses. The concept helps to remind how the risk is distributed across assets, but to equalize the risk across the assets is not a good investing opportunity to prevent losses.

In chapter 7, different extensions to the results in chapter 6 were outlined. Additionally to the 'pure' risk budgeting models, it was shown that the risk budgets can be calculated through a desired distribution assumption through the simulation of returns. In general, extensions to more distributions or copulas are possible: there are no bounds, as risk contributions can be calculated through the sample of simulated returns. However, the investigation has shown, that the simulation of returns does not display a significant different performance compared to the historical sample of returns.

As the ERC portfolios do not hold what they promise, a new idea, which abdicates portfolio optimization technique, but focus also on risk, was also examined. The focus on the stability of the assets as an alternative 'risk' criteria is an interesting approach. The portfolio is constructed with a binary switching method. However, this method either show significant higher returns compared to the minimum risk or ERC portfolios. As the volatility is significantly higher, the Sharpe ratio is lower. Moreover, the stabilizing of the assets before applying a portfolio optimization technique was also investigated. It seems to be a good alternative, as in almost all portfolios the returns can be improved and the risks reduces.

Another idea of clustering assets pairwise in binary risk contribution portfolios based on their individual risk was explored. It unveiled that the hierarchical clustering method outperforms the ERC portfolios in both datasets. In the German dataset, the higher returns are also statistically significant. Thus, this method can be seen as a prospect of the risk contribution idea, as the equalizing of risk contributions seems to have not many advantages to the minimization of risk. The hierarchical clustering models combine assets with the lowest risks according to their risk budgets and are therefore closer to the minimum risk approaches. This idea seems to be promising, as the 'risk' can be individually defined by the investor and the portfolio technique is intuitively understandable. Moreover, as the approach does not depend on an optimizer, the portfolio should be less sensitive to estimation errors.

In the following, further research ideas are outlined.

Based on the performance results, it can be concluded that the risk budgeting models are not suited for an investment universe of homogeneous assets, such as the German equities dataset. It has to be studied how the models perform in an investment universe of different asset classes (e.g. of each asset class one instrument or index such as bonds, equities, gold), equities from different countries or an equal amount of individual assets in the portfolio (like two equities/two bonds, etc.). Thus, it has to be well-conceived which assets should be included in the portfolio.

Another idea, based on the hierarchical optimization study, is to at first divide the assets of an investment universe into clusters and then obtain the equal risk contribution portfolio or the hierarchical portfolio. The clusters can be obtained based on different criteria, like the euclidean distances between the assets, or ordering the assets according to their eigenvalues (similar to the idea of maximum entropy of Meucci (2009)). It would also be interesting to analyze the results of portfolios, which are build of clusters based on risk factors, like the Fama-French three factors, macroeconomic or statistical factors (PCA analysis) and then optimize the ERC or the hierarchical portfolio. This approach would then indirectly build on risk factor diversification, without considering optimization, but an intuitive technique.

Through applying the technique of finite differences in optimization, risk contributions based on other risk measures, like MaxDD, AvDD, LPMs or Spectral Risk Measures, are in general possible. The benefit of equal risk contributions based on other risk measures is however due to the results in this thesis questionable.

From the aspect of robustness, one could also combine the risk contribution portfolio with the robust optimization technique. Thus, to obtain a 'worst-case ERC' portfolio and to study the outcomes.

Concerning the stability portfolio, Würtz et al. (2012b) provide their selves many ideas to use the stability criterion for investment criteria. At first, average returns and average risk measures can be calculated based on the posterior means and variances. They can also be used to calculate a stability performance measure, like the Sharpe ratio or Sortino ratio, or more measures for performance measurement and attribution proposed in (Bacon, 2008). Moreover, it is possible to establish a cumulated stability index, and from the distribution of the changes, measures like Covariance Stability, Value-at-Stability, Conditional Value-at-Stability, Conditional-Drawdowns-at-Stability can be calculated or equal risk contributions to these risk measures are possible ('stability budgeting' or 'stability parity indexation') (Würtz et al., 2012b). The analytics can also be used for rating and ranking investments by assigning a stability score to each instrument. It is also possible to select or cluster assets according to a stability score.

At the end of the day, the risk budgeting models or the diversification of risk across assets seem not to be 'the solution' to prevent from losses in sudden market crashes or bear periods and other alternatives have to be investigated.

A Appendix

A.1 Germany1973 Dataset

Table A.1: Notifications and Asset Names of the Germany 1973 Dataset

Abbreviation	Equity	Abbreviation	Equity
A1	ANDREAE-NORIS ZAHN		
A2	BABCOCK BORSIG	A29	DIERIG HOLDING
A3	DYCKERHOFF	A30	DOUGLAS HOLDING
A4	HAMBORNER REIT	A31	E ON
A5	MANNHEIMER HOLDING	A32	ELKT.LICHT UD.KRTL.
A6	OLDENBURGISCHE LB.	A33	GEA GROUP
A7	PHILIPP HOLZMANN	A34	GELSENWASSER
A8	RAG ABWICKLUNGS	A35	GILDEMEISTER
A9	SCA HYGIENE PRODUCTS	A36	HEIDELBERGCEMENT
A10	WMF WUTBGE.MTWFBK.	A37	HOCHTIEF
A11	AGROB IMMOBILIEN	A38	K + S
A12	ALLIANZ	A39	KOLB & SCHUELE
A13	ANTERRA VERMOGEN.	A40	KSB
A14	ARCANDOR	A41	KUKA
A15	AUDI	A42	KWS SAAT
A16	BASF	A43	LECHWERKE
A17	BAYER	A44	LINDE
A18	BEIERSDORF	A45	MAN
A19	BHS TABLETOP	A46	MUENCHENER RUCK.
A20	BILFINGER BERGER	A47	PILKINGTON DEUTSCHLAND
A21	BMW	A48	RHEINMETALL
A22	CELESIO	A49	RWE
A23	COMMERZBANK	A50	SIEMENS
A24	CONTINENTAL	A51	SUEDZUCKER
A25	CUSTODIA HOLDING	A52	THYSSENKRUPP
A26	DEUTSCHE BANK	A53	TUI
A27	DEUTSCHE LUFTHANSA	A54	VOLKSWAGEN
A28	DEUTZ	A55	WUESTENROT & WUERTT.

A.2 Regressions

A.2.1 Global Dataset

Table A.2: Four-Factor Model Regression Results for the Minimum Risk
Portfolios - Global Portfolio
Signification codes: ***: ≤ 0.01, **: ≤ 0.05, *: ≤ 0.1
If the null hypothesis of the Durbin-Watson test is rejected,
the test statistic is shaded in grey.

Excess return	MV	minCVaR	minCDaR	Naive
α	-0.0001815	-0.0004971	-0.0003404	-0.002109**
β_{MKT}	0.2305504***	0.2123510***	0.1681254***	0.812175***
β_{SMB}	0.1300382***	0.1039935**	0.0594633	0.189775***
β_{HML}	0.0306504	0.0488292	0.0471069	0.077430*
β_{WML}	-0.0065430	0.0289047	0.0844514***	0.024231
R^2	0.4174	0.3757	0.2753	0.8912

Table A.3: Four-Factor Model Regression Results for the Risk Budgeting
Portfolios - Global Portfolio
Signification codes: ***: ≤ 0.01, **: ≤ 0.05, *: ≤ 0.1
If the null hypothesis of the Durbin-Watson test is rejected,
the test statistic is shaded in grey.

Excess return	sampleCVaR	normCVaR	modCVaR	sampleCOV	sampleCDaR
α	-0.0009060	-0.0005878	-0.001113	-0.0007099	-0.0003849
β_{MKT}	0.4565884***	0.3509081***	0.435891***	0.3539351***	0.4058600***
β_{SMB}	0.1871632***	0.1238167***	0.135338***	0.1254494***	0.1023793**
β_{HML}	0.1380471***	0.0420320	0.100467*	0.0398132	0.0635016*
β_{WML}	-0.0035783	0.0344803**	0.072061***	0.0279764	0.0939406***
R^2	0.7413	0.7022	0.693	0.7059	0.6761
DW					

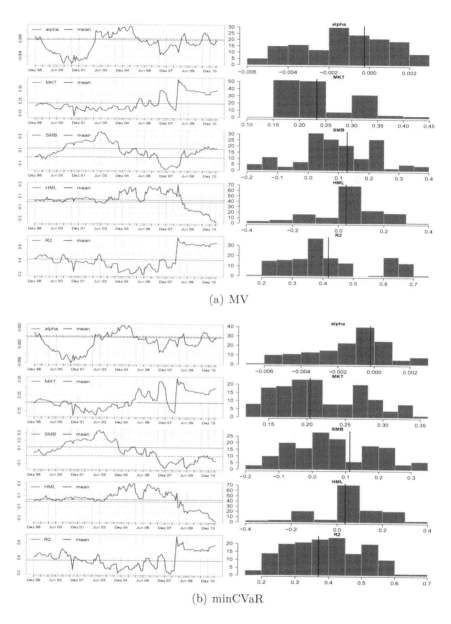

(a) MV

(b) minCVaR

Figure A.1: Rolling Regressions (Global)

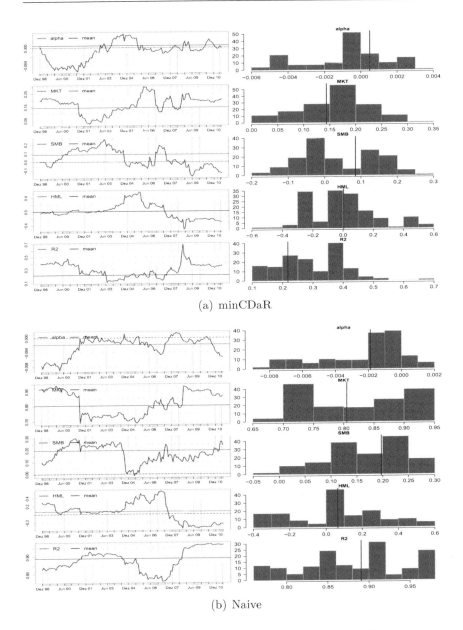

(a) minCDaR

(b) Naive

Figure A.1: Rolling Regressions (Global) - minCDaR and Naive

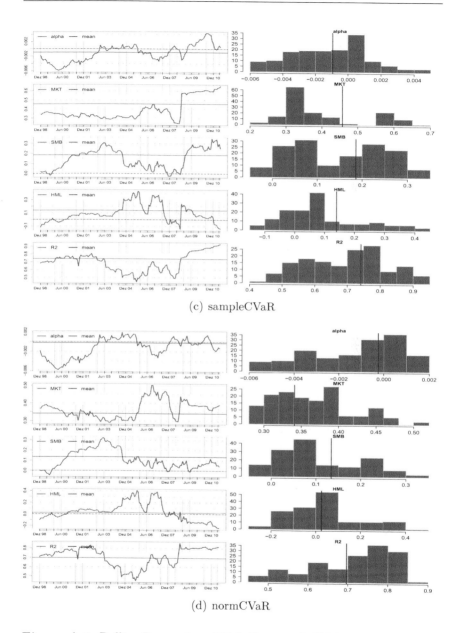

(c) sampleCVaR

(d) normCVaR

Figure A.1: Rolling Regressions (Global) - sampleCVaR and normCVaR

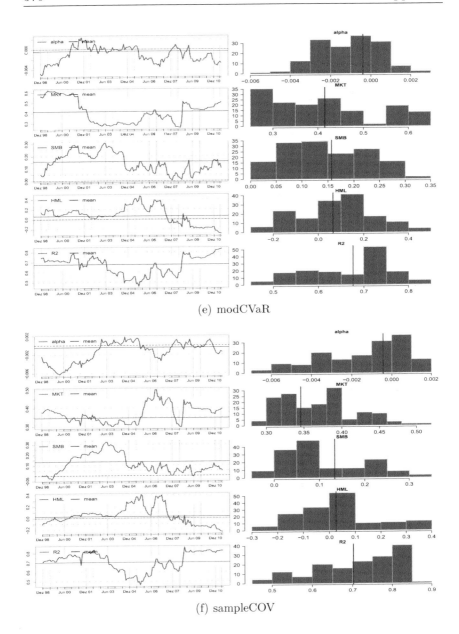

(e) modCVaR

(f) sampleCOV

Figure A.1: Rolling Regressions (Global) - modCVaR and sampleCOV

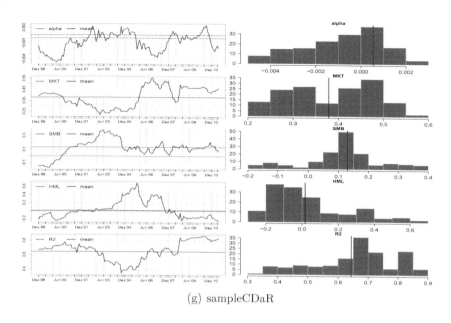

(g) sampleCDaR

Figure A.1: Rolling Regressions (Global) - sampleCDaR

A.2.2 Germany 1973 Dataset

Table A.4: Four-Factor Model Regression Results for the Minimum Risk
Portfolios - Germany 1973
Signification codes: ***: ≤ 0.01, **: ≤ 0.05, *: ≤ 0.1
If the null hypothesis of the Durbin-Watson test is rejected,
the test statistic is shaded in grey.

Excess return	MV	minCVaR	minCDaR	Naive
α	-0.0025575***	-0.001706	-0.003022*	-0.0057175***
β_{MKT}	0.4018051***	0.397128***	0.381805***	0.9027616***
β_{SMB}	0.2890217***	0.244742***	0.216434***	0.3114752***
β_{HML}	0.0581411**	0.031604	0.031955	0.1720652***
β_{WML}	0.0588011**	0.034780	0.068580*	-0.0195986
R^2	0.4626	0.3651	0.2218	0.8741

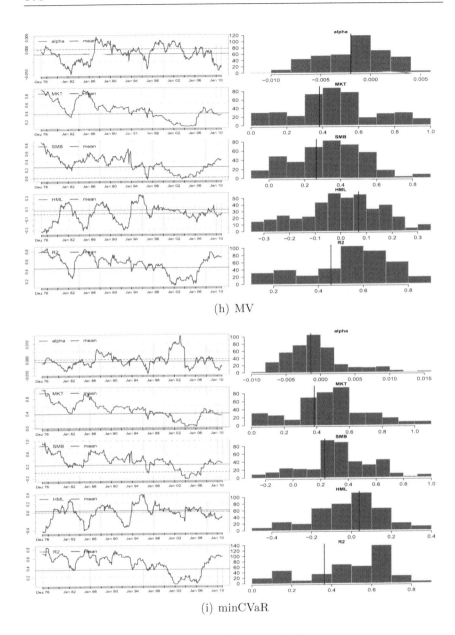

(h) MV

(i) minCVaR

Figure A.2: Rolling Regressions (Germany 1973)

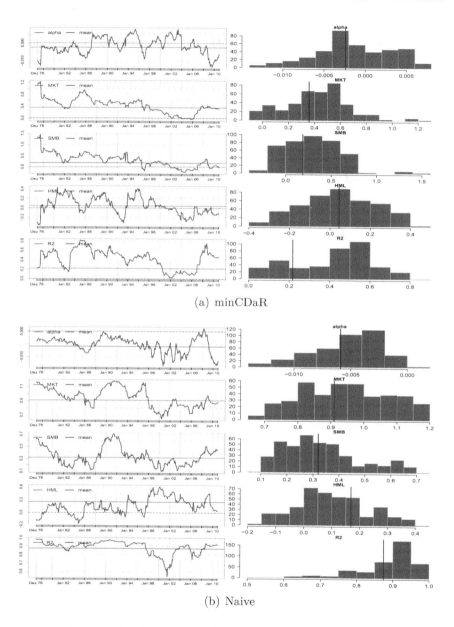

(a) minCDaR

(b) Naive

Figure A.2: Rolling Regressions (Germany 1973) - minCDaR and Naive

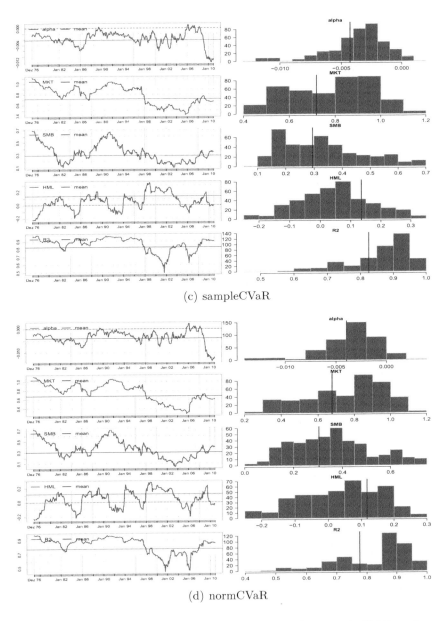

(c) sampleCVaR

(d) normCVaR

Figure A.2: Rolling Regressions (Germany 1973) - sampleCVaR and
normCVaR

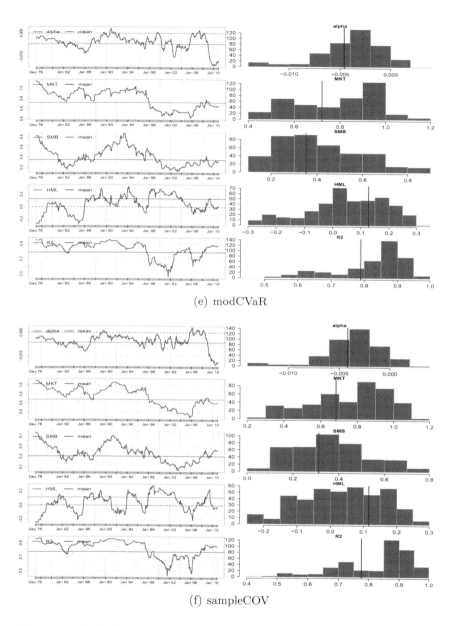

(e) modCVaR

(f) sampleCOV

Figure A.2: Rolling Regressions (Germany 1973) - modCVaR and sampleCOV

Table A.5: Four-Factor Model Regression Results for the Risk Budgeting
Portfolios - Germany 1973
Signification codes: ***: ≤ 0.01, **: ≤ 0.05, *: ≤ 0.1
If the null hypothesis of the Durbin-Watson test is rejected,
the test statistic is shaded in grey.

Excess return	sampleCVaR	normCVaR	modCVaR	sampleCOV	sampleCDaR
α	-0.0046203***	-0.0045980***	-0.0049006***	-0.0047585***	-0.0047101***
β_{MKT}	0.7303896***	0.7001710***	0.7321809***	0.7038672***	0.8008791***
β_{SMB}	0.3097283***	0.3313816***	0.3653961***	0.3379069***	0.2692579***
β_{HML}	0.1291620***	0.1051728***	0.1218723***	0.1048875***	0.1477113***
β_{WML}	0.0352513*	0.0658180***	0.0325744	0.0604960***	0.0670858***
R^2	0.8262	0.7802	0.7906	0.7792	0.8665

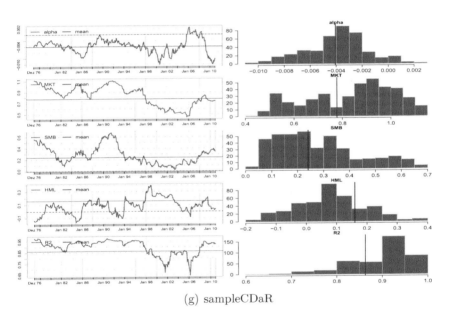

(g) sampleCDaR

Figure A.2: Rolling Regressions (Germany 1973) - sampleCDaR

A.2.3 US Industry Dataset

Table A.6: US Industry Indices of Datastream

US Food Producers	US Leisure Goods
US Fixed Line Telecommunications	US Personal Goods
US Mobile Telecommunications	US Tobacco
US Oil & Gas Producers	US Health Care Equipment & Services
US Oil Equipment & Services	US Pharmaceuticals & Biotechnology
US Industry Forestry & Paper	US Food & Drug Retailers
US Metals & Mines	US General Retailers
US Mining	US Electricity
US Aerospace/Defence	US Gas, Water & Multi-Utilities
US General Industrials	US Nonlife Insurance
US Electronic and Electrical Equipment	US Life Insurance
US Industrial Engineering	US Real Estate Investments & Services
US Industrial Transportation	US Real Estate Investment Trusts
US Support Services	US Financial Services (4)
US Beverages	US Software & Computer Services
US Household Goods	US Technology Hardware & Equipment

Table A.7: Four-Factor Model Regression Results for the Minimum Risk Portfolios - US Industry
Signification codes: ***: ≤ 0.01, **: ≤ 0.05, *: ≤ 0.1
If the null hypothesis of the Durbin-Watson test is rejected, the test statistic is shaded in grey.

Excess return	MV	minCVaR	minCDaR	Naive
α	-0.0039964***	-0.0047238***	-0.0060144***	-0.0034527***
β_{MKT}	0.6347589***	0.6677298***	0.7880170***	1.0111854***
β_{SMB}	-0.0447432	-0.0447057	-0.0724466	-0.0757017**
β_{HML}	0.3643604***	0.3832687***	0.3037618***	0.1613279***
β_{WML}	0.0310535	0.0380060	0.1952289***	-0.0232962*
R^2	0.5855	0.5612	0.6811	0.9408
DW	1.88	1.92	2.013	1.81

Table A.8: Four-Factor Model Regression Results for the Risk Budgeting
Portfolios - US Industry
Signification codes: ***: ≤ 0.01, **: ≤ 0.05, *: ≤ 0.1
If the null hypothesis of the Durbin-Watson test is rejected,
the test statistic is shaded in grey.

Excess return	sampleCVaR	normCVaR	modCVaR	sampleCOV	sampleCDaR
α	-0.0035893***	-0.0036849***	-0.0036355***	-0.0036459***	-0.0034886***
β_{MKT}	0.9529044***	0.9502270***	0.9478406***	0.9460204***	0.9691645***
β_{SMB}	-0.0777308***	-0.0634580***	-0.0862417***	-0.0651882***	-0.0772827***
β_{HML}	0.2039910***	0.2094187***	0.2155394***	0.2077792***	0.1790423***
β_{WML}	0.0073640	0.0130101	0.0085032	0.0024588	0.0634387***
R^2	0.9147	0.9139	0.9037	0.9159	0.9297
DW	1.85	1.86	1.81	1.84	1.90

A.2.4 US MSCI Dataset

Table A.9: Four-Factor Model Regression Results for the Minimum Risk
Portfolios - US MSCI
Signification codes: ***: ≤ 0.01, **: ≤ 0.05, *: ≤ 0.1
If the null hypothesis of the Durbin-Watson test is rejected,
the test statistic is shaded in grey.

Excess return	MV	minCVaR	minCDaR	Naive
α	-0.0024409**	-0.0024770**	-0.0017983	-0.0030030***
β_{MKT}	0.8730338***	0.8816070***	0.9134540***	1.0546861***
β_{SMB}	0.1043305***	0.0979987***	0.2135439***	0.2061630***
β_{HML}	0.3131949***	0.2952613***	0.1248894***	0.0589438***
β_{WML}	-0.0112949	-0.0102850	0.0865019***	-0.0097008
R^2	0.8879	0.888	0.8721	0.9823
DW	1.47	1.50	1.81	2.00

Table A.10: Four-Factor Model Regression Results for the Risk Budgeting Portfolios - US MSCI
Signification codes: ***: ≤ 0.01, **: ≤ 0.05, *: ≤ 0.1
If the null hypothesis of the Durbin-Watson test is rejected,
the test statistic is shaded in grey.

Excess return	sampleCVaR	normCVaR	modCVaR	sampleCOV	sampleCDaR
α	-0.0027804***	-0.0028091***	-0.0028444***	-0.0028212***	-0.0021127***
β_{MKT}	1.0223716***	1.0215170***	1.0245030***	1.0215726***	1.0178969***
β_{SMB}	0.1667880***	0.1661780***	0.1631037***	0.1616980***	0.2136465***
β_{HML}	0.1655231***	0.1741981***	0.1530091***	0.1747183***	0.1801621***
β_{WML}	-0.0126809	-0.0095212	-0.0179715*	-0.0129251	0.0321664***
R^2	0.9784	0.9783	0.9791	0.9781	0.9658
DW	1.90	1.83	1.89	1.84	1.92

A.2.5 German Industry Dataset

Table A.11: German Industry Indices of Datastream

German Forestry & Paper	German Personal Goods
German Metals & Mines	German Pharmaceutical & Biotechnology
German General Industries	German Food & Drug Retailers
German Electronic & Electrical Equipment	German General Retailers
German Industrial Engineering	German Electricity
German Industrial Transport	German Gas, Water & Multi-Utilities
German Beverages	German Nonlife Insurance
German Food Producers	German Life Insurance

Table A.12: Four-Factor Model Regression Results for the Minimum Risk Portfolios - German Industry (Artmann et al., 2012) Signification codes: ***: ≤ 0.01, **: ≤ 0.05, *: ≤ 0.1 If the null hypothesis of the Durbin-Watson test is rejected, the test statistic is shaded in grey.

Excess return	MV	minCVaR	minCDaR	Naive
α	-0.0018117*	-0.0017349	-0.0009996	-0.0037657***
β_{MKT}	0.4948093***	0.4893421***	0.4692628***	0.8377623***
β_{SMB}	0.2828097***	0.2842957***	0.2581782***	0.2166946***
β_{HML}	0.1299990***	0.1324162***	0.1169945***	0.1614137***
β_{WML}	0.0873371***	0.0954225***	0.1219318***	0.0117154
R^2	0.5281	0.5019	0.4331	0.8613
DW	1.93	1.95	2.02	2.02

Table A.13: Four-Factor Model Regression Results for the Risk Budgeting Portfolios - German Industry (Artmann et al., 2012) Signification codes: ***: ≤ 0.01, **: ≤ 0.05, *: ≤ 0.1 If the null hypothesis of the Durbin-Watson test is rejected, the test statistic is shaded in grey.

Excess return	sampleCVaR	normCVaR	modCVaR	sampleCOV	sampleCDaR
α	-0.0034238***	-0.0033911***	-0.0035967***	-0.0034488***	-0.0031726***
β_{MKT}	0.7216799***	0.727471***8	0.7517104***	0.7290885***	0.7233671***
β_{SMB}	0.2547717***	0.2541064***	0.2651891***	0.2532297***	0.2214915***
β_{HML}	0.1551717***	0.1491794***	0.1602824***	0.1500023***	0.1400581***
β_{WML}	0.0557370**	0.0598782***	0.0521448**	0.0541926**	0.0873262***
R^2	0.7968	0.7973	0.7807	0.7973	0.7954
DW	1.97	1.96	1.97	1.96	2.06

A.2.6 German MSCI Dataset

Table A.14: Four-Factor Model Regression Results for the Minimum Risk Portfolios - German MSCI(Hanauer et al., 2013) Signification codes: ***: ≤ 0.01, **: ≤ 0.05, *: ≤ 0.1 If the null hypothesis of the Durbin-Watson test is rejected, the test statistic is shaded in grey.

Excess return	MV	minCVaR	minCDaR	Naive
α	0.0005861	0.0008068	-0.0018781	-0.0039894***
β_{MKT}	0.7893119***	0.7803478***	0.7470136***	1.0430476***
β_{SMB}	0.2917438***	0.2631173***	0.1935652***	0.1394829***
β_{HML}	0.1068890**	0.1079677**	0.1015321**	-0.0090326
β_{WML}	-0.0670286*	-0.0809289**	0.0123738	-0.0728792***
R^2	0.7833	0.785	0.6989	0.9352
DW	2.18	2.27	2.34	2.09

Table A.15: Four-Factor Model Regression Results for the Risk Budgeting Portfolios - German MSCI(Hanauer et al., 2013) Signification codes: ***: ≤ 0.01, **: ≤ 0.05, *: ≤ 0.1 If the null hypothesis of the Durbin-Watson test is rejected, the test statistic is shaded in grey.

Excess return	sampleCVaR	normCVaR	modCVaR	sampleCOV	sampleCDaR
α	-0.0033053***	-0.0034091***	-0.0033503***	-0.0034472***	-0.0029573**
β_{MKT}	0.9760775***	0.9801274***	0.9875107***	0.9807599***	0.9840028***
β_{SMB}	0.2022080***	0.2156396***	0.2030587***	0.2156369***	0.1685165***
β_{HML}	0.0630651**	0.0673648**	0.0521590*	0.0672921**	0.0677733**
β_{WML}	-0.0683882***	-0.0623872**	-0.0612070**	-0.0636919**	-0.0555719**
R^2	0.9268	0.925	0.9282	0.9253	0.9351
DW	2.14	2.13	2.17	2.14	2.03

A.3 Robustness Study

Table A.16: Minimum and Maximum Portfolio Weights for the Minimum Risk Portfolios in the Empirical Dataset (%)
These are the minimum and maximum estimated portfolio weights across 175 optimizations per asset.

Asset	weights	MV	minCVaR	minCDaR
SPCOMP	max	6	8	16
	min	0	0	0
FRUSSL2	max	3	8	15
	min	0	0	0
DJES50I	max	3	4	12
	min	0	0	0
FTSE100	max	5	8	30
	min	0	0	0
TOKYOSE	max	4	5	19
	min	0	0	0
MSEFLA	max	1	1	13
	min	0	0	0
MSEEUR	max	5	15	7
	min	0	0	0
MSASXJ	max	2	8	11
	min	0	0	0
JPMUSU	max	72	84	96
	min	0	0	0
JPMEIU	max	15	21	40
	min	0	0	0
MLHMAU	max	98	94	92
	min	11	0	0
JPMGCOC	max	59	64	85
	min	0	0	0
GSCITOT	max	4	11	20
	min	0	0	0
Average	max	21	26	35
	min	1	0	0

Table A.17: Minimum and Maximum Portfolio Weights for the Risk
Budgeting Portfolios in the Empirical Dataset (%)
These are calculated as the minimum and maximum estimated portfolio weights across 175 optimizations per asset.

Asset	weights	sampleCVaR	sampleCDaR	normCVaR	modCVaR	sampleCOV	Naive
SPCOMP	max	8	11	7	17	7	8
	min	3	1	3	3	3	8
FRUSSL2	max	8	7	6	9	6	8
	min	2	1	2	2	2	8
DJES50I	max	7	9	6	7	6	8
	min	2	1	2	2	2	8
FTSE100	max	10	16	7	9	7	8
	min	2	1	3	2	3	8
TOKYOSE	max	11	12	7	14	8	8
	min	2	1	2	1	3	8
MSEFLA	max	5	12	5	5	5	8
	min	1	0	1	1	1	8
MSEEUR	max	11	8	10	11	9	8
	min	1	0	1	1	1	8
MSASXJ	max	10	9	7	14	8	8
	min	2	0	1	2	2	8
JPMUSU	max	39	63	31	51	31	8
	min	0	5	0	0	0	8
JPMEIU	max	30	40	29	35	29	8
	min	0	2	0	0	0	8
MLHMAU	max	68	62	55	72	52	8
	min	12	4	17	3	16	8
JPMGCOC	max	34	40	33	35	31	8
	min	2	1	2	2	3	8
GSCITOT	max	15	27	13	20	13	8
	min	2	0	3	0	3	8
Average	max	20	24	17	23	16	8
	min	2	1	3	1	3	8

Bibliography

Aas, K., Haff, I. H., and Dimakos, X. K. (2005). Risk estimation using the multivariate normal inverse Gaussian distribution. *Journal of Risk Finance*, 8(2).

Acerbi, C. and Tasche, D. (2002). Expected Shortfall: A Natural Coherent Alternative to Value at Risk. *Economic Notes of Banca Monte dei Paschi di Siena SpA.,*, (31(2)):1–10.

Alexander, G. J. and Baptista, A. M. (2002). Economic implications of using a mean-VaR model for portfolio selection: A comparison with mean-variance analysis. *Journal of Economic Dynamics & Control*, (26):1159–1193.

Alexander, G. J. and Baptista, A. M. (2004). A Comparison of VaR and CVaR Constraints on Portfolio Selection with the Mean-Variance Model.

Alexander, G. J. and Baptista, A. M. (2006). Portfolio Selection with a drawdown constraint. *Journal of Banking & Finance*, (30):3171–3189.

Allais, M. (1953). Le comportement de L'homme rationnel devant le risque: Critique des postulats et axiomes de L'école americaine. *Econometrica*, 21 (1953):503–546.

Allen, G. C. (2010). The Risk Parity Approach to Asset Allocation. *Callan Investments Institute, Callan Associates*.

Álvarez, L. G. and Luger, R. (2011). Dynamic Correlations, Estimation Risk, and Portfolio Management during the Financial Crisis. *Working Paper*.

Amenc, N., Goltz, F., and Lodh, A. (2012). Alternative Equity Beta Benchmarks. *EDHEC-Risk Institute Working Paper*.

Amenc, N., Goltz, F., Martellini, L., and Retkowsky, P. (2010). Efficient Indexation: An Alternative to Cap-Weighted Indices. *EDHEC-Risk Institute*.

Amenc, N., Martellini, L., Goltz, F., and Sahoo, D. (2011). A Long Horizon Perspective on the Cross-Sectional Risk-Return Relationship in Equity Markets. *EDHEC-Risk Institute*, (December).

Amihud, Y. and Mendelson, H. (1986). Asset pricing and the bid-ask spread. *Journal of Financial Economics*, 17(2):223–249.

Andersson, F., Mausser, H., Rosen, D., and Uryasev, S. (2001). Credit risk optimization with Conditional Value-at-Risk criterion. *Mathematical Programming*, (Series B 89):273–291.

Ang, A., Hodrick, R., Xing, Y., and Zhang, X. (2006). The Cross-Section of Volatility and Expected Returns. *Journal of Finance*, 61(1):259–299.

Ang, A., Hodrick, R., Xing, Y., and Zhang, X. (2009). High Idiosyncratic Volatility and Low Returns: International and Further U.S. Evidence. *Journal of Financial Economics*, 91:1–23.

Arrow, K. J. (1971). *Essays in the theory of risk-bearing*. Markham Pub. Co, Chicago.

Artmann, S., Finter, P., Kempf, A., Koch, S., and Theissen, E. (2012). The Cross-Section of German Stock Returns: New Data and New Evidence. *Schmalenbach Business Review*, 64:20–43.

Artzner, P., Delbaen, F., Eber, J., and Heath, D. (1999). Coherent measure of risk. *Mathematical Finance, 9 (3):203–228*, (9 (3)):203–228.

Asness, C., Frazzini, A., and Pedersen, L. H. (2011). Leverage Aversion and Risk Parity. *AQR Working Paper*.

Avramov, D. and Zhou, G. (2010). Bayesian Portfolio Analysis. *Annual Review of Financial Economics*, 2(1):25–47.

Bacon, C. R. (2008). *Practical portfolio performance: Measurement and attribution.* Wiley, Chichester and England and Hoboken and NJ, 2 edition.

Baker, M., Bradley, B., and Wurgler, J. (2011). Benchmarks as Limits to Arbitrage: Understanding the Low Volatility Anomaly. *Financial Analysts Journal*, 67(1):40–54.

Baker, N. L. and Haugen, R. A. (2012). Low Risk Stocks Outperform within All Observable Markets of the World. *Working Paper*.

Bali, T. G. and Cakici, N. (2008). Idiosyncratic Volatility and the Cross Section of Expected Returns. *Journal of Financial and Quantitative Analysis*, 43(1):29–58.

Bali, T. G., Cakici, N., Yan, X., and Zhang, Z. (2005). Does Idiosyncratic Risk Really Matter? *The Journal of Finance*, 60(2):905–929.

Ball, R. (1978). Anomalies in relationships between securities' yields and yield-surrogates. *Journal of Financial Economics*, 6(2/3):103–126.

Banz, R. W. (1981). The relationship between return and market value of common stocks. *Journal of Financial Economics*, 9(1):3–18.

Barra, M. (2010). The Perils of Parity.

Barry, D. and Hartigan, J. A. (1993). A Bayesian Analysis for Change Point Problems. *Journal of the American Statistical Association*, 88(421):309–319.

Basu, S. (1977). Investment performance of common stocks in relation to their price-earning ratios: A test of the efficient market hypothesis. *The journal of finance : the journal of the American Finance Association*, 32(3):663–682.

Bawa, V. S. (1975). Optimal Rules for Ordering Uncertain Prospects. *Journal of Financial Economics*, 2:95 121.

Behr, P., Güttler, A., and Miebs, F. (2008). Is Minimum-Variance investing really worth the while? An analysis with robust performance inference. *Working Paper*.

Ben-Tal, A. and Nemirovski, A. (1998). Robust convex optimization. *Math. of Operations Research*, (23(4)):769–805.

Ben-Tal, A. and Nemirovski, A. (2000). Robust solutions of Linear Programming problems contaminated with uncertain data. *Math. Prog*, (88(3)):411–424.

Benartzi, S. and Thaler, R. H. (2001). Naive diversification strategies in defined contribution saving plans. *The American Economic Review*, 91(1):79–98.

Bernard, C., Chen, J. S., and Vanduffel, S. (2013). All investors are risk averse expected utility maximizers. *Working Paper, University of Waterloo, Canada*.

Bernoulli, D. (1954). Exposition of a New Theory on the Measurement of Risk. *Econometrica*, 22(1):23–36.

Bertsimas, D., Lauprete, G. J., and Samarov, A. (2004). Shortfall as a risk measure: properties, optimization and applications. *Journal of Economic Dynamics and Control*, 28(7):1353–1381.

Bertsimas, D. and Sim, M. (2004). The Price of Robustness. *Operations Research*, (52(1)):35–53.

Best, M. J. and Grauer, R. R. (1991). On the sensitivity of mean-variance-efficient portfolios to changes in asset means: Some analytical and computational results. *The review of financial studies*, 4(2):315–342.

Bhansali, V., Davis, J., Rennison, G., Hsu, J., and Li, F. (2012). The Risk in Risk Parity: A Factor-Based Analysis of Asset-Based Risk Parity. *The Journal of Investing*, 21(3):102–110.

Black, F. (1972). Capital Market Equilibrium with Restricted Borrowing. *The Journal of Business*, 45(3):444–455.

Black, F., Jensen, M. C., and Scholes, M. (1972). The Capital Asset Pricing Model: Some Empirical Tests. In Jensen, M. C., editor, *Studies in the Theory of Capital Markets*, pages 79–121. Praeger, New York.

Black, F. and Litterman, R. (1992). Global Portfolio Optimization. *Financial Analysts Journal*, 48(5):28–43.

Blitz, D., Pang, J., and van Vliet, P. (2012). The Volatility Effect in Emerging Markets. *Working Paper.*

Blitz, D. and van Vliet, P. (2007). The Volatility Effect: Lower Risk without Lower Return. *Journal of Portfolio Management*, (Fall):102–113.

Bonanno, G., Caldarelli, G., Lillo, F., and Mantegna, R. (2003). Topology of correlation-based minimal spanning trees in real and model markets. *Physical Review E*, 68(4).

Bonanno, G., Caldarelli, G., Lillo, F., Miccich, S., Vandewalle, N., and Mantegna, R. N. (2004). Networks of equities in financial markets. *The European Physical Journal B - Condensed Matter*, 38(2):363–371.

Bonanno, G., Lillo, F., and Mantegna, R. N. (2001). High-frequency cross-correlation in a set of stocks. *Quantitative Finance*, 1(1):96–104.

Bondt, W. F. M. d. and Thaler, R. H. (1985). Does the stock market overreact? *The Journal of Finance*, 40(3):793–805.

Booth, D. G. and Fama, E. F. (1992). Diversification Returns and Asset Contributions. *Financial Analysts Journal*, 48(3):26–32.

Boudt, K., Carl, P., and Peterson, B. G. (2011). Asset Allocation with Conditional Value-at-Risk Budgets. *Working Paper, University of Leuven*.

Boudt, K., Peterson, B. G., and Croux, C. (2008). Estimation and Decomposition of Downside Risk for Portfolios with Non-Normal ReturnsBoudt. *The Journal of Risk*, 11(2):79–103.

Boynton, W. and Oppenheimer, H. R. (2006). Anomalies in Stock Market Pricing: Problems in Return Measurements. *The Journal of Business*, 79(5):2617–2631.

Brennan, M. J., Chordia, T., and Subrahmanyam, A. (1998). Alternative factor specifications, security characteristics, and the cross-section of expected stock returns. *Journal of Financial Economics*, 49(3):345–373.

Breusch, T. S. and Pagan, A. R. (1979). A simple test for heteroscedasticity and random coefficient variation. *Econometrica : journal of the Econometric Society, an internat. society for the advancement of economic theory in its relation to statistics and mathematics*, 47(5):1287–1294.

Breymann, W. and Lüthi, D. (2011). *ghyp: A package on generalized hyperbolic distributions.*

Briand, R., Nielsen, F., and Stefek, D. (2010). Portfolio of Risk Premia: a new approach to diversification. *The Journal of Portfolio Management*, 36(2):17–25.

Brida, J. G. and Risso, W. A. (2010). Hierarchical structure of the German stock market. *Expert Systems with Applications*, 37(5):3846–3852.

Bridgewater Associates, L. P. (2010). Engineering Targeted Returns and Risks.

Brinkmann, U. (2007). *Robuste Asset Allocation*. PhD thesis, Universität Bremen, Bremen.

Broadie, M. (1993). Computing efficient frontiers using estimated parameters. *Annals of Operations Research*, (45):21–58.

Brodie, J., Daubechies, I., De Mol, C., Giannone, D., and Loris, I. (2008). Sparse and Stable Markowitz Portfolios. *ECB Working Paper*, (936).

Brown, S. J., Goetzmann, W. N., and Ross, S. A. (1995). Survival. *The Journal of Finance*, 50(3):853–873.

Bruder, B. and Roncalli, T. (March 2012). Managing Risk Exposures using the Risk Budgeting Approach. *Working Paper, HQ Trust GmbH*.

Bry, G. and Boschan, C. (1971). *Cyclical analysis of time series; Selected procedures and computer programs*. National Bureau of Economic Research and distributed by Columbia University Press, New York.

Bucay, N. and Rosen, D. (1999). Applying Portfolio Credit Risk Models to Retail Portfolios. *Algo Research Quarterly*, (Vol. 2, No. 1):9–29.

Bunn, A., Korpela, M., Biondi, F., Campelo, F., Mérian, P., Qeadan, F., and Zang, C. (2012). Dendrochronology Program Library in R.

Burghardt, G., Duncan, R., and Liu, L. (2003). Deciphering Drawdowns. *Risk*, pages 14–17.

Byrne, A. and Brooks, M. (2008). Behavioral Finance: Theories and Evidence. *The Research Foundation of CFA Institute*, 3(1):1–26.

Campbell, J. Y. (2000). Asset Pricing at the Millennium. *The Journal of Finance*, 55(4):1515–1568.

Campbell, N. A. (1980). Robust Procedures in Multivariate Analysis I: Robust Covariance Estimation. *Journal of the Royal Statistical Society, Series C*, 29(3):231–237.

Campello, M. G. J. R. C. R. H. (2010). The real effects of financial constraints: Evidence from a financial crisis. 97(3):470–487.

Carhart, M. M. (1997). On Persistence in Mutual Fund Performance. *The Journal of Finance*, 52(1):57–82.

Carl, P., Peterson, B. G., Boudt, K., and Zivot, E. (2012). *PerformanceAnalytics: Econometric tools for performance and risk analysis*. R package version 1.0.4.4.

Carrasco, M. and Noumon, N. (2012). Optimal Portfolio Selection using Regularization. *Working Paper, University of Montreal*.

Carvalho, R. L. d., Lu, X., and Moulin, P. (2012). Demystifying Equity Risk–Based Strategies: A Simple Alpha plus Beta Description. *The Journal of Portfolio Management*, 38(3):56–70.

Chalabi, Y., Setz, T., and Würtz, D. (2011). Stability Analytics of Vulnerabilities in Financial Time Series. *Econophysics ETH Zurich, Working Paper*.

Chalabi, Y. and Würtz, D. (2012a). Flexible Distribution Modeling with the Generalized Lambda Distribution. *Working Paper, Institute for Theoretical Physics, ETH Zurich*.

Chalabi, Y. and Würtz, D. (2012b). *gldist: An Asymmetry-Steepness Parameterization of the Generalized Lambda Distribution*. R package version 2160.2.

Chan, L. K. C., Karceski, J., and Lakonishok, J. (1999). On Portfolio Optimization: Forecasting Covariances and Choosing the Risk Model. *The Review of Financial Studies*, 12(5):937–974.

Chauvet, M. and Hamilton, J. D. (2006). Dating Business Cycle Turning Points. In Milas, C., Rothman, P., and Dijk, D. v., editors, *Nonlinear time series analysis of business cycles*. Elsevier, Amsterdam and and Boston.

Chaves, D., Hsu, J., Li, F., and Shakernia, O. (2011). Risk Parity Portfolio vs. Other Asset Allocation Heuristic Portfolios. *The Journal of Investing*, 20(1):108–118.

Chaves, D. B., Hsu, J., Li, F., and Shakernia, O. (2012). Efficient Algorithms for Computing Risk Parity Portfolio Weights. *The Journal of Investing*, 21(3):150–163.

Cheklov, A., Uryasev, S., and Zabarankin, M. (2003). Portfolio Optimization with Drawdown Constraints. In Scherer, B., editor, *Asset and Liability Management Tools, Risk Books*. London.

Cheklov, A., Uryasev, S., and Zabarankin, M. (2005). Drawdown Measure in Portfolio Optimization. *International Journal of Theoretical and Applied Finance*, (Vol. 8, No. 1):13–58.

Chong, C. Y. (2011). Effect of Subprime Crisis on U.S. Stock Market Return and Volatility. *Global Economy and Finance Journal*, 4(1):102–111.

Chopra, V. K. and Ziemba, W. T. (1993). The Effect of Errors in Means, Variances, and Covariances on Optimal Portfolio Choice: Good mean forecasts are critical to the mean-variance framework. *Journal of Portfolio Management*, 19(2):6–11.

Clarke, R., Silva, H. d., and Thorley, S. (2006). Minimum-Variance Portfolios in the U.S. Equity Market. *The Journal of Portfolio Management*, 33(1):10–24.

Clarke, R., Silva, H. d., and Thorley, S. (2011). Minimum Variance Portfolio Composition. *The Journal of Portfolio Management*, 37(2):31–45.

Çobandağ, Z. and Weber, G. W. (2011). Risk Modeling In Optimization Problems Via Value at Risk and Conditional Value at Risk. *Working Paper, Middle East Technical University.*

Cochrane, J. H. (2005). *Asset pricing.* Princeton Univ. Press, Princeton and NJ, rev. ed. edition.

Cottin, C. and Döhler, S. (2009). *Risikoanalyse: Modellierung, Beurteilung und Management von Risiken mit Praxisbeispielen.* Studienbücher Wirtschaftsmathematik. Vieweg + Teubner, Wiesbaden, 1 edition.

Cvitanic, J. and Karatzas, I. (1994). On Portfolio Optimization under "Drawdown" Constraints. *IMA Lecture Notes in Mathematics & Applications 65,* pages 77–88.

Da Costa, N., Cunha, J., and Da Silva, S. (2005). Stock selection based on cluster analysis. *Economics Bulletin,* 13.1:1–9.

Danthine, J.-P. and Donaldson, J. B. (2005). *Intermediate Financial Theory.* Academic Press Advanced Finance. Elsevier textbooks, s.l, 2 edition.

Das, G., Gunopulos, D., and Mannila, H. (1997). Finding similar time series. In *Lecture Notes in Computer Science,* pages 88–100.

Das, N. (2003). Hedge Fund Classification using K-means Clustering Method. *9th International Conference on Computing in Economics and Finance,* (July 11-13).

Davis, J. L. (2001). Mutual Fund Performance and Manager Style. *Financial Analysts Journal,* 57(1):19–27.

Demey, P., Maillard, S., and Roncalli, T. (2010). Risk-Based Indexation. *Lyxor Whitepaper.*

DeMiguel, V., Garlappi, L., Nogales, F. J., and Uppal, R. (2009a). A Generalized Approach to Portfolio Optimization: Improving Performance by Constraining Portfolio Norms. *Management Science*, 55(5):798–812.

DeMiguel, V., Garlappi, L., and Uppal, R. (2009b). Optimal Versus Naive Diversification: How Inefficient is the 1/N Portfolio Strategy? *Review of Financial Studies*, 22(5):1915–1953.

Desai, H., Ramesh, K., Thiagarajan, S. R., and Balachandran, B. V. (2002). An investigation of the informational role of short interest in the Nasdaq market. *The journal of finance : the journal of the American Finance Association*, 57(5):2263–2287.

Di Matteo, T., Aste, T., and Mantegna, R. (2004). An interest rates cluster analysis. *Physica A: Statistical Mechanics and its Applications*, 339(1-2):181–188.

Dichev, I. D. (1998). Is the risk of bankruptcy a systematic risk? *The Journal of Finance*, 53(3):1131–1147.

Diether, K. B., Malloy, C. J., and Scherbina, A. (2002). Differences of opinion and the cross section of stock returns. *The journal of finance : the journal of the American Finance Association*, 57(5):2112–2142.

Dose, C. and Cincotti, S. (2005). Clustering of financial time series with application to index and enhanced index tracking portfolio. *Physica A: Statistical Mechanics and its Applications*, 355(1):145–151.

Douglas, G. W. (1969). Risk in the equity markets: An empirical appraisal of market efficiency. *Yale economic essays*, 9(1):3–45.

Dow, J. and Werlang, S. R. d. C. (1992). Uncertainty Aversion, Risk Aversion, and the Optimal Choice of Portfolio. *Econometrica*, 60(1).

Dowd, K. (2002). *Measuring market risk*. Wiley, Chichester.

Dowd, K. (2005). *Measuring market risk*. Wiley, Chichester, 2 edition.

Dowd, K. and Blake, D. (2006). After VaR: The Theory,Estimation and Insurance Applications of Quantile-Based Risk Measures. *The Journal of Risk and Insurance*, 73(2):193–229.

Draper, N. R. and Tierney, D. E. (1973). Exact formulas for additional terms in some 1mportant series expansions. *Communications in Statistics*, 1(6):495–524.

Drobetz, W. (2001). How to avoid the Pitfalls in Portfolio Optimization? Putting the Black-Litterman Approach to Work. *Journal of Financial Markets and Portfolio Management*, 15(1):59–75.

Duda, R. O., Hart, P. E., and Stork, D. G. (2001). *Pattern classification*. Wiley, New York, 2 edition.

Easley, D., Hvidkjaer, S., and O'Hara, M. (2002). Is information risk a determinant of asset returns? *The journal of finance : the journal of the American Finance Association*, 57(5):2185–2221.

Easley, D. and O'Hara, M. (2004). Information and the cost of capital. *The journal of finance : the journal of the American Finance Association*, 59(4):1553–1583.

Easley, D. A., Kiefer, N. M., O'Hara, M., and Paperman, J. B. (1996). Liquidity, information, and infrequently traded stocks. *The journal of finance : the journal of the American Finance Association*, 51(4):1405–1436.

Easley, D. A. and O'Hara, M. (1987). Price, trade size, and information in securities markets. *Journal of Financial Economics*, 19(1):69–90.

Eeckhoudt, L., Gollier, C., and Schlesinger, H. (2005). *Economic and financial decisions under risk*. Princeton University Press, Princeton and N.J.

El Ghaoui, L., Oks, M., and Oustry, F. (2003). Worst-case Value-at-risk and Robust Portfolio Optimization: A Conic Programming Approach. *Operations Research*, 51(4):543–556.

ElGhaoui, L. and Lebret, H. (1997). Robust Solutions to Least-Squares Problems with Uncertain Data. *SIAM J. Matrix Anal. Appl.*, 18(4):1035–1064.

Ellsberg, D. (1961). Risk, Ambiguity, and the Savage Axioms. *[[Quarterly Journal of Economics]]*, 75(4).

Elton, E. J. (2003). *Modern portfolio theory and investment analysis*. J. Wiley & Sons, New York, 6 edition.

Elton, E. J., Gruber, M. J., and Blake, C. R. (1996). Survivorship Bias and Mutual Fund Performance. *The Review of Financial Studies*, 9(4):1097–1120.

Erdman, C. and Emerson, J. W. (2007). bcp: An R Package for Performing a Bayesian Analysis of Change Point Problems. *Journal of Statistical Software*, 23(3):1–13.

Erdman, C. and Emerson, J. W. (2008). A fast Bayesian change point analysis for the segmentation of microarray data. *Bioinformatics*, 24(19):2143–2148.

Fabozzi, F. J. (2007). *Robust Portfolio Optimization and Management*. Wiley, New York.

Fabozzi, F. J. and Francis, J. C. (1979). Mutual Fund Systematic Risk for Bull and Bear Markets: An Empirical Examination. *The Journal of Finance*, 34(5):1243–1250.

Fabozzi, F. J., Huang, D., and Zhou, G. (2010). Robust portfolios: contributions from operations research and finance. *Annals of Operations Research*, 176(1):191–220.

Fabozzi, F. J., Kolm, P. N., Pachamanova, D., and Focardi, S. M. (2007). Robust Portfolio Optimization: Recent trends and future directions. *The Journal of Portfolio Management*, 33(3):40–48.

Fama, E. F. (1965a). Portfolio Analysis in a Stable Paretian Market. *Management Science*, 11(3):404–419.

Fama, E. F. (1965b). The Behavior of Stock-Market Prices. *The Journal of Business*, (38(1)):34–105.

Fama, E. F. (1995). Size and book-to-market factors in earnings and returns. *The Journal of Finance*, 50(1):131–155.

Fama, E. F. and French, K. R. (1992). The Cross-Section of Expected Stock Returns. *The Journal of Finance*, 47(2):427–465.

Fama, E. F. and French, K. R. (1993). Common risk factors in the returns on stocks and bonds. *Journal of Financial Economics*, 33(1):3–56.

Fama, E. F. and French, K. R. (1996). Multifactor explanations of asset pricing anomalies. *The Journal of Finance*, 51(1):55–84.

Fama, E. F. and French, K. R. (2004). The Capital Asset Pricing Model: Theory and Evidence. *The Journal of Economic Perspectives*, 18(3):25–46.

Fama, E. F. and French, K. R. (2010). Luck versus Skill in the CrossSection of Mutual Fund Returns. *The Journal of Finance*, 65(5):1915–1947.

Fama, E. F. and French, K. R. (2012). Size, value, and momentum in international stock returns. *Journal of Financial Economics*, 105(3):457–472.

Fama, E. F. and MacBeth, J. D. (1973). Risk, Return, and Equilibrium: Empirical Tests. *The Journal of Political Economy*, 81(3):607–636.

Fan, J., Zhang, J., and Yu, K. (2012). Vast Portfolio Selection With Gross-Exposure Constraints. *Journal of the American Statistical Association*, 107(498):592–606.

Fantazzini, D. (2004). Copula's Conditional Dependence Measures for Portfolio Management and Value at Risk. *Working Paper, University of Konstanz*.

Fastrich, B., Paterlini, S., and Winker, P. (2013). Constructing Optimal Sparse Portfolios Using Regularization Methods. *Working Paper, University of Gießen*.

Fennema, H. and Wakker, P. (1997). Original and Cumulative Propspect Theory: A Discussion of Empirical Differences. *Journal of Behavioral Decision Making*, 10:53–64.

Filzmoser, P. and Gschwandtner, M. (2013). Multivariate outlier detection based on robust methods.

Filzmoser, P., Maronna, R., and Werner, M. (2008). Outlier Identification in High Dimensions. *Computational Statistics and Data Analysis*, 52:1694–1711.

Fishburn, P. C. (1964). *Decision and value theory*, volume 10 of *Publications in operations research*. Wiley, New York, [nachdr.] edition.

Fishburn, P. C. (1970). *Utility theory for decision making*, volume 18 of *Operations Research Society of America. Publications in operations research*. Wiley, New York.

Fisher, K. and Statman, M. (1997a). Investment Advice from Mutual Fund Companies: Closer to the Talmud than to Markowitz. *The Journal of Portfolio Management*, 24(1):9–25.

Fisher, K. and Statman, M. (1997b). The Mean-Variance Optimization Puzzle: Security Portfolios and Food Portfolios. *Financial Analysts Journal*, 53(4):41–50.

Foresti, S. J. and Rush, M. E. (2010). Risk-Focused Diversification: Utilizing Leverage within Asset Allocation. *Wilshire Consulting*.

Fortin, I. and Hlouskova, J. (2010). Optimal Asset Allocation Under Linear Loss Aversion.

Frazzini, A. and Pedersen, L. H. (2010). Betting Against Beta. *Working paper, AQR Capital Management, New York University and NBER (WP 16601)*.

Freimer, M., Kollia, G., Mudholkar, G. S., and Lin, C. T. (1988). A Study of the Generalized Tukey Lambda Family. *Communications in Statistics - Theory and Methods*, 17(10):3547–3567.

Frost, P. A. and Savarino, J. E. (1988). For better performance. *The Journal of Portfolio Management*, 15(1):29–34.

Fu, F. (2009). Idiosyncratic risk and the cross-section of expected stock returns. *Journal of Financial Economics*, 91(1):24–37.

Gilli, M., Maringer, D., and Schumann, E. (2011). *Numerical methods and optimization in finance*. Academic Press, Waltham.

Goldfarb, D. and Iyengar, G. (2003). Robust Portfolio Selection Problems. *Math. of Operations Research*, 28(1):1–38.

Goltz, F. and Le Sourd, V. (2010). Does Finance Theory Make the Case for Capitalisation-Weighted Indexing?

Gonzalez, L., Powell, J. G., Shi, J., and Wilson, A. (2005). Two centuries of bull and bear market cycles. *International Review of Economics & Finance*, 14(4):469–486.

Gordon, S. and St-Amour, P. (1999). *A Preference Regime Model of Bull and Bear Markets*. PhD thesis.

Goyal, A. (2012). Empirical cross-sectional asset pricing: a survey. *Financial Markets and Portfolio Management*, 26(1):3–38.

Griffin, J. M. and Lemmon, M. L. (2002). Book-to market equity, distress risk, and stock returns. *The journal of finance : the journal of the American Finance Association*, 57(5):2317–2336.

Grootveld, H. and Hallerbach, W. (1999). Variance vs downside risk: Is there really that much difference? *European Journal of Operational Research*, 114:304–319.

Grossman, S. J. and Zhou, Z. (1993). Optimal Investment Strategies for Controlling Drawdowns. *Mathematical Finance*, (Vol. 3, No. 3):241–276.

Guastaroba, G., Mansini, R., and Speranza, M. G. (2009). Models and Simulations for Portfolio Rebalancing. *Computational Economics*, 33(3):237–262.

Guillermo, J. O. and Matesanz, D. (2006). Cross-Country Hierarchical Structure and Curreny Crises. *International Journal of Modern Physics C*, 17(3):333–341.

Hadar, J. and Russell, W. (1969). Rules for Ordering Uncertain Prospects. *American Economic Review*, 59(1):25–34.

Hallerbach, W. G. (1999). Decomposing Portfolio Value-at-Risk: A General Analysis. *Tinbergen Institute Discussion Papers*, (99-034/2).

Hamada, M., Sherris, M., and van der Hoek, J. (2006). Dynamic Portfolio Allocation, the Dual Theory of Choice and Probability Distortion Functions. *ASTIN Bulletin*, 36(1):187–217.

Hamelink, F. and Hoesli, M. (2004). Maximum drawdown and the allocation to real estate. *Journal of Property Research*, (Vol. 21, No. 1):5–29.

Hamilton, J. D. (1989). A New Approach to the Economic Analysis of Nonstationary Time Series and the Business Cycle. *Econometrica*, 57(2):357–384.

Hanauer, M., Kaserer, C., and Rapp, M. S. (2013). Risikofaktoren und Multifaktormodelle für den deutschen Aktienmarkt. *Working Paper*.

Hanisch, J. (2006). *Risikomessung mit dem Conditional Value-at-Risk*. PhD thesis, Univ, Hamburg and Jena.

Hanoch, G. and Levy, H. (1969). The Efficiency Analysis of Choices Involving Risk. *The Review of Economic Studies*, 36(3):335–346.

Hanoch, G. and Levy, H. (1970). Efficient Portfolio Selection with Quadratic and Cubic Utility. 43(2):181–189.

Hansen, L. P. (1982). Large Sample Properties of Generalized Method of Moments Estimators. *Econometrica*, 50(4):1029–1054.

Harding, D., Nakou, G., and Nejjar, A. (2003). Pros and cons of "Drawdown" as a Statistical Measure of Risk for Investments. *AIMA Journal*, pages 16–19.

Harding, D. and Pagan, A. R. (2002). Dissecting the cycle: a methodological investigation. *Journal of Monetary Economics*, 49:365–381.

Harmantzis, F. and Miao, L. (2005). On the Impact of Heavy-Tailed Returns to Popular Risk Measures: Evidence from Global Indices. *Working Paper, Stevens Institute of Technology*.

Harmantzis, F. C., Miao, L., and Chien, Y. (2006). Empirical Study of Value-at-Risk and Expected Shortfall Models with Heavy Tails. *Journal of Risk Finance*, 7(2):117–135.

Hartigan, J. A. and Wong, M. A. (1979). Algorithm AS 136: A K-Means Clustering Algorithm. *Journal of the Royal Statistical Society, series C*, 28(1):100–108.

Harvey, C. R. (1989). Time-Varying Conditional Covariances in Tests of Asset Pricing Models. *Journal of Financial Economics*, 24(2):289–317.

Haugen, R. and Heins, A. J. (1972). On the Evidence Supporting the Existence of Risk Premiums in the Capital Market. *Wisconsin Working Paper*.

Haugen, R. A. and Baker, N. L. (1991). The efficient market inefficiency of capitalization-weighted stock portfolios: Matching the market is an inefficient investment strategy. *The Journal of Portfolio Management*, 17(3):35–40.

Haugen, R. A. and Heins, J. (1975). Risk and the Rate of Return on Financial Assets: Some Old Wine in New Bottles. *Journal of Financial and Quantitative Analysis*.

Hellmich, M. and Kassberger, S. (2011). Efficient and robust portfolio optimization in the multivariate Generalized Hyperbolic framework. *Quantitative Finance*, 11(10):1503–1516.

Huber, P. J. (1981). *Robust statistics*. Wiley, New York.

Huberman, G. and Jiang, W. (2006). Offering versus Choice in 401(k) Plans: Equity Exposure and Number of Funds. *The Journal of Finance*, 61(2):763–801.

Inker, B. (2010). The Hidden Risks of Risk Parity Portfolio. *GMO White Paper*.

Jagannathan, R., Schaumburg, E., and Zhou, G. (2010). Cross-Sectional Asset Pricing Tests. *Annual Review of Financial Economics*, 2(1):49–74.

Jagganathan, J. and Ma, T. (2003). Reduction in Large Portfolios: Why Imposing the Wrong Constraints Helps. *Journal of Finance*, 58(4):1651–1683.

Jegadeesh, N. and Titman, S. (1993). Returns by Buying Winners and Selling Losers: Implications for Stock Market Efficiency. *Journal of Finance*, 48(1):65–91.

Jen, E. (2001). Working Definitions of Robustness. *SFI Robustness*, (RS-2001-009).

Jensen, M. C. (1968). The performance of mutual funds in the period 1945-1964. *Journal of Finance*, 23(2):389–416.

Jobson, J. D. and Korkie, B. (1980). Estimation for Markowitz Efficient Portfolios. *Journal of the American Statistical Association,* 75(371):544–554.

Jöhri, S. (2004). *Portfolio Optimization with Hedge Funds: Conditional Value-At-Risk And Conditional Drawdown-At-Risk For Portfolio Optimization With Alternative Investments.* Master thesis, ETH Zurich, Zurich.

Jorion, P. (1985). International Portfolio Diversification with Estimation Risk. *The Journal of Business,* 58(3):259–278.

Jorion, P. (1986). Bayes-Stein Estimation for Portfolio Analysis. *Journal of Financial and Quantitative Analysis,* 21(3):279–292.

Jorion, P. (2007). *Value at Risk: The New Benchmark for Managing Financial Risk.* McGraw-Hill, New York, 3 edition.

Kahneman, D. and Tversky, A. (1979). Prospect Theory: An Analysis of Decision under Risk. *Econometrica,* 47(2):263–292.

Kapler, M. (2012). Systematic investor toolbox. `https://github.com/systematicinvestor/SIT`.

Kassberger, S. and Kiesel, R. (2007). A fully parametric approach to return modelling and risk management of hedge funds. *Financial Markets and Portfolio Management,* 20(4):472–491.

Kaufman, L. and Rousseeuw, P. J. (1990). *Finding Groups in Data: An Introduction to Cluster Analysis.* Wiley, New York.

Kaya, H. (2012). The Bayesian Roots of Risk Parity in a Mean-Risk World. *Working Paper, Neuberger Berman.*

Kaya, H. and Lee, W. (2012). Demystifying Risk Parity. *Neuberger Berman white Paper.*

Kim, D. (2011). Relevance of Maximum Drawdown in the Investment Fund Selection Problem When Utility is Nonadditive. *Journal of Economic Research,* (16):257–289.

Kleeberg, J. M. (1995). *Der Anlageerfolg des Minimum-Varianz-Portfolios : eine empirische Untersuchung am deutschen, englischen, japanischen, kanadischen und US-amerikanischen Aktienmarkt.* Uhlenbruch, Bad Soden/Ts.

Knight, F. H. (1921). *Risk, uncertainty and profit.* PhD thesis, NY, Cornell Univ, Boston and New York and Ithaca.

Konno, H. and Yamazaki, H. (1991). Mean-Absolute Deviation Portfolio Otimization Model and Its Applications to Tokyo Stock Market. *Management Science*, 37(5):519–531.

Kothari, S. P. and Warner, J. B. (2001). Evaluating Mutual Fund Performance. *The Journal of Finance*, 56(5):1985–2010.

Krokhmal, P., Palmquist, J., and Uryasev, S. (2002a). Portfolio Optimization with Conditional Value-at-Risk Objective and Constraints. *The Journal of Risk*, (Vol. 4, No. 2):11–27.

Krokhmal, P., Uryasev, S., and Zrazhevsky, G. (2002b). Comparative Analysis of Linear Portfolio Rebalancing Strategies: An Application to Hedge Funds. *Journal of Alternative Investments*, (Vol. 5, No. 1):10–29.

Krokhmal, P., Uryasev, S., and Zrazhevsky, G. (2003). Numerical Comparison of CVaR and CDaR Approaches: Application to Hedge Funds. In W. T. Ziemba, editor, *The Stochastic Programming Approach to Asset Liability and Wealth Management*. AIMR/Blackwell Publisher.

Kuutan, E. (2007). *Portfolio Optimization Using Conditional Value-at-Risk and Conditional Drawdown-at-Risk.* Bachelorthesis, University of Toronto, Toronto.

Lakonishok, J., Shleifer, A., and Vishny, R. W. (1994). Contrarian investment, extrapolation, and risk. *The Journal of Finance*, 49(5):1541–1578.

Laux, H. (2003). *Entscheidungstheorie*. Springer-Lehrbuch. Springer, Berlin, 5 edition.

Ledoit, O. and Wolf, M. (2003). Improved estimation of the covariance matrix of stock returns with an application to portfolio selection. *Journal of Empirical Finance*, 10(5):603–621.

Ledoit, O. and Wolf, M. (2004a). A well-conditioned estimator for large-dimensional covariance matrices. *Journal of Multivariate Analysis*, 88(2):365–411.

Ledoit, O. and Wolf, M. (2004b). Honey, I shrunk the Sample Covariance Matrix. *The Journal of Portfolio Management*, 30(4):110–119.

Lee, C.-F., Lee, J., and Lee, A. C. (2010). *Handbook of quantitative finance and risk management*. Springer, Boston.

Lee, W. (2011). Risk-Based Asset Allocation: A New Answer to An Old Question? *The Journal of Portfolio Management*, 37(4):11–28.

Lee, W. (2012). Risk On, Risk Off. *The Journal of Portfolio Management*, 38(3):28–39.

Lehmann, B. N. (1990). Residual risk revisited. *Journal of econometrics*, 45:71–97.

Levell, C. A. (2010). Risk Parity: In the Spotlight after 50 years. *General Research, NEPC*.

Levy, H. (1994). Dynamic Correlations, Estimation Risk, and Portfolio Management during the Financial Crisis. *Journal of Risk and Uncertainty*, 8(3):289–307.

Levy, H. (2006). *Stochastic Dominance: Investment Decision Making Under Uncertainty*. Springer Science+Business Media, Incorporated.

Levy, H. and Markowitz, H. M. (1979). Approximating expected utility by a function of mean and variance. *The American Economic Review*, 69(3):308–317.

Levy, M. (2009). Almost Stochastic Dominance and stocks for the long run. *European Journal of Operational Research*, 194(1):250–257.

Lindberg, C. (2009). Portfolio optimization when expected stock returns are determined by exposure to risk. *Bernoulli*, 15(2):464–474.

Lintner, J. (1965a). Security Prices, Risk, and Maximal Gains From Diversification. *The Journal of Finance*, 20(4):587–615.

Lintner, J. (1965b). The Valuation of Risk Assets and the Selection of Risky Investments in Stock Portfolios and Capital Budgets. *The Review of Economics and Statistics*, 47(1).

Lisi, F. and Otranto, E. (2009). Clustering Mutual Funds by Return and Risk Levels. In Corazza M., P. C. E., editor, *Mathematical and statistical methods for actuarial sciences and finance*. Springer.

Litterman, R. (1996). Hot Spots and Hedges. *Goldman, Sachs & Co., Risk Management Series*.

Little, P. (2010). Risk parity 101. *Research Note, Hammond Associates*.

Lobo, M. S. and Boyd Stephen (2000). The worst-case risk of a portfolio. *Unpublished Technical Report*.

Lohre, H., Opfer, H., and Ország, G. (2011). Diversifying Risk Parity. *Working Paper, HQ Trust GmbH*.

Loschi, R. H., Cruz, F. R. B., and Arellano-Valle, R. B. (2005). Multiple Change Point Analysis for the Regular Exponential Family using the Product Partition Model. *Journal of Data Science*, 3(3):305–330.

Lunde, A. and Timmermann, A. (2004). Duration Dependence in Stock Prices. *Journal of Business & Economic Statistics*, 22(3):253–273.

Ma, C. and Wong, W.-K. (2010). Stochastic Dominance and Risk Measure: A Decision-Theoretic Foundation for VaR and C-VaR. *European Journal of Operational Research*, 207(2):927–935.

Magdon-Ismail, M. and Atiya, A. F. (2004). Maximum drawdown. *Risk*, (Vol. 17, Nr. 10):99–102.

Mahdi, E. and McLeod, A. I. (2011). *portes: Portmanteau Tests for Time Series Models*. R package version 1.07.

Maheu, J. M. and McCurdy, T. H. (2000). Identifying Bull and Bear Markets in Stock Returns. *Journal of Business & Economic Statistics*, 18(1):100–112.

Maillard, S., Roncalli, T., and Teiletche, J. (2010). On the properties of equally-weighted risk contributions portfolios. *The Journal of Portfolio Management*, 36(4):60–70.

Malkiel, B. G. and Xu, Y. (2002). Idiosyncratic risk and security returns. *Working Paper, University of Texas at Dallas*.

Mandelbrot, B. (1963). The Variation of Certain Speculative Prices. *The Journal of Business*, (36(4)):394–419.

Marathe, A. and Shawky, H. (1999). Categorizing Mutual Funds Using Clusters. *Advances in Quantitative Analysis of Finance and Accounting*, 7:199–211.

Markowitz, H. (1952). Portfolio Selection. *The Journal of Finance*, 7(1):77–91.

Markowitz, H. (1959). *Portfolio Selection: Efficient Diversification of Investments*. John Wiley, New York.

Mausser, H. and Rosen, D. (1999). Applying Secario Optimization to Portfolio Credit Risk. *Algo Research Quarterly*, (Vol. 2, No. 2):19–34.

McCulloch, J. H. (1986). Simple consistent estimators of stable distribution parameters. *Communications in Statistics - Simulation and Computation*, 15(4).

McNeil, A. and P., F. R. E. (2005). *Quantitative Risk Management: Concepts, Techniques, and Tools*. Princeton Series in Finance.

Mendes, B. V. d. M. and Brandi, V. R. (2004). Modeling drawdowns and drawups in financial markets. *Journal of Risk*, 6(3):53–69.

Mendes, B. V. d. M. and Leal, R. P. C. (2005). Maximum Drawdown: Models and Applications. *The Journal of Alternative Investments*, 7(4):83–91.

Merton, R. C. (1980). On Estimating the Expected Return on the Market: An Exploratory Investigation. *Journal of Financial Economics*, 8:323–361.

Messikh, R. J. and Oderda, G. (2010). A Proof of the Outperformance of Beta Arbitrage Strategies. *Working Paper*.

Meucci, A. (2007). Risk Contributions from Generic User-Defined Factors. *Working Paper, IRES*.

Meucci, A. (2009). Managing diversification. *Risk*, (Vol. 22 No. 5):74–79.

Meucci, A. (2010). Exercises in Advanced Risk and Portfolio Management-With Step-by-Step Solutions and Fully Documented Code. *Review*.

Miccichè, S., Bonanno, G., Lillo, F., and Mantegna, R. N. (2003). Degree stability of a minimum spanning tree of price return and volatility. *Physica A*, 324:66–73.

Michaud, R. and Michaud, R. (2008a). Estimation Error and Portfolio Optimization: A Resampling Solution. *Journal of Investment Management*, 6(1):8–28.

Michaud, R. O. (1989). The Markowitz Optimization Enigma: Is 'Optimized' Optimal? _Financial Analysts Journal_, 45(1):31–42.

Michaud, R. O. (1998). _Efficient Asset Management: A Practical Guide to Stock Portfolio Optimization and Asset Allocation._ Harvard Business School Press, Boston.

Michaud, R. O. (2009). Are Good Estimates Good Enough? No. _Investment Management Consultants Association._

Michaud, R. O. and Michaud, R. O. (2008b). _Efficient asset management: A practical guide to stock portfolio optimization and asset allocation._ Oxford University Press, New York, 2 edition.

Miller, E. M. (1977). Risk, uncertainty, and divergence of opinion. _The journal of finance : the journal of the American Finance Association_, 32(4):1151–1168.

Miller, M. H. and Scholes, M. (1972). Rates of return in relation to risk: A re-examination of some recent findings. _Studies in the theory of capital markets : [papers of the Conference on Modern Capital Theory, held at the University of Rochester in August, 1969, augmented by several closely related papers]_, pages 47–78.

Mittnik, S. and Rachev, S. T. (1993). Modeling asset returns with alternative stable distributions. _Econometric Reviews_, 12(3):261–330.

Mizuno, T., Takayasu, H., and Takayasu, M. (2006). Correlation networks among currencies. _Physica A: Statistical Mechanics and its Applications_, 364:336–342.

Mossin, J. (1966). Equilibrium in a capital asset market. _Econometrica_, 34(4):768–783.

Natarajan, K., Dessislava, P., and Sim, M. (2006). A Tractable Parametric Approach to Value-at-Risk Optimization. _Working Paper, Berkley-NUS Risk Management Institute._

Neukirch, T. (2008a). Alternative Indexing with the MSCI World Index. *Working Paper, HQ Trust GmbH.*

Neukirch, T. (2008b). Portfolio optimization with respect to risk diversification. *Working Paper, HQ Trust GmbH.*

Neumann, J. v. and Morgenstern, O. (1944). *Theory of games and economic behavior.* Princeton Univ. Press, Princeton.

Ning, H. (2007). *Hierarchical Portfolio Management: Theory and applications.* PhD thesis, Erasmus University Rotterdam, Rotterdam.

Onnela, J.-P., Chakraborti, A., Kaski, K., and Kertész (2002). Dynamic asset trees and portfolio analysis. *The European Physical Journal B - Condensed Matter,* 30(3):285–288.

Onnela, J.-P., Chakraborti, A., Kaski, K., Kertész, J., and Kanto, A. (2003). Dynamics of market correlations: Taxonomy and portfolio analysis. *Physical Review E,* 68(5).

Ortobelli, S., Huber, I., and Schwartz, E. (2002). Portfolio selection with stable distributed returns. *Mathematical Methods of Operations Research,* 55(1):265–300.

Pagan, A. R. and Sossounov, K. A. (2003). A simple framework for analysing bull and bear markets. *Journal of Applied Econometrics,* 18(1):23–46.

Page, S. and Taborsky, M. (2010). The Myth of Diversification: Risk Factors vs. Asset Classes. *PIMCO Viewpoints.*

Pástor, Ľ. and Stambaugh, R. F. (2003). Liquidity risk and expected stock returns. *The journal of political economy,* 111(3):642–685.

Pearson, N. D. (2002). *Risk budgeting: Portfolio Problem Solving with Value-at-Risk.* John Wiley & Sons, New York.

Poddig, T., Brinkmann, U., and Seiler, K. (2005). *Portfoliomanagement: Konzepte und Strategien: Theorie und praxisorientierte Anwendungen mit Excel.* Uhlenbruch, Bad Soden.

Poddig, T., Dichtl, H., and Petersmeier, K. (2003). *Statistik, Ökonometrie, Optimierung. Methoden und ihre praktische Anwendung in Finanzanalyse und Portfoliomanagement.* Uhlenbruch, Bad Soden.

Poddig, T. and Unger, A. (2012). On the robustness of risk-based asset allocations. *Financial Markets and Portfolio Management,* 26(3):369–401.

Podolsky, P., Johnson, R., and Jennings, O. (2010). The All Weather Story.

Pratt, J. W. (1964). Risk Aversion in the Small and in the Large. *Econometrica,* 32(1/2):122–136.

Qian, E. (2005a). Risk Parity Portfolios: Efficient Portfolios Through True Diversification. *PanAgora Asset Management.*

Qian, E. (2005b). Risk Parity: The Original. *PanAgora Asset Management.*

Qian, E. (2006). On the Financial Interpretation of Risk Contribution: Risk Budgets Do Add Up. *Journal of Investment Management,* 4(4):41–51.

Qian, E. (2010). Risk Parity: The solution to the unbalanced portfolio. *PanAgora Asset Management.*

Quiggin, J. (1982). A Theory of Anticipated Utility. *Journal of Economic Behavior and Organization,* 3:323–343.

R Core Team (2012). *R: A Language and Environment for Statistical Computing.* R Foundation for Statistical Computing, Vienna, Austria. ISBN 3-900051-07-0.

Rachev, S. T., Menn, C., and Fabozzi, F. J. (2005). *Fat-tailed and skewed asset return distributions: Implications for risk management, portfolio selection, and option pricing.* John Wiley & Sons, Hoboken and N.J.

Recchia, R. (23.02.2010). *Robust asset allocation problems: a new class of risk measure based models.* PhD thesis, Università di Pisa, Pisa.

Rockafellar, R. and Uryasev, S. (2000). Optimization of conditional value-at-risk. *The Journal of Risk*, 2(3):21–41.

Rockafellar, R. T. and Uryasev, S. (2002). Conditional value-at-risk for general loss distributions. *Journal of Banking and Finance*, 26(7):1443–1471.

Roll, R. (1977). A critique of the asset pricing theory's tests. *Journal of Financial Economics*, 4(2):129–176.

Roncalli, T. and Weisang, G. (2012). Risk Parity Portfolios with Risk Factors. *Working Paper,*.

Rosen, D. and Saunders, D. (2010). Risk factor contributions in portfolio credit risk models. *Journal of Banking & Finance*, 34(2):336–349.

Rosenberg, B., Reid, K., and Lanstein, R. (1985). Persuasive evidence of market inefficiency. *The Journal of Portfolio Management*, 11(3):9–16.

Rothschild, M. and Stiglitz, J. (1970). Increasing Risk: I. A definition. *Journal of Economic Theory*, 2(3):225–243.

Rothschild, M. and Stiglitz, J. (1971). Increasing Risk II: Its Economic Consequences. *Journal of Economic Theory*, 3(1):66–84.

Roy, A. D. (1952). Safety First and the Holding of Assets. *Econometrica*, 20(3):431–449.

Rubinstein, A. (2002). Irrational diversification in multiple decision problems. *European Economic Review*, 46(8):1369–1378.

Sarykalin, S., Serraino, G., and Uryasev, S. (2008). Value-at-Risk vs. Conditional Value-at-Risk in Risk Management and Optimization. *Tutorials in Operations Research, INFORMS.*

Scaillet (2004). Nonparametric estimation and sensitivity analysis of expected shortfall. *Mathematical Finance*, 14(1):115–129.

Schachter, B. and Thiagarajan, S. R. (2011). Risk Parity - Rewards, Risks and Research Opportunities. *The Journal of Investing*, 20(1):79–89.

Scherer, B. (2010a). More than you ever wanted to know about conditional value at risk optimization. In Satchell, S., editor, *Optimizing Optimization*, pages 283–299. Elsevier, London.

Scherer, B. (2010b). A note on the returns from minimum variance investing. *Journal of Empirical Finance*, 18(4):652–660.

Schmeidler, D. (1989). Subjective Probability and Expected Utility without Additivity. *Econometrica*, 57(3):571–587.

Schmidt-von Rhein, A. (1996). *Die moderne Portfoliotheorie im praktischen Wertpapiermanagement*. PhD thesis, Univ, Bad Soden/Ts.

Schneeweiß, H. (1967). *Entscheidungskriterien bei Risiko*, volume 6 of *Ökonometrie und Unternehmensforschung*. Springer, Berlin.

Scutellà, M. G. and Recchia, R. (2010). Robust portfolio asset allocation and risk measures. *4OR*, 8(2):113–139.

Seiler, K. (2008). *Phasenmodelle und Investmentstilanalyse von Hedgefonds und Investmentfonds*. P. Lang.

Sereda, E., Bronshtein, E., and Rachev, S. F. F. (2010). Distortion Risk Measures in Portfolio Optimization. In Guerard, J. and Markowitz, H., editors, *Handbook of portfolio construction*. Springer, New York and London.

Shanken, J. (1992). On the estimation of beta-pricing models. *The Review of Financial Studies*, 5(1):1–33.

Sharpe, W. F. (1964). Capital Asset Prices: A Theory of Market Equilibrium under Conditions of Risk. *The Journal of Finance*, 19(3):425–442.

Sharpe, W. F. (2002). Budgeting and Monitoring Pension Fund Risk. *Financial Analysts Journal*, 58(5):74–86.

Shawky, H. A. and Marathe, A. (2010). Stylistic Differences across Hedge Funds as Revealed by Historical Monthly Returns. *Technology and Investment*, 2:26–34.

Sheikh, A. and Qiao, H. (2010). Non-Normality of Market Returns: A Framework for Asset Allocation Decision Making. *The Journal of Alternative Investments*, 12(3):8–35.

Soyster, A. L. (1973). Convex Programming with Set-Inclusive Constraints and Applications to Inexact Linear Programming. *Operations Research*, 21(5):1154–1157.

Stattman, D. (1980). Book values and stock returns. *The Chicago MBA: A Journal of Selected Papers*, 4:25–45.

Stoyanov, S., Samorodnitsky, G., Rachev, S. T., and Ortobelli, S. (2005). Computing the portfolio Conditional Value-at-Risk in the Alpha-Stable case. *Working Paper*.

Stoyanov, S. V., Rachev, S. T., and Fabozzi, F. J. (2010). Computational aspects of risk estimation in volatile markets: A survey. *Annals of Operations Research*, 176(1):293–309.

Stracca, L. (2002). The Optimal Allocation Of Risks Under Prospect Theory. *European Central Bank Working Paper*, (161).

Stubbs, R. A. and Vance, P. (2005). Computing Return Estimation Error Matrices for Robust Optimization. *Axioma Research Paper*, (001).

Subrahmanyam, A. (2010). The Cross-Section of Expected Stock Returns: What Have We Learnt from the Past Twenty-Five Years of Research? *European Financial Management*, 16(1):27–42.

Tamura, R. (2007). *Rdonlp2: an R extension library to use Peter Spelluci's DONLP2 from R*. R package version 0.3-1/r4954.

Tasche, D. (1999). Risk contributions and performance measurement. *Working Paper, Munich University of Technology.*

Tobin, J. (1958). Liquidity Preference as Behavior Towards Risk. *The Review of Economic Studies,* 25(2):65–86.

Tola, V., Lillo, F., Gallegati, M., and Mantegna, R. N. (2008). Cluster analysis for portfolio optimization. *Journal of Economic Dynamics and Control,* 32(1):235–258.

Torrence, C. and Compo, G. P. (1998). A Practical Guide to Wavelet Analysis. *Bulletin of the American Meteorological Society,* 79:61–78.

Tütüncü, R. H. and Koenig, M. (2004). Robust Asset Allocation. *Annals of Operations Research,* (132):157–187.

Tversky, A. and Kahneman, D. (1992). Advances in Prospect Theory: Cumulative Representation of Uncertainty. *Journal of Risk and Uncertainty,* 5:297–323.

Uryasev, S. (2000). Conditional Value-at-Risk: Optimization Algorithms and Applications. *Financial Engineering News,* (14):1–5.

van Vliet, P., Blitz, D., and van der Grient, B. (2011). Is the Relation Between Volatility and Expected Stock Returns Positive, Flat or Negative? *Working Paper.*

Wang, I. and Zheng, P. (2010). Rebalancing, Conditional Value at Risk, and t-Copula in Asset Allocation. *Working Paper.*

Ward, J. H. (1963). Hierarchical Grouping to Optimize an Objective Function. *Journal of the American Statistical Association,* 58(301):236–244.

Weber, E. and Johnson, E. (2003). Decisions under uncertainty: Psychological, economic, and neuroeconomic explanations of risk preference. In Glimcher, P., Camerer, C., Fehr, E., and Poldrack, R., editors, *Neuroeconomics: Decision making and the brain.* Elsevier, New York.

White, H. (1980). A heteroskedasticity-consistent covariance matrix estimator and a direct test for heteroskedasticity. *Econometrica*, 48(4):817–838.

Würtz, D., Chalabi, Y., Chen, W., and Ellis, A. (2010). *Portfolio Optimization with R/Rmetrics*. R package version 2130.80.

Würtz, D., Chalabi, Y., and Locher, D. (2011). Stabile Portfolios in Krisenzeiten: Investitionen auf der Diversifikationslinie. *Schweizer Personalvorsorge*, 10:1–2.

Würtz, D., Chalabi, Y., and Locher, D. (2012a). Stabile Portfolios in Krisenzeiten: Investitionen auf der Diversifikationslinie als alternatives Portfolio-Paradigma. *Neue Zürcher Zeitung*.

Würtz, D., Chalabi, Y., and Setz, T. (2012b). Stability Analytics: New Directions in Active Portfolio Management. *Econophysics ETH Zurich, Working Paper*.

Würtz, D. and Rmetrics Core Team (2011). Rmetrics - Portfolio Selection and Optimization.

Xiong, J. and Idzorek, T. (2011). The Impact of Skewness and Fat Tails on the Asset Allocation Decision. *Financial Analyst Journal*, 67(2):23–35.

Yaari, M. E. (1987). The Dual Theory of Choice under Risk. *Econometrica*, 55(1):95–115.

Yamai, Y. and Yoshiba, T. (2002). Comparative Analysis of Expected Shortfall and Value-at-Risk: Their Estimation Error, Decomposition, and Optimization. *Monetary and Economic Studies*, 20(1):87–122.

Yen, Y.-M. (2010). A Note on Sparse Minimum Variance Portfolios and Coordinate-Wise Descent Algorithms. *Working Paper, Institute of Economics, Academia Sinica, Taiwan*.

Zangari, P. (1996). A VaR methodology for portfolios that include options. *JPMorgan RiskMetrics Monitor First Quarter*, pages 4–12.

Zeileis, A. and Hothorn, T. (2002). Diagnostic checking in regression relationships. *R News*, 2(3):7–10.

Zhang, J. and Maringer, D. (2009). Improving Sharpe Ratios and Stability of Portfolios by Using a Clustering Technique. *Proceedings of the World Congress on Engineering, WCE*, 1:1–6.

Zhang, J. and Maringer, D. (2011). Distributing weights under hierarchical clustering: A way in reducing performance breakdown.

Zhu, S. and Fukushima, M. (2009). Worst-Case Conditional Value-at-Risk with Application to Robust Portfolio Management. *Operations Research*, 57(5):1155–1168.

Zivot, E. (2011). R-script: portfolioEsDecomposition.r. http://faculty.washington.edu/ezivot/research/ portfolioEsDecomposition.r.

Made in the USA
Middletown, DE
20 May 2019